MEMORIÆ VIS:

ESSAYS *in* CELEBRATION
of ARTHUR R. EVANS

MEMORIÆ VIS:

ESSAYS *in* CELEBRATION
of ARTHUR R. EVANS

EDITED BY ERASMO LEIVA-MERIKAKIS

AND ERDMANN WANIEK

SCHOLARS PRESS

ATLANTA, GEORGIA

1993

MEMORIÆ VIS:
ESSAYS in CELEBRATION
of ARTHUR R. EVANS

EDITED BY ERASMO LEIVA-MERIKAKIS
AND ERDMANN WANIEK
© 1993
SCHOLARS PRESS

Library of Congress Cataloging in Publication Data
Memoriæ Vis: essays in celebration of Arthur R. Evans/ edited by
    Erasmo Leiva-Merikakis, Erdmann Waniek.
        p. cm. — (Scholars Press homage series)
        ISBN 1-55540-851-6 (cloth)
        1. European literature—History and criticism. 2. Art and literature.
I. Evans, Arthur R.   II. Leiva-Merikakis, Erasmo, 1946–
III. Waniek, Erdmann.   IV. Series.
809'.894—dc20   93-3343
                                                             CIP

Printed in the United States of America
on acid-free paper

"Tout fait l'amour." Et moi, j'ajoute,
Lorsque tu dis: "Tout fait l'amour":
Même le pas avec la route,
La baguette avec le tambour.

Même le doigt avec la bague,
Même la rime et la raison,
Même le vent avec la vague,
Le regard avec l'horizon.

Même le fil avec la toile,
Même la terre avec le ver,
Le bâtiment avec l'étoile,
Et le soleil avec la mer.

GERMAIN NOUVEAU, *Le baiser*

IN MEMORIAM

CATHERINE EVANS
1926 – 1989

THOMAS LYMAN
1926 – 1992

T A B L E *of* C O N T E N T S

Arthur and Tass Evans
photographed by Henry Sharp,
November, 1985.

ARTHUR EVANS, MINIATURIST

"I have all along had much ambivalent feelings about the project: so grateful to my friends; and so conscious of my unworthiness: I am no scholar, no teacher, simply a reader of books, and a dreamer." This is how Arthur R. Evans, the person whose luminous presence among us this collection of essays celebrates, characterized himself some time ago in a letter to me. "I am deeply moved by the generosity of my friends," he added. "The range and diversity of the contributions are what appeals to me most. Thank you."

I suppose the preface to a scholarly *Festschrift* is the place for an editor soberly to sketch biography and talk bibliography, to present a cogent rationale for these particular essays appearing together between the covers of this particular book, to show how this balances that and how a serious effort has been made to give fair representation to at least the salient aspects of the proposed theme.

But Arthur Evans, the friend and – despite his own self-appraisal – the scholar and teacher to whom these pages are offered, has always been wary of overarching theories that try to explain too much, of the kind of academic discourse that swallows up person into idea, image into theory, sound and color into abstracting concept, God into theology.

In this sense, it would be discourteous to the friend we honor either to put him shrilly into the center of attention (like a good fisherman, he has always favored the silent periphery) or to turn up the accustomed professorial music of the academy, forgetting that the root of *Festschrift* is *festal*. I do not think the contributions will be found lacking in substance, variety, or relevance. But here at the threshold, rather than belabor *them* I prefer to introduce Arthur Evans to those who do not know him and perhaps evoke certain echoes in those who do. I do not so much intend to talk about him as allow him to speak for himself, giving us snatches and snapshots, as it were, of those things he likes best and that most passionately concern him. To do this, I will simply let the voice captured in his letters to me be heard at slightly wider range. I hope Arthur will not hold it against me if, by copying his words, I propose that you consider him not so much as an individual but, precisely, as a quiet voice inviting us to share his vision.

Der liebe Gott steckt im Detail, we read in one of the essays:
"The dear Lord hides in the details." I know no one with better claim
than Arthur Evans to this aphorism as summing up the intellectual
and affective habits of a lifetime. The search for transcendence with a
human face, the patience of a warm gaze that incubates faces, poems,
and life-journeys until they yield their unique bounty, the delicate
probing of every undulation of a poet's unique physiognomy until the
whole spiritual landscape lights up from within: this caressing of the
details, this turning over of even the smallest stone in the garden, will
at once be recognized by all who know Arthur Evans as his particular
"habit of being" which, beyond any specific knowledge, is, I dare say,
the intimate vision he communicates to his students and friends by
a kind of happy contagion. Our epigraph from Germain Nouveau's
"Le baiser," which speaks of "the gaze that makes love to the horizon,"
evokes this noble manner of relating to creation.

If he can say, "I am no scholar, no teacher," I think it is because he never set out intentionally to be these things. His students,
among whom I have sat, embark on one of his seminars as others go
to gather wild berries or to trek in the mountains. His area of scholarly
research in the last few years – the literature of adventure as a means
of self-transcendence – is, in fact, emblematic of his own life, which has
dedicated all its energies to the hunt for the better, the more beautiful,
the more lasting self, sought not in a mirror but in the transparency of
the other.

"I am a professional generalist," he once said to me. The object
of his search has always been a human reality too vibrant and overflowing for strict disciplinary specification. Nevertheless, European
literature has been for Arthur Evans the privileged hunting ground
for archetypes of existence. He walks in that forest with a fondness for
each separate tree, and this is why I call him a "miniaturist," an epithet
I think he will not disdain.

Perhaps a few titles from his published work will convey some
idea of the serenity of his approach, of the wide range of his interests
and competence, and of the keynote of all his endeavor: always to
contemplate persons, unique faces, lives and works, and to attempt
to bring these into intelligible relationship to one another:

The Literary Art of Eugène Fromentin: A Study in Style and Motif.
"The Myth of Pygmalion and Modern Painting: Balzac's *Chef-d'Oeuvre*

Inconnu." "Hunters in the Snow: A Winter Landscape in Pieter Brueghel and John Berryman." "A Nautical Metaphor in Dante and Claudel." "Firmitas et Robur: The Column and its Meaning in Claudel's Work." "Erich Auerbach as European Critic." "Physiognomische Theorie und heroische Porträts" (on Stefan George). "The Path of Misrah or the Dilemma of Power in Ernst Jünger's *Heliopolis.*" "The Self-Portrait in Max Beckmann." "Assignment to Armageddon: Ernst Jünger and Curzio Malaparte on the Russian Front, 1941-43." ...Never a word too much, never a flashy construct aiming at self-promotion.

I have learned from Arthur Evans not to look for the Meaning of Man, but instead to bestow patient and loving attention on the life of one person with a proper name and face: Georg Trakl, Arthur Rimbaud, Simone Weil, Charles Baudelaire, Dante Alighieri, Elisabeth Langgässer, Patrick White, Blaise Pascal, to name only a few of the profound souls to whom he introduced me in earnest. His silent appreciation of all things beautiful glows in my memory as permanent correction to my logorrheic tendency. The critic, Arthur Evans suggests, does best to allow the splendor of the contemplated form to shine through his own words.

If you want to know something about Dante's universe, the gist of his "method" would have it, spend all your leisure hours for one week savoring one canto of the *Commedia*, letting the images, ideas, and emotions of the language be your guide, following them where they would take you. If you want to know something about the climate and aesthetics of French literature at the beginning of the twentieth century, throw away the manuals and take off the next year to do little else with your free time but read all of Proust, preferably out loud. (For this man, who fulfils Josef Pieper's every dream, leisure is work and work leisure!) But what if one should die in the meantime, the anxious graduate student would gasp, and leave unread so many books of criticism, one of which might provide the clue to the "real Proust"? My friend, the quiet voice replies, Proust is as Proust says; and in any event it does not matter: *Der liebe Gott steckt im Detail.* This conspiracy, this sacred bond between the divine presence and the concrete detail, proves in the long run, I further learned, that only the present moment of life – and therefore every moment of life – is worth living. Simplistic, unambitious, unproductive reasoning? On the contrary! A desperately needed therapy.

Details, eloquent details. When Arthur first found out about our project in his honor, he had a double reaction. First, the mixture of embarrassment and gratitude we have seen. But, almost immediately, the keen concern that some colleague or former student might be neglected from the list of those invited to contribute. This is indeed the place for an editor to beg the pardon of anyone who may have been so treated despite our efforts to the contrary. But the point is this knack for attending to the reality of the other, this habit of approaching living human bonds with all the devotion and sense of the crucial that many of our contemporaries expend only on actions aimed at the public eye.

Details: In recent years a controversy has broken out in French letters regarding the treatment given by her family to Camille Claudel, a very talented sculptor and one-time mistress of Auguste Rodin, as well as the sister of the famous Catholic poet and diplomat, Paul Claudel. The unfortunate woman went mad, some say as a result of Rodin's megalomania and cruelty, and she spent the greater part of her long life locked away in a second-rate institution in the provinces, where her brother, wealthy and enjoying an international reputation as a restorer of religious poetry in the modern world, rarely visited her. A long-time admirer of Claudel's poetry, Arthur got wind of the newly published findings and, although already suffering from the "annoyances" of Parkinson's, he wrote me in longhand a detailed letter full of passionate concern for the fate of Camille Claudel: "As you know I greatly admire Paul Claudel's works (some of them, that is; no great poet, unless it be Victor Hugo, wrote so much bad poetry!); I think *Cinq grandes odes* can be compared with *Four Quartets*... *Tête d'or* is not unworthy of Rimbaud. But Claudel, the man, is someone I have trouble with. His aggressive Catholicism can be quite intolerable. I recall my disappointment upon reading his *Journal*: there is very little *caritas* in the day-to-day entries.... I must get to the bottom of this scandalous matter." The situation is, to Arthur, all the more ironical as "Camille was the archetypal source, the model for those great Claudelian women. In *Le soulier de satin*, Dona Prouhèze at one moment is made to limp by her guardian angel, and Camille had a slight limp!" And he concludes his remarks with his characteristic interest in physiognomy: "In Reine-Marie Paris' book there is a frontispiece, a photo of Camille in her youth. At the end of her account there is another photo taken of Camille just a few months before her death. It is heart-breaking to look at: an old woman, her spirit broken, shabbily dressed, staring aimlessly."

Such effortless integration, rare enough in our day, of scholarly curiosity and Christian compassion again surfaced on another occasion when Arthur was relaying to me a single sentence that had struck him concerning the daughter of James Joyce, like Camille Claudel hospitalized for insanity. When Joyce asked C.G. Jung "to explain the difference between his own mental state and hers, Jung is said to have replied, 'You dive, she falls.'" Infinitely more than just a compelling linguistic *trouvaille*, this quotation expresses Arthur Evans' interest in borderline states of human consciousness as the locus of both poetic creativity and the utter fragility of man.

If Arthur will have no truck with religious triumphalism in the style of Paul Claudel or in any other form – he who, when in Paris, went to daily Mass at Saint-Séverin or the Greek Catholic parish of Saint-Julien-le-Pauvre together with his wife – neither is he indulgent with the reigning tone in academia with regard to the religious dimension, without which he considers the whole endeavor of humanism to be unimaginable: "What I miss most in academics is a tragic sense of life, a search for God, a religious sense.... Without these one cannot help but lack generosity, largesse.... There are splendid *aperçus*, touching on some of these points in George Steiner's remarkable essay on Anthony Blunt.... I wrote Steiner a note upon reading that essay, telling him that almost alone among modern secular critics he possessed a 'tragic sense of life.' There are things I don't like about Steiner, but he seems almost alone in being *sérieux*. Everyone else is ironic. In fine, artists and writers are religious; critics, academics are not.... Shame on critics!"

The search for charity in the artist, the search for some analogue of faith in the professor.... In the case of Arthur Evans, these cannot be isolated from a third quest: the search for justice in the political scene. There is only one time of the day when Arthur is not to be disturbed: the evening news hour. The turn of events near and far engages him as intensely as a sonnet of Baudelaire or the vacant sadness on the face of Camille Claudel. In the early '80s he wrote me: "Where are the outcries, where are the demonstrations in support of the Irish hunger-strikers? God help them, these extraordinary young men. Will such extremes bring the English to their knees? Can anything move Margaret Thatcher, *cette dame de fer*? I have supported my Jewish and Black friends; where are they now?... It's time for the Brits to get out!"

More details: Arthur Evans possesses a singular talent for quoting from his voluminous reading, a practice he once apologetically referred to as his "unpunished vice" just before yielding to it with relish. His art of the perfect citation has always been to me an index both of a prodigious memory at the service of attentiveness in reading and of the generous maieutic role he enjoys between his friends and the unexplored horizons these have yet to make their own. At one point, as I described to him my translation work on the highly compressed distichs of Angelus Silesius, he responded not only encouragingly but relating the seventeenth-century German mystical poet to – of all people – Baudelaire, the nineteenth-century decadent: "My favorite distich of Angelus Silesius, and one which could serve as the *locus classicus* of the phenomenon of synaesthesia, is:

> *Die Sinnen sind im Geist all ein Sinn und Gebrauch:*
> *Wer Gott beschaut, der schmeckt, fühlt, riecht und hört ihn auch.*

How far superior this *pensée* is to the far more famous verses of Baudelaire on the 'stereoscopy' of the sensations:

> *O métamorphose mystique*
> *De tous mes sens fondus en un!*
> *Son haleine fait la musique*
> *Comme sa voix fait le parfum!"*

When some time later I told him of my delight in the study of Hebrew, particularly at watching the incessant dance of the vowels, light as snowflakes, all about the sturdy consonants, he again had the perfect quotation for me, which of course expressed my opaque intuition in a fully developed form, adding much else besides. The source was *The Adventurous Heart* of Ernst Jünger, a writer who, along with André Malraux and Curzio Malaparte, has been the subject of his meditations for many years. The hub of the quotation is this truly genial insight: "The true magic of the word speaks in the vowels, while it assumes a more bodily fullness in the consonants.... We are lacking a theory of sounds, which I envisage as operating in the sense of Goethe's theory of colors, that is, unscientifically." As I read this, I not only experienced the rare satisfaction of feeling thoroughly understood, but I knew as well that Arthur had just invited me, through the mask of

Jünger, to undertake a new project: developing an unscientific, "poetic" theory of the sounds of human language!

His dominant intellectual passion is, thus, a pursuit for the details of poetry and culture, for the "problem of style in individual works and as a phenomenon of cultural change," as he himself describes his "professional interests" in an update to his *curriculum vitae* for the Department of Romance Languages at Emory University. But I would venture to say that the driving force behind the very patience that has always fueled both his personal search and his scholarly research is the spiritual conviction he attributes to the poetry of a Paul Claudel and a St.-John Perse: "Over against the *Zeitgeist*, both of these affirm the sacred character of the word and the dignity of life." And at once he proceeds to quote from Perse's essay "On Dante": "Without poetry, the human breath would never reach its plenitude either of aspiration or of restoration. To breathe with the world remains the poet's proper, mediating function. Such is in truth the secret primacy of the poet."

Poetic sublimity, however, makes a home with smiling humor in the interior household of this humanist. In the painful letter (painful, that is, to me) Arthur wrote me in the early summer of 1979, informing me he had recently been diagnosed as having a mild case of Parkinson's Disease, he concludes on an upbeat by telling me that, on individual days of the week, a number of friends "are all going to Mass for me – so, what with a prayer crusade and L-Dopa, I shall before long be the *Übermensch* that Nietzsche was looking for." Humor being a catalyst that leads to higher places, he at once quotes Hemingway: "Every man can be broken, but he mends; and it's just in those broken parts that he mends the strongest." But, in the case of Arthur Evans, this strength that blossoms out of woundedness reveals a far different source and contour than Nietzsche's or Hemingway's. And so a few years later, at a time when the Parkinson's was no longer mild and in the midst of his distress over his wife's grave condition, he wrote me with humble confidence: "I, on the other hand, am a 'reed shaken by the wind.'" Even at a moment of indescribable sorrow, humor is like a breeze that softly moves the boat. In this same letter, dated August 13, 1987, he slips in: "Tass will meet with her oncologist – I had never heard of this term, this medical specialty before, so I kept hearing 'ontologist'!!"

In the departmental update mentioned above, he likewise follows his irrepressible instinct for the playful aside, adding a marginal quip as commentary on the fact that, for years, he had been dividing his teaching assignment at Emory between the Department of Romance Languages and the Graduate Institute of the Liberal Arts: "Un pied en Bourgogne, un pied en Champagne," though he leaves us in suspense as to which university department corresponded to which French province. And, gently reproaching the humorless formats of the academic world, he concludes the *curriculum vitae* by adding parenthetically – smuggling it in, as it were – the fact that that year he had read all of Proust's mammoth novel on the labyrinth of memory for the second time, hinting in this way that this was the year's accomplishment he was proudest of.

IN A LETTER in which he confesses to me being "frightened by the prospect" of a *Festschrift* in his honor being published, Arthur tells me he was much relieved at hearing Tass say: "Don't worry, Art, they'll never be able to find the funds necessary to publish it!" But as a result of an astounding confluence of generosities which I have only in some sense coordinated, it appears that this work of celebration is indeed about to see the light of day. The event is to be attributed, more than to any other individual, to the imagination and energy of this very Tass Evans, writing whose name here fills me with deep emotion, who even as she was reassuring her husband of the project's probable failure was secretly hoping for its success with her usual peevish sparkle. Catherine Evans has not lived to see the finished product. But this volume, whose leaves are gathered together into unity by the powerful hands of Augustinian *memoria,* bears a dedication in her name. For, in the *lata praetoria memoriae*, that "wide treasure-house of the memory," there are nothing but real presences. *Tanta vis est memoriae*, writes the Bishop of Hippo in the magnificent tenth book of the *Confessions, tanta vitae vis est in homine vivente mortaliter!* "How great the *memoriae vis,* our power of memory, how great is the power of life in man even as he lives but a mortal existence!"

My mortal existence once took me and my wife to the offbeat Greek island of Andros, where the Evanses with their sons were enjoying a portion of their sabbatical year. There, on the shores of the Aegean, Arthur and I endlessly discussed my impending doctoral dissertation on the Austrian Expressionist poet, Georg Trakl, whom he had revealed to me – conversations which Tass referred to as "trakling away." Then, in the evening, we ate fried fish in the village, in a tiny taverna whose owner's pride and joy was an authentic Stradivarius hanging inexplicably on the wall, being cured with waftings of garlic and olive oil. Though I did not, of course, realize it then, I now think it hung over us there as a smiling fruit, a gracious sign from the Muses, from *la Muse qui est la Grâce*. And under it there, feasting, we still all are...

A FEW WORDS are, after all, in order regarding the organization of the book. An initial section contains contributions that bear a more personal character or are creative pieces. This is followed by four essays of a philosophical nature, all of them dealing with the theme of fullness of humanity as something to be attained by the crafted integration of the faculties of the soul. A third section offers five essays on poetry and poets, and it presents interpretations of specific texts. Section IV then passes over into the prose genre; its three contributions again consider specific texts. The four essays of Section V offer the reader different possibilities in critical methodology, from the structuralist to the religious. There follows a section grouping three essays on art history and interpretation and an original collage. A final section leaves the reader questioning the world around us today. And a striking poem by Paul Evans, by way of epilogue, strives to break open the reader's memory – break it open like a fertile field that is turned over for sowing – and leave it suspended in the resonant silence of contemplation, which is perfect act because it is perfect receptivity. This poem is, to me, the verbal equivalent of a postcard here on the desk before me, which Arthur Evans once sent me from Chartres and which Paul has never seen. It shows the "contemplative life opening her book," a figure from the thirteenth-century sculptural program of the north portal. Once, sitting in the garden of the Evans home in Atlanta – a place we jestingly called "the garden of the Finzi-Continis" because of its secluded spaciousness – Arthur explained to me how in his family everyone tried to integrate the active and the contemplative lives. The poem "Passion/ Sun(Son)" is an eloquent fruit of that attempt.

Memoriae vis: "the power, the vitality, of memory." The contributors to this collection of essays were in no way held to elaborating any specific theme. A man, not a theme, was to be the point of convergence. This very fact makes it astonishing that, in various ways, nearly

xix

every contribution touches on the theme of memory. I believe this has to do both with the spirit of humanism that breathes through these pages (for humanism is rooted in a living tradition and thus is the bane of amnesia) and with the character of the man the essays honor. On both counts, everywhere there filters through a keen sense of an experience, a discovery, a word, a work, an image, a face, an idea, a landscape, a love, that memory salvages from the ephemeral to the eternal moment by embracing it both firmly and tenderly. A few examples, by section, will suggest the common thread.

"Envois to the Man": In a series of imagined letter-fragments to Arthur Evans, John Leavey reconstructs with linguistic playfulness, and through the recalling of literary texts, the memory (*mémoir!*) of his debt to his teacher. Wallace Fowlie offers us an autobiographical essay that remembers the reading of literature as an exploration of and a search for the self in the eternal moment created by great art.

"The Roots of Beatitude": Richard Parry points to the need of going beneath the "veneer of sophisticated skepticism" to rediscover that reason can in fact know truth, and that this knowledge is the deepest satisfaction possible to man, according to Plato. In its highest form, virtue is an active imitation of Immortal Beauty itself, for which our *eros* yearns, remembering its dazzling attraction from a time of pure spiritual existence. This active memory of the highest and most desirable reality is what moves a soul to be noble and exert herself ever upwards. Desire for carnal beauty is a repressed desire for eternal Beauty, which the philosophical memory must recover: Freud in reverse!

"The Shape of Ecstasy": John ter Haar commemorates Goethe's love-affair with Bohemia. The Goethe poem he interprets itself memorializes – and thus eternalizes – a moving experience of Goethe's in Prague.

"Self's Shades and Shadows": Michael Riley shows how, both in Kafka and in Chesterton, the question "Who am I?" – the attempt to remember one's identity – emerges as the chief motor-force of the plot of their stories and novels. John Dunaway introduces us to Vladimir Volkoff, a French writer from a Russian émigré family, who, through the apparently minor genre of the detective-story novel, can continually astonish the reader by reminding him that the full depth and background of life are fraught with mystery, human and divine. Volkoff shatters the crystal-palace perfection of much Western aesthetics by reminding us by unconventional fictional methods that true transcendence is not produced by man but comes solely from man's break-through to God, itself only the obverse of God's breakthrough to man. In this and other ways, Volkoff exhibits his Eastern Orthodox heritage. Memory, or better, remembering, is approached by Maximilian Aue on the paradigm of select short stories of Hugo von Hofmannsthal as an attempt at discovering the true self. But remembrance of the real self occasions a crisis: the loss of the accustomed self and its tight connections with the socio-historical context. Aue applies Kierkegaard's distinction between *Erinnerung,* as a relating to the essential as a result of reflection, and *Gedächtnis,* as a spontaneous remembering of what could just as well be forgotten.

"The Elusive Hunt": Erasmo Leiva-Merikakis culls the moral implications of the act of reading as formulated in T.S. Eliot's critical essays, animated as these are by an active memory of the living Christian tradition and dogma. Erdmann Waniek and Cristina de la Torre lucidly analyze three versions of a folktale as modalities of the European collective memory.

"Through the Magic Mirror": Dorothy Joiner suggests that Bosch's paintings present a particularly intense "condensation" of many elements of the mystical tradition (Kabbalah, Gnosticism, fairy-tales). In this sense, the paintings are a graphic compendium, a creative memory of religious culture. The artist's memory is seen to be "associative," as Freud suggests for dreams. Through an analysis of specific paintings, Carlos Rojas reconstructs Picasso's quest for his father and, hence, for his own identity and vital source. The memory of his father's renunciation of art weighs guiltily upon Picasso, and this leads him to exercise a, literally, creative memory in the act of painting. Repeatedly he paints an anonymous man with a long, sad face whom he later identifies with shock as his father. The magic of art thus reunites what had been sundered. The memory of the father is resurrected in the art at the same time that that same memory provides the impulse that produces the work of art. Thomas Lyman evaluates his own first encounter with Malraux's theory that only the present can give meaning to past works of art. History is transcended the moment when the beholder's passion reanimates in an art-work the original passion that had created it. Lyman retraces his own itinerary as art historian and the way it was affected by Malraux's ideas. The only authentic history, it is suggested, may be autobiography – a form of "history" that puts the present in touch with, not a theoretical past, but a transcendent present that wills into existence a far broader world than that which meets the uncreative eye.

"Recalling the Present": James Young uses the historian's memory in an unusual but presently most relevant application. In the context of the AIDS epidemic, he compares the many ready "cures" and solutions being offered to the desperate with the long history of panaceas and nostrums that he fully documents, beginning at the end of the eighteenth century. In another article, Daniel Taylor asserts that the present role of Christian humanism is to remind the "escapist" Church of the necessity of engagement in the world, and to remind the "secularistic" non-believer, who is merely escaping in the opposite direction, of man's need for transcendence and an eternity of life and love. The Christian humanist keeps alive the memory of what the Church at her best has been and can still be for the life of the world.

ONE OF THE CHIEF INSTIGATORS of this tribute was Tom Lyman. In February I learned of his sudden death with great sadness. To Tom goes the singular merit of having been a gentle gadfly at all stages of the project save the last. His perseverance in seeing his dear colleague Arthur Evans honored is in itself the most eloquent testimony of a life well lived. May his memory too, then, be celebrated in these pages.

Erasmo Leiva-Merikakis
Aix-en-Provence and San Francisco
July, 1992

ARTHUR R. EVANS DIED ON SEPTEMBER 7, 1992.

ACKNOWLEDGEMENTS

THE EDITORS – Erdmann Waniek is taking over responsibilities as I am writing this – are profoundly grateful to many persons. First, and most obviously, I thank all those who responded so promptly and generously to the invitation to contribute. I am especially indebted to you for a patience that really deserves the more poignant name of forbearance. And only Danny Smartt himself knows the extent of my gratitude to him for having not only transcribed the entire manuscript as a labor of love, but given me the continual benefit of his intelligence and humor. I owe his friendship to our common effort.

xxiii

E.L.-M.
July, 1992

THE AUTHORS RESPONDED most swiftly when called upon in the essential, concluding stages of preparing this volume, and for this they yet again deserve the editors' gratitude. Robert Evans and his wife, Judith Martens, designed the volume, and Robert faithfully recorded all necessary changes as well. Throughout, Harry Gilmer of the Scholars Press has been a valuable critic and ready support. I greatly benefitted from James McMahon's unstinting advice and from Elizabeth Soilis' unfailing secretarial assistance. Finally, and perhaps most crucially, we must thank Emory University for the generous gift which has made the publication of this volume possible.

E.W.
February, 1993

I. ENVOIS *to the* MAN

LETTER from a FRIEND

Aug. 26th, 1986

Dear Erasmo,

Excuse my not replying instantly. I'm an old war horse small town reporter, long retired. I don't understand your Chicago system nor word processors. Expept on Lou Grant reruns.

Art and I grew up togbther in Mpls. We still get together when he can return here. And I phone and write him frequently. My Mom had Parkinson's and I took care of her.

-O-

We haven't DONE much in adult years , except to chat. But one last thing, in the fall of '42, does come back to me tonight. Just before both Art and I went into the Army.

Two things held us togbther. Writing and sports. And we played a lot of sandlot pickup tackle football.

Our final game in '42 was a 30-18 win, just before all of us scattered to the four military winds.

The crucial point was that Art directed a victory, despite being kicked in the head very early. He was the quarterback.

Not until late in the game, did he finally give us a play that sounded like alphabet soup. I escorted him to a blanket on the sideline.

His uncle, a doctor, put him in the hospital for 5 days with a concussion.

Good luck on the book,

your signature

BY JOHN P. LEAVEY, JR.

12 JUNE 1986

a letter indebts in your memory. The request calling for a celebration of you "as a gesture of gratitude" declares a theme *(Gedanke)* of memory (symbolic reconstitution, tradition, remembering of beloved ...). In your name, in memory of you, on memory, the letter demands a gift, a gift of remembrance *(Gedächtnis, Gedenken)*. Remembrance of indebtedness recalls letters of indebtedness, the letter bearing and dissolving its gift in itself, a letter of Seneca (split in two for Dante) who accurately writes, a gift is not without the recognition of a debt, here a debt from an unending conversation that will never have taken place. This series of letters I here sign severally and with love and affection will have taken up, only to defer, that conversation. From Seneca, to Dante, Rimbaud, and Trakl, the three you taught me, I write them today in the name of the obscene gesture, under the seal of your pain, *paralysis agitans.*

23 JANUARY 1976

Some days before my father's death, the gift of an *envoi.* "What we can learn from Erich Auerbach's example is something of that severe joy *(res severa verum gaudium)* which he must surely have felt in every page he wrote" ("Erich Auerbach as European Critic," *Romance Philology* 25 [1971]: 215). Your *envoi* I detach here, a dispatch citing from memory a letter of Seneca, whose letters end with a contribution *(mercedulam* [Letter 6]), a payment, as is the custom, for this letter *(et aliquid, ut institui, pro hac epistula dependendum)*, although it will not be charged to the repayment or debt *(solutum)* – I gave it to you from you yourself *(dedi de tuo tibi* [Letter 8]) – a small gift as is my custom *(ut more meo cum aliquo munusculo epistulam mittam* [Letter 10]), the seal of a saying *(si illi signum suum inpressero, id est aliquam magnificam vocem perferendam ad te mandavero* [Letter 13]), the envoi of a daily donation *(cotidianam stipem* [Letter 14]) the hand stretches out to receive, the *envoi* that closes *(claudere)* the letter that cannot be closed without paying the price *(tibi valedicere non licet gratis* [Letter 17]), the letter that begins to be folded *(conplicare* [Letter 18]) or must be broken open again *(resolvenda* [Letter 22]) for the gift of the *envoi.*

I. ENVOIS TO THE MAN

break open these folded seals, *envois*

the plane was late, I imagine. Vicki and I went to the Waverly Hotel for brunch, and I planned to see you for a short time before the flight to Gainesville. I was just returning from Chicago, where Derrida delivered a lecture on *Geschlecht*, on Heidegger, the hand, and Trakl. I finished translating the piece only a few days before the conference, since Jacques was working on it close to the beginning of March. And I also had my brief paper to complete as well. It was on translating Derrida, on the *envoi* whose wandering disrupts assured destination – destinerrance – that indebts in the fold of the letter to be broken open again, in the apocalyptic seals (not) to be broken open to reveal the indebtedness of translation.

      Here the conversation was to have taken place, brief, only an hour or so. Vicki has been the conduit of contact for us for quite some time. And for that I owe her much thanks. She always lets me know how you are. And I to you, as you wrote me. We did talk, of plans, of my trip, of Vicki and other friends. And you asked me a simple question

      – Did I know much about Parkinson's Disease?

      – Only that the loss of physical control would be the most difficult thing to live with.

      The conversation never took place, the gift never exchanged. The debt accumulates. The letters continue.

severe joy. In letter 23, Seneca exhorts *ad bonam mentem*, you and me, to the sound mind. (Lucilius is addressed, but the addressee, even you and I, is not to be restricted, cannot be restricted. Seneca is already split. In these letters I cannot control addressee or sender. I occupy all places at once. And by apostrophe, you as well.)

      – *Mihi crede, verum gaudium res severa est.*

      Believe me, Seneca writes, the statement that follows is to be believed, the statement of the severe joy that is the fundament (*fundamentum*), no, rather the culmination (*culmen*), of the sound mind: do not take joy in vain things (*vanis*).

      – I do not want to rob (*detrahere*) you of many pleasures (*multas voluptates*), of gladness (*laetitiam*). It is to be born within you (*intra te*), in your house (*tibi domi*), that true joy that is a severe thing, a severe thing that can only be *de tuo*, from the best of you, you yourself, *te ipso et tui optima parte.*

And to acquit the debt (*solvendi aeris alieni*) (Seneca's, but also ours, but also the debt of the letter itself [*hanc epistulam liberare*] in its folding, under seal, but always broken to be read), there is the gift, the gift of a life saying as the explanation of one by Epicurus: *Id agendum est, ut satis vixerimus.* To live as if we already will have lived enough, that is the stake. That is the *envoi.*

The debt accumulates on its own

"In my book of memory, in the early part...there comes...*Incipit vita nova.*" During which "my body was afflicted by a painful disease... I was forced to lie in bed like a person paralyzed." I mention, only like Dante to leave out, the epistle. Thus does Dante begin his *Vita nuova.*

But I want to invoke the noble, writing memory (*mente*) that does not wander or err: *la mente che non erra ...o mente che scrivesti ciò ch'io vidi* (*Inf.* II:6, 8). The English translations I consulted (Sinclair, Sayers, Ciardi, Mandelbaum) all translate *mente* as "memory" at this location, possibly to distinguish this from the earlier *l'animo mio* still in flight (*Inf.* I:25). In the *Purgatorio*, this confidence in *mente* writing without errancy begins to falter.

– Right before reaching the other shore (*riva*) of Lethe, right before being dunked (*e mi sommerse*) by Matilda, I hear the *Asperges me,* the song I cannot remember, nor write (*che nol so rimembrar, non ch'io lo scriva*) (*Purg.* XXXI:97-101).

And in the beginning of the next canto:

– my eyes (*li occhi miei*), staring into the eyes of Beatrice, quenched all the senses.

But the memory is not restored. Lethe obliterates. Eunoë restores.

– A greater care (*maggior cura*), Beatrice says to Matilda, often deprives the memory (*la memoria priva*), perhaps it clouded his mind's eyes (*la mente sua nelli occhi oscura*). Eunoë will restore his stunned power (*la tramortita sua virtù*).

– I was remade (*rifatto*) from those waters (*Purg.* XXXIII:124-45).

So the writing of the *mente,* the writing or the *mente,* is not without errance. It can be clouded.

Immediately after, in the opening lines of the *Paradiso, mente* and *memoria* are distinguished once again.

– Our intellect (*nostro intelletto*) goes so deep drawing near its desire, the memory (*la memoria*) cannot follow. But the matter of my

6

song (*matera del mio canto*) will be what my mind (*mia mente*) can treasure of what I saw (*vidi*) in that highest kingdom (*Par.* I).

But memory fails at the end of desire, and so too our speech at the outrage suffered (*'l parlar nostro, ch'a tal vista cede, / e cede la memoria a tanto oltraggio*). Not all, but as the passion impressed (*la passione impressa*) in a dream, remains to the mind (*mente*), so grant it, my mind (*mia mente*), my memory (*mia memoria*), just a spark of what I saw, of what appeared. Insufficient were my own wings (*ma non eran da ciò le proprie penne*), but my mind was struck by a refulgence in which came its wish (*se non che la mia mente fu percossa / da un fulgore in che sua voglia venne*) (*Par.* XXXIII:55-60, 68-73, 139-41).

Thus I write in the errance of memory at the end of desire, where memory, obliterated and restored, is remade, only to fail at the outrage that strikes it.

The question of Dante, then, in the end:

– Am I struck dumb, mind paralyzed, agitated in the refulgence of a desire?

Envoi: the obscenity (what is in opposition to the scene, or what is off scene) of the *Commedia* is the lurching release of all *mente*, mind as memory's failure to write without errance, without desire. *Mente come paralysis agitans.*

25 DECEMBER 1986

the off-scene is what cannot be in proportion to the scene. As the always broken seal of the scene, the off-scene makes the scene visible, able to be seen. *Obscenus*, adverse, opposite in position. Obscene, then, is positions. And the obscene gesture is the positional scene, the site of the positional opposition: *ob-scene*. Paralysis agitans – the obscene gesture itself. Paralysis that is opposedly agitating. Let me shorten this to what Derrida calls *paralyse*, "a certain movement of fascination (fascinating fascinated), a movement that analyzes what prevents and provokes at once desire's step [*pas*] into the labyrinth that it itself is – not [*pas*]" ("Ja, ou le faux-bond," *Digraphe*, No. 11 [1977]: 89).

26 DECEMBER 1986

Commedia, the writing of paralyse

17 JANUARY 1987

Again,

– if I remember well (*si je me souviens bien*)…the severity of the new hour, yes (*Oui, l'heure nouvelle est au moins très sévère*).

JOHN P. LEAVEY, JR.

The memory of the poison, the deliriums, the impossible morning – from *Une saison en enfer* I want to extract only a few phrases:
– *Plus de mots*
– *Il faut être absolument moderne.*
– *Point de cantiques* ....

No more words (*plus de mots*) in the labyrinth of more words (*plus de mots*). This moment of *paralyse* in Rimbaud (but in French uncontrollably) leads to the incorporation of the dead, of death. To the question of self-knowledge, of nature, the paralysing response of (no) more words – *J'ensevelis les morts dans mon ventre.* I bury deep in my belly the dead words (*mots, morts, les mots morts*). Self-knowing is the incorporation of *paralyse.*

And if self-knowing is to be absolutely modern (the obscene memories [*les souvenirs immondes*] are effaced), the refusal of hymns (*point de cantiques*) is also the position, the point, of hymns (*point de cantique*), the position of the vigil (*la veille*), of the old loves (*vieilles amours*): *tenir le pas gagné.* Yes, keep to the pace won, to the step already taken. But also keep to the *no* gained, to the *paralyse* gained. Such is the vigil point, the vigil to possessing the truth dans une âme et un corps, *in one soul and one body,* the vigil of *paralyse, paralyse* itself.

– I paralyse

18 JANUARY 1987
Trakl. He read Rimbaud. Paralysed.

18 JANUARY 1987
– And a distant friend writes you a letter (*Auch schreibt ein ferner Freund dir einen Brief*). In a dream. (*Der Spaziergang.*)
– Of night.
– In winternight (*Winternacht*), the stars configure ill omens (*Deine Sterne schliessen sich zu bösen Zeichen*). The darkness (*die Finsternis*) petrifies its steps (*Mit versteinerten Schritten*) as it trudges along.
– In the night (*Die Nacht*) of the sung wild cleft (*wilde Zerklüftung*), a petrified head (*Ein versteinertes Haupt*) storms the sky.
– In submission to the night (*Nachtergebung*), by night (*nachts*), the earthly wandering (*Erdenwallen*) turns into the dream, the room to grave.
– in *Föhn*, the white night (*die weisse Nacht*) comes along quietly, transforms the pain and torment of stony life (*Des steinigen Lebens*) into purple dreams.

– In the night song (*Nachtlied*), speechless (*sprachlos*), there is the blue that stiffens, the vast power of the silence in the stone (*Gewaltig ist das Schweigen im Stein*), the still mirrors of truth (*stillen Spiegel der Wahrheit*).

Paralyse of night, of the dream wrapped in its night, in its derangement. But the night mirrors the truth, provokes and prevents truth. Rimbaud paralysed self-knowing, Trakl the dream.

– *Traum und Umnachtung.* In the past tense, remembered, a family scene, the *Geschlecht* of the dream. As Derrida points out, the translation of this term will never have been done, even in German.

– *Am Abend*, in the evening, not quite night.

– In the evening the father became old, the mother's face stone (*versteinerte das Antlitz der Mutter*), and the curse of the degenerate *Geschlecht* (*der Fluch des entarteten Geschlechts*) pressed on the young boy.

9

The curse of degenerate birth, of degenerate descent, of the dream, that is what pressed on the young boy.

– *Erinnerte er sich.* He, the father, the young boy – but here it, *der Traum*, an apostrophe to the dream, what the title says – it recalls childhood and the sister in the blue mirror (*Aus blauem Spiegel*). The self-recollecting dream, as if dead, tumbles into darkness (*ins Dunkel*), its mouth broken open, and its dreams, the dreams of the dream, filled the old house of the fathers.

The lineage here, the dream of the dream, its *Geschlecht*, includes the old house of the fathers.

– The dream spoke the source of the blue (*die ehrwürdige Sage des blauen Quells*)…with a stone mouth (*mit steinernem Munde*), and recognized its own face, surrounded with night (*sein umnachtetes Antlitz*), in the child's. Over it the shadows of night fell like stones (*die Schatten der Nacht fielen steinern auf ihn*).

The stone mouth paralyzes, that is, recognizes itself in its own generation, but generation in stone that is itself the dream's *Umnachtung*.

– The dream was turned into a stone pillar by the blue rustle of the gown, and the nightlike form of its mother stood in the door (*Das blaue Rauschen eines Frauengewandes liess ihn zur Säule erstarren und in der Tür stand die nächtige Gestalt seiner Mutter*). Darkness struck its brow (*die Finsternis schlug seine Stirne*). It saw its own bloody shape *starrend von Unrat*, what Getsi rightly translates as "rigid with excrement." It loved more the stone works – tower and grave.

– O cursed *Geschlecht* (*O des verfluchten Geschlechts*). The father's voice, harsh, rang out (*klang*). From paralyzed (*erstarrten*) hands fruit and tools of the displaced *Geschlecht* (*entsetzten Geschlecht*) fell and decayed (*verfielen*). There was the seer surrounded in the night (*Ein umnachteter Seher*), an unseeing seer, deranged in prophecy, paralyzed in seeing. O children of the Night, O dark *Geschlecht* (*dunklen Geschlechts*), O, the cursed (*der Verfluchten*), eyes broken.

– Sleep is deep in dark poisons (*in dunklen Giften*). The white, stone face of the mother is there. And the sister's eyes of stone (*der steinernen Augen der Schwester*). On the nighted brow of the brother (*auf die nächtige Stirne des Bruders*) trod her madness. The bread turned to stone in the mother's hands. A purple cloud clouded its head (*Purpurne Wolke umwölkte*); the dream, of stone (*steinern*), fell upon its own blood and image, dropped into the emptiness (*ins Leere*). Night swallowed (*verschlang*) the cursed *Geschlecht* (*das verfluchte Geschlecht*).

The dream is swallowed into the Night, into the white that swallows, clouds in purple, names the source of the blue that turns to stone, the *Geschlecht* of the dream, the family scene, sex, and lineage, the wide-open mouth into which it falls – stoned eyes broken.

dream – paralyse

27 JANUARY 1987

Envois. Paralyse – the last word, the word always spoken as if it had already been spoken, at the tower. The logic of the last word:

– *le dernier mot.* The obscene word. Paralyse. The watchword, the ordering word, *le mot d'ordre* is *plus de langage*, (no) more language.

– *plus de langage contraignant ou affirmatif, c'est-à-dire plus de langage – mais non: toujours une parole pour le dire et ne pas le dire* (*Après coup*, 93). No more language is to say no more language; saying and unsaying in a word.

– already no longer speaking and yet not the beginning of some other thing.

– the last word cannot be a word, cannot be the absence of word, cannot be any other thing but a word.

– I became stone. I was the monument and the hammer that breaks it (*Le dernier mot*, 77-78).

Paralyse. The last signature. Always (un)signed as if it will already have been signed. *Envoi.*

I sign here out of your own teaching. The debt will have continued. I sign for both of us in the obscene that will always have been on the scene, in the paralyse of my affection

– without saying a word

MEMORY

BY WALLACE FOWLIE, DUKE UNIVERSITY

Dear Art, we have been friends for well over thirty years. I no longer write articles such as those traditionally published in a festschrift. As a way of honoring you, may I contribute these pages from a "work in progress," a continuation of reminiscences about the past, which, if they are ever completed and published, I would like to call: *Memory: a fourth attempt.*

11

W e call it now "stream of consciousness," but through the centuries, memory, for want of a better term, has been referred to as flowing water. During these past ten years I have descended into that stream more often than I have stayed on its banks, on the solid ground of day-by-day life. Currents of the past are indeed deep, and at times I have struggled hard to raise my ghosts, watery figures mist-covered, in order to join them and walk again with them.

Self-writing, with which I am now unashamedly allied, is, in a fundamental sense, mimesis. It has its grandeur and its misery too. But it has the music of human life. I can still hear the waves breaking on South Beach in Popham, which I heard when I was nine years old, as clearly as I hear this morning, at the age of seventy-seven, the cars rushing along Chapel Hill Boulevard on their way to Chapel Hill or to Durham.

The eternal moment: that is the sole subject of autobiography. I am who I was. Life is a narrative, and self-writing is narrative discourse, whether I am recalling a specific episode, or the words of a friend, or thoughts that rise up again and again in my consciousness. When I say to myself: 'observe each day as it comes in, and celebrate it as if it is an aubade,' I am really saying, 'observe age as it comes in, and make it serviceable.'

I pursue a lonely conception of this book and often ask myself as I resume daily work on it: where is its grand design? I persevere because I am the sole custodian of the figures of my life. Those invisible presences play their part as I rehearse the repetitive patterns of living. There was, of course, at the beginning an original text, a first occurrence. But then, each year, each decade, the original text is reworked.

For Dante it became one of his one hundred cantos, written perhaps in Verona, in his exile from Florence. For Ezra Pound it became one of his *Pisan Cantos*, also written in exile, and possibly in Rapallo.

Such master craftsmen as they were are examples for minor writers who live in far less dramatic exiles. From such writers, and from others: St. Augustine, Pascal, Thomas Merton, I have learned that what I have been seeking I have already found. From the writing of these pages I know that I am going to where I am. Circularity in time and space is the mode of my existence as I recall words and sites, figures and sounds, desolation and jubilation.

Places, real places where I once lived, are more real than the town in which I now live. They haunt me and draw me back through intervening spaces: a street in Boston, a hotel in Nice, a eucalyptus tree in Taormina, a movie house in New Haven, New York's Central Park, Golden Hill in Colorado. Paris is my pillar of cloud and fire.

For many years I have lived so close to Dante that I now behold life in images of journeying, and especially in images of *descent*. And yet I am related to no hero, to no protagonist comparable to Dante. Wherever I am, it is a place of no thoroughfare. If I had the strength of no purpose, I would drop all props and wander forth. Then I would feel more related to a hero and more able to resist this need to write of the self.

In retrospect I can remember clearly the unique power of Paris. It obliterated for me all personal affairs, all personal attachments. I had read *Le Père Goriot* and *Le spleen de Paris*, and thus in the streets of Paris I dreamed not of myself but of Balzac's Eugène de Rastignac and *le vieux saltimbanque* of Baudelaire. There I learned to think of books as artifacts, as objects not related to me but to truth, and when I came upon the sentence (I believe it is Flaubert's) *Tout ce qu'on invente est vrai* ("Everything invented is true") I knew I had discovered a major key to the art of reading and the art of teaching. The old writers of France: Villon and Ronsard, Voltaire and Nerval, were *revenants* for me whom I welcomed in my *promenades*, whom I accosted at times and on whose marginal intellectual worlds I poached.

Autobiography is fiction of a special breed. One picture is always clear to my mind when I hear the word "autobiography": a young man from his province en route to the city (and the city is usually Paris). Flaubert, Balzac, Stendhal, of course, but also James Joyce, Rimbaud, Hart Crane, Samuel Beckett.

The personal growth in each of these famous cases is unique,

12

and that is what autobiography means. In this shocking comparison I am making with these big names and accomplishments, my own personal growth, if I can call it that, is linguistic. I study words in order to become more human. Words at first not understood, but spoken over and over again until I have learned them by heart. Separate isolated words at first, in this process of turning myself into a human being, and then whole poems (*Mémoire* of Rimbaud, *Vergine Madre*, canto 33, *Il Paradiso*), then whole scenes from Molière and Racine.

The usual cycle in a man's life of exile and return to the home base, is, in my case, the cycle of exile and a further exile in a new place. There has been no return home. Boston-Cambridge to Connecticut (Taft School and Yale), to Chicago, to Vermont (Bennington), to Colorado (Boulder), to North Carolina (Durham). And now to Duke, where I still teach long after I should have legally retired, I contemplate the next (and last?) move, one not too far from this place of favorite courses, and medicine, and the thwarted hope of building a chapel on Campus Drive (which I had planned to call "Chapel of the Angels" to offset "the Blue Devils").

13

My essays and books of literary criticism are today my quarries. Thanks to them, this new text I am writing can be stabilized. Let me be self-writer now and not critic.

Whatever this chronicle is, whatever it becomes, I know it is rooted in the reading of literature, and in the exercises I have written about French writers and Dante. There has been little or no influence of other autobiographies. Almost nothing from Rousseau and Yeats. Some, it is true, from Thoreau, and some from Henry Adams. And that is because I already know their woods and their cities. I remember the fields and ponds of New England. I remember Boston and Paris, the Virgin of Notre Dame and Louisberg Square.

This fictional guise I am calling autobiography is made up of conventions and mythologies that frame half-truths. A meeting of minds took place – not in reading Rimbaud, but in trying to explain him in a classroom. The presence of others around me, of your lives – innocent despite all their worldliness and sophistication – has forced me into moments of self-identification. I would never have written about Rimbaud if I had not taught him. I would never have written a memoir-book, if I had not half-memorized *Une saison en enfer*. The artful flashes that fill *Une saison* portray man rather than one man. The narrator in that book is also the protagonist – as Proust was once in *A la recherche* so gloriously, so ruthlessly. With such models which I observed by teaching them, I have been forced to exhibit myself twice over: an outworn self, and a new self created by these words. Self-scrutiny leads me to beings outside myself. How futile to hope for any total autobiographical image!

As an older narrator I learn now to manipulate pseudo-autobiographical forms. Have I reread too often? Have I thought too steadfastly of the past? Have sentences and rhythms of Rimbaud (*L'automne déjà!*) persisted too long in my memory? There is a covert religion at work in Rimbaud's text. One day in the future it will lie exposed for all to see. All men are one. Every text, even *Une saison,* will be demystified.

Without the support of literature, no one can have an image of humanity, no one can have a theory of life. Books of science will lead into literature, but they lack the splendor, the portentous truths of *Four Quartets*, of Ulysses, of Pascal's *Pensées*. It is, after all, racial memory that counts – the transmission of experience from generation to generation: Boethius to Dante to Chaucer to Machiavelli. Only after such a genealogy will a man begin to comprehend such a term as *fortuna*.

We are continuous from generation to generation. The embryo that turned into the child I once was, and which is now an old man, will not have reached its end at my death. Concerned as we are with our bodily changes, we easily forget the transmigration of our soul that is also taking place when we breathe and when we will no longer breathe.

I rarely watch sunsets, but each morning for the past thirty years I have watched the sunrise, even when there is no visible sun if a grey mist covers it. I have seen it rise over Lake Como and Mount Etna, over house tops in Paris, and over the distant Mediterranean in Saint-Paul-de-Vence. At such unusual mornings as those in my life, I joined the coming of dawn in my eyes, to the inner light of my spirit as it strove to pierce the darkened mystery of words on the page of a notebook.

Light veils of clouds have allowed me to converse more frankly with Dante and Montaigne, with Saint John in Patmos, and Jules Laforgue in his Pierrot complaints. Such men have been my fellow travelers. And they often kept me outside the major movements of my plot. Now that I look back more often than I look forward, I journey back on the road of ancestry, to emperors or pontifices, to gallows' victims and court jesters. I must be after some theory of recovery I am unable to resurrect. A seminal source in the sun, perhaps. A myth fostered in my childhood as I walked on paths around Walden. I have moved from pagan learning to letters of Paul.

14

Truth is to be found in autobiographical fable. I try to hear voices that echo in the pages of this narrative, and often recognize them to be echoes of my fledgling selves. I remain principally an early naïve persona.

The old image of life as a river flowing along and being fed by tributary streams, and whose entrance into the sea is death, is an archetypal image long in the race of men. The growth of the river accumulating riches is the preparation for annihilation, for expansion and then dissolution. It fits perfectly the nature of tragedy, which is life-death. As a child I watched the mouth of the Kennebec River at the sea, and now I am writing that experience. The shift from a scene of real living water to lines of real living words.

I am waiting now for a climactic flood that will fulfill the action lived heretofore as an obscure drama. The Charles River of my childhood, and the more prosaic Rhône River I have watched in later years, are less significant to me than the river of *Le bateau ivre*. In that river and in the river of Rimbaud's *Mémoire*, I felt the beatings of the world's mighty heart. They were the outlet toward something noble and beautiful.

It is hard to force on to a river some arbitrary plot manipulation. My flood will come as the answer to prayer...

March-April 1986
Durham

THE CONCISEST TENANT

BY FRANK MANLEY, EMORY UNIVERSITY

She thought it was her husband scratching the headboard in a fragment of dream she could not remember, and then she was awake hearing the same sound. It was over her head. She lay in bed and looked at it and saw nothing but darkness and the sound coming from it like the sound of her own thoughts. "The rat is the concisest tenant," she thought, the words rising up unbidden. "It pays no rent." She thought of it as a secret presence.

She struck her husband on the arm. "Get up," she said. "There's a rat in the house." He stirred beside her, and she struck him again.

"What happened?" he said.

"Listen."

They listened to the sound on the slope of the roof over their heads.

"Squirrels on the roof," her husband said, and turned over to go to sleep. She smelled the whiskey. It was inside the bed like the smell of something under the covers. She thought of their marriage. That's what it smelled like. She struck him again and kept striking him until he sat up.

"What's the matter?" he asked. It was clear he had already forgotten.

"It's night," she said, "Squirrels sleep at night."

"So what?"

She got up and turned on the light and saw what it was and ran out of the house into the yard. The noises of insects exploded around her. They seemed like stars. Every individual voice she heard was like the sound of a star. Her heart rose up in her throat. It was as though she had never been outdoors at night, had never seen stars or heard the myriad voices. There were so many. She had never known there were so many. It was like a miracle.

Then her husband came out and said, "Bat. It's flying all over."

She saw that he had propped open the screen door with a paddle and was taking a screen out of a window, and she said, "What are you doing? You crazy or what? I'd rather have bats. What you think you're letting in there?"– thinking of all the sounds she was hearing, each with a different kind of body.

"Get the screen back," she told her husband. "I'll get the front door," and she ran and kicked out the paddle and slammed the door after her. It was only then that she realized that she had not locked it out. She had closed herself up inside with it. The bat came reeling across the ceiling. She ducked behind a chair just as her husband came in and saw it staggering toward him and immediately backed out.

"What are we going to do?" he asked from the other side of the door, and she thought, he's still drunk.

Looking back, it was the moment her whole life had changed. She knew she could not rely on him. Whatever had to be done she would have to do herself.

"We can't just leave the house," she heard her husband say through the screen. And then it came to her.

"Get in the bedroom, and turn off the light," she said. Her husband had turned on all the lights in the house.

"What good does that do?" her husband asked. And then he said, "I know. I'll hit it."

"With what?"

"A shovel."

"What?"

"A broom. A broom will kill it."

"Not in my house you won't."

"A motel then. Go to a motel and call the exterminator."

And she said, "Get in the bedroom, and close the door so it can't get in there." And he got in the bedroom, and she crept about the house as under an invisible ceiling two or three feet from the floor. The bat dipped and fluttered in the air space over her, herded from room to room as she turned out the lights behind it and closed the door, driving it forward, the bat always leaving the darkenend room seeking the light ahead as though guided by a tropism until they ended up in the kitchen.

The door was closed. In the dark the bat could be anywhere. She slid on her rump across the tiles, keeping her head down for fear it would seek out her hair as bats are said to do, having a mysterious affinity for human hair, particularly the hair of a woman. Bats are covered with lice and vermin. If it ever touched her, she would never get clean. She would have to shave her head and wash it with kerosene. Besides getting rabies. Bats carried rabies, that was well known. Look how they fly, jerking this way and that. She would foam at the mouth and die slowly in spasms. Then she was at the white hulk of the refrigerator.

It looked like a marble sarcophagus. She reached up for the handle and flung the door open. The room filled with color and light and the odor of cold. She was momentarily comforted by it. Then she felt the bat sweep past her, the wings in her ear like leather gloves rubbing each other, scraping and squeaking. Then it was inside the refrigerator, seeking the light, and she slammed the door on it.

She rose to her full height and went into the bedroom. Her husband had already fallen asleep. He stirred when she got in bed beside him and asked what happened. She said, "I froze it," but he was too drunk and too sleepy to know what that meant. She lay beside him listening to him breathe. Her eyes were open, and she could see in the dark. She was thinking not of the bat but of the rest of her life. The two seemed related.

The next morning she got up while her husband still slept. He looked like something deposited in her bed by a truck. She went into the kitchen and stood beside the refrigerator listening. Then she eased the door open a crack. It was still dark. She opened it a little more. The light came on, and she quickly closed it. This was not at all what she had imagined. She imagined something clean and painless, swift as a scalpel to the throat, innocent as poison gas, cold and antiseptic. She leaned her head against the door and thought of never opening it again. She would go to the bedroom and get dressed, take whatever money they had, and get in the car and go somewhere, as far as she could, and change her name and get a job and start a new life.

She opened the door to look again. The bat was on its side on the grill beside a container of green beans. The container had been knocked over, and beans were scattered about like garbage, some under the bat and some on top. Its shoulders were hunched, one wing folded under its body. The other was partially extended. She saw the delicate membranes, more delicate than the web of flesh between her own fingers. The skin was pink and coated with a thin coating of down. It was fawn colored and matted in places where it was wet. The veins were blue and thin as a spider web. The maraschino cherries looked like gobbets of blood. There was juice everywhere.

She closed the door again, thinking never to open it. She would have them take it away and buy a new one. Then she went and got the Scott towels. She opened the door and picked up the bat with a triple layer of towels. She took it in the bathroom and flushed it down the toilet. It seemed more fitting than to throw it out in the garbage. She would not bury it, but she acknowledged that it had been something more than green beans or maraschino cherries. Then she got a garbage can. It was half full, and she lined it with a plastic bag and began emptying out the refrigerator – the leftover meals they had together and the food yet uneaten – the unbroken eggs, the unopened packages and jars. It was all tainted, even the fruits and vegetables. It had all been touched and polluted. Her whole life. It was not just the bat.

She began weeping and humming a tune to herself. When she finished filling the garbage can, she tried to lift it, but it was too heavy. She put a throw rug under it and dragged it across the floor, rolling it on its rim over the threshold out on the back porch. She closed the door on it and began washing out the inside of the refrigerator, knowing that she would never be through. It filled with pink suds. She rinsed it. The suds were still pink. She kept rinsing it. Then she scrubbed it with Lysol, washed it again and scrubbed it with Pinesol.

19

She heard her husband flush the toilet. Then she heard his heavy tread. She thought of getting inside the refrigerator and closing the door, but she knew that was futile. She was already that hollow herself. She began humming again and forced herself across the room to the breakfast table. She sat down at one of the places she had set the night before. The plate in front of her was empty. It shone dully in the light. I will sit here the rest of my life, the woman thought. I will starve to death.

MISSING HALLEY'S COMET

BY RICKS CARSON, PACE ACADEMY, ATLANTA

for Arthur Evans

Strike your tongs again, God!
Blister the sky with firefalls –
Drive me to Palomar in a limousine –
Ice in my vodka, serve me caviar –
Do anything you like
But I will not look
At heaven tonight
Where a Phoenix rock
Drags its tail across the eye.
After such fiery grace
Are you proud of his dance,
The Parkinson shuffle
And slide?

When your comet buzzes,
I'll draw the curtain
And we'll pass the evening
In talk of purple grackles
Strutting by the hedge,
Plucking threads of wool
Snagged from winter coats –
Of how those scraps crimp
The edge of their notes –

And how their coarse clucks
Rise up in rusty screeches
Like metal in distress,
Then at last of how revenge
Seizes up a hinge.

20

TRIPTYCH

BY EMILIA NAVARRO, EMORY UNIVERSITY

I. Interior.

(remembering Hammershøi)

Round earthenware jug. White pebble, kept for a forgotten reason.
Flock of terracotta pots riding an oak table.
A nomad rug. Tender sun. P. m. December.

21

II. Sick Child.

Echoes through the leaves of the tall tree by the window.
Voices passing, merging. Weave of sibilants from the past.

Good words. Compañero. Gracia. Amigo.
Spying on the other world, grownups, and soldiers, and books.

III.

A tight walk through the woods, Sunday morning.
No dog or child, gloves in hand. Striding, striding.
Other woods, not the same. Where the firs sang black
woven phrases, glinty snow somewhere,
plains and rocks below.
Another, another. Other words, new crocuses
to reach for, more, more, a new tongue for the oracle.
To retell the quotidian, bread, and cloud, and orange.

Another tongue. A new language to name echoes
and haloes.

Another language. To share like wine and absence.

SINGING HERBERT'S "EASTER"

BY DANIEL SMARTT, SWARTHMORE COLLEGE

EASTER[1]

Rise heart; thy Lord is risen. Sing his praise
Without delayes,
Who takes thee by the hand, that thou likewise
With him mayst rise:
That, as his death calcined thee to dust,
His life may make thee gold, and much more just.

Awake, my lute, and struggle for thy part
With all thy art.
The crosse taught all wood to resound his name,
Who bore the same.
His stretched sinews taught all strings what key
Is best to celebrate this most high day.

Consort both heart and lute, and twist a song
Pleasant and long:
Or since all musick is but three parts vied
And multiplied;
O let thy blessed Spirit bear a part,
And make up our defects with his sweet art.

I got me flowers to straw thy way;
I got me boughs off many a tree:
But thou wast up by break of day,
And brought'st thy sweets along with thee.

The Sunne arising in the East,
Though he give light, & th'East perfume;
If they should offer to contest
With thy arising, they presume.

Can there be any day but this,
Though many sunnes to shine endeavour?
We count three hundred, but we misse:
There is but one, and that one ever.

T he way a poem such as "Easter" is printed on a page influences the way we read it – not only through the type face, punctuation, and so forth, but also by the very fact of its presence on a page. The concreteness of black ink on white paper, the critical distance provided by the margins of the page, and the placement of the last line in clear view, all negotiate the frontier between the poem's time and my time. For the poet, these are factors that take shape only at the end of the gestation period of the poem, but for me, the reader, they precede the beginning of my acquaintance with it. However, the normal, circumscribed process of reading a poem on a page is not the only mode of acquaintance with it. Other modes may parallel the poet's relationship with the work – may draw people together around the text – in ways that normal reading does not. With this in mind, and out of joy in Arthur Evans and George Herbert, I offer these notes about music, kinesthesia, and "Easter."

My first awareness of the poem came through music. I sang in a church choir that was preparing Ralph Vaughan Williams' *Five Mystical Songs*[2] for baritone solo, chorus, and orchestra. The first two songs are settings of the two halves of "Easter"; the soloist sings the entire text (with some repetitions), while the choir only hums or sings on an "ah," or repeats brief phrases from the text. Our rehearsal process was typical for these productions: the choir practiced the choral parts for many weeks before the soloist, and finally the orchestra, were brought in during the final rehearsals. As a chorister, I learned first the lines of text given to the chorus, then those lines from the soloist's part that I needed to know for cues, tempo changes, finding proper notes, etc. During the weeks leading up to that performance (and often during the fifteen years since), I would find myself singing or reciting bits of the text … aloud or silently, during all sorts of daily activities, but particularly the cadenced activity of walking.

Only in the final rehearsals, after I knew some passages intimately, did I come near encountering the full text in order. My acquaintance with the poem came slowly, not from top to bottom, but in random order, a few words at a time. Whereas the composer had had the entire poem before him on one page, and even our audience would have the printed text and would only be obliged to wait a few minutes while the musicians entwined it with the composer's musical thoughts, we choristers saw the text only as through a glass darkly. That is, we heard it iterated, but only in the excruciatingly slow motion of music, and hidden under the bushel of the diction of a soloist who was facing away from us. At the same time, although we did have the text printed before us, it was not all in one place, in the two-dimensional form that the composer and the audience had. It was laid out over a dozen pages, effectively in one dimension, in the very score from which we were busy singing. Furthermore, not only does the music present the text slowly, even repeating certain lines and phrases, but the rehearsal process also added its own decelerations, stops, and repetitions.

From another point of view, however, the musical setting of a text offers choral singers a luxury that is not quite like any other. The text itself becomes a vessel of human communion. Gathered around it, as it were, the singers share a great deal: a time and place; a rate of action; similar physical attitudes, breathing, and mechanics of vocal production; and the inflections of the text itself dictated by musical performance. Sometimes the text embodies thoughts in which the singers find an additional level of common ground, whether it be best described as spiritual, sentimental, warlike, or something else. At such times (I speak from my own experience, though I have heard it echoed by others) the richness of the process as a *symbol* of human community, and its complexity as an *example* of human community, make the pleasure of good choral singing almost unbearable.

One of those who would echo my experience was George Herbert himself. By all accounts, no one ever took more pleasure in choral music – anticipated or remembered in tranquillity – than he. He was a passionate amateur musician throughout his life (1593-1633). His biographer, Izaak Walton, tells us:

> His chiefest recreation was Musick, in which heavenly Art he was a most excellent Master, and did himself compose many divine Hymns and Anthems, which he set and sung to his Lute or Viol; and, though he was a lover of retiredness, yet his love to Musick was such, that he went usually twice every week on certain appointed days, to the Cathedral Church in Salisbury; and at his return would say, That his time spent in Prayer, and Cathedral Musick, elevated his Soul, and was his Heaven upon Earth: But before his return thence to Bemerton, he would usually sing and play his part, at an appointed private Musick-meeting; and, to justifie this practice, he would often say, Religion does not banish mirth, but only moderates, and sets rules to it.[3]

Although the biography is highly contrived to fit Walton's desire for a new, Protestant hagiography, Herbert's poems confirm his alleged love of music-making.[4] This passion was nurtured from his youth. The musical evenings at his mother's house in Chelsea attracted such luminaries as John Bull and William Byrd, and during George's school days at Westminster and then at Cambridge, the everyday musical fare included recent works by Tallis, Tye, Byrd, and Gibbons (Charles, 1977, pp. 42-43 and 163). Herbert became an accomplished lutanist, and probably set his own texts.[5] Nor was he disinclined toward choral singing. His book of poems, *The Temple*, includes a number of items that can only be read as psalms and hymn texts, including the last three stanzas of "Easter." Furthermore, as Amy Charles asserts, "That the singing men of Sarum sang the burial office for Herbert at Bemerton conveys the impression that it was choral music that transported him from earth to heaven" (1977, p. 165).

Herbert's sense of the dynamics between mirth and religion helps to explain certain peculiarities of both his poetic production and his trips to Salisbury. In recent years, students of his writing have concentrated on conflicts and inconsistencies within his poetic voice.[6] Herbert was evidently torn between early aspirations, on the one hand, steeped in splendid Anglican rite and reared among the elite young men of the kingdom, and on the other hand, his growing commitment to a life of humble ministry. Although he had once aspired to the highest ranks of civil service, in 1630 he became rector at Bemerton, a ramshackle parish whose church stands less than two miles from Salisbury Cathedral. Over the three years until his death, his health permitting, he would make his trips to Salisbury for what was apparently only a second-rate musical experience.[7] Yet in his twice-weekly round trips on foot, he evidently found satisfaction of a deep, personal need. Since most of his poetry was written as personal devotional meditation, and since it contains so many echoes of his musical passion, going to Salisbury would appear to have served a purpose in his life similar to that of his writing.

It seems safe to speculate that he contemplated lines of poetry and music as he walked. The journey to the cathedral, by daylight, probably would have taken the spry but frail pastor a half hour or a little more. It was surely dark by the time he set out for home after the "Musick-meeting" (except perhaps in high summer), and so the return trip was probably slower. He often walked alone. It is inconceivable that his return trip, at very least, was not usually accompanied by music playing in his head, or that the rhythm of walking and the rhythm of music would not coincide. He must have done some composition of both poetry and music during his walks.

THIS SPECULATION strikes me as especially applicable to "Easter." When I eventually became familiar with the poem on the pages of a book, I shared with Herbert, in my own way, the frame of mind of a choral musician. I fancied myself enfranchised thereby to criticize Vaughan Williams' settings, and particularly the division of the poem into two songs. The composer could point to the text itself for license: the first three stanzas beg to be taught to sing, and the last three are the song. But the real reason for dividing them probably lay in the metric division of the poem. One glance at the text printed on a page makes it clear that the last three stanzas obey a regular, hymnic meter, while the first three have a lopsided or syncopated rhythm, with two lines of four syllables injected among four others of ten syllables each. The composer certainly could not adapt one simple strophic form to accommodate all six stanzas, but was virtually forced to use a strophic form for the latter ones.[8]

But splitting the poem in two snaps a lovely, delicate strand that weaves it together, namely, the plot. It isn't much, but anybody who loves Herbert knows not to tamper rashly with anything lovely or delicate, because in those qualities lies much of his enduring appeal. The poem's story concerns Easter morning before dawn: rising, singing, stretching, tuning instruments, gathering flowers and boughs, bringing perfume, and seeing the dawn, but finding that the sought-for one is already gone. Its primary allusion is to the three Marys coming to the tomb of Christ and finding it empty. The "perfume" refers directly to one of them, Mary Magdalene, who had once wasted a bottle of costly perfume by opening it to anoint Christ's feet.[9]

Some features of the poem are perhaps more evident to the choral musician than to the standard reader. For instance, the first three stanzas of "Easter" happen in darkness, the last three in light; from the point of view of one accustomed to singing while walking, this helps to account for the difference between the irregular, rambling, stumbling meter in the first three stanzas and the perfect cadence in the last three. The instant of sunrise comes at the beginning of stanza five, in the line, "The Sunne arising in the East." That this is the only line Herbert left unchanged from the earlier version of the poem[10] would seem to suggest that he considered it the one on which the rest of the poem pivots – perhaps that he composed it first. This out-of-order pro-

26

cess is familiar to anyone whose knowledge of a poem is mediated through musical performance. Furthermore, Herbert may have wanted to keep "The Sunne arising in the East" because he was quietly pleased with himself for a stroke of cleverness that singers would appreciate, namely, the synesthesia embodied in the sequence of vowels in the line. When one sings the word "sun," one modifies the "uh" vowel to "ah," and similarly, "in" is pronounced "een." As sung, "The Sunne arising in the East" has only two vowels, the neutral vowel "ah" in the first half of the line, and the brightest vowel, "ee," in the second half, with the shift coming in the center of the line. In other words, Herbert uses the vowels to paint the moment of sunrise in the middle of the word, "arising."[27]

Rising, singing, stretching, and walking in the dark are things that countless musicians, including Herbert, have done over nearly twenty centuries of Easters. One is tempted to imagine "Easter" being inspired in the hours before dawn: in the grogginess and stiffness, the cold, quiet, and dark, the perfumes and gathering light of early morning. The kinesthetic dimension of the stumbling meter of the early stanzas contrasted with the perfect cadence of the rest may likewise have come to him as he walked to Salisbury in the afternoon and walked back after dark, singing to himself and putting words together. When one comes to know the poem slowly, out of order, piecemeal, set to music and movement, one at least follows in Herbert's footsteps, whereas starting from his finished product is rather like taking a path on which one hopes to pass the poet coming the other way. He was the first to sing his Easter hymn, and we read it in at least a valid way when we sing it, too.

NOTES

1 C.A. Patrides, ed., *The English Poems of George Herbert* (Totowa, NJ: Rowman and Littlefield, 1974), pp. 61-62. The point of view expressed here would argue for a date during the Bemerton years. See note 9 below.

2 London: Stainer & Bell, 1911.

3 Izaak Walton, *The Lives of John Donne, Sir Henry Wotton, Richard Hooker, George Herbert & Robert Sanderson* (Oxford: Oxford University Press, 1927), p. 303. Walton had not known Herbert, and first published the biography in 1670, some thirty-seven years after the poet's death.

4 The third stanza of "Easter" is a good example. There is a considerable critical literature on the subject. See Rosalie J. Eggleston, *A Study of Some Relationships Between Late Renaissance Music and* The Temple *of George Herbert* (Ph.D. dissertation, University of New Mexico, 1969). Amy Charles has dealt with it in several publications, such as "George Herbert: Priest, Poet, Musician," in *Journal of the Viola da Gamba Society of America*, IV (1967), pp. 27-36, and *A Life of George Herbert* (Ithaca: Cornell University

Press, 1977), especially pp. 51 and 163-66. See also Elsky, 1981, cited in note 6, below.

5 Charles, 1977, p. 166, citing Herbert biographer John Aubrey.

6 Martin Elsky gives a helpful summary of recent Herbert criticism in "Polyphonic Psalm Settings and the Voice of George Herbert's *The Temple*" in *Modern Language Quarterly,* 42 (1981), pp. 227-46. A key work is Barbara Leah Harman, "The Fiction of Coherence: George Herbert's 'The Collar'," in *PMLA,* 93 (1978), pp. 865-77.

7 Eggleston, pp. 178, 182, and Charles, 1977, p. 165. During that period, interpersonal friction had depressed the musical life of the Salisbury Cathedral in a way that the urbane and sophisticated Herbert could not possibly have failed to notice or to deplore.

8 In his final product, the first song is through-composed, with no repeated melodic material and stanza divisions only barely marked. In the second song, two stanzas are given almost identical melody and length, while the last is different enough to announce a sermonic moral in the text that seems to look back over the whole.

9 Herbert was intensely devoted to his mother, whose name was Magdalene. At her death in June, 1627, he expressed his grief in a long poem in Latin and Greek, *"Memoriae matris sacrum,"* in which he addressed her with lengthy allusions to Mary Magdalene, including holy women coming to her tomb, unbound hair, and perfumed oil. The gathering of flowers and herbs figures again and again there as well. It seems plausible that George Herbert's process of writing "Easter," probably a few years later, involved his revisiting the memory of the separation from Magdalene Herbert.

10 Preserved in MS Jones B 62 in Dr. Williams' Library, Gordon Sq., London; reprinted in Patrides, ed., p. 62n.

28

II. THE ROOTS *of* BEATITUDE

"THE ANGUISH of BEATITUDE": HAPPINESS and PAIN

BY DEAL W. HUDSON, FORDHAM UNIVERSITY

I t has been said that unhappiness is more easily described than happiness. "Happiness," said de Montherlant, "writes white," while for Tolstoy every family's unhappiness provided a new story to tell. Unhappiness also has the advantage of fastening our attention quickly; we warm immediately to a character who suffers and struggles toward the light, while the stories of happy people can seem boring, except in the hands of a great writer. The world of literature thrives in this purgatory of conflict and surprise. How many readers of the *Commedia* enter Paradise?

31

Philosophers, apparently, have felt more at home in discussing happiness. Few of them have noticed any special rhetorical challenge attached to the subject. Those who have – Augustine, Boethius, Rousseau, Kierkegaard, Nietzsche – are even more persuasive for avoiding strictly didactic forms of communication. Until a century ago most philosophers spoke easily and expansively about happiness; speculative treatises on happiness were commonplace until Kierkegaard's time. But since the middle of the nineteenth century there has been a noticeable decline of such philosophical analysis.[1] Philosophers seem to have adopted the attitude of poets and novelists in finding it more rewarding to consider the multiplicity of human unhappiness, in its doubt, despair, and alienation. This change is significant. For centuries philosophers treated happiness as the pivotal issue for determining the ideal shape of human life and society. As the *summum bonum* happiness specified the basic elements of a morally good life, offered directives to statesmen who wished to rule wisely, and guided clerics whose job was the care of souls on their journey to the beatific vision.

For the present, happiness carries very little philosophical weight, a situation which, I think, is unfortunate but deserved. This lack of critical, historical, and systematic reflection about happiness is moving us closer toward making private and inscrutable one of the most important realities in human life. For example, Alasdair MacIntyre has recently issued a warning about the dangerous effects of this fragmentation on our language about virtue.[2] The pursuit of happiness does not end because philosophers stop talking about it; it continues to underlie our knowledge of what we are and our intentions about what we want to become. If there is sloth, fear, or confusion about these, the problem may lie with our vague and misleading conceptions of happiness. The meaning of happiness needs once again a public airing.

A revival of philosophical reflection about happiness, however, must begin by untangling from its tradition the erroneous premises which have led the way to this dead end. We must avoid the "little mistakes in the beginning" that have plagued all subsequent thinking about happiness. One of these mistakes has been the failure to imagine the role of pain in the formation of the happy life. The idea of happiness has been limited by the so-called "positive" divorce between most theories of happiness and the experience of emotional, psychological, and physical pain. This divorce has caused some modern thinkers to conclude that the pursuit of happiness is a frivolous concern. In *The Tragic Sense of Life*, Miguel de Unamuno writes that it is necessary to choose between love and happiness, and that those who choose happiness are incapable of love because they are unwilling to suffer: "The satisfied, the happy ones, do not love; they fall asleep in habit, near neighbor to annihilation."[3] Of course, this charge against happiness is a great deal more serious than saying that it is aesthetically uninteresting. Happiness, for Unamuno, disengages us from life by destroying our readiness for moral action and our capacity for spiritual devotion. Happiness is a pretense to ignore the tragic sense of life.

Unamuno's attitude finds support throughout the history of the idea of happiness. From Aristotle through Locke and Bentham to the present, the typical picture of the happy life is one in which pain is largely excluded for the happily contented few who by a rare combination of good luck, talent, and effort have succeeded in "having it all." This is not to say that happiness is always strictly identified with pleasure. For Aristotle happiness is an activity, not a feeling, but an activity always accompanied by the greatest pleasure.[4] Pain tears at the fabric of happiness with its harmonious interconnections of internal goods, external goods, and good fortune. For example, a person who exercises his virtue grudgingly, or who loses his health or wealth, cannot be happy. Happiness belongs to the person who possesses all of life's goods without being deprived of them, because this loss would cause pain. A truly happy person, for Aristotle, is a fortress of invulnerability against misery, excepting cases of the worst ill-fortune. The crown of human happiness is the virtue of contemplation because it is delight of the surest kind and the supreme exercise of our highest faculty – the rational mind.

The development of this ideal from Aristotle into the patristic and medieval periods adheres closely to the picture of happiness found in the *Nicomachean Ethics*. However, some important adjustments were necessary in order to align it with the Christian virtues of faith, hope, and love. As the idea of happiness within the medieval synthesis became weighted heavily toward the perfection of eternal beatitude, the concern of philosophers and theologians for happiness in this world naturally diminished. But it can be asked what effect this transposing of eudaimonism into Christian terms had on the picture of earthly happiness. One might expect that the pain of the present life would be further separated from happiness by the concentration on the life to come.

Augustine's first extant writing is a dialogue entitled *On the Happy Life*. Although it should not be expected to contain his most mature reflections on happiness, it does reflect clearly the Aristotelian position. Augustine argues that between happiness and misery there exists no middle ground. Misery signifies a lack, the frustration of a desire, and since a happy person possesses all the goods that the soul rightly desires, misery must signify unhappiness.[5] Augustine infers from this that happiness consists in possessing God, not in seeking God, because seeking implies a lack. Indeed, in his later years, Augustine will refuse to apply the term "happiness" to temporal life at all, for only in eternal life can all of the soul's desire be fulfilled in the vision of God. The only happiness we have in this life, he says in *The City of God*, is in virtue of hope.[6]

Thus pain, misery, and suffering become a dividing line not only between happiness and unhappiness, but also between life in this world and the happiness of eternity. With his characteristic sense of proportion, Thomas Aquinas would soften this distinction and speak of a worldly happiness, which is imperfect, as well as of an eternal, perfect happiness. Pain, however, is still the issue. Any happiness to be enjoyed in this world is imperfect because it "cannot completely exclude misery," which belongs by necessity to the present life because here "the desire for the good cannot be fully satisfied."[7] Following Aristotle, Aquinas stresses the pleasure, or joy, of happiness. Joy is our delight in possessing what is good, and joy grows to its greatest pitch when we possess God. By being transposed into eternal terms, the invulnerability of happiness is made complete. What Aristotle only hinted at concerning the god-like character of happiness emerged full-blown in Aquinas' discussion of the grace of beatific vision. Only in the actual presence of

God is all human desire satisfied, all longing stilled, all motion brought to rest, and all pain terminated.

Both Aristotle and Aquinas wanted to retain pleasure as one of the goods of human life. Aristotle sneered at the Cynics' argument that a person could be happy "even on the rack" provided he was good, calling it nonsense (NE 1153b). Indeed, one alternative to the problem of pain in happiness is suggested by the Cynics and Stoics who placed happiness entirely in the realm of moral goodness: pleasure, they maintained, has nothing whatever to do with happiness. This fundamental difference with Aristotle's eudaimonism is overlooked because of his oft-quoted definition of happiness as "activity in accordance with virtue." The remainder of that definition is usually not considered: "All the other goods are either necessary prerequisites for happiness, or are by nature co-workers with it and useful instruments for it" (NE 1099b). Pleasure is among those other goods along with such things as wealth, health, honor, and friendship.

Epicurus made pleasure the *summum bonum*, but he so closely tied it to virtue that even the Stoic Seneca praised him. Epicurus considers pain an evil, "yet not every pain is of a nature to be avoided on all occasions…. [F]or under certain circumstances we treat the good as evil, and again, the evil as good."[8] This willingness to recognize pain as a good hits at the heart of the matter, although there arises the Stoical tendency which is too severe to be satisfying. A happiness which is synonymous with only moral development stands aloof from what people commonly associate with the idea – the most desirable of all lives. The views espoused by Seneca, Cicero, and Marcus Aurelius are persuasive only, as has been noted before, within a civilization in decline, where the only possible domain left open to establishing order and harmony is within one's private life. Cicero himself was forced to admit that pleasure was a good, albeit one closely knit into virtue.

If ignored too long the affections have a way of asserting their importance, and sometimes in explosive fashion, as the hedonism of the eighteenth century was to show. Excluding pleasure from happiness can only serve to make happiness available to ascetic temperaments alone; it cannot provide the foundation of a general theory. At the same time, to make pleasure identical with happiness, as did Epicurus and many of the Renaissance and Enlightenment philosophers, leaves the problem of pain still unsolved. These later hedonistic versions of happiness, beginning with Lorenzo de Valla and moving through Locke and Helvétius to Bentham, lose sight of the close connection between virtue and happiness which even Epicurus stressed. Happiness became contentment or satisfaction with one's own life regardless of the attainment of real moral goods. For example, the contentment of the happy life began to float freely in a world of equally worthwhile objects. One became contented by possessing whatever one *valued*, rather than by having one's choice directed by the judgment of prudence and the other moral virtues. Because of this slippage, Mill found it necessary to break with Bentham's teaching and posit once again the primacy of prudent choice in the experience of pleasure, even to the point of admitting that pain is sometimes preferable: "Better a human being dissatisfied than a pig satisfied; better to be a Socrates dissatisfied than a fool satisfied."[9]

It was not long after Mill and the evolutionary philosophy of Herbert Spencer that the large-scale deliberations on happiness dried up, and serious minds began to produce popular "how-to" manuals. Two of the most interesting and representative are Bertrand Russell's *The Conquest of Happiness* (1930) and John Cowper Powys' *The Art of Happiness* (1935). Indeed, both of these books demonstrate how badly thinking about happiness had deteriorated. Russell centered his entire book round his newly-baptized virtue of "zest"[10] and Powys argued that happiness is a kind of "conjuring-trick or magical auto-suggestion whereby, in spite of any circumstances, one can self-induce 'positive' feelings about life and the world."[11] This is a happiness gone wild whose "invulnerability" bullies the world into yielding contentment. But it is typical of contemporary popular books on happiness to offer techniques of creating and maintaining "good feelings" regardless of a person's actual character and the state of the world. The "mind-cure" approach to happiness has enjoyed a long and healthy life in the American consciousness thanks to a distorted understanding of the pragmatism of William James by the tradition of "positive thinkers."[12] An unhappy life and circumstances were to be transformed not by effort of moral reform but simply by a change of "attitude" toward them.

This psychological overhauling can bring a person contentment, but at the cost of prudence, which is the disposition of the mind to recognize what is real. By shutting this window upon reality, the positive thinker can easily begin to nurture a delusion. Certainly it is this kind of escapism that Walker Percy lampoons in his *Lost in the Cosmos: The Last Self-Help Book*. Percy asks why so many people are depressed in a world of "unprecedented opportunities." His answer, though troubling, provides hope for those who, in spite of therapy, good friends, and religious piety, continue to feel unaccountably dragged down by life. "Any person, man, woman, or child, who is not depressed by the nuclear arms race, by the modern city, by family life in the exurb, suburb, apartment, villa, and later in a retirement home, is himself deranged."[13] Here is the same concern for a genuine engagement with the world that was seen in Unamuno, except that Percy does not reject happiness in the name of love. Instead he attempts to shatter the many magical versions of the self which are removed from concrete existence by their use of signs.

The mind-over-matter approach of the positive thinkers to happiness is a kind of perverted Stoicism. Its tranquillity results not from the incantation of formulas and slogans – a curious reversal in the direction of resignation. A happy person is not required to live according to the directive of nature and to bear the pain of contact with the world; his newly-acquired thought patterns magically filter out what is negative to consciousness and reshape the world to make it yield pleasure, regardless of concrete circumstances. Even Nietzsche, the greatest prophet of self-creation, repeatedly warned against using the desire for happiness as an escape from suffering: "How little you know of human *happiness*, you comfortable and benevolent people, for happiness and unhappiness are sisters and even twins."[14]

Nietzsche accused Christians of inventing "heaven" and its "eternal beatitude" as an escape from the suffering of the world. Although he admired the power of Christian contemplatives to suffer monastic discipline, Nietzsche regarded their professed intention of preparing for the afterlife as a sign of inner weakness. Happiness was for him *the feeling of power*, the "new virtue" which endures the thought of eternal recurrence with the greatest suffering and the richest laughter.[15] Yet, there was an overcoming of the self which could not anesthetize itself to the experience of finitude. Compared to Nietzsche, Russell's "zest" or, more recently, Paul Kurtz's "exuberance," sound a rather superficial and bourgeois note.[16]

What these modern versions of happiness have in common is their attempt to emphasize the *power* of the subject in coping with the external conditions which endanger happiness. This, in spite of its problems, is helpful and important. Taking into account this subjective character will make happiness seem less static and more tensive, less the achievement of perfection than the straining toward a goal. It also may provide the key for reinterpreting the history of happiness from a perspective off the dead-center of the pleasure/pain divide. Placed under this light both Boethius and Aquinas reveal that, in spite of some statements to the contrary, they have modified their Aristotelian eudaimonism and moved toward a worldly happiness which includes and even makes positive use of *pathos*. For them, a person's power to be happy lies in his capacity for passion, his capacity to suffer the world, not magically to recreate it.

Of course, it was the problem of suffering that caused Boethius to write his famous *Consolation of Philosophy*.[17] According to Aristotle's standards Boethius should have considered his happiness to have been destroyed by his imprisonment and impending execution. But Lady Philosophy tells Boethius that no person can ever be certain of happiness until he has suffered misfortune (*CP* 22); "adverse fortune is more beneficial to men than prosperous fortune" because, by removing the objects of idolatry, it "turns them around and forcibly leads them back to the true good" (*CP* 40). Human happiness contains a constant undercurrent of "anxiety" and "bitterness" because its enjoyment of external goods cannot be guaranteed. Misfortune is often fortunate because it causes us to reaffirm the only basis upon which our happiness can be securely forged – our self and God.

Boethius, it can be said, was helped by Stoicism to present a view of happiness which is more akin to the Christian answer to the problem of pain. In this world a happy person should expect to suffer and in suffering be reminded of what counts the most. Perhaps no one carried this lesson further than Søren Kierkegaard, who remarked that God's judgment falls upon those who do not suffer rather than those who do. Misery need not be excluded from the kind of life which is called "happy": as Nietzsche said, in his usual ironic manner, happiness and unhappiness are "sisters." Thomas Aquinas came to a similar conclusion from another route. Like Boethius, he may seem to accept the separation between pain and happiness, but he actually attempts to bring about a reconciliation.

Aquinas knew very well that he was breaking with the classical tradition in some of his questions concerning the Passion of Christ (*ST* III, 46-52). In order to affirm the teaching that Christ's pain was the greatest which could be suffered, Aquinas dealt with the Stoic and Aristotelian objection that the man of virtue suffers very little. Christ, he argued, suffered not only the greatest bodily pain but also the greatest sadness (*tristitia*) at his death. The whole man underwent the Passion. But though the intellect suffered, Christ was not hindered from enjoying the perfect vision of the Father during his death. His Passion did not prevent the full enjoyment of the beatific vision (*ST* III, 46, 7).

Again, Aquinas cited Aristotle's objection that sadness must subvert pleasure and therefore delight: "It cannot therefore be," Aristotle would say, "that Christ's soul wholly suffered and rejoiced at the same moment." But that is exactly what Aquinas did argue. The contrary states of pain and joy co-exist with Christ's earthly beatitude. His pain derived from the soul's connection to the body, and his delight from the intellect which remained united to the vision of God (*ST* III, 46, 8).

Earlier in the *Summa* Aquinas had prepared for this interpretation by giving a new twist to the Aristotelian view of pleasure and pain. Aristotle teaches that an intense amount of pain will drive out pleasure; he pictures the two as if they were on the opposite ends of a see-saw. Aquinas stays close to this conception but amends it in an important way, one consistent with the presence of affective contraries in the Passion of Christ. Sorrow, he says, is the contrary of every pleasure, but the same disposition can give rise to contrary emotions (*ST* I-II, 35, 4). In this case the pursuit of pleasure and the avoidance of sorrow – one affirming, one negating – are joined together through the presence of virtue. Thus, Aquinas shows that sorrow can be a good when the human appetite is distressed by the presence of evil in itself or someone else (*ST* I-II, 39, 4). "Some sadness is praiseworthy…when for example it proceeds from a holy love; this occurs when a man is saddened over his own, or another's sin" (*ST* III, 46, 6). Sorrow strengthens moral character because its presence reinforces our recognition and rejection of what is evil. Aquinas, thereby, widens the scope of a happy life to include not only pleasure and joy but a specific range of suffering as well. Greek pleasure gives way to Christian "passion," not only in the literal sense of unending suffering but also in the generic sense of *being acted upon*. Here Aquinas takes warrant from Augustine's remark that there "was no better way to cure our misery than the Passion of Christ" (*ST* III, 46, 3).

Aquinas' concern with happiness in this world is remarkable for a medieval theologian. In his questions on the spiritual life, he asks "whether the rewards described in the Beatitudes belong to the present life?" Yes, a Christian should look for divine aid in procuring a happiness *in via*; such a present happiness is naturally to be expected as fruit from a tree when the leaves begin to turn green. "For when a person begins to make progress in the acts of the [infused] virtues and the gifts, one can hope that he will attain the perfection which belongs to the journey and that of the destination" (*ST* I-II, 69, 2). But these gifts do not come as pleasures to be enjoyed but as a passion with both joy and sorrow intermingled in their train. Happiness *in patria*, of course, has a perfect character: there, joy is complete and cannot be lost to sorrow. Still, as a realist Aquinas distinguished between the two orders of happiness not simply to glorify what is perfect but to estimate soberly what can be expected of this life, even at its best. The extremes of hedonism and moralism solved conceptual confusion but did not present a picture of the happy life which would satisfy anyone but an established elite, whether a protected leisure class or an educated, disciplined few.

It is a pity that such insight into happiness has had such little influence on the generally accepted notions. A look into the history of Christian spirituality would uncover a continuous, deepening reflection in this direction. However, the general direction of philosophical reflection about happiness between the fifteenth and eighteenth centuries can be summarized by citing John Locke: "*Happiness*, then, in its full extent, is the utmost pleasure we are capable of, and *misery* the utmost pain; and the lowest degree of what can be called happiness is so much ease from all pain, and so much present pleasure, as without which any one cannot be content."[18] Some cynical conclusions would follow from this notion. Immanuel Kant dissociated the idea of happiness from ethical motivation altogether and, echoing Pascal, thought that happiness was hardly attainable by man: "For his own nature is not so constituted as to rest or be satisfied in any possession or enjoyment whatsoever."[19] Freud concurred in his *Civilization and Its Discontents* that "one feels inclined to say that the intention that man should be 'happy' is not included in the plan of 'Creation'," and he concluded dryly: "Unhappiness is much less difficult to experience."[20] This is disconcerting, especially when one bears in mind that both of them believe it impossible for a human being not to desire happiness. Happiness, from their vantage point, is a "Catch 22." Human desire wants what it cannot have in this life, an unrealizable goal of never-ending pleasure and satisfaction, the dream of Lockean *immediacy*.

Mortimer Adler has recently argued that the way out of this dilemma is to do away altogether with any element of contentment in happiness. His version of going back to Aristotle defines happiness as "a whole life enriched by the cumulative possession of all real goods that every human being needs and by the satisfaction of those individual wants that result in obtaining apparent goods that are innocuous."[21] Certainly this has the advantage of being an "objective" view, but it still sets happiness apart from pain and makes it contingent upon misfortune, as Adler himself admits. Even further, can all the subjective color-ings of a happy life be treated in this way? Wouldn't it be just as absurd to call a person happy who was not satisfied with his life as it was for Aristotle to describe him happy while being tortured upon the rack? The prudent collecting of life's goods does little justice either to the role of passion in happiness or to the devotion toward a transcendental object which itself is the source of all goodness and human happiness.

Thomas Aquinas preserves both. By working from the theological datum of the presence of eternal beatitude within Christ's Passion, Aquinas was able to move beyond the limits of Aristotle's eudaimonism. The final end of the human person for Aquinas is not happiness, eternal or temporal, but God Himself.[22] Thus happiness on earth does not have to carry the impossible weight of perfection, and the desire for immediacy is recognized as an undeniable and universal appetite for the vision of God. For the present we must suffer what Jacques Maritain calls the "anguish of beatitude," which springs from the inescapable circumstance that "the largest and most abounding life will always be something very small, compared with the dimensions of man's heart."[23] Worldly happiness will be, as Boethius describes, "shot through with bitterness" because life in this world is a tragic unfolding toward what is to come.

40

NOTES

1 One notable exception is Wladyslaw Tatarkiewicz, *Analysis of Happiness*, trans. Edward Rothert and Danuta Zielinski (The Hague: Martinus Nijhoff, 1976). For a critical survey of the concept of happiness in Western thought see V. J. McGill, *The Idea of Happiness* (New York: Frederick A. Praeger, 1967).

2 Alasdair MacIntyre, *After Virtue: A Study in Moral Theory* (Notre Dame, Ind.: Univ. of Notre Dame Press, 1981), 64.

3 Miguel de Unamuno, *The Tragic Sense of Life in Men and Nations*, trans. Anthony Kerrigan (Princeton: Princeton University Press, 1972), 225.

4 Aristotle, *Nicomachean Ethics*, 1099a. Hereafter cited as *NE*. The translation used is by Martin Ostwald (Indianapolis: The Bobbs-Merrill Co., 1962).

5 St. Augustine, *The Happy Life*, trans. Ludwig Schopp (St. Louis: B. Herder Book Co., 1947), 71.

6 St. Augustine, *The City of God*, trans. Marcus Dids (New York: Random House, 1950), 680; BK.19.20.

7 St. Thomas Aquinas, *Summa theologica* I-II, 5, 3. Hereafter cited as *ST*. Translations are from the Blackfriars edition, ed. Thomas Gilby, O.P. (New York: McGraw-Hill Book Co., 1963-1980).

8 Epicurus, *Letters, Principal Doctrines, and Vatican Sayings*, trans. Russel M. Geer (Indianapolis: The Bobbs-Merrill Co., 1964), 56.

9 John Stuart Mill, *Utilitarianism* (Indianapolis: The Bobbs-Merrill Co., 1957), 14.

10 Bertrand Russell, *The Conquest of Happiness* (New York: Horace Liveright, 1930), 158-75.

11 John Cowper Powys, *The Art of Happiness* (New York: Simon and Schuster, 1935), 44.

12 Donald Meyer, *The Positive Thinkers: A Study of the American Quest for Health, Wealth, and Personal Power from Mary Baker Eddy to Norman Vincent Peale* (Garden City, N.Y.: Doubleday & Co., 1965), 315-24.

13 Walker Percy, *Lost In the Cosmos: The Last Self-Help Book* (New York: Farrar, Straus, & Giroux, 1983), 75.

14 Friedrich Nietzsche, *The Gay Science*, trans. Walter Kaufmann (New York: Penguin Books, 1985), 270.

15 Friedrich Nietzsche, *Daybreak*, trans. R. J. Hollingdale (Cambridge: Cambridge Univ. Press, 1982), 68. Also, Friedrich Nietzsche, *Thus Spoke Zarathustra*, trans. R. J. Hollingdale (New York: Penguin Books, 1985), 101.

16 Paul Kurtz, *Exuberance: An Affirmative Philosophy of Life* (Buffalo: Prometheus Books, 1985).

17 Boethius, *The Consolation of Philosophy*, trans. Richard Green (Indianapolis: The Bobbs-Merrill Co., 1962). Hereafter cited as *CP*.

18 John Locke, *An Essay Concerning Human Understanding* (New York: Dover Publications, 1959), 340.

19 Quoted by McGill, 92-93.

20 Sigmund Freud, *Civilization and Its Discontents*, trans. James Strachey (New York: W.W. Norton & Co., 1961), 23-24.

21 Mortimer Adler, *Ten Philosophical Mistakes* (New York: Macmillan Publishing Co., 1985), 134.

22 For further discussion, see Alan Donagan, *Human Ends and Human Action: An Exploration in St. Thomas's Treatment* (Milwaukee: Marquette University Press, 1958).

23 Jacques Maritain, *Integral Humanism*, trans. Joseph W. Evans (New York: Charles Scribner's Sons, 1968), 56.

41

EROS and MORAL PERFECTION
in PLATO'S MIDDLE DIALOGUES

BY RICHARD D. PARRY, AGNES SCOTT COLLEGE

I n Book IV of Plato's *Republic* we find an account of virtue which has few rivals in its combination of density in expression and profoundness of conception. In what follows I shall outline this account, draw out some of its implications, and complete it with some of Plato's most brilliant passages from the *Symposium* and *Phaedrus*. What is offered here is not a scholarly inquiry, although it is based upon contemporary British and American scholarship. It is rather a stepping back from the detailed search through the text and an attempt to report, in less technical language, on what has been found. Plato has given us a powerful view of human life in these dialogues; I hope to call attention to some of its depth and wisdom for the benefit of the general reader.

PLATO'S ACCOUNT of virtue can be called psychological. In this sense, it differs in a subtle but important way from most modern accounts of virtue. Modern philosophy attempts to define the acts which are morally correct by specifying either the rule such acts should follow or the consequences such acts should provide. Plato, by contrast, identifies virtue with having a certain disposition. Disposition is distinguished from action in that the former is the capacity and proclivity to act (i.e., it is the source of action). The virtue of courage, for example, is the capacity and proclivity to act in certain ways – ways not always foreseeable, not always specifiable by a rule. What medieval thinkers called *habitus,* or dispositions, are what we moderns might call qualities of character. Of course, since these dispositions naturally give rise to certain kinds of actions, if one never performed virtuous acts, one could not be said to have the disposition of virtue. Still, Plato identifies virtue with the deeper source of the actions; virtue is a way of being – morally speaking, a style of life.

Dispositions as inner sources of action are attributed by Plato to the soul. As a consequence, Plato's account of virtue tells us what the soul of the just person will be like. It is an account of the character of the just person seen from his interior life. As Glaucon says, "What I desire is to hear what each of them [justice and injustice] is and what potency and effect each has in and of itself dwelling in the soul."[1] As we shall see, this account is also an account of happiness. The person who possesses in the soul the virtues of justice, wisdom, courage, and self-control is also and always the person who is happy in a sense that includes but is not exhausted by our notion of pleasure.

Before Plato can give an account of virtues as dispositions he must first have a theory about the soul, its parts and its structure. This kind of theory is sometimes called a moral psychology and tells about those assumptions that a moralist is making in recommending one way of life over another. Generally, a moral psychology tells us something about reason and its functions, about the role of the will, and about that recalcitrant source of most moral conflict, the passions. Plato has something to say on all of these subjects.

43

In an extended argument in the *Republic* (435c-441d), Plato tells us that the soul has three parts – or clearly distinguishable functions. For clarity's sake we can begin by distinguishing between function and disposition. A function is the ability to do certain actions – e.g., to reason or to carry out decisions – which is not acquired or learned; dispositions are acquired. A function is simply the ability to act; the notion does not imply that the action is good or bad, well done or badly done. A disposition, on the other hand, is either a tendency to do well or a tendency to do ill. In Plato's inventory of psychological functions, there is first of all reason, which calculates consequences and takes forethought for the whole soul. It frequently finds itself at odds with the second part of the soul – the passions. Thought by Plato to consist primarily of the desires for food, drink, and sex, the passions seek immediate fulfillment while reason has the job of looking out for undesirable consequences. The conflict between the two is classic and is the very beginning of moral thought for Plato. The resolution of the conflict is one of the results Plato wishes to provide with this account of virtue.

The third part of the soul is a less familiar notion in modern moral psychology. It is called *thymos*, or *thymoeidês*, and is usually translated 'the spirited part.' *Thymos* is a character of Greek warriors – an aggressive principle impelling one to adventure across the forbidding seas, to join in awful battle. Plato makes it an ally of reason in its conflict with the passions. As can be imagined, *thymos* does and does not correspond to our notion of will.

Plato's tripartite soul can be seen as an inventory of psychological functions. Each person must have these three functions for living a life. Reason gives us the long view about courses of action; *thymos* carries out our conception of the best course of action – whether that conception comes from reason or not; the passions provide the bodily existence. But the three also entail three distinct kinds of needs. Given that we have these three functions, our life is also characterized by three kinds of emotional needs and their corresponding satisfactions. To begin with the passions, it is obvious that we need the satisfactions afforded by fulfilling our desires for food, drink, and sex. (Plato allows, in the best kind of life, for what to us would appear to be the sublimation of the latter.) As well, we need a life which has the satisfactions of *thymos* – one which enjoys adventure, aggressive play, and risks. Finally, our lives need the satisfaction of reason – its desire to discover, solve, resolve, and contemplate. A life lacking one of these three kinds of satisfactions is much poorer than a life with all three. Plato seems wise in recommending all three; he only seems unwise when we stop to think what has been left out. Much of the plausibility of the position depends on his ability to adapt this tripartite division to include other needs, notably personal affection.

44

After giving us this inventory of psychological functions, Plato quickly turns to his account of virtue in the soul (*Rep.* 441d-448e). Virtue is that set of dispositions which perfect these psychological functions. These functions become virtuous by acquiring the capacity and proclivity to function well or correctly. Thus, wisdom is reason's ruling in the soul with knowledge of what is good for the three parts and for the whole formed by the three parts. Wisdom is the disposition for reason to make long-term policy for one's life and short-term decisions within it, armed with insight into what is truly beneficial for reason, *thymos*, and the passions – as well as for the polity formed by the three. This sort of disposition is best appreciated when it is contrasted with, say, the disposition to give over policy and decisions to the passions. Heedless of the other, none with any sense of the good of the whole, the passions as rulers are the very picture of folly. There may be more to wisdom than rule by informed reason – but not much more. Our greatest hesitancy may be that no place is arranged for experience of life. But then if one really *knew* what was for the good of the parts and the good of the whole, experience might not seem so greatly needed.

Courage is the quality of the spirited part. When *thymos* follows the lead of reason about what is to be feared and what is not to be feared, a person is courageous. *Thymos* becomes virtuous when it habitually points its aggressive and adventurous energies towards the goals reason sanctions. Presumably reason guides the *thymos* so that it is aggressive against the passions – and against other people – only when one's real interest is threatened. Since one's real interest is one's stable disposition to act wisely, courageously, temperately, and justly, a courageous person has the disposition to fend off those influences which would undermine these dispositions. Real courage is the courage to preserve virtue, the courage to persevere in a way of life.

Temperance is that condition of soul that results when the extravagant appetites and the ebullient *thymos* are controlled by the wise and naturally moderate reason. But Plato has a more profound notion of this virtue as well. One is temperate when all parts of one's soul agree to reason's rule. One is temperate, then, when the appetites, for example, are accustomed to recognize that reason knows best what are the limits to each drive and the proper balance among them all. Striving each for its own fulfillment, each passion has the disposition to defer to the deeper insight of reason.

Finally, justice is the state of soul achieved when each part of the soul has the disposition to perform its proper function and not to interfere with the functions of the other parts. In the first instance, this virtue means that the appetites seek their own satisfactions without attempting to rule in the place of reason. One seeks, for example, such food as the appetite for food wants – in whatever variety and quantity – as long as doing so does not keep reason from exercising its benevolent rule over the psychic commonwealth. Reason must control these satisfactions so that the good of other appetites, of the *thymos*, and of reason itself is achieved. However, it should not be overlooked that justice works – by implication – in another direction. It would be equally unjust for reason to constrain the appetites in favor of its own narrow interests. Reason rules to achieve the good of all, not just its peculiar good. Thus, an ascetic repression of the appetites is not at all just, even if one achieved thereby the superficial peace needed by reason to read, study, puzzle, or contemplate. This implication is rendered less secure by what Plato says about sublimation. But even at that, there must be a difference between sublimation and repression. The latter is clearly unjust usage of an appetite.

There are several ways to see the value of this reign of justice in the soul. In the first place, it allows each part of the soul to enjoy the maximum satisfaction consistent with the welfare of the whole. Thus reason not only rules; it pursues all those activities whose achievements constitute its satisfaction. Lively intellectual interests of all sorts must be included here. When there is justice among parts of the soul, reason pursues all those activities by which it discovers truths, facts, aspects, viewpoints – each with its own satisfaction. All these activities lead towards that final goal – the goal that Plato holds is the deepest motive of reason – the discovery of that truth which will crown all the others. Even to imagine such a conception of reason we would have to go well below our contemporary veneer of sophisticated skepticism. There, at the most suppressed levels of our own intellectual endeavors, we will recognize a touching hope that it will all fit together...someday. And if we would admit it, this hope is the deepest motivation which keeps us working at the details. Only despair prompts us to disavow, in public at least, this early, Hellenic desire. But its satisfaction would be, for Plato, the deepest satisfaction.

46

The soul with justice also gives its due to the *thymos*. The aggressive principle – the spirited part – has its peculiar needs for adventure, risk, going beyond the familiar and comfortable. The *thymos* of the warrior not only took him into battle; it also started him off from home on the voyage across the pathless sea. Part of the adventure was the satisfaction that comes from meeting and overcoming the unknown. If a life without the satisfaction of reason would have no insight, no direction, the life without the satisfaction of *thymos* would be flat, confined. Even the joys of reason would become circumscribed.

Finally, with justice in the soul, one's life will enjoy the satisfactions of the passions, without the excess that turns satiety into revulsion. While the satisfaction of the passions is an integral part of the just life, its internal limitation implies that satisfying the passions will not disrupt the other parts of the soul. Thus, when each part of the soul receives its due, one's life is fulfilled intellectually, aggressively, and passionately. All of these satisfactions are balanced against one another so that none crowds out the others. If we suppose that there are no other parts of the soul, then such a life is emotionally fulfilled in all the ways possible for fulfillment.

A life which satisfies all the known emotional needs of the soul would be the most pleasant life. And Plato is Greek enough to appreciate that pleasure is an important motive in leading the virtuous life. He even argues that the virtuous life is more pleasurable than the vicious life by a factor of 729 – an amount of pleasure so great as to seem exhausting (*Rep.* 587e). In any event, Plato is clearly arguing that the variety of distinct pleasures in the well-ordered soul is preferable to the intense but one-sided pleasures – marred by regret and remorse – of the unbalanced soul.

However, this fulfillment of all known desires is only the most superficial reason that Plato has for recommending justice in the soul. It does not touch the center of his conception of happiness. Plato's more profound reason for recommending justice goes deeper, to the concept of well-being or well-functioning. Plato says in Book I that each thing has its function (*ergon*) and performing that function well is virtue (*aretê*) for that thing (*Rep.* 353b ff.). It is natural then for Plato to say that virtue is doing well; he also says that it is happiness. What really recommends justice in the soul is that each of the parts is performing its function well. Each part has attained the perfection of its nature. Each part's reaching natural perfection is good in itself even if we leave out the satisfactions that accrue to each from justice in the soul.

Perhaps the best way to appreciate this notion of perfection is to use an analogy from athletics: a gymnast. Having reached top form, she has attained a kind of natural perfection. She lifts and propels herself in and out of, around, over, and under the bars, arcs through the air, and lands at the intended spot. Her performance shows a perfection of those muscular functions that most of us use every day in a – literally – pedestrian way. Moreover, her performance can be appreciated quite apart from whatever satisfaction accrues either from seeing it or from executing it. What really recommends the performance and its underlying bodily condition is the fact that it is a perfection of certain physical functions. The satisfactions are subsequent to, and flow from, recognizing the perfection.

So with the perfected soul. What really recommends it is the performance of which each of the chief functions of the soul is now capable. In such a life one's reason would make, for example, good decisions about short-term actions and long-term policy. The decisions would be good not only as product but also as process – good not just because they proved to be right. The ability to reason well is good also because it gives rise to a certain kind of performance: one gathers evidence thoroughly and efficiently; one weighs it judiciously; one draws from the evidence no more and no less than what is warranted. One's reasoning is – in the mathematicians' telling word – elegant.

The other two parts of the soul would have similar style. Not only would they be successful in their service to the psychic commonwealth; their performance would show a perfection of the underlying function. *Thymos* would be perfected aggression, neither

47

excessive nor deficient; if it were expressed as risk-taking adventure, it would not be aimless thrill-seeking but the pointed and balanced exercise of a well-trained human function. And the passions – recognizing, through the aid of reason, an internal limit – would become what passions ought to be. Not lost in uncontrolled self-indulgence or ascetic repression, their exercise would be proportionate to their real need. In sum, each function would have reached its top level of performance.

Such a life would show a deftness at being human that would clearly be a kind of perfection. Plato calls this life happy – *eudaimon*; literally put, it is 'well-geniused.' A life-long performance of this sort would be as graceful, adroit, and fitting as that of the gymnast. It would be the spiritual equivalent of the Olympic athlete. And if it could be frozen into one moment – rendered in sculpture rather than in drama – it would have all of the spiritual balance and harmony, energy and ease to which the fifth-century athletic statues are the physically ideal equivalent.

At this, the second level of understanding of Plato's account of virtue in the soul, we might think that we have all the recommendation necessary. A life built of dispositions to perform at this level – a life based upon the ability and proclivity to be an Olympic hero of the spirit – such a life seems to have the highest possible recommendation. Not only is it the most satisfying life, it is the most fitting, graceful, and well-done. But there is yet another level of understanding of virtue in the soul.

This deepest level is reached in Plato's account when he explains how one establishes virtue in the soul. The process is portrayed as one of imitation. One sees an exemplar which constitutes both a set of directions and a motivation. Not only does the exemplar act as a model of what is to be imitated, but it shows what is to be imitated as more attractive than any alternative. Plato's exemplars for virtue are the Forms of justice, courage, temperance, and wisdom – what he calls (*Rep.* 500c-d; pp. 735-36) the eternal realities:

> For surely…the man whose mind is truly fixed on eternal realities has no leisure to turn his eyes downward…but he fixes his gaze upon the things of the eternal and unchanging order, and seeing that they neither wrong nor are wronged by one another, but all abide in harmony as reason bids, he will endeavor to imitate them and, as far as may be, to fashion him-

self in their likeness and assimilate himself to them. Or do you think it possible not to imitate the things to which anyone attaches himself with admiration?... Then the lover of wisdom associating with the divine order will himself become orderly and divine in the measure permitted to man.

Gazing upon the Forms, the virtuous person sees ideal exemplars of justice, courage, wisdom, and temperance. They are used as models – the way a painter uses a model – to fashion the corresponding virtues in the soul. Becoming and remaining an Olympic hero of the spirit is finally based upon imitation of these ideal Forms. The best reason for having justice in the soul – the highest recommendation – would seem to be that such an arrangement – besides providing satisfaction to all parts of the soul, besides being the perfection of all the functions of the soul – is an imitation of these Ideals. Indeed, we recognize the perfection of the soul as perfection just because we compare it to the Ideals of justice, wisdom, courage, and self-control. And we would strive for this perfection of soul because we are inspired by these Forms; it is their perfection we wish to embody.

Unfortunately, in the *Republic* the ideas of this passage remain little more than a hint. We are never given a detailed account of the way in which the just person is to use the Forms to create the just order in his soul – nor then of the way in which the Forms are the final motivation for acquiring justice in the soul. In fact, it is in his two dialogues on love *(eros)* that Plato tells us the most about acquiring virtue in one's soul. The *Symposium* and the *Phaedrus* together give us a unified account of a relationship between lovers which has become sublimated into a spiritual bond for the purpose of acquiring and fostering virtue. In this account, a Form is the inspiration which motivates the lovers in their pursuit. The Form in question is not the Form of justice – as might have been expected from the *Republic* – but the Form of beauty, for it is beauty which is the object of *eros*. While nothing is said about imitation of the Form of beauty, it is clear that the chief motivation of the lover is his vision of the Form of beauty together with his desire to reproduce it in himself and in others.

The *Symposium* begins this account of acquiring virtue with Socrates' speech to the assembled celebrants. In fact, in an intriguing and dramatic move, Socrates quotes his teacher in these matters of love, Diotima, the Mantinean seeress. She says that all love – even earthly love – is always love of something beautiful; she relates how a person conceives and brings forth in the presence of beauty and only in the presence of beauty (*Sym.* 206 c-e). When the person is of the physical type, he marries a beautiful woman and brings forth children. When he is of the spiritual type, he falls in love with a youth – especially if the youth has spiritual beauty – and brings forth by speech and beautiful conversation virtue in the soul of the beloved (*Sym.* 209 b-c).

These passages are remarkable – almost breathtaking – for their mixture of sexual and birthing images. The lover is pregnant with virtue in his soul; but this pregnancy is also an erotic tension which can only be relieved by spiritual discourse with a beautiful youth. This parturition, which is also a consummation, is completed in creating the beauty of virtue in the soul of the beloved. How this conversation might actually bring forth virtue is given a most charming exposition in Alcibiades' speech about Socrates. Conversation with Socrates is not just all talk, as Alcibiades learned to his chagrin. In their conversation, however, talk gave way to spiritual, not carnal, knowledge. By an ironic reversal, the physically beautiful Alcibiades came to see the beauty of the ugly Socrates' soul:

> Whether anyone else has caught him in a serious moment and opened him, and seen the images inside, I know not; but I saw them one day, and thought them so divine and golden, so perfectly fair and wondrous, that I simply had to do as Socrates bade me.[2]

The beloved's desire to imitate these images is quite explicit; in this way the virtue-child is born.

What, after all, makes a memorable teacher beloved? What makes us want to imitate such a person? Is it not that this is the one whose life exemplifies that which is taught? It is not this teacher's words but what the words reveal about the person that is so cogent – or rather the way that the teacher's life embodies the meaning of the words. The teacher's conversation is treasured because it is a sacramental sign of the inner person. Just as no serious symbol is a mere symbol, so, with such a teacher, no serious conversation is mere conversation.

So far we have seen how earthly love is an inspiration to virtue. Still, we have not yet seen what role Forms have to play in this account. Diotima has saved the best for the last, for now she tells Socrates that earthly love is really striving for contemplative union with the most authentic beauty, the Form of the beautiful. One may realize this striving through initiation in the mysteries of love. First the lover, rightly initiated, learns to love more and more abstract things, moving from love of beautiful bodies to beautiful souls, thence to beautiful customs and laws, and thence to the beauty of knowledge.

> When a man has been thus far tutored in the lore of love, passing from view to view of beautiful things, in the right and regular ascent, suddenly he will have revealed to him, as he draws to the close of his dealings in love, a wondrous vision, beautiful in its nature; and this, Socrates, is the final object of all those previous toils. [*Sym.* 210e; p. 205]

This beauty is the Form of beauty. It does not come to be nor pass away; nor does it suffer any of the other vicissitudes of the beauty that is seen with the eyes (*Sym.* 211a). Perhaps most remarkable of all, it is not a quality found in another substance. Nothing but undiluted, pure beauty, it is not even in anything else – not in face nor hands nor knowledge. It is hard to decide whether what makes this latter claim so remarkable is the metaphysical implication that there is a substanceless quality or the moral and psychological implication that supreme love has an object which is not personal in any way whatsoever.

The effects of contemplating this unearthly beauty are automatic and profound. At this point the soul experiences the most authentic genesis of virtue, quickened by the most authentic beauty. Diotima says:

> Do but consider…there only will it befall him, as he sees the beautiful …, to breed not illusions but true examples of virtue, since his contact is not with illusion but with truth. So when he has begotten a true virtue and has reared it up, he is destined to win the friendship of Heaven; he, above all men, is immortal. [*Sym.* 212a; pp. 207-9]

At last we see the third level of understanding of Plato's account of justice in the soul. One seeks the perfection of the soul's function as the natural outcome of seeing the ideal in the Form. The life-long performance of the just soul is indeed striking, good in itself apart from whatever satisfaction it affords – although the satisfactions are not negligible. But finally it is striking because it is an embodiment of, a reflection of, the Form of beauty – a love which is our most profound motivation and our most primordial.

It is a love so profound that, in the companion dialogue, the

51

Phaedrus, Plato says its origin antedates our earthly existence. Before we had bodies, our souls – in the form of winged chariots – paraded with the gods, beyond the empyrean; and in this divine progress, our souls gazed upon the Forms (*Phdr.* 247c-e). The Form we saw the clearest was the Form of beauty (*Phdr.* 250 b). It left the strongest impression on our memory; in our earthly life, this memory is awakened by *eros.*

Having seen the Form of beauty in his previous, non-bodily life, the lover is reminded of it when he sees earthly beauty. Then do the "wings of his soul" sprout and he desires to return to the eternal realities: "Such a one, as soon as he beholds the beauty of this world, is reminded of true beauty, and his wings begin to grow; then is he fain to lift his wings and fly upward."[3] Since he cannot leave this world, he stays transfixed by his memory-glimpse of the unearthly beauty. Truly distracted, he appears mad: "…but inasmuch as he gazes upward like a bird, and cares nothing for the world beneath, men charge it upon him that he is demented" (*Phdr.* 249e; p. 496).

The strength of his memory of the Form of beauty will deter-mine what kind of lover this recollector of beauty will become. If the memory is dim, then he will pursue the beloved merely as an object of physical lust. However, if the memory of the Form of beauty is fresh and strong, he will treat the beloved with awe and reverence as though that one were the "holy image of a deity" (250e-251b). It is the latter kind of lover, moderated by memory of the Form of beauty, that seeks the spiritual perfection of the beloved (252e ff.). The account of their spiritual union has many surprising and even puzzling aspects. Not the least of these is the way that Plato attributes all of the eccentric behavior of the late-fifth-century lover (252a) as well as his extravagant psychosomatic reactions – shuddering, sweating, fever (251b) – to an as-yet-unrecognized memory of the Form of beauty. The true lover comes to see the real cause of this divine madness and to control his behavior accordingly (254b). Finally, if the lover and beloved remain chaste, "their days on earth will be blessed with happiness and con-cord, for the power of evil in the soul has been subjected, and the power of goodness liberated; they have won self-mastery and inward peace" (*Phdr.* 256b; p. 501).

By way of a conclusion we can reflect on the remarkable way that *eros* becomes transformed in Plato's account. Treated as a mere passion in the *Republic,* love, in *Phaedrus* and *Symposium,* becomes the driving force for acquiring virtue. In turn, what at first looked like a lonely task of self-perfecting becomes the goal of two lovers' devotion

52

to one another. However, in order that lovers may have this devotion, *eros* must cease being a selfish passion. In its radicalness, Plato's design for this transformation rivals his plans for marriage and family in the ideal city. We know that something revolutionary is afoot when he tells us that the true object of *eros* is not the body, nor even the soul of the beloved, but the Form of beauty; the beloved becomes simply the beneficiary of this love of the Form. By displacing the beloved, Plato makes the first step toward a notion of selfless human love. First of all, the Form of beauty, when it is at last seen as the real object of love, will disarm *eros* of its selfish need for physical possession of the beloved. The awe and reverence inspired by the Form is transferred to the beloved; one could no more possess the beloved whom one held in awe and reverence than one could possess the Form that one so regarded. Second, in these dialogues, *eros* begins to look like benevolence as the lover, eschewing sexual intercourse, seeks the spiritual improvement of his beloved. Inspired by the Form of beauty, the lover wishes to replicate the Form in the soul of the beloved. In this way, the lover achieves a kind of passionate detachment not unlike the passionate detachment of the artist who wishes his painting to be the best possible embodiment of inspiration. The lover who wishes nothing more for the beloved than a beautiful soul can be fairly described as benevolent – wishing the very best for his beloved and rejoicing in it.

Moreover, it is the fact that this Form is the Form of beauty that enables Plato to complete the somewhat improbable transition from *eros* to benevolence. For now we can see how the Form is the model for spiritual beauty. It not only motivates the lover but shows those qualities of soul that should be fostered, if we believe – as Plato does – that beauty is defined by harmony, balance, and symmetry. Beneath the beauty that one can see with the eyes – literally, aesthetic beauty – with its harmony, balance, and symmetry, there is, for the lover, the spiritual beauty defined by the harmony, balance, and symmetry among the parts of the soul. The balance and harmony of the parts of the soul constitute a beauty that also is justice for each of the parts – each receives its due. It is at this point in Plato's thought that what we call aesthetic becomes what we call moral. Moreover, this spiritual beauty is the precondition for treating other people justly or, as we would say, for being fair – using one of our older words for beautiful.

Finally, as *eros* becomes benevolent it also becomes contemplative. In the *Symposium*, the final revelation of the Form of beauty is achieved in a contemplation which is comparable to the gaze of the

53

lover upon the beloved (*Sym.* 211d). The *Phaedrus* talks movingly about the lover's gazing upon his beloved, admitting a flood of passion into his soul; and this vision is a reminder of that previous vision of the beautiful itself: "…whole and unblemished likewise, free from all alloy, steadfast and blissful were the spectacles on which we gazed in the moment of final revelation; pure was the light that shone around us" (*Phdr.* 250c; p. 497). This prototype of the loving gaze seems to be *eros* purified, come into its own. In the *Symposium, eros* culminates in a mystical vision combining both love and knowledge; Plato seems to say that *eros* is, paradoxically, the desire to gaze upon fundamental reality in an unobstructed vision. In a reverse Freudianism, we might conclude that all of the pricking desire for firm young flesh is really a suppressed longing for eternal beauty. The longing is never satisfied by possessing the flesh; it is only by gazing upon the eternal beauty that the longing will be fulfilled.

54

In closing, we might measure the remarkable transformation that *eros* has undergone by comparing it to contemplation in Christian neo-Platonism. Noting some similarities as well as differences will help us to see what *eros* has become and what it has not become. The notion of *eros* which seeks its ultimate satisfaction in gazing upon a non-material beauty may make us think immediately of meditation and the interior life. But we must be careful to observe that, in the *Symposium*, Plato's account has nothing to do with retiring from the active life. The vision of the Form of beauty is part of the generative act of bringing forth a virtue which, in turn, is meant to be public and civic. Nor is this contemplated beauty a person in any way, as it is for the Christian neo-Platonist.

Still, there are similarities, if we confine ourselves just to the vision itself – similarities well illustrated by the vision enjoyed by two contemplatives of a different sort, St. Augustine and St. Monica at Ostia. In Book IX of the *Confessions* we read of their conversation about the eternal Wisdom – in some important respects the counterpart to Plato's Forms. Although the eternal Wisdom is Christ, it also contains the exemplars – the Forms – of all material things. Ascending in their thoughts from the lowest to the highest material objects – to the stars themselves – they arrive at the conception of that eternal Wisdom by which all these other things are made. And then they move from the conception to the reality: "and while we were thus talking of His Wisdom and panting for it, with all the effort of our heart we did for one instant attain to touch it …"[4] Not only is this Wisdom the eternal truth about the world and the creatures in it; contemplating it is also the ultimate satisfaction of desire – the object of the strongest longing of their hearts.

Since this vision is a foretaste of the afterlife, the apt comparison is with the *Phaedrus*. Augustine might envy Plato's ability to describe the vision of Forms in the divine progress; but still, the vision that is had by souls destined to belong to mortals is quite insecure. Most, apparently, cannot maintain their gaze; and thus they lose their wings and descend to a cycle of reincarnation. It is clear that Plato does not intend that the end of human life, for most mortals at least, be an eternal contemplation; the real purpose of the vision is to ground the task of perfecting virtue in this life. On the other hand, Augustine firmly holds the vision that he and Monica shared but for a moment to be the end of human life; when mortals have finally attained it, they break out of earthly existence and securely gain eternal life. Augustine hints that this latter is an endless act of understanding, an eternal unfolding: "...and if this could continue, and all other visions so different be quite taken away, and this one should so ravish and absorb and wrap the beholder in inward joys that his life should eternally be such as that one moment of understanding for which we had been sighing – would not this be: *Enter thou into the joy of thy Lord?*" (p. 165).

In this contrast we ourselves are left with two prospects. The dramatic events of the *Republic, Symposium,* and *Phaedrus* are set in the bright Hellenic afternoon; Plato has yet to fail at his Syracusan experiment. It is still possible to suppose that *eros* can be harnessed to become the driving force of perfect virtue in this life. Augustine writes in the Hellenistic twilight; his own struggle with *eros* has left him with scars he recognizes will keep him from perfect moral virtue. In Book XIX of *The City of God* he persuasively presents a case for despairing of anyone's being able to attain moral virtue; it is a tragic vision of human life that he, of course, believes will be redeemed. Nevertheless, the beauty of Plato's account of virtue is not dimmed for us even if we recognize the necessity for that belief.

55

NOTES

1 *The Collected Dialogues of Plato,* ed. Edith Hamilton and Huntington Cairns (New York: Random House, 1961), 606; *Rep.* 358b-c.

2 *Lysis, Symposium, and Gorgias,* trans. W.R.M. Lamb (London: Heinemann Ltd., 1932), 223-25; *Sym.* 217a.

3 *The Collected Dialogues,* p. 496; *Phaedrus* 249e.

4 *The Confessions of St. Augustine,* trans. F.J. Sheed (New York: Sheed & Ward, 1942), 164.

ROYCE and the METAPHYSICS of COMMUNICATION

BY ANGEL MEDINA, GEORGIA STATE UNIVERSITY

For Arthur, in celebration of loyalty and community.

N ot many philosophers today are willing to speculate about the future of reason, and not many, among those who are willing to do so, can envision any alternatives beyond a deeper mech-anization of human life. I feel intellectually at home among human scientists who look, however dim their hopes, for a future with many alternatives. Anyone for whom science does not exhaust reason, for whom reason can be operative in service, in dialogue, in drama, or in ritual, is my kin amidst a world of strangers. The theme of community thus makes its first appearance in this discussion, and it need not be abandoned here for it can point the way to the heart of Royce's doctrine.

I. Metaphysics and Idealism in Royce

The primary concerns of Josiah Royce were undoubtedly metaphysical. However, his metaphysics did not originate from a desire to perceive the ultimate shape of the cosmos; its source was instead an overriding sense of the cosmic significance of morals. In his world system, cosmic purpose is clearly subordinated to moral purpose. The natural world order, in its evolutionary incompleteness, could never give rise to any self-sufficient or final purposes; but if one places above that order the moral universe of man and his fellows, an absolute ground must be in-troduced in order to avoid at the moral level the same indeterminacy and relativism that affects the physical world. In the interplay of human beings with nature, no individual purpose could be considered a pur-pose, no individual thought a thought, no individual error an error, unless they can be integrated in a transcendent unity and harmony.

It should be understood, then, that for Royce the cosmos can be known to be orderly and law-abiding only by virtue of an appeal to a transcendental "rational will" or absolute. The existence and the con-stant possibility of novelty and mutations in the cosmos indicate that, however this ultimate "will" may be framed, it must be considered a "free will." Hence, all regular and harmonious pictures of the world, other than the mysterious order attributed to the inner experience of the absolute, will be, of necessity, mere abstractions from that order. They can be meaningful only within modes of experience other than those of the absolute.

To confirm these claims, Royce needed to set up a variety of levels of experience relative to which all possible world views would make sense as coherent, if abstract, systems of meanings. His method of correlating world pictures to finite modes of experience was not then, it would seem, a way of accounting for metaphysical doctrines other than his own but more likely a means of attributing the necessity and abstract regularity of the cosmos to a subjective mode, or modes, of apprehension. In so doing, Royce was negating the traditional claims of purely cognitive cosmic world views to be acknowledged as the final metaphysical order on the strength of the worldly regularities and necessities made apparent through them. Regularity and necessity are only the aspects that the world presents to an abstracting experience, the human, insofar as this experience is based on habits.

57

One more important observation can be made in this context. The justification of a multiplicity of world pictures, Royce's early contribution to the emerging sociology of knowledge, did not completely undermine the moral and metaphysical elements of his system. The latter were intended to coexist with indeterminism in the physical realm and with pragmatic diversity and evil in the moral realm. Precisely how this coexistence was possible is something that Royce could not and did not explain satisfactorily in terms of the teleological idealism of *The World and the Individual* (1900-1902). But the subsequent development of his thought led him away from all standard forms of idealism and even of metaphysics. That is why interpreters of his thought must handle those two concepts with care when they apply them to him. Both notions, that of idealism and that of metaphysics, undergo a tremendous transformation in Royce, one that carries him forward into the mainstream of our present concerns and our most pressing problems.

The key to Royce's uniqueness as a metaphysician was his clear awareness of the principles of social psychology newly developed by James Mark Baldwin in a vastly influential work: *Social and Ethical Interpretations in Mental Development: A Study in Social Psychology* (New York, 1897). The fears and concerns of a Californian childhood in the days of the Gold Rush had determined the moral, rather than cosmic, nature of the absolute in Royce's doctrine. The debt to Baldwin determined his envisioning of all conscious striving as an act, not of a subsistent mind but of a self-creating will that, moment by moment, produces differences within itself and communicatively bridges them. In individual men the communicative will grows into a life plan, not a substantial soul. In groups of men it constitutes communities. In the absolute it reconciles all differences of meaning and conflicts of interests.

It is appropriate to emphasize here that, even in their early characterizations, neither the human mind nor the absolute is a substance for Royce. In this surely lies the key to his contribution to a new kind of metaphysics. Faced with the challenge of evolutionist thought, metaphysics was called upon in Royce's time to explain the continuity and consistency of moral effects in the world without any recourse to the category of substance which had been always its principal instrument. Royce alone among his contemporaries responded to the challenge without reducing the moral will to the realms of either purely pragmatic or utopically ideal intentions.

After the publication of *The World and the Individual*, his efforts toward the discovery of concrete instances of the communicative will led Royce to the singling out of an attitude, loyalty, that seemed to make the continuity and consistency of this will formally possible. Next, he tried to isolate the communicative will at work in an institutional setting. In modern society, where geographic and social mobility are rampant, the communicative will seems to be merely incidental or marginal. Only in areas where the spirit of localism has preserved its strength are people attracted to each other in ways effective enough to counter an apparently generalized self-estranging egoism. Royce felt that a resurgence of provincial architecture and art, history, folklore, and festivities was needed to shore up the communicative will in America. However, the clearer his concrete understanding of this will became, the more ambiguous and remote the absolute appeared to be.

In a book that has reestablished the origins of American sociology as a fertile ground for intellectual history, R. Jackson Wilson explains this aspect of Royce's development:

> The ideal of the absolute was always distressingly remote in Royce's thought. In the philosophy of loyalty and its integral provincialism the absolute became not only remote but vestigial. Loyalty was an individual good and loyalty to loyalty was an absolute law only in the sense of being categorical. The absolute was not nearly so necessary to Royce's work on loyalty as it had been to his earlier philosophy, and the province had only the barest connection with an infinite self of all

selves. As the absolute dwindled, Royce's emphasis on working forms of human community grew. In the end the absolute
practically disappeared from his thought and was replaced by
the community.[1]

In the course of this transition we see the teleological idealism of Royce
become a philosophy of communication. The emphasis shifts from the
affirmation of the reality of a final harmonious "will" in the moral realm
to the requirement for a commitment to harmony among all empirical
wills as a necessary condition for the very existence of the moral realm.
This transition, however, did not make Royce's philosophy any less
metaphysical. And neither can it be said that the sociology of knowledge that survived this philosophy has subsisted as a theory without
metaphysics. What Royce produced during the last period of his life,
and what the sociology of knowledge has been constantly revealing and
applying, is a new fundamental ontology of interactive or communal
subjectivity.

This new ontology is devoted to an explanation of the nature
and modes of operation of human subjects that are not substances. The
metaphysics of nonsubstantial subjectivity does not postulate any new
entities or energies in the world but only an autonomous level of the
social tendencies that bind living beings to each other. In this higher
sphere, common organic and even physical energies are directed to the
production of novel meaningful effects; new ends appear that bear no
direct relationship to the interaction between man and nature. In fact,
these ends, whether they are technical or expressive or political, could
not be called ends in the traditionally accepted sense of "telos," for they
are not put forward in order to be fulfilled but rather to be transcended, so that human life may interpret itself anew in the positing of further goals.

It would be impossible in the space of these comments to
present in detail the metaphysics of the communicative will to which
Royce gave classical expression in *The Problem of Christianity* (1913).
An imperfect, but loyal, account of it might be summed up in the
following two principles:

A. *Communication is for community.*

The medium of highly diversified actions and signals, on which ride the
waves of our everchanging forms of life, is not primarily an instrument
of species adaptation or progress. The conventions by means of which

men relate to nature presuppose a profound adaptability of men to each other; it is this adaptability that produces the rule-guided behavior from which hypotheses and theoretical constructs are framed. The German philosopher Karl-Otto Apel has recently pointed to Royce as the first author to make systematic use of this insight:

> Royce made it clear [that] indispensable conventions about the meaning of concepts needed in science presuppose that there are not only cognitive operations, such as perceptions and conceptions, which rest on an exchange between man and nature, but also cognitive operations, such as interpretation of signs, which rest on an exchange between men in a "community of interpretation."[2]

The meaning of the term "interpretation," in Royce's technical use of it, makes references to the multiplication of means in the achievement of the same ends and to the multiplication of ends themselves in human life. Through such multiplication it becomes obvious that, except for some biological givens, human life does not have to have the same shape or structure in all the members of the species. The forms of life thus made available through differentiation can be shared.

These peculiar features of human life place the fact of linguistic communication in a new light. Original human language is a form of covenanting about new forms of life to be explored in community. In primitive peoples all language that is not made unnecessary by interaction is sacred. As we move from prehistory to history, this sacred character remains attached solely to written language, to the scriptures that attempt to preserve forever the novelty of sacred conventions.

What makes these facts so important is that conventions about forms of life are not understood, nor are they to be understood, by reference to any mentalistic representations or any ulterior motives which themselves could not be shared. All the understanding that is necessary about conventions is achieved in the sharing itself, in the adoption and repetition of modified actions.

All modern conceptions of human thought, whether rationalistic or empiricist, were caught in the difficulty of translating both simple and complex physical events into conscious events that would adequately represent them. Even less persuasive were the attempts of these schools to explain communication as the transmission of private conscious events from one mind to another. Royce's discovery of the communicative character of action was a fortunate finding. It allowed

60

him to break with centuries of epistemological solipsism, but most of all it became the basis for the first fully developed metaphysics of community. Some recent philosophers, Wittgenstein for example, have achieved as much in the realm of epistemology; to my knowledge, only three (Scheler, Ortega, and Jaspers) have worked out complete and consistent metaphysics of community. The core of this metaphysics in Royce is constituted by the second principle that transpires in *The Problem of Christianity*.

B. *Community is for communication.*

The multiplication of forms of life by convention involves for Royce the existence of a radical ambiguity at the very heart of interactive consciousness. Through this ambiguity one can explain both the inevitability of dissent and the ultimately moral character of all conflicts. In the earlier Royce, ambiguity existed only at the level of the cosmos, the world of description. In the lawfulness and regularity of this world, were implicit both a reference to purposeful design and an indication of incompleteness. Thus, a free will could relate to the world by producing irregularities which would become the source of new orders. In the later Royce, communicative interaction shares some of the characteristics of the moral world, the world of appreciation, but it also shares in the ambiguity and incompleteness of the world of description. The lawful and regular conduct made possible by conventions is always ambiguous and incomplete – it produces only partial interpretations of life.

61

To be sure, it is conventions that impart a new life to the members of the community living by them; it is conventions also that require that no new life be begun without a covenant. Such, to Royce, is the root of the original sin: the "law of members" that lean toward new life clashes with the sacred agreements of the communicative will. Without freedom to innovate, new spontaneous actions and syntheses of interaction would never give rise to covenants. These antinomies can be seen most clearly in the new means/end relations born through covenants. On the one hand, the participants in free interaction become ends for each other because their wills are identified with the general will. On the other hand, each one of them is only an instrument of the communicative will and must will to die to himself to make it work.

II. Existential Elucidation and the Human Sciences

Recent existentialism and hermeneutical philosophy have further elaborated the metaphysics of the communicative will. The communicative process of life-building and development is not just a string of conventional and uncoventional actions. Covenants, of necessity, lead to what Jean-Paul Sartre has called the "totalization" of the covenanted life. The life that man builds through innovation and agreement grows very quickly toward the absorption of its own boundaries. Some of these boundaries (such as birth, love, and atonement) are intimately related to the communicative process itself. Others, like death and suffering, depend to a large degree upon the facilities and difficulties that the cosmos presents to a life of inventiveness and communication.

The tendency toward the absorption of its boundaries transforms the communicative life from a mere process of rule-following behavior into a process of elucidation of complete existential projects. Formally, human life, both individual and social, takes shape thereby as a being towards its boundaries, viz. a being that suspends some of its fixed, organic activities in the interest of producing and transmitting to fellow men original interpretations of its relations to its limits. From this existential perspective, the whole of human culture emerges as a continuing narrative account, a history, of the conversion of our stark existential limits into a rich diversity of symbolic reasons for being.

From their very beginnings, the Human Sciences have been deeply involved in questions of existential elucidation. Myths, religious narratives, and epic literature contained in ancient times robust versions of steady communicative life; in modern times it was left to sociology, and to its literary surrogate, the novel, to trace the explosive power of diversification of the communicative will. The growth of the modern individual toward a life of his or her own is a distinctly communicative phenomenon which has been recently compared with the birth of the hero in the context of the ancient cosmogonies:

> Defoe's *Robinson Crusoe* is a characteristic bourgeois odyssey that...proves the superiority of the novel over the epic....
> Hegel gives us a beautiful analysis of epic poetry and the stages of its development, from the cosmogonies to the epics centered around a single hero.... Here, man has recourse only to himself, he carries out his project of self-creation in terms of his own forces. One could laugh at Defoe's narrowmindedness, characteristic of the English bourgeoisie, when he re-

creates the prejudices of his own country on a desert island. But, in fact, the path from *Robinson Crusoe* to *The Phenomenology of the Mind* is a direct one.[3]

What have been the contributions of American sociology to the use and development of the method of existential elucidation? The image of American sociology as a sophisticated use of statistics in the service of administrative techniques is, as everybody knows, not only quite recent but quite inexact. If one reads between the lines in Wilson's book (cited above, n. 1) on the birth of sociology in this country, a thesis about the growth toward existential elucidation implicit in the development of American sociology as a human science can be adumbrated.

63

Human life in America is the most glaring manifestation of the cultural phenomenon of modern individualism. An explanation of this phenomenon principally in terms of survival greatly muddles it, since not all varieties of individualism could be easily explained in those terms. According to Wilson, there are two types of individualism at the root of our national character. One is represented in the vast "scramble for repute, place and power"[4] typical of people whose lives were founded in total freedom. The other is embodied in the ideal of the transcendent individual, the legitimate heir of the pilgrims. The work of William Graham Sumner justified the life style of the adventurous man of enterprise, the conqueror of nature; but one generation before, Thoreau and Emerson had justified in equally fervent language a style of life characterized by detachment, privacy, and the cultivation of the moral sense in contemplative submission to nature.

The coexistence of these antithetical ideals within the rising expectations of early American life would be difficult to understand if one failed to see that "the mythic figure of the transcendent individual was a moral and aesthetic counterpart of the ideal free entrepreneur."[5] Both types of men represent an exercise in self-creation, both seek, though in different ways, the help of "nature" to break the molds of tradition and society. Any guilt feelings that might be generated by the particularism of these endeavors are promptly stifled by calming assurances that society will share, in time, in the riches of a new form of life. As Emerson wrote:

> A thought does not dart into the mind of the recluse scholar who rejoices at the discovery of a new truth but I am presently in acquaintance with it and also made wiser. The merchant does not earn a pittance by his commerce without enlarging

the wealth of his customers the community.[6]

An appropriate symbolic illustration of the coexistence of these two types, both forms of existential elucidation that will remain invariant in our society, is given by Herman Melville in his novel *Pierre; or, The Ambiguities*. America is represented in this book by a building known as the "Church of the Apostles," a New York edifice prematurely aged by two consecutive changes in the character of its neighborhood. Into it, after a purifying retreat in the woods, comes Pierre, a young esquire who had divested himself of his rank and all of his possessions. The building had been intended to shelter a throng of believers, one in mind and in heart; instead it is inhabited by a split crowd of busy merchants, who operate at the street level, and of shabby, unrecognized intellectuals, who occupy the upper rooms. The "Church of the Apostles" is, in Melville, a tragic symbol not only because of the total insulation of its two breeds of "parishioners," but because neither of these two sectors can truly have any hope of achieving its goals. The moralizers must live with the grim realization of their inability to be relevant; the pragmatists know in their hearts that their methods will never lift them above the rabble.

The years from 1860 to 1920, which saw the birth and consolidation of American sociology, constitute a rare period of awareness of the inevitable failure of individualism. That awareness is not generalized, but signs of recognition of the marginality of the individual voice and of the mass psychology hiding behind competition abound in all quarters. Women, the young, the dispossessed, conservatives and progressives, religious people and agnostics, they all show, in various degrees, a nagging uneasiness about the amorphousness of their culture and the fragility of their roots.

The initial task of the newborn science was, hence, to reveal and restore the sources of the richest values in the culture before they were swept by the oncoming tide of industrialism and urbanization. The search for value led each one of the major figures of this foundational period to different communal wellsprings of authentic existential elucidation. Charles Sanders Peirce looked at the genteel elite for some relief from the common credence that "greed is the great agent in the elevation of the Universe."[7] For Baldwin it was the communal character of the "ideal self" that balanced the individualism of our habits and the social conformity built into our tendency to adaptation. Edward Ross sought insistently for interpersonal means of social control such as public opinion, the influence of art in the creation of ideas, education, and the example of extraordinary individuals. Royce's trust in the moral component of communication has been shown above. And Granville Stanley Hall reconstructed with incredible devotion the communal experiences of his "boy life" in the little town of Ashfield in the hills of western Massachusetts.

It is particularly moving to witness Hall's attachment to the place and memories of his boyhood. Wilson observes that Hall "never cut himself loose from childhood despite many years of European travel and study, two marriages, a distinguished professorship, and thirty years as a university president with an international reputation" (p. 117). It may be that Wilson expects too much from marriage, professorships, and even university presidencies; on the other hand, Hall's attachment to his genetic community was not just a matter of sociological method. He and, to a great extent, all the others mentioned were attempting to elucidate their existence while freeing themselves through sociology from the illusions of their epoch.

The happy union of existential elucidation and sociology seems to come to an end with the new avalanche of individualism and upward mobility created by technological explosion and war in the second and third quarters of our century. The consensus sociology of this period seems to be interested only in those forms of action and motivation that have lost all cultural and psychological peculiarity and can be quantified as manifest functions. Yet, even during these years, sociology performed important tasks in partial areas of existential elucidation.

In the area of the sociology of knowledge, for example, reflection about our elites and their direction has been stimulated by the excellence of American intellectual history in the postwar years, and by the continued controversies in political science about elite and countervailing power structures and about the end of ideology. Furthermore, our conventional sociologists have made great strides, greater perhaps than in any other advanced society, in the understanding of the social situation of ordinary people facing their boundaries. The sociologies of the young and of the aged, of leisure, of mass communication, of religion and death, have reached maturity in these years and are perhaps the most promising areas of future research and interpretation. Finally, our racial problems and the gravity of our urban situation have created an urgent concern for the community forms of the future, a concern that other societies, more confident of their past, are not yet able to feel.

These reflections on Royce can conclude, then, in a tone of

confidence. Perhaps the worst days of individualism are over. The conflicts created by individualism are likely to lessen if circumstances – and the Human Sciences themselves – help make us aware that individualism, greed, and violence, are not "natural" to human life, but rather psychosocial phenomena willfully manipulated by unscrupulous minorities. If the awareness of this fact continues to grow, it will have a powerful therapeutic effect on the most harmful aspect of those psychosocial phenomena.

There will always be conflicts and ambiguities in our existential elucidation. Yet, as the late Royce taught us, the restoration of the sense of community can bring to bear powerful moral restraints on particularistic attitudes. Individualism and the sense of community are the most profound existential constants of our human life, and we are due for a swing of the pendulum toward the latter. If, and when, this swing comes about, the metaphysics of communicative interaction will yield the full measure of its promise.

NOTES

1 R. Jackson Wilson, *In Quest of Community: Social Philosophy in the United States, 1860-1920* (New York: Oxford University Press, 1970), p. 165.
2 Karl-Otto Apel, "The A Priori of Communication and the Foundation of the Humanities," in *Man and World,* 5 (1972), p. 8.
3 F. Feher, "Is the Novel Problematic?," in *Telos,* 15 (Spring 1973), p. 53.
4 Wilson, p. 21.
5 Wilson, p. 22.
6 Emerson, *Journals,* III, p. 29. Quoted by Wilson, *ibid.*
7 "Evolutionary Love," in *The Monist* (1893), quoted by Wilson, p. 56.

PERCY'S *LOST in the COSMOS*: MEMORY, SACRAMENTALITY, and COMMITMENTS in the PRESENT

BY VICTOR A. KRAMER, GEORGIA STATE UNIVERSITY

Percy's oblique fiction concerns itself with the odd manifestations experienced by his protagonists as they observe peculiar things in a world which is strangely turned in upon itself. These protagonists sense that something is radically wrong with themselves and society and they also sense that they must seek answers to the dilemmas which they face. Thus, Percy's heroes seek ways to understand the peculiarities they experience, yet to do so is extremely difficult because so many others within their world seem to have forgotten so much about life that nothing even appears wrong.

Life, Percy's protagonists sense, must have been more satisfying for earlier generations who could live more in the immediate yet with an awareness of the transcendent. For his fictional inhabitants of the present moment, however, living seems largely bounded by regular consumption and by an extreme abstractedness which provides comfort. Such life often appears satisfying because humankind has developed so many different ways to consume experiences and to affix labels; yet the haunting feeling remains that something is terribly wrong. This is why Percy's major characters frequently long to be elsewhere or to find their true selves; yet these characters have been lulled, like the majority in the contemporary world, into the belief that life is something which can be controlled and manipulated. Percy's fictional world is, therefore, full of characters who have frequently lost contact with the beauty of life itself. Instead, for such characters abstraction, consumption, and faith in things or systems of thought outside themselves have caused them to lose contact with the natural as a gift which provides glimpses of the transcendent. Such Percy characters have frequently lost the ability to discern what it means to live in a particular place and to have a special, even a sacramental, mission. What these protagonist-searchers learn is that to remember who they are, they first must learn to see their own lives, and the lives of others, as the results of combinations of gifts and choices which connect them with the living past, the present, and which also move them into the future – all as part of an ongoing process. But the only way to accomplish this is not to be obsessed either by the past or by the future.

Percy's dissatisfaction with psychoanalysis and his skepticism about what science may deliver are clearly expressed in many of his essays and throughout the fiction. His novel *The Thanatos Syndrome* (1987) demonstrates these things by satirizing, through plot and setting, contemporary society while the novel is imagined as taking place in the mid-1990s. Perhaps more forcefully in this novel than earlier, Percy demarcates a vision of a society which can easily become forgetful of what is most important. Aiming to manipulate (even unto death), this future society forgets about the present. Throughout such a prophecy about the future, Percy allows reverberations of the Third Reich to remind readers of contemporary America's contempt for the uniqueness of persons. The non-fiction of *Lost in the Cosmos*, which immediately precedes this novel, is its foreshadowing.

In *Lost*, Percy investigates many of the sicknesses of the present moment which bring about our forgetfulness and thus cause individual persons to be so lost. Percy's insights, through story and also throughout the unusual mixture of non-fiction and fiction in *Lost in the Cosmos*, suggest that if individuals are to find themselves, it will be possible only if they learn to live well in the present.

If humankind clouds the present with abstractions or diverts attention to some utopian vision of the future it will remain lost. Strangely, however, Percy also always reminds readers through both his non-fiction and his novels that mystery must remain at the core of living: acceptance of that mystery is ultimately what allows persons to find themselves. Percy's tongue-in-cheek method of providing questions and answers, to be checked as exercises in *Lost*, ironically reveals what he really believes. For some of the more important questions, there are no easy answers. Even worse, humanity seems to have forgotten this fundamental fact.

I

PERCY'S *Lost in the Cosmos: The Last Self-Help Book* combines theorizing
– about the nature of contemporary man, about language and semiotics, and why humankind seems so amazingly lost – with fiction entitled
"A Space Odyssey." Percy includes meditations about contemporary
abstractedness (the very thing which causes humankind to be so lost),
ironic answers to man's dilemma, and storytelling, which is his best
way of suggesting the answers which he is convinced that we as a culture so desperately need. Percy's funny subtitle implies he realizes that
this will not be the "last self-help book," but he ironically suggests that
if readers are attentive it might be a way of recovering a sacramental   69
view of the universe. His most important advice stresses that we should
attempt to forget about the self if we are to find our way.

All of Percy's fiction builds on the same theme – the slow
education of an *isolato* adrift in a world which seems to be quite content with its drifting. Percy is convinced that humanity at the present
moment exists in an extremely difficult situation because it so frequently
insists on acting as though it is possible to be an "autonomous self."
In *Lost in the Cosmos* Percy reminds readers that humankind will remain
lost as long as it lets such a conviction remain a ruling assumption.
Just as in his novels, Percy provides a key in *Lost in the Cosmos* which
may unlock the puzzle of lostness if readers are willing to admit that
their true selves can never be autonomous ones. Above all, Percy insists
that we must honor the world in its mystery. This essay examines how
this idea is fundamental to *Lost in the Cosmos*.

Percy insists that to be human is to be aware of the need to
reflect and to share with one another in celebration. Such experience
brings people together and makes it possible for individuals to have
insights into key experiences. A basic problem in the contemporary
Western world, however, is that so many have forgotten how to live
sacramentally moment by moment, and thus much human experience
seems meaningless or ambiguous. Key experiences (initiation, work,
death, communion with others) seem to blend with everything else,
and the result is that, for many, life is bland and boring. In a counter-
move, all kinds of unusual measures are sought to find ways out of
such a frightening existence while ironically these measures largely
insure still more *lostness*.

VICTOR A. KRAMER

Percy realizes that what is essential about human experience resides in personal experience and the facts of personal lives, yet for so many who remain lost, the means of interpreting personal experience have also been lost. As Bernard Cooke argues in his *Sacrament and Sacramentality*, what mankind needs is "a hermeneutic of experience."[1] If mankind's experience day by day is to serve as "word of God," thereby giving insight into one ultimate story, then every action and every experience should have meaning. In times past official religious teaching, scripture, liturgical celebrations, and so forth came to our aid. Today, Percy argues, such aids are largely not available because people have cut themselves off from such means of interpreting experience in a post-Christian and frequently post-religious age. It is as if women and men have forgotten the best of the past and, what is worse, do not care about the present. *Metanoia* is not possible if we are not concerned about the present.

Percy's concerns are clearly Christian, yet he is also fully aware of the fact that a Christian interpretation of life does not "make sense" in the eyes of the contemporary world. "Only in faith," says Cooke, can a Christian interpretation of life make sense, but already at the beginning of Christianity "Paul tells the Corinthians that the paradoxical wisdom of Christianity is a stumbling-block for the Jews and pure nonsense to the Greeks" (*op. cit.,* 35). What follows is an analysis of *Lost in the Cosmos* and of Percy's concern about what has gone radically wrong for contemporary man, why modern humankind seems to be so violently dislocated, and how, through a sacramental awareness (especially through friendship and commitment to others), we might again begin to find our way.

Readers of Walker Percy have frequently accused him of being caustic, even unwilling to admit the value of the "progress" so characteristic of our present moment. However, it is not a matter of being sarcastic or angry because of what he sees; it is more a matter of Percy's fear that as a culture we run the risk of being enveloped in a gigantic sea of apparent comfort, convenience, materialism, and abstraction. His essay "Southern Comfort" (1979) suggests that the Sunbelt – that rim looming ever larger from Los Angeles to Atlanta – is the inevitable wave of the future.[2] While it may be too soon to predict whether this will be good or bad, depending upon the combination of events which actually take place in the next several decades, Percy says that the South has emerged from its preoccupation with racial issues and that in fundamental ways the South of the present moment may resemble the South of 1820 more than that of 1920. Its diversity, its ability to react as a region and as a contributing part of the nation "might even leaven the lump," he says. By this he means that, at the present moment of the history of the world, all the necessary ingredients do exist for finding ourselves and for making a proper contribution for the benefit of others. His fictional heroes certainly undergo such potential for change. Such hopeful thoughts might apply equally well to American culture as a whole.

We also know that there is a darker side to Walker Percy, a side that acknowledges original sin, man's obsession with himself, and his obsessive tendency in the present century to continue to set out upon paths of destruction of others, and ultimately of self-destruction. Clearly the present moment is a curious one, fashioned more by technology and science than by faith. Percy, as someone trained as a scientist (chemistry major at Chapel Hill, M.D. at Columbia), has made a profession of observing the present century, a century poised, it seems, between two possibilities. On the one hand are abstractions (such as in science) and the selfish concerns (of individuals) which will insure continuing lostness. On the other hand is a possibility of a reawakened awareness of reality as experienced because of a respect for the immediacy of a world to be loved and accepted, not manipulated or endlessly worried about in an egocentric manner. Percy's humor, revealed in the fiction and in the funny meditations of *Lost*, are a satiric way of reminding readers that they cannot always bend the world to their individual likings. So often when this is attempted disaster follows. (Could this be why Percy's characters seem to thrive on disasters – something bigger than themselves takes over, and they can suddenly *be*, and no longer have to worry about what they appear to be, or what they should *do*?)

Percy has written essays about the mystery of language. Many of these pieces are collected in *The Message in the Bottle*, essays which frequently are designed to remind readers that something fundamentally wrong has occurred since the Renaissance, during which time man has apparently become more sure of himself and of his ability to investigate and build (both machines and structures, and structures of thought). Like Henry Adams who pondered the amazing loss of faith during the nineteenth century as machines grew ever larger, Percy (aware of such facts, too) ponders the curious fact that while contemporary humankind purports to be immensely comfortable, it is, in fact, getting crazier and crazier as it inhabits condominiums from Birmingham to Los Angeles. In the desire for control humankind has apparent-

71

ly forgotten about life.

Percy believes that we have lost contact with, or forgotten about, something fundamental to our nature; most basically this is the need for recognition of others as persons and of the corresponding need – which all persons should have – to acknowledge the sacramentality of all life. Percy also knows that most readers do not want preaching, even though they may sense that life is sacred and may long for an awareness of the transcendent. *Lost in the Cosmos*, subtitled "The Last Self-Help Book," is Percy's way of gently showing readers that progress may not be progress after all. Of what good, he implies, is progress, if one's eternal awareness of the sacramental is lost? Progress is meaningless if we cannot honor the mystery of life itself.

72

Lost in the Cosmos is a catalogue of what Percy considers wrong with the contemporary world. This bemused report is one of humankind apparently unable to figure out what has gone wrong; but if Percy suggests that modern humanity is lost, his implication is that deep within himself man senses he is lost from something, and that therefore he is in dire need of being bound back to whatever will allow him to be found. Above all, Percy is convinced, humankind needs a sacramental view of the world.

II

ONE OF THE fundamental patterns reiterated throughout Percy's fiction is that of a hero engaged in attempts to understand himself within a world which makes so little sense. Such a hero, whether it is Binx Bolling in *The Moviegoer*, or Will Barrett in *The Second Coming*, finally has to pursue a search for something fundamental which will allow him to begin to function in a society which is caught up in its meaninglessness and in numerous activities which overshadow the true self. In this fiction Percy's heroes are archetypal figures who undergo trials of alienation because they are separated from an awareness of a larger pattern; first they are lost, and then slowly, slowly, parts of answers come to them. It is as if they slowly remember that they are part of a larger whole.

Such an awareness of a fundamental need to go beyond self (and models of self) is at the base of Percy's meditations throughout *Lost in the Cosmos* too. The contemporary world described in this book is one in which characters are both ignorant of self and in desperate need of appearing to be more sure of themselves. But if the true self is lost, covered over by false selves which compete for attention and pleasure – a kind of temporary false transcendence – how does one begin to find oneself? Percy hints that reverence for, and with, other persons is the answer. This is the core of what he says in all his fiction, including *The Thanatos Syndrome*.

For a character like Will Barrett in *The Last Gentleman* Percy imagines that it was as if he had been for years convinced that he really could engineer his life. And the fact is that such characters do inhabit the contemporary world, one so complex and comfortable that it frequently appears they do really engineer existence. Yet, as Percy is fond of reminding readers, such hope is delusionary. It is like the group dynamics which Will chooses to walk away from. As *The Last Gentleman* proceeds, Will does seem to believe sincerely that he will marry Kitty, go to work for Mr. Vaught, settle down in the suburbs, and live happily ever after. That, of course, does not happen; and what does occur is that Will puzzles through Sutter Vaught's journal; he meets Val, the sister who has become a Sister; and he witnesses the baptism of Jamie.

At the end of the novel, Father Boomer appears, and Jamie's baptism takes place, and in the final part of the book everything changes: Val has insisted that baptism is necessary; she has charged Will with the responsibility of making sure that measures would be taken to insure "the economy of salvation." But all of this is highly mysterious for Will within a fictional situation where apparently the religious beliefs of Val, on the one hand, and the skepticism of Sutter Vaught (the near-suicide doctor philosopher) on the other, seem to be irreconcilable.

Percy's point must be that there is a world of sacramental awareness which does have validity, yet such awareness exists within a world which can never be fully explained by science or psychology. The scene in the hospital at the end of this novel (the end of Jamie's quest, and perhaps the true beginning of Will's which will only be concluded twenty years later in *The Second Coming*) could not be more prosaic. In an ordinary hospital room a more or less graceless priest performs his function as priest by baptizing Jamie. This is a very simple ceremony, yet as a sign it speaks much more than the words prescribed reveal. There is a fundamental reorientation, and Will is therefore introduced to a mystery. The sacramental reality of this particular moment casts light on all the preceding actions in Percy's novel. Key movements in *Lost* function in the same way: Percy insists that men are called to act because of their responsibility to others and because of the placement of particular persons in particular circumstances. When they cease to think only about themselves, then the whole cosmos takes on a different look.

In *The Message in the Bottle* Percy wrote about the dilemma of a Christian novelist who has, metaphorically, found the treasure of great price hidden in an abandoned trunk in the attic of an old house. Such a writer rushes out into a city street to announce his miraculous find, only to discover that no one is there. All the inhabitants of the modern city have, he finds, moved to the suburbs (and now seem to be making plans to move to another planet). Even more amazing, like Binx in Gentilly, or the Vaughts near their golf course setting, these people are perfectly happy to be just where they are, and certainly they do not want to be disturbed by news from some other realm. Yet I think what Percy is telling his readers, over and over, is precisely this: we are lost because we refuse news of the transcendent, and we miss that news because we forget who we are – persons with responsibilities to other persons. The news is there on a daily basis, if we would accept it.

It is interesting that in the trade edition of *Lost in the Cosmos* Percy included one epigraph. It is from Nietzsche and outlines the plight of contemporary men "unknown...to ourselves." In the paperback edition Percy has added an epigraph from St. Augustine: "O God, I pray you to let me know my self."[3] This significant addition suggests what is at the core of Percy's odd and elegant book. Once one peels away the cleverness of Percy's format it is clear that the writer remains compassionate about his lost fellow travelers who sometimes seem so lost that such a lost self would as soon forget itself as find itself.

In the dozen short chapters which open *Lost in the Cosmos* Percy entertains readers with questions about the "amnesiac" self; the "self as nought" (trying to inform itself by possession of things, or pursuit of fashion); the self "surprised to find it lives somewhere"; the fearful self (afraid of being found out, afraid of being with another, trying to escape the predicament of shyness); the promiscuous self; the envious self; the bored, depressed, and (significantly) the impoverished self in a world overflowing with things to make the self happy. In all these exercises Percy outlines fundamental ways in which, despite all our knowledge, technology, and material goods, mankind seems to remain fundamentally lost. Percy then includes a "Semiotic Primer of the Self," forty pages which he calls an "intermezzo" and which he suggests can be skipped "without fatal consequences." Clearly, however, he implies in this essay, and in other parts of the book, that semiotics may provide a key for finding one's way in the cosmos. He hastens to inform readers that "Semiotically, the self is literally unspeakable to itself. One cannot speak or hear a word which signifies oneself, as one can speak or hear a word signifying anything else...." In Percy's view, once "the unprecedented appearance of the triad in the Cosmos" was recognized, and we became conscious of ourselves, our history took a dangerous swerve into its lostness: thus,

> The self perceives itself as naked. Every self is ashamed of itself.
> The semiotic history of this creature thereafter could be written in terms of the successive attempts, both heroic and absurd, of the signifying creature to escape its nakedness and to find a permanent semiotic habiliment for itself – often by identifying itself with other creatures in its world.
> Among Alaskan Indians, this practice is called totemism. In the Western world, it is called role-modeling.[4]

75

Percy raises many questions in this essay, and one of his strongest implications (both in this "Primer," and throughout his fiction) is that man's lostness is keyed in with the "solitary absorption with self" and that to find a way beyond self seems mankind's most important need.

Percy's language in this semiotics essay is especially important: "What is the nature of the catastrophe of the self?" His final rhetorical question in a long series is this: "Is it a turning from the concelebration of the world to a solitary absorption with self?" (109). The word "concelebration" seems to be extremely significant. Isolation seems to be what Percy finds most alarming, and this is what he is most fearful about with regard to science, abstraction, technology, and materialism run rampant. It is not an accident that Percy allows statements by Mother Teresa of Calcutta to give a focus to his chapter 12: affluent Westerners seem to be "sad and poor, poorer even than the Calcutta poor" (82). This chapter is, significantly, arranged to precede immediately the "intermezzo on semiotics."

In the light of the chapters which follow the "intermezzo" Percy does have a message for his readers. Could it be, he asks, that humanity has found all kinds of ways of getting away from reality by becoming too absorbed with the self? Should that self be more concerned with others? Chapters 13 and 17 trace how the contemporary self places itself in relation to the world while it continues to have problems when it "orbits" that world; and how certain persons are (apparently) exempted, such as scientists who don't have to take account of themselves; and how, nevertheless, the self (which steadfastly thinks itself to be autonomous) remains lonely; and, finally, how this autonomous self is possessed of both a spirit of the erotic and a secret love of violence, and how this could (literally) be devastating in a nuclear age.

As presented by Percy such facts indicate that contemporary man is sad, frustrated (maybe, crazy?), and is disappointed in myriads of ways: so much so that, among other things, he is faced with "the sudden and unprecedented appearance of florid sexual behavior and the overt and covert practice of violence to the point of rendering cities unlivable" (187), millions killed in wars, and the very real threat of complete self-destruction.

Does Percy provide any hope? The answer is yes; but some readers will probably lack the patience to perceive this because Percy's method remains so indirect. At the same time, *Lost in the Cosmos* is an important analysis of the contemporary moment for it reminds us of our propensity for selfishness when so turned in on ourselves. It also serves as a gloss on Percy's fiction. Significantly, the last two sections, "A Space Odyssey," are fiction, an imagined voyage of a manned vehicle which escapes the nuclear destruction of future earth to return centuries later to a darkened planet to discover only a remnant of the human species still alive. Here, surprisingly, Percy does provide hope. We can choose, he suggests.

III

PERCY'S FICTIONAL ODYSSEY spins out a situation where finally a choice has to be made between abandoning the broken planet and carrying on in some particular out-of-the-way place. This is Percy's way of indirectly making readers think about the present dilemma. The impassioned speech of Abbot Leibowitz, an echo of Walter M. Miller, Jr.'s *A Canticle for Leibowitz,* suggests what Percy wants his readers to hear, believe, and choose; man

> ...somehow encountered a catastrophe, God alone knows what, used his freedom badly, and chose badly – perhaps chose himSELF, the one thing he can never know of itself, rather than God – and has been in trouble ever since. [247-48]

Percy's Abbot Leibowitz, who insists that the crew of the returned spaceship must go to Lost Cove, Tennessee, also insists that humanity does always continue to have the promise of God, and that we must therefore remain in faith on this earth. The abbot also explains that choosing to go to an out-of-the-way place in Tennessee may seem exceedingly strange, but this is a way to choose something other than a dream for utopia (and thereby to remain lost); it is a paradox:

> The only reason, from your point of view, is that you have no choice. You know now that if what I say is not true, you are like the gentiles Paul spoke of: a stranger to every covenant, with no promise to hope for, with the world about you and no God. You are stuck with yourselves, ghost selves, which will never become selves. You are stuck with each other and you will never know how to love each other. Even if you succeed, you and your progeny will go to Europa and roam the galaxy, lost in the Cosmos forever. [250-51]

Therefore, Percy's Abbot insists that humankind must choose between being lost forever and finding themselves by choosing to be children of God.

The Abbot also proposes that a church-sanctioned marriage for the Captain of the returned spaceship and the mother of his children, Dr. Jane Smith, is immediately called for, and that all survivors should, forthwith, go to Lost Cove, Tennessee. It is all pretty improbable. But Percy obviously thinks that man's current selfish situation is preposterous as well. He concludes this book by providing some final "Thought Experiments" wherein he explains that Judaism, Protestant Christianity, and Catholic Christianity all seem to be preposterous in the face of our expanding scientific knowledge; but even more preposterous, Percy states, is any "New Ionia," a colony dreamed about on a different planet where a new and guiltless race could emerge.

Percy's "Space Odyssey," like Walter Miller, Jr.'s A Canticle for Leibowitz, upon which it is based, is a parable. It is Percy's way of warning and teaching. Percy is saying we must avoid making still more wrong choices. We cannot dream our way away from the fact that we remain wayfarers in the city of man.

Percy clearly wants readers to realize that it is a commitment to the here and now, and not to some imagined otherness or abstraction, which may bring salvation. The problem is, he keeps insisting, that many individuals keep insisting they really have all the necessary answers. It is precisely such an individual's refusal to concelebrate the given world in all its mystery which makes him keep thinking he can build his own private way of coping. As a storyteller Percy knows that even in storytelling, no full answers are forthcoming; yet at the same time he reminds readers that a sacramental view of the world, a concelebration of the mystery of the world, makes far more sense than any abstraction or temporary transcendence (through science, or even art).

As noted above, Percy uses Mother Teresa's commentary about the sadness throughout the affluent West to suggest that something is quite wrong in Western society (chapter 12, "The Impoverished Self"). Are we poor because we have forgotten about others?

> ...Western society is an ethic of power and manipulation and self-aggrandizement at the expense of the values of community, love, innocence, simplicity, values encountered both in childhood and in non-aggressive societies (e.g., the Eskimo). As Ashley Montagu says, adulthood in the Western world is a deteriorated and impoverished childhood. [81]

Whether we check this as the correct "answer" or not, it does suggest a lot about contemporary society, a society of loners, adventurers, and temporary transcenders – near suicidal in their frustration. In contrast, to grow up would mean we would remember that we are not alone.

Percy's Mother Teresa of Calcutta might be compared to Sister Val in *The Last Gentleman*. Both opt for the here and now. As affluent Westerners we remember the apparent peculiarity of Sister Val's conversion and her own father's disgust with her generosity when she established a school for Negroes. It simply made no sense to him for her to give her money away "to Niggers," yet her decision to spend the money (he had given each of his children $100,000) in such a surprising fashion stands as a symbol for what the New Testament suggests that all Christians should do. As a parable, the actions of Percy's fictional Sister Val speak to all affluent Westerners.

In *Lost in the Cosmos* Percy's sentiments are clearly with the characters who choose to remain on Earth with all its troubles. The real difficulty – and Percy insists we must remember this – is to see the world as *both* "mysterious" and "sacramental" (157). He stresses that we have to enter into the dance without the abstractions that seem so unfortunately to doom so many to a cosmos of abstractions. Significantly, within *Lost in the Cosmos*, chapter 13, "The Transcending Self," is placed strategically after the "intermezzo" on semiotics, and this chapter is perhaps the pivotal point for all these meditations. The scene is a corn dance at a Taos Indian pueblo in the 1940s. Percy imagines a cast of ten characters, all as witnesses, or participants, in relation to the imagined event. A prosaic Father-Boomer-type of Catholic priest, "hardly afire with love of God and fellow man... yet aware too of his failings and accordingly staking a good deal on the mercy of God" (139), seems to be the key.

This priest is another one of Percy's "wayfarers," and while he "accepts his identity as a pilgrim," he (like all of us) "dreads the likelihood of being assigned to the Hopi reservation, the true boondocks." Semiotically, Percy reports, this imagined wayfarer has deceived himself by acquiescing in the *sign* and role with which the world invests him. He should, instead, be more concerned with the *signified*. As a person with a priestly vocation, he should act accordingly. Such seems to be the message Percy provides for all wayfarers: each one, as a pilgrim, must accept homelessness. In so doing they may begin to find and accept their creatureliness and limitations. Then in a paradoxical way, they may find their true selves as they live in their own Lost Coves. Without perhaps expecting so much for the self, and with a recognition of what can be done without abstraction and technology, we may even begin again to pray, as did St. Augustine.

Exiled from Eden, we are castaways: Percy tells us this, but he also implies that while exile is certain, the good news of man redeemed – if we but have the good sense to listen to the news – remains available. Man's exile, the Fall, is therefore a fall into abstraction. The way to re-enter the Garden, at least as part of a holding action, is to choose to live sacramentally in the reality which God has given us.

Percy's reference to James Agee in *Lost in the Cosmos* is paradigmatic. If Agee were living now, Percy asks, would he choose to be an apartment dweller in Greenwich Village (a kind of protest against the establishment and his employment in Rockefeller Center in the offices of *Fortune, Time,* and *Life*), or would he make some other choice:

> Where would you rather be if you were James Agee now and alive and well: stumbling around Greenwich Village boozed to the gills, or sitting on the front porch of a house on a summer evening in Knoxville? [154]

To "play" the role of artist (still another abstraction), Percy implies, can very easily get in the way of being an intact person. The point is that while Agee must have had doubts about the accuracy of what language or gesture can represent, he (as the model of an artist who sought to blend art and life) must also have been aware that a role assumed, if played too self-consciously, can be problematic. The real need as artist, and as human being, is "to live an intact though difficult" life.

Percy mentions Simone Weil, Martin Buber, and Dietrich Bonhoeffer as writers "who have become themselves transparently before God and managed to live intact though difficult lives." This is a hint for all who would find themselves. Some, such as Flannery O'Connor, "have even outdone Kierkegaard and seen both creation and art as the Chartres sculptor did, as both dense and mysterious, gratuitous, anagogic, and sacramental" (157). Through story, Percy informs us that such an apprehension of reality – "dense" and "sacramental" – is the way individuals must apprehend the entire universe as well as other selves, selves that are fearful and lonely, selves that keep so frantically acting as if they were not lost.

Percy tells us that we will remain *lost* just as long as we think we have all the answers. If we can bring ourselves to understand that we will not make a perfect world with faster computers and bigger convention hotels, maybe humankind can then begin to find a world beyond the world we have tried so hard to fashion into a paradise but which has proven to be only our labyrinth. Another way to say some of this might be to stress that the city of man, as St. Augustine would call it, has many virtues and attractions, but there is another whole city beyond the visible one. Percy would remind us that we have to be aware of both.

The problem, as for example it was for Uncle Jules in *The Moviegoer,* is that in this society it is possible to become so comfortable in the city of man that we can literally forget about the city of God as even a remote possibility. Percy says only an "ex-suicide can contemplate cosmic mystery" (78). What he wants his readers to realize is that the entire cosmos is given to us to celebrate, to be in wonder of. Yet the only way to understand (or even begin to make sense) of that world is to enter into it. Percy writes:

> The non-suicide is a little traveling suck of care, sucking care with him from the past and being sucked toward care in the future. His breath is high in his chest.
>
> The ex-suicide opens his front door, sits down on the steps, and laughs. Since he has the option of being dead, he has nothing to lose by being alive. It is good to be alive. He goes to work because he doesn't have to. [79]

It is precisely the person who can laugh and not be a bundle of cares who can assume a sacramental view of the universe. Such a person ceases to be lost.

Luckily, characters like Val in *The Last Gentleman*, and persons such as Mother Teresa, writers such as Flannery O'Connor and Walker Percy, will not let us forget that we have an obligation to ourselves and to others, and above all that obligation is to remember that we must make commitments in the here and now. If we do not make commitments, we can easily veer off into still more abstraction, or pleasure, or depression, or consumption, or impoverishment, and thereby remain lost. If we do, perhaps we will, like St. Augustine, pray "'O God, I pray you to let me know my self.'" The paradox, of course, is that an awareness of self is found through an awareness of others.

Percy's work as essayist and novelist reminds readers of what is going wrong in a world where humankind apparently has so manipulated things that we attempt to ignore some of the fundamental facts about the self – not the least of which is that members of humankind must remember that they have an obligation to live in the present and with others. This means that such living also necessitates commitments in the present. These commitments (rather than commitments to theory, to consumption, or to the vague future) are what will allow us to live well and thereby, again, to find ourselves.

NOTES

1 Bernard Cooke, *Sacraments and Sacramentality* (Mystic, Conn.: Twenty-Third Publications, 1983), 31.
2 See also "Random Thoughts on Southern Literature, Southern Politics, and America's Future," *Georgia Review,* 32 (1978), 499-511.
3 *Lost in the Cosmos: The Last Self-Help Book* (New York: Pocket Books, 1984), 5.
4 *Lost in the Cosmos: The Last Self-Help Book* (New York: Farrar, Straus, Giroux, 1983), 108-9. Subsequent page references given in parentheses refer to this edition.

III. THE SHAPE *of* ECSTASY

ASPIRATIONS TOWARD ANONYMITY:
VALÉRY and RILKE

BY WALTER A. STRAUSS, CASE WESTERN RESERVE UNIVERSITY

A t the very beginning of the twentieth century we can observe quite clearly in Paris and in Vienna the gradual liquidation – or perhaps transformation – of the culture of the nineteenth century, and we can see it in terms of distinct contrasts. There were, in 1900, other cultural and intellectual centers in Europe, particularly Berlin, Prague, and London. Yet the juxtaposition of Paris and Vienna brings into focus many of the principal intellectual preoccupations of the modern world – the death pangs of the older and more secure culture of the nineteenth century, birth pangs and agonies of a state of mind that we have been obliged to regard as characteristic of the twentieth. Naturally, this did not happen overnight. The final decade of the nineteenth century, which in itself was the product of multiple historical, intellectual, and cultural forces, ushered in the process of change; there is an acceleration of this in the five years or so preceding the outbreak of the First World War, which interrupts the accumulated momentum of those artistically very fertile years 1908-14; and there is a resumption of the dynamics, colored by the dark experience of the War, during the five years or so that follow the ces-sation of the inter-national hostilities. By 1925 the twentieth century is, so to speak, full-fledged, and we have been trying to come to terms with it ever since. That may well be the moral of our Tale of Two Cities.

LET ME OUTLINE as succinctly as possible the fundamental and decisive contrasts in the two city-profiles. The first thing that strikes the observer of the period 1900-14 is the difference in artistic "personality" between Paris and Vienna. Paris in 1900 had become the undisputed Mecca of painters and sculptors, continuing and seemingly perpetuating the traditions of innovation and mastery that had manifested themselves there since the 1820s and more particularly since the 1870s. The great accomplishments of this earlier period were to culminate in the work of Cézanne and the invention of Cubism during the first decade of this century. Music definitely played a secondary role, despite the activities of Debussy, Ravel, and Satie (and of Stravinsky after 1911), this subordinate status of music being altogether characteristic of

French culture since the end of the seventeenth century. As a matter of fact, the most visible and noteworthy aspect of music in Paris during that period tends to be focused on the ballet – another French legacy – in which the "plastic" dimensions of music are overshadowed by the dramatic. The situation is quite different in Vienna. Vienna at the turn of the century was the musical capital of the world, the center of musical gravity being situated in opera and, if you will, operetta. Everything in Vienna, one might say, aspired to the condition of the theater, and toward musical dramatics in particular; the popularity of the symphonic music of the nineteenth century, with its strongly emotive and dramatic accents, bears witness to this predilection for theatricalism; and Mahler's symphonies are strongly marked by the implicit histrionics of Viennese culture. Even the great musical pioneers of the new radical Vienna School of composers after 1906-7 – Schönberg, Berg, and (to a lesser extent) Webern – develop and grow out of the atmosphere of a supercharged theatricality. Innovations in the plastic arts, particularly in architecture and painting, must be relegated to second place, though they are significant in relation to the artistic mood of *fin de siècle* Vienna.

The second point of contrast is to be found in the sharply divergent nature of the historical and political experience of France and Austria and in the virtually antithetical temper of the two capital cities around 1900. Vienna can only be described as being in a state of political stagnancy, ruled by an inflexible emperor, lulled into a false security by the illusion of past glories and future preëminence. The most eloquent and trenchant observer of this state of affairs is Robert Musil, who described this tragicomic paralysis two decades later in his novel *The Man Without Qualities*. Yet Musil was only one of the several minds who dissected the "Kakanian" (as he called it) psyche. The Viennese writers of that period, virtually all of them members of the well-to-do bourgeoisie and most of them uneasily assimilated Jews, were all disenchanted, disaffiliated, or even pessimistic. How else could the new clinical science of psychoanalysis ever have come into being? No such equivalent in France: the political and social atmosphere was entirely different. The Third Republic, established in 1871 after eight decades of political struggle, after weathering several crises in the late 80s and 90s, had emerged triumphant, relatively stable and secure after the traumatic Dreyfus Affair: the republican and liberal elements were finally in the ascendancy. The society was fluid and bourgeois-republican, not stagnant like the bourgeois-aristocratic society of Vienna. Proust's great novel, *Remembrance of Things Past*, documents (along the way) the kaleidoscopic shifts in the social fabric. And Proust's novel is principally concerned with a hero who finds his vocation, whereas Musil's novel is about a man without qualities (or properties) – a man of extraordinary possibilities who does not progress from virtuality to actuality, as Proust's hero does.

Somewhere in all this lies the dilemma of the will directing the vision; or, in other terms, the dilemma of aesthetics and ethics seeking to find an adequate balance. In Vienna, the tendency is for aesthetics, for artistic experience, to absorb moral inquiry into what Professor Schorske has astutely labeled a narcissism: a phenomenon which, it seems to me, comes about more by default than by an operation of intellectual energy. Yet the narcissistic strain is strong in France also, as a legacy from the Symbolists; it is clearly in evidence in Gide, Valéry, and Proust, to name the most distinguished literary creators of that period. And yet it is a different kind of narcissism; it is always in dialectical tension with the pressures of a middle-class and progressivistic society. It strives to overcome itself, to strike a balance between the claims of the self and those of the community. In brief, its critique is more sharply focused on a concrete reality: Gide's attempted transvaluation of ethical values, Proust's dissection of snobbery, even Valéry's quest for a purity of consciousness – all these are directed toward the resilient body of a mobile society whose dynamics Bergson was trying to redefine. The isolation of the artist (another legacy of the nineteenth century) had come to mean by the beginning of the twentieth century in France that the artist and the bourgeois had "agreed to disagree" and that the battle lines were clearly drawn.

The Viennese ambience is totally different: the artist, especially the performing artist, was the darling and ornament of the aristocracy and the upper bourgeoisie, a sort of glorified lapdog whose estrangement took the form of an alienation *within* his class (to paraphrase Schorske again). It is no wonder, then, that the energies of the Viennese artists and intellectuals were oriented toward problems that were socially peripheral though they may have been intellectually crucial. In vain does one search in Vienna for social or political renewal: enterprises such as Émile Durkheim's sociological and anthropological investigations, Péguy's Catholic socialism and philo-Semitism, Georges Sorel's political radicalism – ingredients of the continuing historical and political consciousness of France during the nineteenth century – are utterly absent in Vienna. Instead, Vienna excels in the socially more marginal critiques of language, as exemplified by Karl Kraus, Fritz

Mauthner, and finally Ludwig Wittgenstein. Vienna contributes an ongoing critique of positivism, as in Ernst Mach and again in Wittgenstein, but without deviating significantly from a positivistic position, whereas in France the dominant philosophical figure is Henri Bergson, the arch-enemy of positivism. Perhaps the Viennese contradiction can best be exemplified by the polarity between psychoanalysis and Zionism as responses to a modern sense of discontent and discrimination in a supposedly enlightened culture, the one gravitating toward a gloomy truce with modern mediocrity, the other seeking a flight from modern bigotry.

And yet the two disparate and discordant phenomena now – toward the end of the twentieth century – appear to be more complementary than contradictory. The common element in both cultures – Paris and Vienna – was the necessity of coming to grips with the new historical and intellectual realities of their epoch, even though this was accomplished in different ways. (The contemporary bourgeois world has become more stagnant, more Viennese, one might say; and yet some of the admirable curiosity of which the French have always been such excellent exponents has not been entirely dissipated.) What can be gained from a closer inspection of Paris-Vienna around 1900 is the impulse that motivated the best French and Austrian minds similarly – namely, the desire "to see through," in H. Stuart Hughes' phrase. That, I would argue, is always an achievement, no matter how favorable or dismal the surrounding contexts may be.

THE TOPIC I HAVE chosen makes a modest attempt to establish a bridge between Paris and Austria (though not exactly Vienna). The nexus is the poet Rainer Maria Rilke, who was born in Prague in 1875, spent much of his life in France and Switzerland, with frequent and extensive travels in Italy, Spain, Scandinavia, Russia, and Egypt: a man who sought out solitude by periodic displacement. Paris played a special role in his life; it was the one metropolis in which he resided for a long time (periodically between 1902 and 1907 and more or less continually from 1907 to 1914); and it was the city in which the crucial and critical years of his creative career had their setting. The French poet with whom Rilke will be compared and contrasted is Paul Valéry, four years older than Rilke and temperamentally very different, who lived in Paris until his death in 1945. He thus represents a stable counterpoise to the restless meandering and the rootlessness of Rilke. The two poets enjoyed a brief friendship in the 1920s; they met in Switzerland in 1924 and several times afterward. But it is not the friendship nor the poetic and intellectual affinities between the poets that constitute the main subject of my essay. It is rather the contrast of two prose works that concerns me, both of them autobiographical in nature, Valéry's *Monsieur Teste* and Rilke's *The Notebooks of Malte Laurids Brigge*.

These are prose works by writers who are primarily poets, and each work occupies a very special niche in the development of its creator. They are works of fiction written by artists whose principal interests are lyrical, meditative, and philosophical – not narrative – and therefore the two works represent unexpected and yet significant departures from the two men's normal creative habits. In Valéry's case the various fragments comprising the *Teste* cycle bear witness to an ongoing process of self-inspection which, curiously enough, attains an unprecedented degree of abstraction (something one does not normally expect from fiction) in the quest of the self meditating and exploring the limits of self-consciousness. In Rilke's case, self-examination is also central, but situated in a context of anguish, fear, and uncertainty that demand of the Rilkean persona, Malte Laurids Brigge, the most concrete and painful inventory of the self in its relation to the world. In other words, it is miles apart from Valéry's ironic detachment, which tends to conceal the personal crisis that had made possible the creation of the persona of M. Teste. It is as though both Rilke and Valéry felt the need to come to grips with their own poetic and intellectual identities by choosing the byways of fiction, by the detour of narration, which provided a kind of objective distance from the compositional exigencies of lyrical poetry: how to shape the self, tentatively and experimentally, so that the newly-shaped self could once more shape the poetry that was within him. This was not merely a newly-shaped self, but a new self, a purified self: one that would also embody a certain anonymity that characterizes the poet, and especially the Orphic poet. Both works exercise autobiography in quest of its own annulment, for the sake of its own transcendence: two prolonged fictional monologues seeking to dissolve the individual voice in cosmic language.

I BEGIN WITH Rilke's *The Notebooks of Malte Laurids Brigge*. It was written between 1903 and 1910, precisely at the time during which Rilke in his *Buch der Bilder* and especially in his *Neue Gedichte* was breaking new ground for himself as a poet. For here, in the French capital, he first began to expand the horizon of his sensibility in the direction of a greater visual and plastic concreteness in his poetry. Paris taught Rilke how to see and, ultimately, how to give things seen and felt more pre-cise plastic form. In this respect, Malte Laurids Brigge's notebook paral-lels Rilke's affective transformation. Malte writes, near the beginning of the book:

> I am learning to see. I don't know why it is, but everything penetrates more deeply into me and does not stop at the place where until now it always used to finish. I have an inner self of which I was ignorant. Everything goes thither now. What happens there I do not know.

In effect, the deepening sensibility is generating an "inner" transforma-tion, since Malte is for the first time in his life reaching toward a new inwardness; he thus initiates a slow but radical mutation of his entire personality. That is, in brief, the theme of the *Notebooks*: the difficulty of charting inwardness, once the exploration has begun. Of the parallel achievement of Rilke, namely the poetry written during those years, nothing is said in *Malte Laurids Brigge*; consequently, we must be careful not to identify author with persona. For Rilke, *Malte Laurids Brigge* was a "watershed" (as he termed it later); that is to say, it is the record of a transition to something else – namely, the *Duino Elegies*, begun in 1912 and completed in 1922 – and thus indicates that the poetic accomplishments of Rilke between 1904 and 1908 did not con-stitute a resting-point for him. *The Notebooks of Malte Laurids Brigge* attempts to get at the core of this personal and artistic transmutation by way of the alter ego of Malte, witness of the realignments in Rilke's artistic personality.

The external factors that played a major role in defining this new Rilkean sensibility are all closely associated with the arts. First of all, there was Rilke's contact with Auguste Rodin from 1902 onward: the discovery of the artist who could make plastic objects of great beau-ty. And somewhat later there was the revelation of Cézanne's painting, made possible by the retrospective exhibit of the painter's work in the Salon d'Automne of 1907 (a year after Cézanne's death), which elicited extensive comment from Rilke in his letters, such as:

> I was only convinced that there are personal inner reasons that place me more contemplatively in front of pictures that per-haps not so long ago I would have passed with only casual interest.... It isn't even painting that absorbs my interest...it is the turning [Wendung] in these painting that I recognized,

90

because I myself had reached this same turning point in my own work...

But it was not only a matter of seeing art works, but also a matter of living in the city of Paris, observing its throbbing populace, its squalor, its gloom. Rilke's attitude toward Paris in *Malte Laurids Brigge* is as ambivalent as Baudelaire's had been fifty years earlier, and indeed the specter of Baudelaire hovers over the early sections of Rilke's narrative. Not only does it contain a direct tribute to Baudelaire's poem "Une Charogne," but the spirit of Baudelaire's "Tableaux parisiens" and of his prose poems known as *Le Spleen de Paris* is ubiquitously present, that spirit so superbly articulated in the following three short excerpts:

> Fourmillante cité, cité pleine de rêves,
> Où le spectre en plein jour raccroche le passant!
> ["Les sept vieillards"]

and (from the prose poems):

> Multitude, solitude: equal terms, and convertible by the active and fertile poet. Whoever does not know how to populate his solitude does not know either how to be alone in a busy crowd. The poet enjoys that incomparable privilege of being able, in his own manner, to be himself and someone else. ["Les foules"]

> This life is a hospital in which each patient is possessed by the desire to change beds.
> ["Anywhere Out of the World"]

That same melancholy and anguish of living in the modern city, for which Baudelaire was the first to find the right verbal rhythms and articulations, infuses Malte's experience and clothes it in the colors of mortality, fear, and the macabre. The very opening of *Malte Laurids Brigge* stands under the shadow of death: "So, then, the people do come here in order to live; I would sooner have thought one died here. I have been out. I saw: hospitals..." and, a little later: "The street began to smell from all sides. A smell, so far as one could distinguish, of iodoform, of the grease of pommes frites, of fear." The keynote is thus sounded on the first page; the rest of the work is the episodic account of Malte's confrontation with fear, death, and emptiness, and his efforts to penetrate beyond the disintegration of his self into at least the prospect of a renewal.

The originality of *Malte Laurids Brigge* as a work of fiction lies in Rilke's attempt to mould a different kind of reader, one who would adjust and relate himself to the text in a new way. Quite possibly Rilke's relative indifference to prose fiction enabled him to conceive the reader's task in an unorthodox way. When his Polish translator, Witold Hulewicz, asked his advice concerning the problems of translating the work, Rilke replied:

> In *Malte* the problem cannot be that of making the manifold evocations precise and independent. Let the reader not communicate with their historical or imaginary reality, but let him communicate through this reality with Malte's lived experience: for Malte lets himself become involved with these things as one lets a passer-by in the street or a neighbor leave an impression. The connection lies in the fact that those who happen to be conjured up are marked by the same frequency of life's intensity as the one which at that moment vibrates in Malte's being.... This book should be *received*, not comprehended in its detail. Only *in that way* will everything attain its correct intonation and intersection.

Rilke thus requests that the reader set aside the habit of testing the mimesis of the fiction, as he had been trained to do by the imitators of reality who dominated the novel of the nineteenth century, in favor of a participation – more passive in this instance than active – in the *Erlebnis*, the lived experience, of the hero, not necessarily by identifying with Malte, but with the quality of his life. In some ways, this action of moulding the reader parallels the exhortation that concludes Rilke's famous sonnet "Archaïscher Torso Apollos" of 1908: "Du mußt dein Leben ändern." Yet the parallel is not altogether exact; the task of self-transformation as enjoined by Rilke's poetry, especially by the *Duino Elegies* and the *Sonnets to Orpheus*, is more absolute. *Malte* remains a transitional and preparatory landmark in the re-orientation; it registers the process of alteration in the hero and asks the reader to "communicate" with it.

What is the nature of this alteration? In the same letter, Rilke speaks of the efforts of young Malte, "to make his life, which is continually receding into the invisible, intelligible to himself beyond appearances and images; he finds these appearances and images now in his own reminiscences of childhood, now in his Parisian environment, now in the recollections culled from his reading. And all this, *wherever*

it may have been experienced, has the same valence for him, the same
duration and presence." Thus, Rilke continues, past and future become
present: everything is turned inward by Malte and illumined only
by the "spotlight of his heart"; all things experienced by Malte are
"vocabulary-words of his distress." In the process of dissolving the
habitual categories of self-orientation, time and space are internalized;
and names, too, lose their conventional reference – and become anonymous, so to speak. Rilke writes: "Therefore it would only lead to error
if the figures indicated were to be given a more particularized existence;
let everyone adapt them to his own way of seeing; and whoever cannot
adapt them can still experience enough from the tension of these anonymities." Anonymities: the outer world is un-named in this inward-
turning experience, in order to be re-named in the *Duino Elegies*. *Malte
Laurids Brigge* is poised along the vibratory wave as it moves downward, rounds the trough, and swings upward again.

93

    The Notebooks of Malte Laurids Brigge is quite unlike any narra-
tive work written before that time – again I stress Rilke's lack of commitment to "fiction" as practiced in the eighteenth and nineteenth
centuries. For most readers, it is fictionalized autobiography; but that
does not alter the fact that it is fiction – that is, invention, make-believe.
Even autobiography, particularly since Jean-Jacques Rousseau's
Confessions, has intersected with fiction, at least insofar as a retrospective view of an author's life requires a selection and arrangement of the
reminiscences that constitute autobiography. In that sense, an autobiog-
rapher creates (or at least re-creates) his own self; and in *Malte* Rilke
creates a self-in-transition. The process of transition, when viewed from
the perspective of the present tense – from the vantage point of immediacy – cannot be understood except as a discontinuous process; hence
the episodic character of the narrative in *Malte*. Consequently, the first
half of the *Notebooks* is a series of notations, in the course of which
several dominant themes emerge. As I mentioned above, the keynotes
of the book are the consciousness of death and an ill-defined fear
linked to death and to a dislocation of the self: experiences of the
grotesque, distortions of identity (this is particularly striking in the
mirror scene, where the young Malte recalls how the mirror "usurped"
the reality of the beholder – a frightening triumph of image, or mask,
over face). Along with the experience of anguish there is the counter-
motif of a new beginning: learning how to see; a new sensibility of space;
the encounter with the occult; and, most particularly, an acute awareness of the intimacy of "things." Malte once speaks of "things which are

meant only for one individual and which do not let themselves be said." Here lies the crux of Malte's dilemma: how to say, how to articulate; how does one *write* such an experience? The initial phase of the experience is passive, with an intimation of something greater to come:

> For a while yet I can write all this down and express it. But there will come a day when my hand will be far from me, and when I bid it write, it will write words I do not mean. The time of that other interpretation will dawn, when not one word will remain upon another, and all meaning will dissolve like clouds and fall down like rain. Despite my fear I am yet like one standing before something great, and I remember that it was often like that in me before I began to write. But this time I shall be written. I am the impression that will change. Ah, but a little more, and I could understand all this and approve it. Only a step, and my deep misery would be beatitude.

This expectation of a transformation of misery into bliss leads into the second half of the *Notebooks*, in the course of which Malte attempts to convert the passive anonymity into something active. The movement is not really completed by the end of the *Notebooks*, but one gets the impression that Malte has advanced. It would not be wrong to say that the transformation is not to be accomplished until the *Duino Elegies* reach their final shape in 1922. But a great deal of new terrain has been annexed by the time Malte's quest breaks off. There is, for instance, the recognition that "God is but a direction of love, not an object of love" and that it will be necessary "to think with the heart." Here Rilke is anticipating his 1914 poem "Wendung" in which he will declare: "Werk des Gesichts ist getan, / tue nun Herz-Werk." And closely related to this discovery is one of Rilke's favorite ideas, also sketched out in *Malte*, that loving is greater than being loved. This conviction is fleshed out in Rilke's version of the Parable of the Prodigal Son, with which *Malte* concludes. Along the way, there have also been aesthetic discoveries, notably in the anecdote about the death of the poet Felix Arvers, who delayed his dying moment in order to correct an error of diction. Malte observes, "He was a poet and hated approximations." But most strikingly the second part of the *Notebooks*, with its profusion of anecdotes and stories, is a probing of the art of narrative itself. In recounting the story of the false Tsar Grisha Otrepyov, Malte begins to fill in gaps not accounted for by the tradition, and then comments: "…This event is in no way outmoded. One could imagine a present-day narrator who might lavish much care upon the final moments; and he would not be wrong to do so," and then he continues the narrative in the present tense. It is precisely this present-ness of narration, this abandonment of the conventional narrative categories of time and space, that Malte aspires to in his struggle with narration. In Rilke-Malte the enterprise is transitional, and perhaps necessary as such, because it liberated Rilke toward the poetry that he was to undertake two years later; and indeed, just after the termination of the work, he wrote to his publisher, "Poor Malte starts so deep in misery and, in a strict sense, reaches toward eternal bliss; he is a heart that strikes a whole octave: after him all songs are possible." For other novelists, despite their unfamiliarity with *The Notebooks of Malte Laurids Brigge*, these same reassessments of the temporal and spatial problems of fiction were to become a central preoccupation. I need only mention Proust, Mann, Joyce, Virginia Woolf, and Faulkner, among others.

95

In a letter to Rodin written during the composition of *Malte*, Rilke gave a powerful expression to the contrast between writing poetry and writing prose, as a kind of distillation of his creative experience during those years:

> In writing poetry you can be helped and even carried away by the rhythm of external things; for the lyric cadence is that of nature: of water, of wind, of the night. But to find the rhythm of prose one must descend into oneself and find the anonymous and multiple rhythm of the blood. Prose wants to be built like a cathedral; in it one is truly without name, without ambition, without help: up there in the scaffolding, with nothing but one's consciousness.
>
> And think of it: in that prose I know now how to make men and women, children and old people. I have particularly evoked women by creating carefully all the things around them, leaving a blank which would be no more than a word, were it not for the fact that, if one moved about it with tenderness and all the way, this void becomes vibrant and luminous, almost like one of your marbles.

To write prose: to descend into the depths of one's being; to find the multiple and anonymous rhythm of the blood; to build like a cathedral – surely we are closer to Proust here than to Valéry. So let us unstitch the phrase and re-tailor it for Valéry's needs: to penetrate the inner recesses of the intellect; to find the multiple and anonymous rhythms of consciousness; to build like a theorem, or perhaps like a Greek temple – and there we have the graph of Valéry's dynamics. The common denominator remains "anonymity."

MONSIEUR TESTE is, by any standard, an anomaly. It is actually a series of fragments, some of them more fully worked out, some of them merely in the form of sketches. The first of them, which is the most cohesive of the pieces, entitled "La soirée avec M. Teste," was written when Valéry was only 24 (in 1895) and marks a temporary halt, or even paralysis, in his activity as a poet; it signals the onset of a prolonged period of literary silence (which was nevertheless a period full of intensive private "researches" that was to last until 1917). Prior to the invention of M. Teste, Valéry had written a group of highly accomplished, almost precocious, poems (now known as *Album des vers anciens*) which had earned the admiration and endorsement of his early mentor, Stéphane Mallarmé. An intellectual crisis appears to have ensued, in which Valéry, possibly under the influence of Mallarmé, put in question the entire problem of the creative act; the immediate results of this self-examination were the essay on Leonardo da Vinci's "method," and then M. Teste. Valéry's meditation on Leo-nardo's notebooks – this intensive contact with a mind that was both scientific and artistic, fascinated by problems of observation and composition, and above all with an artist who regarded his art as "cosa mentale" – prompted Valéry to devise "his own" Leonardo out of the substance of the notebooks, that is to say, to construct and "valérize" the great Italian creator. Similarly, the invention of M. Teste a year later is another link in the chain of self-projections of its author, whose final avatar was to be his "own" Faust (*Mon Faust*, he called the work) during the final years of his life.

The parallel with Rilke is striking. Here we have two poets, highly gifted in their early production, who some time in their twenties experience the need for a radical self-examination and self-transformation. They both have recourse to narrative prose, a mode somewhat alien to their artistic temperaments, as an intermediary and as a mediating device. And that prose is fictional, tending toward the autobiographical, but with a strong impulse to dissolve the personal in the anonymous. In this respect both works are highly unorthodox. *Monsieur Teste* gravitates toward essay and aphorism, *Malte Laurids Brigge* toward the parable.

Valéry's preoccupation with the figure of M. Teste remains intermittent over the first four decades of the twentieth century, whereas

Rilke brings Malte to literary life during a period of six years and then passes beyond him in favor of a new persona that was later to reveal himself as Orpheus. Valéry's *Monsieur Teste* continues to be an "essay," in the Montaignean sense of the term: a try-out, an attempt…and a temptation. Valéry added three more brief sections in the 1920s and provided an important preface for the 1926 edition; and the posthumous edition of *Monsieur Teste* in 1946 has five additional fragments to round out the Teste "cycle."

Who and what is *Monsieur Teste*? Valéry referred to the work as "a manuscript found in a brain," thus making a polite bow to Edgar Allan Poe's "MS Found in a Bottle" – or, one might add, in a pot. The old French word "teste" meant "pot" as well as "head," a heady metaphor; and "teste" subsequently contracted into the current spelling, "tête." But the title also puns on the English word "test," for its hero is a test: that is, an "essay" as well as a test case. And, most importantly, he is "testis," Latin for witness, therefore an observer, one who testifies.

This M. Teste is the creation of an intellectual fantasy – hence a necessary and possibly a "supreme" fiction, a fiction that proposes the existence of a pure consciousness, a disincarnate intellect existing and functioning in the world of men. He owes something to Descartes' *Discourse on Method* and to Edgar Allan Poe's cerebral detective, Auguste Dupin – two unlikely bedfellows, who nevertheless have in common a passion for mathematical analysis. There is, of course, something preposterous, even monstrous, in all this, and Valéry was perfectly aware of it; in a sense, he was writing a piece of abstruse science fiction ("Voyage to the Center of the Brain," perhaps?). For this kind of fiction makes all anecdotal narrative (which Valéry detested) totally impossible and superfluous. M. Teste, as a pure mind, is all potentiality without action; he is, as Valéry states in the preface, "le démon même de la possibilité." He can witness the external world, and he can be witnessed by others in that world, but there cannot be any interrelation or intersection of the two entities, because our normal intercourse with the world goes through our senses, through our body, and M. Teste does not exist as a body (though, for fictional purposes, he *has* one). As a musical notation, M. Teste would be all staccato, never legato. A pure consciousness would be, so to speak, a mathematical organ, detached and independent of any phenomenon to which it might apply itself; and its mode of operation would be simply the unfolding of its forms and a series of transformations of these structures relative to the object being contemplated, since an indefinite set of pos-

sibilities is inherent in the pure intellect. Hence Valéry's characterization of Teste as the demon of possibility. The whole enterprise is
demonic; the demon of possibility is a fascinating *impossibility*; hence
also the need for fiction, which makes the impossible momentarily
possible and offers it as a subject for contemplation.

The various sketches and fragments that constitute the *Teste*
cycle are held together – not firmly – by the magnetic center, which is
Teste himself. We come to perceive him through a few persons associated with him, mainly the Narrator, admittedly an aspect of Valéry
himself, who functions as friend and interlocutor of M. Teste. This
Teste-monitor describes him as follows:

> M. Teste was perhaps forty years old. His speech was extraor-
> dinarily rapid, and his voice quiet. Everything about him was
> fading, his eyes, his hands. His shoulders, however, were mili-
> tary, and his step had a regularity that was amazing. When he
> spoke he never raised an arm or a finger: he had *killed his pup-
> pet.* He did not smile, and said neither hello nor goodbye. He
> seemed not to hear a "How do you do?"

Contingency and mechanical action do not exist in this "essence" of the
mind. The Narrator has observed him closely during an evening spent
at the Opéra, in the street and in his modest lodgings. M. Teste is first
perceived as perfectly detached from his surroundings at the foyer of
the Opéra, bodies and architecture forming, as it were, only disjunct
elements of his consciousness. His few remarks are clipped and precise,
become more extensive and precise, then become more extensive as
the dialogue moves out of the gregarious setting of the Opéra into the
street; they finally consolidate into a monologue as M. Teste is in the
process of falling asleep: "I am being and seeing myself, seeing me see
myself, and so forth." Reflectivity has become reflexivity: the mirrors
are finally turned inward upon themselves. Moving from the Opéra
hall to the hall of mirrors, M. Teste is shown to be a closed system.

This closed system is, nevertheless, lucid and transparent.
In a section presented as M. Teste's "Log-Book," the self inspects the
self. One of the entries is called "The Man of Glass," recalling distantly
Cervantes' story, and at closer range, Mallarmé's transparencies: "So
direct is my vision, so pure my senses, so clumsily complete my knowledge, that I see through myself from the extreme edge of the world
down to my unspoken word." But he also notes the impossibility of
attaining truth by the process of self-reflection. Any truth is simply a

rearrangement of the coördinates of the virtually infinite possibilities that exist in the mind:

> It is impossible to receive the "truth" from oneself. When we feel it forming (it is an impression), we form at the same moment *another and unaccustomed self*...of which we are proud...or jealous... (This is the last word in inner politics.) Between Self clear and Self cloudy, between Self just and Self guilty, there are old hatreds and old accords, old denials and old supplications.

Alas, poor Yorick – and alas poor M. Teste! The problem is Hamletic to begin with – "thus conscience doth make cowards of us all." In a way, it is the same problem that Valéry faces all over again in the famous poem "Le cimetière marin," in which, discarding the pale cast of thoughts, he opts for "Il faut tenter de vivre." M. Teste seems to be caught on the horns of this dilemma: how to reach the end of his series of thoughts. That last thought, no matter what its content, would then constitute the "supreme," the ultimate thought, because it would cancel out the series: "This would amount to being able to die of a certain thought, simply because there is no other to follow." Here we also see the Faustian element in M. Teste: to carry an enterprise to its absolute limit.

99

This evidence of the Log-Book is particularly valuable since it gives us access to the innermost anomaly of M. Teste's consciousness – a dimension of perception that is unavailable to the Narrator-friend. But there is also the charming testimony of his wife, Emilie, who ap-provingly quotes a remark of her father-confessor (another observer of M. Teste), who characterizes him as "a mystic without God." A remarkable observation: M. Teste is a consciousness that has all the potential required to encounter or unite with a greater consciousness than himself, but encounters only himself: not a plenitude, but a nothingness. After all, a void too can be transparent.

So M. Teste, like Malte, is troubled by the threat of nothingness at the center of awareness; and for both Valéry and Rilke the struggle with the specter of emptiness energizes these two works of the imagination, these two prolonged monologues with potential, provisional and fictional selves. The unconventional forms of these two works are best explained, as I have tried to show, out of the particular self-interrogation that both artists imposed on themselves at a critical point in their development. The fact that *M. Teste* and *Malte Laurids*

Brigge have, incidentally or accidentally, opened new directions for later fiction – such as Maurice Blanchot's abstract novels or mental states on the one hand, and Sartre's odyssey of existential nausea on the other hand – all this is beyond the scope of this paper. What does matter, however, is that in both writers a process of depersonalization or anonymization disrupts the stabler identities that preceded, and that it transmutes the voices of Valéry and of Rilke into a new language revitalized with more intricate multiple rhythms having wider reverberations.

THE TWO POETS finally met in Switzerland in 1924. By that time, Valéry had broken his long silence and begun publishing again: the long poem *La Jeune Parque*, the twenty-one poems under the title *Charmes*, and the two platonic dialogues on architecture and on the dance. Rilke had become interested in the poems as early as 1921, and began translating them, as well as the dialogue *Eupalinos ou l'architecte*. All this was happening about the time when Rilke was reaping his own harvest, which was even more abundant than Valéry's, in 1922: the completion of the *Duino Elegies* and the composition of the two cycles of the *Sonnets to Orpheus*. Coincidentally with Rilke's friendship with Valéry, and probably as a result of his preoccupation with Valéry's poems, Rilke began several cycles of poems in French; and during the same years he also rendered most of Valéry's *Charmes* into German, with extraordinary sensitivity, especially when one considers the great linguistic difficulties of Valéry's poetic language and its archetypal Frenchness. Valéry reciprocated by publishing some of Rilke's French poems in his review *Commerce*. Notwithstanding their temperamental differences, as evidenced by the comparison of *Malte* and *M. Teste*, the two poets maintained a friendship based more on mutual admiration than on intimacy. Valéry was to confess later, "All that side of existence which I knew nothing about, or which I decided to ridicule, Rilke presented to me in a charming way." Rilke's French poems, by the way, are not in any clear-cut sense "influenced" by Valéry's poems. Temperamentally Rilke falls somewhere between Verlaine and Mallarmé; but actually his French poems are unique and bear the unmistakable personal imprint of their creator.

Yet occasionally these poems touch on themes that Valéry also favored, and the most striking of these is that of Narcissus. The story of this youth, who fell in love with his image and who drowned in the attempt to kiss his reflection in the water, is well known; it played an important role in seventeenth-century art and literature and was revitalized in Symbolist literature and afterward by Mallarmé, Gide, and Valéry. It should be evident from my earlier account of *M. Teste* that the work is really a variation on the Narcissus theme – the doubling of Narrator and M. Teste, and more pointedly the self-speculations ("speculation" is a word derived from the Latin word for "mirror") of M. Teste himself. And in Malte's experience the self-examination and the mirror play an analogous role. So it is, in a sense, the Narcissus theme that both poets hold in common. But there is also a difference. Modern poetry has refurbished many of the old myths and given them, if not always a new interpretation, at least a new context and emphasis. The Narcissus myth and the myth of Orpheus stand in close relation to each other. While Narcissus is solipsistic and self-enclosed, Orpheus is prophetic and cosmic. Narcissus represents a short-circuited version of the Orphic journey: the poet passes through a stage of self-inspection and self-fascination, and encounters self-annihilation at the climactic moment. The Orphic poet descends into himself, into hell, into death, in search of Eurydice – and returns from hell and death, but without Eurydice, into the upper world, where he is dismembered by the Maenads, only in order to become, as Mallarmé proclaimed so eloquently, "Tel qu'en Lui-même enfin l'Eternité le change." His symbolic descent into darkness and death are the prerequisites for an illumination and a resurrection.

101

Valéry in one of his early poems celebrates Orpheus but then passes him by in favor of Narcissus; and the Narcissus motif provides a continuous thread through his early poem "Narcisse parle" of 1891 to his *Cantate de Narcisse* of 1938 and even beyond that, into the *Mon Faust* of his final years. In the long poem, *Fragments de Narcisse*, written between 1919 and 1926, Narcissus, like M. Teste, in the ultimate play of self-reflection, as darkness descends over the pool in which he beholds his image, perceives the void and the cancellation of the series of reflections:

> Mon âme ainsi se perd dans la propre forêt,
> Où la puissance échappe à ses formes suprêmes...
> L'âme, l'âme aux yeux noirs, touche aux ténèbres mêmes,
> Elle se fait immense et ne rencontre rien...
> Entre la mort et soi, quel regard est le sien!
> . . . .

Hélas! corps misérable, il est temps de s'unir.
Penche-toi... Baise-toi. Tremble de tout ton être.
L'insaisissable amour que tu me viens promettre
Passe, et dans un frisson, brise Narcisse, et fuit...

My soul thus loses itself in its own forest / Where the power
slips from its supreme forms... / The soul, the black-eyed
soul, touches the very darkness / It makes itself immense and
yet encounters nothing... / Between death and oneself, what a
glance it bears! /... Alas! wretched body, it is time to unite
... / Lean forward... Kiss yourself. Tremble in all your being! /
The ungraspable love that you came to promise me / Passes
on, and in a tremor, breaks Narcissus, and vanishes...

With Rilke, the Narcissus-Orpheus sequence reasserts its
proper progression: Narcissus dissolves in nature and prepares the way
for the Orphic apotheosis. Of the three poems on the Narcissus theme
written in April 1913, this brief one condenses excellently Rilke's
dialectic of the coincidence of opposites: Narcissus exudes beauty and
reabsorbs it; his downward movement toward the water of the pool
closes a circle, and thus transcends itself. Thus Rilke's Narcissus-
movement is really upward, in contrast to Valéry's:

Narziss verging. Von seiner Schönheit hob
sich unaufhörlich seines Wesens Nähe,
verdichtet wie der Duft vom Heliotrop.
Ihm aber war gesetzt, daß er sich sähe.

Er liebte, was ihm ausging, wieder ein
und war nicht mehr im offnen Wind enthalten
und schloß entzückt den Umkreis der Gestalten
Und hob sich auf und konnte nicht mehr sein.

Narcissus vanished. From his beauty rose / incessantly the
nearness of his being, / concentrated like the scent of the heli-
otrope. / But it had been decreed that he would see himself.
He loved back into himself what had emanated from him /
and was no longer contained in the open wind / and closed
rapturously the cycle of shapes / and transcended himself and
could no longer be.

Rilke's final Narcissus poem, in French, and written in 1924, ends with
two questions:

Où tombe-t-il? Veut-il, sous la surface
qui dépérit, renouveler un centre?

Whither does he fall? Is it his wish, under the surface / which
gives way to him, to renew a center?

The word "renew" marks the sharpest difference between Rilke and
Valéry. For Rilke the poetic question turns around the possiblity of a
total regeneration of the self, for which Orpheus is cast in the role of
a patron saint; for Valéry, the attainment of that center is the demise
of consciousness, yet also a liberation from the circularity of thinking.
Rilke's Narcissus indeed resembles the Angels of his *Duino Elegies*,
who are described as

Spiegel: die die entströmte eigene Schönheit
wiederschöpfen zurück in das eigene Antlitz

mirrors, drawing up their own
outstreamed beauty into their faces again.

The Angel, as Rilke tells us in his famous letter to his Polish translator,
is "the creature in whom the transformation of the invisible we are
performing already appears complete." To put it another way, he is
Narcissus surmounted; and Orpheus is the prophet of that transcen-
sion, and the way toward it.

IT LOOKS AS THOUGH the distance between Switzerland and Paris turned
out to be very large; but even so, Valéry and Rilke found their way
toward each other, because they shared a certain amount of common
purpose and common ground. Perhaps in some ways they are complementary. If Rilke ever had a home – somehow that word seems inappropriate for the migratory songbird that he was – it was the Château
de Muzot in Switzerland. Yet if he had a favorite city, that city was
Paris. Valéry's birthplace was on the shores of the Mediterranean, but
his literary home became and remained Paris. Despite all of Rilke's
ambivalence toward cities, toward Paris – an ambivalence not shared
by the urbane Valéry – Paris was, in those years, the great magnetic
pole for all artists: that Paris of the final years of "la belle époque," of
the great moment of the late Cézanne and the early Picasso, of Débussy,
of Stravinsky and the Ballets Russes, and of Gide, Proust, and Valéry.
Rilke, with all his differences in background, language, and sensibility,
belonged there too. It was the place where "all songs were possible."

THE QAṢIDA of IMRU' AL-QAYS

TRANSLATED AND ADAPTED BY EDWARD B. SAVAGE,
UNIVERSITY OF MINNESOTA

Introduction

The *Qaṣida* of Imru' al-Qays is the first of seven odes collected in the *Mu'allaqāt*, known as *The Seven Golden Odes of Pagan Arabia*. Dating from the historical period just prior to the advent of Islam, these odes were the combined product of oral as well as, possibly, written tradition, and derived from the poetry contest held each year as part of the pagan religious ceremonies performed around the Black Stone of the Ka'bah in Mecca. The seven odes judged the best were accordingly hung on the Ka'bah, the practice to which the name *Mu'allaqāt* (or "suspended") refers.

Little is known of the life of Imru' al-Qays, which may be the cause of the legends which have grown up around his name. He was born early in the sixth century A.D., the son of Hujr, a tribal chieftain of Najd. The writing of the first golden ode of the *Mu'allaqāt* was the occasion of al-Qays' banishment by his father from Najd. According to Arab custom, a young man was allowed to love, but he was not allowed to make his love public. The *Kitāb al-Aghāni* also reports that Hujr went so far in the judgment of his son as to order a freedman to murder him. But Imru' al-Qays evidently was a favorite of the people, so much so that the freedman slew an elk instead and returned with the eyes to Hujr as proof of the young poet's death. It is appropriate for the writer of the story to associate the large beautiful eyes of the elk with those of "the Poet of Sorrow," as Imru' al-Qays has sometimes been called. During the period between his banishment and his father's death, al-Qays was also called "al-malik al-dillīl" or "the Wandering King," a title which suits him really better than "the Poet of Sorrow," for the independence of his life and actions fits his aristocratic nature, and the role of a wanderer his highly poetic soul as well as his close familiarity with the desert.

After his father's death, Imru' al-Qays evidently became a man of some prominence. His father Hujr had stipulated that the son who did not weep upon hearing of his death should obtain the inheritance. When al-Qays was informed, he was playing at draughts, and refused

104

to listen until his game was finished and won. Since all his brothers had wept ostentatiously, al-Qays inherited the estate. In 530 he was summoned to Constantinople by Justinian for service against the Persians. Here he practiced (probably cursorily) a mode of Jewish-Christian faith. Sometime between 530 and 540, he died in Ankara on an expedition for the Emperor. It is reported that Justinian, incensed by the fact that al-Qays made love to his daughter, sent him a gift in Ankara of a poisoned cloak which was the cause of his death. Authorities have refuted this, however, by claiming that there is no record of any princess of this description at either the court of Justinian or of his successor Justin II.

Imru' al-Qays' contribution to Arabic prosody is considerable: he is credited with first submitting Arabic verse to fixed rules of scansion and rhyme, and of introducing the use of the *qaṣida* (where the poet asks two friends to stop and weep as he tells his tale), thus adding the characteristics of the dramatic monologue to the ode which was originally limited to the *rajaz*, or a simple retelling in some form of rhymed verse of the event which forms the subject of the ode. To this extent, al-Qays did much to formalize Arabic verse.

The rhyme scheme used by our poet demands that all the lines of the poem end with the same consonant, and that each line be divided into two hemistichs. (His ode has eighty-three lines, all ending with "li.") Syntactically, a sentence is supposed to be contained within one full line, and no word is supposed to be divided between two hemistichs. Even in a highly inflected language like Arabic, such strictures in rhyme and syntax invite mannerism and artificiality, characteristics which plague much later Arabic verse. Al-Qays, however, not only takes liberties in both syntax and form (he was, after all, establishing the rules), but also tempers the formalism with the natural imagery of the desert, balancing sophistication with earthiness, spirituality with sense.

For Imru' al-Qays appeals first and foremost to the senses; by his constant reaction to and presentation of sensory impressions, he is capable of communicating with the modern Western reader by means of pictures which are by nature strange and foreign, but vivid and emotionally attractive under his hand. Also, he is unique among the Pre-Islamic poets in that he deals almost exclusively with his own reaction to the familiar theme of forbidden love, a tale we are expected to know, while the six other poets depend largely upon tribal feuds, diplomatic missions, or complicated desert customs.

The present translation attempts to convey not only the literal meaning and the rich desert imagery of the poem, but some idea of the

EDWARD B. SAVAGE

metrics and style as well. Recreating al-Qays' rhyme scheme is, of course, impossible in English. I have, however, attempted to approach that rhyme scheme by casting the poem in terza rima, hoping to preserve some sense of the continuous rhyme of the original. I have tried also through alliteration, assonance, and repetition to reinforce this continuity as well as to recreate some idea of the sound of the original.

Imagery in the Pre-Islamic poets poses some problems due to the unfamiliarity of Western readers with desert customs and traditions. I have, however, eschewed lengthy footnotes, choosing rather to extend the image by including, as clearly and economically as I could, the unfamiliar connotations in the text. Arabists, I hope, will excuse this liberty in the interest of maintaining some of the rushing continuity essential to the poem's roots in oral tradition.

The era of the Pre-Islamic poets is short and brilliant, only about sixty years, and dies with the birth of Islam and the start of the Arabian Empire. In this short space, however, they have given us a unique experience, one in which an unknown region becomes familiar, and one in which Nature has been presented both as a stimulation to the active mind and as an avenue to a new and vibrant sensibility. In Imru' al-Qays particularly, there is a passion to probe through the shell of existence into the unknown and, most important of all, to experience new sensory and intellectual thrills.

THE *QAṢIDA* of IMRU' AL-QAYS

Stay, – oh friends, and listen while I mourn
My love of Saktilliwa, in the land
Of Hawmal and Dakhoul, a ruin born
In the palm of Al-Maqrat and Tudeh. Sands,
Sifted by desert South Winds, buried deep   5
Her house; but now the walls, brushed by the hand
Of love-sick North, lie silent, as in sleep.
Like pepper seeds, the dung of the wild white ram
Lies scattered in the courtyards where I weep.
The hour I realized her caravan   10
Had left me there alone, I stood beneath
The talah trees, clawing my brain, like a man
Scratching the handallah, rattling death
In its poisonous seeds, killing the worm
Who, grown greedy, wriggles to the teeth   15
Which clench the handal-tainted meat, to squirm
And die a death that he himself would deal.
          My friends, astride their horses, in their turn,
Stood round me in a ring, saying, "Heal
Your wounds with patience. Sorrow kills."   20
          I wept, and weeping, cried, "The only weal
For me is shedding tears. But what avails
My weeping, when, alas, the tears I shed
For love wash clean the ruin which impales
My love? I went from 'Um Hawairith's bed   25
The same, and from the breast of 'Um Rabab.
When these two women moved, my sense was led
To follow, their bodies so with scent enwrapt
The air, that sweeter sighed no soothing North,
Swollen with karen-flowered beds of Nagd.   30
Remembering such love, my eyes pour forth
A flood of tears which, look you, flowing, sting
My throbbing throat, and reach my body's girth
To wet my sword, which rusts in languishing."
          Happy days unrivalled are but few,   35
And mine are fewer, but as I begin
Recalling other women, days, and true
Delights, the day at Darat Juljili

Surpasses all of them. That day I slew
My she-camel to feast my lusty eye   40
On virgins, wet and shining. So unhinged
I stood, the clever wenches, sleek and sly,
Carried off my saddle. But first they singed
The camel fat (like silk close-woven, her fat);
When they had filled their bellies, something tinged   45
Their senses, and they flung the sizzling meat.
I gaped in wonder, and wonder to this day.
                    Not less enticing was Annaiza. Heat
Of love for her possessed me as I lay
Within her howdah. As we tossed about,   50
The rocking of the camel made her say,
All close, "Sir Bumble, if you don't watch out,
You'll end my camel-riding days for good!"
And when the howdah used to lurch, she'd shout,
"Now you have done it! Stop! Go down! How could   55
You wound my camel so? Now stop! Let loose!"
                    On fire, I begged, "Let loose the reins. Why should
I go, when fruits untasted lie, the juice
Of which I know, and cannot lying leave?
Unleash my lust! How can a maid refuse   60
What mothers giving suck or on the eve
Of childbirth granted? One put by her brat,
All decked with charming baubles, to receive
My wantonness, and when our love waxed hot
The hungry child, whimpering at her back,   65
Was silenced with her breast while I begat
Its brother down below."
                    One day in track
Of sporting game, I laid Annaiza down
Against a hill, but she, loath to unpack
Her goods, resisted, swore she would disown   70
Our love and leave me. "So her ladyship
Is on her high-horse?" Then I changed my tone
To gentler words. "Put by the smarting whip
Of your disdain, and if you plan to quit
Me, do it kindly then, and let me slip,   75
Not plunge into despair. But if your wit
Has fashioned female nonsense that I play

108

The fool and rule my heart for such a chit
As you, forget it. If in any way
You hate me, send my body far from yours.   80
Just know I know those tears betray
No virgin scruples. Each salty arrow pours
More smart into my sorrow-stricken breast.
Each spreads to yet unwounded parts and scores
New wounds." In such a vein do poets wrest   85
A virgin of her gold, so I am told.

       Once a virgin guarded in her nest
Like to a hatching egg by brothers bold
(As feathering hens guard their eggs to keep
Them warm) I warmed and feathered from the cold   90
In quite another manner. So did I reap
What Patience would allow me, and defied
Her stalwart sentinels who set their cap
To kill me secretly. The sun had died,
And in the sky bright Atthorayya strew   95
Her points like studs which sparkle golden-eyed
In a maid's girdle. When my cunning drew
Me to her side, I found her body bare,
Save some soft sleeping garment, soft as dew.
She sighed, "My love cannot resist such fair   100
Temptations, though I know your vows have rent
The shame of virgins countless as the air."
And when I led her gently from the tent,
She drew a rudely figured tapestry
Across our fleeing footsteps' testament.   105
The black hair tents soon dropped beneath a sea
Of dewy heaps; we paused upon the sand
Between two little hills. I slipped her free
Of that soft garment with my softer hand,
Then pulled her head down by her two side tresses.   110
Without a sound, as if the breezes fanned
Her body ever closer, so she presses.
Her thighs are fat, her waist and belly thin,
All smooth and tightly made for my caresses.
Her neck and shoulders are of silver sheen,   115
Like polished mirror. When she stands, her lithe
Is like the sugar cane's beside a stream

Untouched by human hand or hanging withe
So palely yellow pure she is. And when
In mocking protest to my love, she'll writhe   120
From my embraces, turn her cheek, and then
When she has charmed me with her side, turns right
Upon me eyes a she-gazelle of Ben
El Wajra turns upon her kids. The white
Hind has not a smarter neck, but that   125
Her neck is full of pearls. The blackest night
Is not so black as is the cloudy jet
Her hair is, falling down like clustered dates
To lend her back more beauty. The plait
Which pulls her black locks upward bates   130
In braids the tamer strands, while yet untamed
Black curls fall down upon her forehead. Straight
And smooth her waist, smooth as a rope hand-framed,
A leg as pure as the ripest sugar-cane
Well-watered, round and richly bending, strained   135
With over-ripeness. When the sun has shone
Full long upon her bed, she wakes to rise,
And from her loosely flowing sleeping gown
The grains of musk are scattered where she lies.
Her thin and fragile fingers curve around   140
My wrist like miswik on the Ishall trees.
The darkest dark of night cannot confound
The light of my love's face, which glimmers as
The solitary lamp upon the mound
Of a pious lonely priest. She fills the eyes   145
Of jaded lovers with a longing lust
So far her beauty and her height surpass
A riper maiden or a mother just
In bloom. My heart cannot forget its longing
For you (though men of my years have often lost   150
The eye to see young beauty). Once in wronging
You, a rival sought at any cost
To rob me of my peace in love, maligning,
But still I thrust his poison from my breast.
          But see! How black and evil is the night 155
Whose curtains fall unceasingly to test
My spirit, rolling in upon my sight

III. THE SHAPE OF ECSTASY

Like sea-waves ever rolling. How she strains
Her length like to the cat who stretches tight
Her drowsy body after sleep. She stains   160
The sky still, shows no sign of the beginning, wains
Not, without end. "Oh Night," I cry, "cease spinning
Darkling hours, let day appear!" And yet
The daylight brings no respite to my pining.
Alas, the stars that sear your black seem set   165
Eternally, fettered by strongest ropes
To the peaks of Yithbilli as in a net.
        But sometimes, shedding woe, I hunt in hope
Of early game while birds still droop and drowse.
My horse, swifter than the antelope   170
And freer, stronger far in running, bows
To none in agile moves, whether attack,
Retreat, skittish or spinning in skirmish, throws
Straight his strength as does a cataract
Plunge straight a stone. And down the saddle slides   175
From off his hide, dull red and shimmering black.
In such a way a slithering raindrop glides
And glances off a black and shimmering stone.
Despite his pallid eye, within him rides
A fury, out of which is sudden thrown   180
A sharp "Saheel!" exploding like the burst
Of water furiously boiling, pregnant grown.
When other mounts, run sluggish, stir the dust
With languid hooves out of the solid land,
My horse speeds far ahead and leaves the first   185
Lost in his wake. When others try a hand
At mounting him, he havocs all, will pitch
The delicate young boy onto the sand,
And in his flight will loosen every stitch
Of the heavier back of a heavy horseman. Round   190
He spins so rapidly he will bewitch
The eye to seem a whirling stone tight-bound
With a well-wrought rope unto a baby's fist,
And as the infant swings the stone around
In ever-quickening circles, twist by twist,   195
So whirls my horse. His girth is like the trim gazelle's,
He gambols like a cub, and when unleashed

EDWARD B. SAVAGE

In a wolf-like trot his legs are swift and well
As slim as any ostrich's. His thighs
Are fully muscled, and his glossy tail   200
So full and reaching near the ground, defies
The daylight peeping through. His sleeky hide,
Surpassing in its silken smoothness, vies
With grooveless stones, used by the early bride
To grind her scented powders, or to squeeze   205
The juices of the handal seed. The dried
Blood of my first game still filligrees
His mane as juices of the hina'a plant

Drip redly from the mouth: the traces freeze
In brownish wisps in old men's beards. I pant,   210
Remembering when we two first met a herd
Of wild white cattle: just as virgins dance
Around and round a phallus stone, all girt
In trailing robes, the heifers frisked. They seemed
– While circling to stampede but soon deferred   215
To left and right around us so they streamed –
A necklace strung from white Yemeni pearls,
Each separated, one from each they gleam
Upon the necks of little blue-blood girls
Like jewels. But to resume my tale, my mount   220
With quickening hooves and lightning gallop hurls
Himself upon the heifers, puts to rout
The leader well before her frantic cry
Can warn the rest. The horse and rider clout
A trundling cow and bull-calf, kill them dry   225
Without the ooze of sweat that blinds and binds
A slower rider.
                        When the feast was nigh
And hunting done, the steaming heaps of viands
Were stewed in a pot or sizzled on hot stones,
So great the kill. Contented, evening finds   230
Us glutted; thus the sleepy eye disowns
Its sight in drowsy wonder at the source
From which my horse's beauty wells, condones
His head and mane but soon descends perforce
In boozy contemplation of that part   235
Below. And while we dozed my noble horse

Slept tied and saddled; no one had the art
Or sense to set him free to graze.
                              But friend,
See! look how the lightning flashes dart
Round the gathering clouds! See how they rend   240
The bosom of the night! The sparks are quick
And glitter like my horse's hooves which send
Out sparks in flight; or like the sudden flick
Of a priest's sputtering lamp when the spout is bent
To nourish with more oil the flagging wick.   245
          Then we lay between Authai'ib's tent
And Darrig, looking at the clouds which spread
As far as we could see. The storm clouds went
Tumbling down the right of Mount Kattan's head
And stretched on the left as far as Sittar and   250
Yathbool. Soon the swollen clouds burst, bled
Their substance on Kuttaifa's parching land,
Bending and pitching the huge Kannahbal trees
Upon their chins. Winds whipped a torrent band
Around Kinnán. Down the mountain's knees   255
The white-foot deer went scuttling. The rush
Of the water ravished Taima'a, left the lees
Of date-palm trunks and pulverized to mush
The huts not built on solid rock. Like a sage
Who raps his aged body in a lush   260
Lined cloak was Mount Thabeer in the torrent's rage.
At dawn Ra'as Al-Muggaimir was as
A web in which was etched the mad rampage
Of the stormy night's debauchery. The grass,
Plants, flowers and trees lay at the mountain's feet,   265
All helter-skelter in a tangled mass
Of color, on the sands of Al-Ghabeet.
And when the sun was up, the circling kites
Swooped crazily to and fro as if replete
With spiced grape-wine. And in the wadi the night's   270
Great carnage lay, of dead and swollen brutes
Caught hapless, buried in their sluggish flights,
Like mud-encrusted plump wild onion roots.

113

GOETHES „ST. NEPOMUKS VORABEND":
KOSMOS eines GEDICHTS

VON JOHN A. A. TER HAAR, UNIVERSITY OF IOWA

Was die Geschichte reicht, das Leben gibt,
Sein Busen nimmt es gleich und willig auf.

TORQUATO TASSO, I, 1

Wer den Dichter will verstehen,
Muß in Dichters Lande gehen.

MOTTO, NOTEN UND ABHANDLUNGEN
DES „WEST-ÖSTLICHEN DIVANS"

Wenn man sich Goethe als Reisenden vorstellt, treten an erster Stelle die zwei großen Wiedergeburts- und Menschwerdungsreisen mit Bestimmungsland Italien in Erinnerung. Es waren Reisen, während derer er sich als Mensch, aber besonders als klassischer Dichter entdeckte.

> Wie mir's in der Naturgeschichte erging, geht es auch hier, denn an diesen Ort knüpft sich die ganze Geschichte der Welt an, und ich zähle einen zweiten Geburtstag, eine wahre Wiedergeburt von dem Tage, da ich Rom betrat. [*Italienische Reise*, Rom, 3. 12. 1786]

Aus der Sicht des Greisenalters hat Goethe, Eckermann gegenüber, den unschätzbaren Wert seiner Romerlebnisse nochmals bestätigt:

> Ich kann es [Prof.Göttling] nicht verargen..., daß er von Italien mit solcher Begeisterung redet; weiß ich doch, wie mir selber zu Mute gewesen ist! Ja ich kann sagen, daß ich nur in Rom empfunden habe, was eigentlich ein Mensch sei. – Zu dieser Höhe, zu diesem Glück der Empfindung bin ich später nie wieder gekommen; ich bin, mit meinem Zustande in Rom verglichen, eigentlich nachher nie wieder froh geworden.[1]

Es besteht denn auch kein Mangel an Literatur, die sich intensiv mit dieser Goetheschen Lebensdimension befaßt hat. Dagegen scheint die Tatsache, daß Goethe nicht weniger als siebzehnmal Böhmen bereiste, weithin ins literarische Unterbewußtsein abgesunken zu sein. Auf jeden Fall wirkt es befremdend, daß Goethes Verhältnis zu dieser bedeutenden Kulturlandschaft relativ wenig Beachtung gefunden hat. Böhmen, das von jeher ein Land der Begegnung verschiedener Völker und Kulturen gewesen war, zog ihn immer wieder in seinen Bann. Und daß es Goethe dabei um weit mehr ging als bloße Erholung durch Badereisen, oder um Flucht aus sächsisch-weimarischer Provinz, beweisen Anspielungen seinerseits, wie: „das gute alte Böhmen," „mein geliebtes Böhmen," und „der magische Kreis des Böhmerlandes," oder „das Böhmen ist ein eigenes Land. Ich bin dort immer gern gewesen." Kein Wunder, daß sich die Gesamtzahl der von Goethe im Böhmerlande verbrachten Tage auf ca. 3 Jahre und 19 Tage beziffert. In Italien dagegen hielt er sich nicht ganz 2 Jahre auf. Immer wieder kehrte er in Franzensbad und Marienbad ein. Doch am liebsten verweilte er in Karlsbad, wo sich die große Welt aus Ost und West traf, und wo der Dichter dreizehnmal als höchst angesehener Gast in aristokratisch-kosmopolitischen Kreisen verkehrte. Hier konnte er freier atmen als in der provinzlerischen Enge des Weimarer Hofes. Wie sich in Karlsbad Politik, Geschichte, Archäologie, Geologie, Mineralogie, Religion und Philosophie mit menschlicher Geselligkeit verbanden, zeigt die folgende Tagebucheintragung aus dem Jahre 1805:

> *20. Juli. Karlsbad.* Am Sprudel, am Neubrunn. Mit Fürst Reuss über die gegenwärtigen politischen Verhältnisse. Mit dem Landgrafen von Hessen über Urgeschichte und Gang der Menschheit. Mit Voght über die höheren Ansichten woraus sich das einzelne herleitet. Der Fürstin Narischkin auf der Promenade vorgestellt. Regnichtes Wetter. Bei der Hoheit zur Tafel. Scherzhafter Ernst über Mineralogie und allerlei Wissenschaftliches. Mit Graf Lepel und Voght spazieren. Das Gespräch fort- und die Thesen heiter durchgesetzt. Visite bei der Feldmarschallin von Kalckstein. Kurze Promenade. Brief von Madame Bethmann.[2]

Als kürzeste Zusammenfassung von allem, was Goethes Verhältnis zu seinem geliebten Böhmerland seelisch bedeutete, sei folgendes Zitat aus einem früheren Brief an seinen Freund Knebel vom 30. 12. 1785 angeführt, in dem das Wiedergeburtsmotiv ebenfalls anklingt: „In's Carlsbad geh ich auf alle Fälle, ich bin dieser Quelle eine ganz andre Existenz schuldig."[3]

Es war dieses existentielle Anderssein, das in glücklicher

Stunde, angeregt von einem böhmischen Kirchenfest, durch Goethes genialen Dichtergeist zu einem einzigartigen Gedicht auskristallisierte:

ST. NEPOMUKS VORABEND
Karlsbad, den 15. Mai 1820

Lichtlein schwimmen auf dem Strome,
Kinder singen auf der Brücken,
Glocke, Glöckchen fügt vom Dome
Sich der Andacht, dem Entzücken.

Lichtlein schwinden, Sterne schwinden;
Also löste sich die Seele
Unsres Heil'gen, nicht verkünden
Durft' er anvertraute Fehle.

Lichtlein, schwimmet! Spielt, ihr Kinder!
Kinder-Chor, o singe, singe!
Und verkündiget nicht minder,
Was den Stern zu Sternen bringe.

Neun Tage nach der St. Nepomuks Vorabendfeier, am 24. Mai 1820, schickte der Dichter sein Nepomuks-Gedicht an seinen Duzfreund, den Komponisten Karl Friedrich Zelter, mit den Worten: „Zum Abschieds-gruß ein Liedlein, welches Du mit Liebe entziffern und beziffern mögest."[4] Ein sinnschwerer Begleitsatz, der mittels der zärtlichen Di-minutivform „Liedlein" und der adverbialen Bestimmung „mit Liebe" manches über des Dichters persönliche Zuneigung zu seinem Gedicht aussagt. Bezeichnend ist weiterhin Goethes Aufruf zur Entzifferung des Gedichts und seiner Geheimschrift durch Deutung der „Chiffren," in denen sich, nach uralter, pansophischer Ansicht, der tiefere Sinn der Natur und Geschichte offenbare. Es ist, als stünde der Dichter vor dem Mysterium seines eigenen Gedichts und bäte den Freund um Aufklärung.

Zelter muß es sofort eingeleuchtet haben, daß es sich bei dem „lieben Nepomukchen," wie das Gedicht nunmehr in der Korrespon-denz der beiden Freunde hieß, um eine der kostbarsten Früchte han-delte, die je an Goethes dichterischem Lebensbaum gewachsen waren. Schon am 2. Juni 1820 läßt er Goethe das Gedicht vertont wieder zuge-hen; es habe sich „auf der Stelle wollen absingen lassen."[5] Bald darauf, am 14. Juni, erfahren wir, wie die schöpferischen Anregungen beider Künstler aus der gleichen geistigen Symbiose mit dem Böhmerland hervorgegangen sind, wenn Zelter schreibt:

Da ich immerfort Dich in Gedanken habe und mir Dein
Weben und Leben wie ein Faden, wie eine schwingende klingende Saite vor der Seele schwebt, so sprang mir das 'Nepomukchen' sogleich entgegen: ich fand mich in Prag auf der
Schützeninsel, die schöne Brücke vor mir, dazwischen den
sanften Strom, der tausend Schiffchen mit hellen Kerzen trägt;
das Frohlocken der Kinder, das Gebimmel und Getön der
Glocken und der ruhige Gedanke, daß mitten in dem poeti-
schen Wirr- und Irrwesen die Wahrheit ruht wie ein schla-
fendes Kind – und das Stückchen stand vor mir.[6]

Was Goethe in Zelters Antwort erhielt, war also weniger eine Entschlüs-
selung seines Gedichts als ein ähnlich verschlüsseltes Parallelerlebnis
in Prosa, das sich eng an seine eigenen Erfahrungen anschloß. Beide
poetische Darstellungen lassen eine merkwürdige Einheitlichkeit von
Gesehenem und Gehörtem erkennen.

Bei aller Ähnlichkeit der Aussage fällt es aber doch auf, daß
bei Goethe das Gesehene stärker in den Vordergrund tritt. Diese
Tatsache entspricht durchaus seiner neuplatonisch inspirierten
Weltanschauung, deren Weltbild alles Erschau- und Erforschbare
allegorisch-symbolisch mit den göttlichen Urbildern verband: „Am
farb'gen Abglanz haben wir das Leben" (*Faust* II, 4727). In der Vielfalt
des irdisch Seienden offenbare sich das absolute Sein, ewig wechselnd
als ein Ausfließen (*emanatio*), in das Gott, der Ureine, sich in zahllosen
Sinnbildern ergießt, um alles Erschaffene kreislaufartig wieder in sich
zurückzunehmen (*regressio*). Nach Goethes neuplatonischem Denken
ist der Mensch das Wesen der Mitte, dessen Streben nach Licht ihn
erlöst, dessen Hang nach dem finsteren Bösen ihn jedoch tragisch
gefährdet. So wird ihm das Auge zum großen Weltorgan, das die
dunkle Erde über die Welt der Symbole mit den lichtvollen, göttlichen
Sphären in Verbindung setzt. Als Dichter mit dem Lynkeus-Auge
erschaut er auch, wie die göttliche, all-beseelende Kraft in Menschen
und Natur lebt und webt, und fühlt sich "zum Sehen geboren, zum
Schauen bestellt" (*Faust* II, 11288/9). Durch die Ausstrahlung des
Göttlichen in die menschliche Seele ist diese umgekehrt auch wesent-
lich am Göttlichen beteiligt, was Goethe zu der uralten, mystischen
Erkenntnis führt, daß Gleiches nur von Gleichem erkannt wird. Diese
alles mit allem verbindende Zusammenschau hat Goethe gleichnishaft
in seinem *Entwurf einer Farbenlehre* ausgedrückt:

Wär nicht das Auge sonnenhaft,
Wie könnten wir das Licht erblicken?
Lebt nicht in uns des Gottes eigne Kraft,
Wie könnt uns Göttliches entzücken?[7]

So weit einige der einleuchtendsten, weltanschaulichen Voraussetzungen, ohne welche das lichtdurchstrahlte Nepomuk-Gedicht kaum
zustande gekommen wäre.

Unentbehrlich für die Entstehung und Deutung des Gedichts
sind weiterhin die kulturlandschaftlichen Voraussetzungen, denn
Böhmen war offensichtlich ein Land, dessen Einklang von Landschaft,
Natur, Kultur und Menschentum Goethes unersättlichem, visuellem
Bedürfnis in hohem Maße entgegenkam. Dort begegnete Goethe dem
von tiefer Schau- und Musikfreudigkeit geprägten Formenreichtum
einer noch katholisch-barocken Volkskultur.

> Zehn Jahre später (15. Mai 1820) bewegt ihn die Abendvorfeier
> des St. Nepomuks-Tags in Karlsbad so sehr, daß er in einem
> Gedicht, „St. Nepomuks Vorabend", nicht nur dem Volks-
> brauchtum bei diesem Fest huldigt, sondern mit starker
> Einfühlung in die katholische Empfindungsart dem Heiligen
> selbst fromme Verehrung darbringt.[8]

So der deutsch-böhmische Dichter Johannes Urzidil, der in seinem
umfassenden Werk *Goethe in Böhmen* dessen Spuren durch seine
Heimat mit Liebe verfolgt und höchst einfühlsam dargestellt hat.

Um noch einiges von der festlichen Stimmung einzufangen,
der Goethe sich am 15. Mai 1820 in Karlsbad hingegeben hatte, sei
– außer der schon zitierten Beschreibung der Prager Nepomuk-Feier
von Zelter – ein späterer Nachhall angeführt aus dem *Fest-Kalender
aus Böhmen: Ein Beitrag zur Kenntnis des Volkslebens und Volksglaubens in
Böhmen.* Das Buch, ohne Veröffentlichungsjahr, trägt im Vorwort das
Datum: „Prag am Dreikönigsfest 1861."

> Schon lange bevor ihn Papst Benedikt XIII. auf Antrag Kaiser
> Karl's VI. am 19. März 1729 heilig gesprochen, verehrte ihn das
> Volk als Schutzpatron gegen Verläumdungen, Anschwärzungen
> und Verkleinerungen und rief ihn zugleich, da er seinen Tod
> in den Fluten der Moldau gefunden hatte, als Helfer gegen
> Wassernoth an. An ihn gerichtete Gebete in deutscher und
> böhmischer Sprache wurden an seinem Grabe aufgehangen
> und mit Eifer abgelesen, und Kerzen und andere Geschenke

ihm geopfert, der Andrang wurde endlich so groß, daß man die Grabstätte, über welcher dreiundneunzig silberne und zum Theil vergoldete Lampen hingen, von denen einige immer brennend erhalten wurden, mit einem eisernen Gitter umgeben mußte. Aus den entferntesten Orten kamen, von ihren Predigern geführt, ganze Gemeinden hierher um Regen zu bitten.[9]

So weit der Rückblick auf die Geschichte der Nepomuk-Feier. Von der Art und Weise, auf welche der 16. Mai noch in der Zeit um 1861 im Prag gefeiert wurde, hat der Autor u.a. Folgendes zu sagen:

> Zur Vigilie schon erglänzt die Kapelle, welche, mit Laub und Blumen geschmückt, über der am 31. August 1683 errichteten Statue des Heiligen auf der steinernen Brücke (der Karlsbrücke) erbaut wird, von Lampen und Kerzen, und die Menge strömt so andachtseifrig herbei, daß an diesem, sowie am nächsten, dem eigentlichen Festabend, die Brücke für Wagen gesperrt werden muß. Am Tage des Heiligen selbst wallfahrtet man zu seinem von Silber schweren Grabmal in der Metropolitane [zum sog. Silbergrabmal im St. Veitsdom]. Die Burghöfe, der wälsche Platz, die Brückengasse, bieten das Bild einer belebten Messe dar. Auf dem Platz vor der königlichen Burg bei der Schloßsteige wird abwechselnd gekocht und gegessen. Alle Bilder und Statuen des Heiligen werden reich bekränzt, man hört nur Lieder zu seiner Ehre.[10]

Das Fest zu Ehren des Prager Chorherrn Johannes von Nepomuk gehörte also in den westslawischen und süddeutschen Ländern zu den beliebtesten Volksfeiern. Damals, wie auch heute noch, war sein Bild an zahllosen Orten, Seen, Plätzen, aber besonders häufig auf Brücken zu finden. Er war 1389 zum Generalvikar, also zum höchsten kirchlichen Würdenträger nach dem Erzbischof von Prag, aufgestiegen, als König Wenzel IV. ihn am 20. Mai 1393 foltern und von der Moldaubrücke ins Wasser stürzen ließ, angeblich, weil er sich geweigert hatte, die Beichte der Königin, der bayerischen Prinzessin Sophie, zu verraten. Die meisten Darstellungen zeigen ihn deshalb mit dem Kruzifix in der Hand, den leidenden Christus mit inniger Teilnahme betrachtend, oder mit der Schweigegeste, weil er das Beichtgeheimnis gewahrt hatte. Sein Heiligenschein enthält 5 Sterne nach den 5 Buchstaben des lateinischen „tacui," „ich habe geschwiegen." Nach der Legende trugen die Wogen der Moldau seine Leiche erbarmungsvoll empor und schwemmten sie an die Oberfläche des Wassers, von hell leuchtenden Sternen umgeben. So konnte der Leichnam des geliebten Priesters vom frommen Volke aufgefunden und geborgen werden.

Aus dieser kurzen Schilderung wird ersichtlich, wie das gläubige Volk spontan dazu kam, Johann von Nepomuk als Schutzheiligen gegen Hochwasser, Feuergefahr, und verschiedene andere Lebensbedrohungen anzurufen. Da die Brücke geistige und konkrete Seinsbereiche des menschlichen Lebens sowohl trennt als verbindet, errichtete man seine Statuen vorzugsweise auf Brücken. Wie die Schwelle, weist der Sinn der Brücke auf Überschreiten von Grenzen, auf Wandlung. Brücke bedeutet symbolhaft ein Hinter-sich-Lassen von Altem und Eintritt in Neuland. Durch sein Märtyrertum hatte Johann von Nepomuk der pilgernden Menschheit den tiefsten Sinn des Lebens vorgelebt: das Leben als Brückenschlag ins Jenseits hinüber, über den gefahrvollen Abgrund des Diesseits. Deshalb wurde der „Brückenheilige" gleichsam selber zur Brücke, zur Transzendenz. Durch die Jahrhunderte hindurch standen seine Bilder in böhmischer und deutscher Landschaft wie versteinerte Gebete um Befriedung von Flüssen, Wildbächen und Seen, oder sie begleiteten vom Straßenrand Pilger, Reisende, Wanderer und Flüchtige. Wie unser Gedicht beweist, lernte auch Goethe, der zeitlebens der Erleuchtung bedürftige Reisende ohne Rast und Ruh, den Brückenheiligen als Lichtgestalt kennen und schätzen.

Zum Schluß gehört zu den kulturlandschaftlichen Elementen, die in Goethes Gedicht eingegangen sind, noch das „Lichterschwemmen." Schon in vorgeschichtlichen Zeiten spielte das Licht eine allbelebende, kultische Rolle. Man sah, wie im kosmischen Drama von Tag und Nacht, Frühling und Herbst, das wachsende und schwindende Licht in immerwährenden Kampf mit der Finsternis verwickelt war. Deshalb war es kein Zufall, daß von den verschiedenen vorchristlichen und verchristlichten Frühlingsfesten, bei denen das Licht eine bedeutende Rolle spielte, das „Lichterschwemmen" mit der Feier des Nepomuks-Tages verschmolzen wurde. Mancherorts stellte man brennende Kerzen auf Brettchen, um sie unter Gesang den Fluß oder Bach hinunterschwimmen zu lassen. Oder die Jugend ließ von innen erleuchtete Häuslein, Kirchlein und Schifflein auf dem Wasser davonschwimmen. Was so gefeiert wurde, bedeutete überall, kosmisch gesehen, das ersehnte Eintreffen des Frühlings, d.h. den Sieg des Lichtes und des Lebens über die Mächte der winterlichen Finsternis und des Todes. Zugrunde liegt hier außerdem die fruchtbare, lebensspendende Zweieinheit von Wasser und Licht als Voraussetzung für das Wiedergeborenwerden zu einer neuen, irdischen und geistigen Existenz. In Fausts morgendlicher Rettung vor dem Selbstmord durch die Osterglocken hat Goethe dieser tiefmenschlichen Sehnsucht nach der Wiederauferstehung ein unsterbliches Denkmal gesetzt.

NACH UNSERER BESPRECHUNG der kulturgeschichtlichen und folklorischen Hintergründe ist es jetzt angebracht, tiefer auf den eigentlichen Sinn des Gedichts einzugehen. Der Thema, Ort und Datum fest umreissende Titel klärt jedoch wenig darüber auf. Gerade deshalb wirkt die festlich leuchtende Eröffnung des Gedichts umso überraschender. Man fühlt sich sofort hingerissen vom Strom sinnschwerer Worte und Eindrücke, die schon in der ersten Strophe horizontale und vertikale Dimensionen bilden. Jene kommen zum Ausdruck in den über die dunklen Tiefen der Tepl dahinströmenden Lichtlein, sowie auch durch die auf der Brücke singenden Kinder; diese, im Glockengeläute von dem auf die himmlischen Sphären hindeutenden Domturm. Die Melodien des Glockenspiels gipfeln in der Entzückung, die sich der feiernden Menschheit mitgeteilt hat; eine Hochstimmung, die von der Klangmelodie der Vokale getragen wird.

121

Auffallend an diesem Gedicht sind die ständig wiederkehrenden, liebevollen Verkleinerungsformen, die Auge und Ohr in der Rhythmik des Ganzen mitschwingen lassen. Goethe, der sich zeitlebens von dem kindlichen Elementarzauber, von der Einheitlichkeit und von der spontanen Naivität des Kindes angezogen fühlte, hat die gesamte Nepomuk-Feier ausdrücklich auf die Kinder zugeordnet. Nur das Kind in seiner Unschuld zeigt sich einer solchen ungeteilten Andacht und Entzückung fähig. Kindsein verbürgt Goethe unverfälschte Echtheit der Empfindung und Sinn für Wahrheit. So sind ihm die Kinder das singende, klingende Herz seines Gedichts.

Um die Mittelstrophe richtig einzuschätzen, werden wir uns kurz mit Goethes pantheisierendem Polaritätsdenken befassen müssen. Diese Lebensanschauung schließt bekanntlich den Streit von Gut und Böse, Licht und Dunkel, Leben und Tod in sich ein. Aus dieser polaren Entzweiung geht immer wieder der Sieg der positiven Seiten des Daseins hervor in der Form einer einheitlicheren Steigerung ins Gute, ins Licht, und ins Leben. Mit dem Begriff der Polarität stoßen wir auf einen Kernsatz Goethescher Lebensanschauung, den er selber anerkannt hat als eine seiner „frühesten Überzeugungen, an denen ich niemals irre geworden bin" (an J.S. Schweigger, 25. 4. 1814).[11] Das eintönig-monistische Einerlei einer materialistisch-homogenen Welt war ihm seit seiner Straßburger Zeit gründlich zuwider. Auch der damit verbundene tote Mechanismus als Naturphilosophie war ihm ein Greuel, und als Dichter des Lebens strebte er danach, den Tod womöglich ins Leben umzubiegen.[12]

Kein Wunder deshalb, daß die Polarisierung von Leben und Tod und die daraus erfolgende Steigerung auch in unserem Gedicht ihren Niederschlag gefunden haben, und zwar in der mittleren Strophe, also im Herzen des Gedichts. Dort erscheint, sicher verklammert zwischen zwei lichterfüllten, das Leben bejahenden Versen, der jähe Einbruch einer tragischen Vergangenheit: der grausame Märtyrertod „unsres Heil'gen," der sowohl die irdischen als die himmlischen Lichter auszulöschen droht. Doch bei dieser tragischen Gefährdung läßt der Dichter es bewenden; es ist ihm, als wären die Festlichkeiten der Menschenkinder gar zu köstlich, daß er sich die Freude daran hätte verderben lassen. Die Lichtlein und Sterne „schwinden" nur anstatt völlig zu entschwinden; der Heilige stirbt nicht, seine Seele „löste sich" bloß. Auch feiert Goethe Johannes von Nepomuk nicht, weil er sich heroisch geweigert hatte, das Beichtgeheimnis preiszugeben, sondern um seiner taktvollen Verschwiegenheit. So wie Goethe sich vor der schaurigen Wirklichkeit des Todes durch die Flucht in die Arme der großen Mutter Natur zu schützen pflegte – z.B. beim Sterben seiner eigenen Gattin – so läßt seine all-umfassende Weltfrömmigkeit es auch hier zu keinem vollständigen Durchbruch vergangener Tragik kommen.

Dafür bricht sich in der Schlußstrophe nochmals das überschäumende Hochgefühl der ersten Strophe Bahn, aber gesteigert zu ekstatisch jubelnden Ausrufesätzen, deren Sprachmelodie vornehmlich von hochgestimmten i-Vokalen getragen wird. Ja, es wäre nicht verfehlt zu behaupten, die Sprache hätte Himmel und Erde in reine Melodie aufgelöst. Dadurch verschiebt sich das Schwergewicht von der beschreibenden zur begeistert imperativen Form, und inhaltlich von visueller Betrachtung zur Melodie des Kindergesanges. Es ist eine Entwicklung, die in rhythmischen Wogen verläuft, und jede Erinnerung an die tragische Vergangenheit hinwegschwemmt. Zugleich erhebt sich das Blickfeld in einem letzten Aufschwung vom dunklen, mit schwimmenden Lichtern übersäten Strom, auf Flügeln des kindlichen Spieles und Gesanges bis in immer himmlischere Sphären, wo aus Kindermund die Verkündigung der höchsten Wahrheit erfolgt. Damit berühren wir das Geheimnis vom Tode unsres Heiligen, vor dem der Dichter sozusagen die philosophischen und sprachlichen Waffen strecken muß. In diesem rätselhaften Bereich halten ihm nur noch gleichnishafte Sinnbilder die Treue. Das „Unbeschreibliche" des Märtyrertodes, und die darauf folgende, überirdische Verklärung hat Goethe also in die uralte Lichtsymbolik der Sterne getaucht. Er läßt den Seelenstern des Brückenheiligen in den bestirnten Himmel hinaufsteigen, um dort in das Sternenheer aufgenommen zu werden. Aus Ehrfurcht vor diesem Mysterium drückt er die himmlische Heimkehr nicht rein faktisch, sondern in der Möglichkeitsform eines frommen Wunsches aus: „Was den Stern zu Sternen bringe." Man wird erinnert an die Schlußzeile der Erläuterungen von Erich Trunz: „In der Mischung von impressionistischen Bildern, zauberischer Süße der Melodie und hintergründiger Weisheit des Geistes eins der erstaunlichsten Lyrica dieser Spätzeit."[13]

Es bleibt gewiß erstaunlich, daß ein böhmisches Heiligenfest den „alten Heidenkönig" – wie sein katholischer Kölner Freund, Sulpiz Boisserée, Goethe einmal nannte – mit einer derartig überwältigenden Begeisterung erfüllen konnte. Der Schlüssel zu diesem merkwürdigen Phänomen wäre wohl zu suchen in Goethes Sensibilität für das, was er Eckermann gegenüber einmal als „die wahren Symbole der Allgegenwart Gottes"[14] bezeichnet hat. Mit seiner nie ermattenden Beobachtungsgabe kam er zu der Überzeugung, daß diese Symbole, oder Urbilder, oder Urphänomene, sowohl in der eigenen Seele, als auch überall in der Welt aufleuchten. Dadurch, daß Äußeres und Inneres ineinander fließen, entsteht jenes Identitätsdenken, das Goethes symbolische Darstellung der Erscheinungswelt in hohem Maße beflügelt. Dies geht besonders aus unserem Gedicht hervor, und weiterhin aus dem folgenden Zitat Eckermanns aus einem seiner Gespräche mit Goethe (26. 2. 1824):

> Hätte ich nicht die Welt durch Antizipation bereits in mir getragen, ich wäre mit sehenden Augen blind geblieben, und alle Erforschung und Erfahrung wäre nichts gewesen als ein ganz totes vergebliches Bemühen. Das Licht ist da, und die Farben umgeben uns; allein trügen wir kein Licht und keine Farben im eigenen Auge, so würden wir auch außer uns dergleichen nicht wahrnehmen.[15]

Wer in solchen schöpferischen Entsprechungen von lichthaftem Auge und lichtdurchstrahlter Natur schauen, fühlen und denken kann, dem kann auch das heiligende Drama altchristlicher Liturgie mit seiner Formen-, Farben- und Lichtfreudigkeit nicht gleichgültig bleiben. Goethes Anteilnahme an dem festlichen Symbolreichtum gestaltet sich zwar pantheistisch und steht durchaus im Zeichen seiner rhetorischen Frage: „Was kann der Mensch im Leben mehr gewinnen, / Als daß sich Gott-Natur ihm offenbare?"[16] Die Symbolerfahrung des Christen jedoch beruht auf einer profilierteren Trennung von Gott und Welt, und muß sich deshalb begnügen mit dem Erleben von dem, was Goethe als „die gottgedachte Spur"[17] bezeichnet hat.

Beide Wirklichkeitserfahrungen vereinigen sich in der Person des wahrhaft begnadeten Dichters, der einen feinen Spürsinn besitzt für die tiefsten, seelischen Regungen des Menschen, für seine Nöte und Bedürfnisse, kurzum, für das zeitlos Wahre, Schöne und Gute, das er in die rechte Form zu bannen weiß, wo immer es ihm begegnet. Dafür ist Goethes „Nepomukchen" ein unsterbliches, bis in unsere dunkle Zeit hineinleuchtendes Beispiel.

ANMERKUNGEN

1 Johann Peter Eckermann, *Gespräche mit Goethe.* Zweiter Teil: 1828-1832, 9. 10. 1828 (Zürich: Artemis Verlag, 1948), S. 188/9.

2 Johann W. Goethe, *Tagebücher* (Zürich und Stuttgart: Artemis Verlag, 1964), S. 265.

3 Johann W. Goethe, *Goethes Briefe,* 3. Auflage (München: C.H. Beck Verlag, 1988 = Hamburger Ausgabe), Bd. 1, S. 498.

4 Johann W. Goethe und Karl Friedrich Zelter, *Der Briefwechsel zwischen Goethe und Zelter,* 2. Bd. 1819-1827, Hg. Max Hecker (Frankfurt: Insel Verlag, 1913; Bern: Neuverlegt bei Herbert Lang, 1970), S. 66.

5 Ebenda, S. 70.

6 Ebenda, S. 76.

7 *Goethes Werke,* Bd. 13, 5. Auflage (Hamburg: Christian Wegner Verlag, 1966 = Hamburger Ausgabe), S. 324.

8 Johannes Urzidil, *Goethe in Böhmen,* zweite erweiterte Ausgabe (Zürich und Stuttgart: Artemis Verlag, 1965), S. 243.

9 O. Frh. von Rheinsberg-Duringsfeld, *Fest-Kalender aus Böhmen* (Prag, 1861), S. 240/1.

10 Ebenda, S. 242/3.

11 Johann W. Goethe, *Goethes Briefe,* Hamburger Ausgabe, Bd. 3, S. 268.

12 Vgl. dazu: Johann W. Goethe, *Hermann und Dorothea,* Gesang IX Urania – Aussicht, Hamburger Ausgabe, Bd. 2, S. 504:
Lächelnd sagte der Pfarrer: 'Des Todes rührendes Bild steht / Nicht als Schrecken dem Weisen und nicht als Ende dem Frommen. / Jenen drängt es ins Leben zurück und lehret ihn handeln; / Diesem stärkt es zu künftigem Heil im Trübsal die Hoffnung; / Beiden wird zum Leben der Tod. [46-50]

13 *Goethes Werke,* Hamburger Ausgabe, Bd. 1, 8. Auflage, S. 695.

14 *Gespräche mit Goethe.* 29. 5. 1831, S. 503.

15 Ebenda, S. 98.

16 Aus dem Gedicht ohne Titel, mit der Anfangszeile: „Im ernsten Beinhaus war's…," entstanden 1826; auch genannt: „Bei Betrachtung von Schillers Schädel," oder „Schillers Reliquien."

17 Ebenda.

A POLYSEMIC READING of STEFAN GEORGE'S
"Wir schreiten auf und ab im reichen flitter"

BY DENIS MICKIEWICZ, EMORY UNIVERSITY
AND ELLEN BRINKS, PRINCETON UNIVERSITY

Wir schreiten auf und ab im reichen flitter
Des buchenganges beinah bis zum tore
Und sehen aussen in dem feld vom gitter
Den mandelbaum zum zweitenmal im flore.

Wir suchen nach den schattenfreien bänken
Dort wo uns niemals fremde stimmen scheuchten
In träumen unsre arme sich verschränken
Wir laben uns am langen milden leuchten

Wir fühlen dankbar wie zu leisem brausen
Von wipfeln strahlenspuren auf uns tropfen
Und blicken nur und horchen wenn in pausen
Die reifen früchte an den boden klopfen.

We step to and fro in the rich flickering
Of the beech allée almost to the gate
And from the bars see outside in the field
The almond tree a second time in flower.

We seek the shadowless benches
The place where alien voices never startled us –
In dreams our arms entwine –
We feast upon the long mild radiance

We feel thankful when in quiet rushing
From the treetops traces of rays drop upon us
And only glance and listen when in pauses
The ripe fruits drop on the ground.

Literal translation
E.B.

*D*as Jahr der Seele (1897) has been regarded as the culmination of George's early Symbolist phase.[1] Indeed, we propose a reading of the fourth poem from the collection, "Wir schreiten..."[2] as a poetological manifesto of George's Symbolist poetics. A similar method of reading can be applied specifically to all the poems of this collection and more generally to the whole corpus of George's work. The poem is a clear example of consistent multilinear progression of thought, a method so prevalent in Modernist texts that it may be regarded as a hallmark of Modernism in general. The multiple semantic tiers are formed in this poem by a relatively dense succession of polysemic words.[3] Such an arrangement allows the reader to follow plots on any one or all of several tracks, at once; and they need not be contradictory or confusing.

The strength of each of the multiple tiers is evidenced by the different critical exegeses of *Das Jahr der Seele*. Gerhart Frommel and Gottfried Benn see these poems as nature or landscape poems.[4] Johannes Klein and Kurt Hildebrandt emphasize the biographical connection of the cycle to George's relationship with and separation from Ida Coblenz.[5] Friedrich Gundolf, a close friend and long-time member of the *George Kreis*, defines the Symbolist nature of the collection as a reflection of an *état d'âme*: "...not ensouled landscapes or landscape-experiences: but a soul which realizes its being and its fate through landscapes...[and] appears as nature."[6] Still others, among them Manfred Durzak and Manfred Gsteiger, read at least some of the poems as poetological symbols of George's aesthetics.[7] These readings vary in sophistication, but they are all linear readings. It is not that the critics fail to appreciate the metaphoric potential of the text. Most readers' confrontation with paradigmatic structures creates the heady awareness of transcending the confines of unilinear thought. However, such an effect is simply filed under the umbrella term "symbolism," without sorting out which semantic magnitudes are being "thrown together." To our knowledge, no multilinear reading of this well-known poem has been attempted.

Failure to acknowledge explicitly the polysemic nature of George's text precludes several semantic dimensions from being weighed into the context recreated by the reader. Although multilinearity allows each interpretative track to stand individually, a simultaneous reading on several discrete and yet compatible levels yields a fuller view of the workings of the designer's mind. Among various possible tracks, we propose to examine "Wir schreiten..." as:

1) denotative of the afternoon stroll of two lovers,
2) a reflection of a state of the soul,
3) a paradigm for the intellectual processes by which George creates art.[8]

Level one presents little semantic resistance for any reader, other than resolving a few ornamental details, such as "reichen flitter" or "tropfen," and tabling such questions as why an almond tree blooms twice, and why it does so in the fall. The apparent accessibility of George's diction accounts for the widespread success of the book.[9] Its denotative power suffices to convey the event – a celebratory stroll in the park. It is a beautiful "Herbstgedicht" even though George himself cautioned against naive literality. In the *Vorrede* to *Das Jahr der Seele*, he warns against searching for the original of the given setting or circumstance:

> In a work of poetry, one ought to…avoid unwisely turning
> back towards the original human or landscape model (*Urbild*):
> through art this original has undergone such transformation
> that it has become insignificant even for the creator, and, for
> anybody else, a knowledge of it would confuse rather than
> resolve anything.

To invest his content with a unique import, the poet models out of his original circumstantial material a special context, "a timeless world isolated from quotidian reality." Not all readers may feel the need to leap to this other level. What is obtained here on the literal or denotational level may have the lingering charm of a pretty snapshot of a pleasant and disarmingly ordinary instance. Many lyricists, indeed, invite readers to commemorate and share a biographical moment in its "naive" form. Additional historical elucidation may, then, enhance its appreciation, but that common sentimental path is dismissed by George as insignificant and confusing. It sidetracks the attention from the more significant, ironic part of his private experience, the part which is related to universal spirituality and to the lyrical efforts of capturing it. These realms must be expressed, however, through the very *realia* they seek to transcend. To serve as an element of conduct, the initial data are screened and recombined, and the words that name these data are chosen to project a special tone of the speaker. Symbolism thus converts an ephemeral fact into an illusion of a general and permanent import.

DENIS MICKIEWICZ AND ELLEN BRINKS

In approaching our topic of concern, namely, the artistic transformation of the *Ur*-model, let us consider the poem along the second
and third levels mentioned above, and use a distinction proposed by
William Butler Yeats (1901) to differentiate between these levels: the
second level features an "emotional symbol" (expressive of an *état
d'âme*); the third level presents a "symbol of ideas" (expressive of the
conceptual paradigm of making poetry).[10] These two levels of interpretation will provide the basis for our characterization of George's
Symbolist approach. Following Yeats' "symbol of ideas" notion,
George's *symbolisme* would be viewed as an extension of the initial
image-object (the *realia* of a park). That process is sustained by the extensive semantic energy of his words.[11] The tri-level semantic reading
we propose includes also the consideration of the sensory or semiotic
features. These entail the sub-lexical semic data, phonational and
syntactic symmetries and asymmetries, kinesthemic effects, and also
the projected effects of the substances and relations suggested by the
images. Doubtlessly, these data encrease further the semantic energy
of the words. The dynamics of these minute expressive data should fill
whatever gaps we create by abstracting three levels of content.

In this way the tone and the bearing of the speaker enter the
plot through the sub-lexical and supra-segmental particles of his delivery. Voiced or imagined, these palpable image-constituents are encoded
to be realized by the user: they inform his delivery (articulation, breathing, dynamics, accentuation, tempo, intonation, etc.). More exactly
than verbal concepts do, such structures combine to form lingering
if unnamed expressive *Gestalten*. Paralleling the simple plot and the
complex theme, these *Gestalten* mimic or provide concrete data for
imagining the festive stance of the speaker and the intensity of his attitude toward the narrated experience. By making the semantic content
more vivid and explicit on all levels, these vocal gestures permeate the
overall lyrical message.

"Wir schreiten…" as "emotional symbol"

LEVEL TWO, then, reads the text as symbolic of an *état d'âme*. (We must
remember that this collection was entitled *The Year of the Soul.*) It is a
ceremonial state whose conditions are either named or exhibited by the
bearing of the persons. The paramount importance granted to the ego
is made manifest by the first person plural pronoun's phraseological
role. It rules the action as a substantive in eight out of eleven instances

128

(lines 1, 3, 5, 7, 8, 9; and twice in line 11). It is emphasized by conspicuous repetition. The phrasal unit ("wir" plus a common bisyllabic verb) stands out as as an anaphora four times, tying together the three stanzas. Moreover, it appears once as a metonym ("unsre arme"), and three times it functions grammatically as the subject without being mentioned (lines 3 and 11 – notable instances of a direct semantic effect of absent words), and once as an object ("auf uns," l. 10). With the austere simplicity and uniformity of the syntax (all stanzas are structured similarly, I and III are syntactically almost identical, and both total the same number of words), the anaphora appears as a semiotically strong figure. The ego-figure is deliberately stylized, and its ceremonial stance becomes central to the lyrical message. In George's case, the poet is equally concerned with projecting visually, in his portraits and photographs, the same deliberate impression of his image. Arthur Evans points in his essay on physiognomic theory and heroic portraits to "Stefan George's conscious stylization of head and bearing after a chosen model of human behavior."[12] Such stylization reveals the theatrical aspect of the will to emphasize the formal side of the character, much as the poet does in his lyrical self-presentation. In both modes, George does not describe things and their settings *per se* but what spiritual states *his* selection of things reflects.

In our poem, such orientation *(Einstellung)* produces a special presentation of the corporeal materiality of the denoted image-objects (the ambience of the park). On the first level, the denotative tier, that process begins with George's favoring of the affective qualities of things over the things themselves. Thus, "wir" is strolling, not merely along a beech allée, but in the quivering light of its leaves. Similarly, the sound of the fruit falling to the ground is chosen over a description of the fruit. The "fremde stimmen" are disembodied intruders. One is reminded of Mallarmé's attempt to convey not the forest, but "the horror of the forest, or the silent thunder afloat in the leaves."[13] This favoring of sensual qualities even on the level of denotation is a step towards suggestive metonymic usage. It has tremendous synaesthetic potential, as colors, light patterns, sounds, and movements are displayed in relation to each other as parts of images. Therein lies George's mechanism of symbolization. The *état d'âme* consists of intense celebrations of the salient tokens of a particularly chosen setting, and the action – repeated and astute – acquires the markings of a solemn ritual.

Although it is not clear at the beginning who the "wir" is, throughout the poem the inseparability of the dual identity of the subject is established as the very essence of the "wir." As George indicates in the *Vorrede*: "...rarely are you and I so very much the same soul as in this book." All activities in this poem – the common denominator between "you" and "I" – are sensual, intensely perceived and shared, and metaphorically all of the substantives can be read as lending a carnal quality to the relation. However, only line seven denotes an affectionate physical contact, and the general stance indicates that in this relationship the overtly Apollonian principle dominates over the metaphorical Dionysian element. (The autumnal sun of this poem sheds light, not heat.)

130

With the second word of the poem nobility of gesture is emphasized: "schreiten" denotes measured steps as in a procession, a stately dance or parade, and carries connotations of formality and control, while "auf und ab" emphasizes repetition and regularity. Ernst Morwitz reports that George saw "in the manner of walking... an unmistakable, distinguishing feature of character."[14] An explicit notion of splendor is transmitted phonationally from another realm ("reichen flitter"). Placed together in the same line, "schreiten... reichen" provide the delivery of the words with a particular bearing (one also hears the related semes *reiten, breiten, streiten*). Such families of semes, breeding in phonological proximity, inform or infect the delivery of a passage with a particular histrionics: in this case, the gait of a *Ritter*.[15] "Reiche[r] flitter" is, among other things, golden flickerings and gleaming sequins or jewels on garments, further defining the identity of the "wir" with decorative pomp. Clothed in the natural made artificial, the *pas de deux* of the "wir" and the light move as one along a beech-avenue, a natural terrain ennobled by planning.

The service words of supposedly low or neutral semantic significance such as the adverbs "auf und ab," "beinah bis," "aussen," "auf uns," "niemals," "nur," "dort wo," "wenn," and "zum zweitenmal," are central for conveying the complex set of attitudes, responses and bearings that comprise the state of the soul. "To and fro" denotes a ritualistic repetition and also confinement. That sense is sharpened by the acuteness of "almost to," and confirmed by the awareness of the "outside." There is a vulnerabiltiy ("upon us"), that seeks total exclusivity ("never," "only") in special places and times ("the place where," "when"). The result is an aloof aristocratic *Haltung,* a bearing that rejects the outside world with determined indifference.

The qualitative-circumstantial adverb "for a second time" marks the only overt ambiguity in the poem. Poetic ambiguities do not lack meaning; they lack restriction of meaning, and function as deliberate invitations for multiple readings. The reader is also compelled to reexamine the context in order to determine which key item denotes an *analogon* (what is copied from reality), and which stands as a metaphor for something else (in this case, the flowering almond tree). The adverb may modify either or both predicates: "we see" and "in flower." More importantly, there is no explanation of how either does happen "zum zweitenmal", i.e., how a second spring takes place in autumn. That somewhat exotic plant (or whatever it metaphorizes) is placed beyond the *Buchengang,* and the gaze of "wir" responds only to it. This ambiguous image cluster unmistakably leads to the multiple planes of the poem's content. On the first level, the "wir" consciously stop short of the gate ("beinah bis zum tore"). Projected as a barrier to the outside world ("feld vom gitter"), it is the artistry of the gate which draws attention. The flowering "mandelbaum" can then be read as an *analogon* – a depiction on the face of the "Gitterwerk." "For a second time blooming" would mean an artistic recreation of the original natural fact: *natura naturans* becoming *natura naturata.*

On the second, spiritual, level, the same image can be tied to a sensation of witnessing a marvel. The almond tree bears often mystical associations in the arts, and blooming is the peak of an aesthetic development. Beholding it "for a second time" is a re-witnessing, a *Wiedererleben,* of an ecstacy. In a Neo-Platonist way, Viacheslav Ivanov connects this kind of epiphany with the universal role of the poet-seer. He links it with "the rapturous tremor of a second sight granted to a lyricist...a recall of a dim memory of some ancient live knowledge which revealed to the seer the mysterious book of the *anima mundi.*"[16] Ascent toward such "light" marks the stirrings of inspiration. Appropriately, this first phase is announced in stanza I. Whether the flowering *état d'âme* is creative or erotic, and the partner in "we" is the Muse or the lover, the inspiration is shared in the "secluded sanctuary" in stanza II, and rewarded in stanza III. Below, we will also discuss "the second flowering" on the third level, as the poet's acquisition of his own identity vs. that of his canonized forebears.

In the second stanza special places of repose are sought. There the required illumination and privacy emphasize the long-held social, existential and spiritual dominion of the "wir" within their own cultivated environment ("dort wo uns niemals fremde...").[17] Seeking the purest light and eschewing the alien voices suggest that the lingering in the garden is a symbol for the rarified culture of the soul. Aware of the

DENIS MICKIEWICZ AND ELLEN BRINKS

proximity of the outsiders (barbarians), the polysemous predicate "scheuchten" foregrounds a multiple referential attitude which is indicative: 1) of the emotional vulnerability of the "wir," 2) of the latent crude force of the "fremde stimmen," 3) of the precariousness of the shelter, 4) of a hidden metaphor for animals vs. hunters (*scheuchen* meaning to "flush out of hiding"), and 5) of a hidden metonymy for carnal love, if *scheu* refers to animals (i.e., a quality describing the skittishness and shyness of an animal). On the first level, then, carnal love would be the original motive for the couple's will for seclusion. On the second level, the notions of confinement and of prey (seme #4) suggest that George's "...bearing shows a restrained strength...whose lordly fierceness took the King of the animals as a model,"[18] and he retreats before the encroaching world. From here, in the words of Friedrich Wolters, "the wide open eye of youth does not turn inward as does that of an observer, or mystic, but gazes from a deepening interior into the world." Evans' research documents further that George shares the double character of the lion: as observed in the early Renaissance, there is *fortezza e clemenza* in such characters.[19]

132

The delicacy of the metonymy, "verschränkte arme," and the raptures expressed as "träume" reveal an eroticism which is experienced as a mutual celebration in a real or metaphorical garden. An unabashed and mutual sensual enjoyment is unmistakably rendered in the kinesthemically most eloquent symmetrical line 8: "Wir *laben* uns am *langen* mild*en* leucht*en*," lays out four rhyming, trochaic, bisyllabic, sense oriented, "easy" phonesthemes, with four common liquid ls resonating the words' semantic consonance. The climactic nature of this line is amplified by its contrast with the preceding asymmetrical, semantically disparate, sibilant and r dominated line 7. As in the first stanza, the reciprocal nature of the light and the emotional state of the "wir" preempt their separation. "Leuchten" stands here for the suspended enjoyment of the experience[20] and also for a lofty distance of its source.

The third stanza projects the experience into a new spiritual dimension. The feeling of gratitude, "dankbar," expresses not only an emotional attitude, but a fully conscious *Weltanschauung*. The gift of the experience is acknowledged. This gratitude, combined with the "search for the shadowless...," brings into relief a spiritual condition: the determination to exit from darkness and to fill an absence, by finding the bright places of repose. If the symbolic value of light is progressively given a sensual, emotional and finally spiritual value, then stanza three can be read as Ivanov's ascension to *realiora*. The motif of thanksgiving becomes coupled with that of mystery. Line 11, "[wir] blicken *nur* und horchen," makes the participants passive witnesses of the marvels. Far from reading the poem as expressive of a melancholic attitude, as many critics have characterized *Nach der Lese*,[21] the "baptism" of light ("strahlenspuren auf uns tropfen," l. 10) is wholly a blessing, literally from above. The "leisem brausen" becomes the delicate sympathetic vibration of the soul and an anticipation of the similarly lightfooted climax, the drops of the "traces of light-beams." The phonemic similarity of "-spuren" to "spüren" carries the lexemes' semantic and sensory fusion into the context. "Radiance" ("strahlen") implies figuratively a synonym for the suffused happiness and joy (cf. the colloquialisms "er strahlt ja" or "sie strahlt übers ganze Gesicht"). Finally, the suspension of the celebration is interrupted only by the acknowledgement of the *Gegengabe*, the dropping of the ripe fruit.

Again, the grammatic layout draws an exact map of the transformation of the role of "wir." It gradually surrenders its substantival predominance. In line 6 "wir" becomes a direct object ("uns"), subordinated to the "stimmen"; in line ten, "strahlenspuren" becomes the subject and "wir" the receiving object; and in the final line, the ego disappears altogether, the fruit being the subject, and earth the direct object. This simple grammatic transformation marks the exact points at which the subject ego yields its position to epiphany and fruition.

The poem as poetological "symbol of ideas"

LEVEL THREE, as consistently maintained as the other two, is the most metaphorical of the three levels. "Wir" in this case represents not two lovers, or a person and his psyche, but the artist and his creative agent, the Muse, and possibly, the ideal reader. The strict delimitation of the terrain now becomes mandatory for reasons of total control rather than for privacy (a mere pre-condition). Manfred Gsteiger notes that the garden motif in early George is a "rather painful attempt to create a new order within a small area – an attempt constantly threatened by failure."[22] As will become evident, the mental walk is a continual marking of boundaries, a control of the disturbing or disruptive elements within and outside the garden, the search for a moment and a *locus* conducive to creative insight. The "schreiten auf und ab" evokes the rhythmic impulses that often precede images and are the signals of immanent, specifically poetic, creation. The motif of rhythmicity is made explicit by the term "in pausen" (line 11). Formal analysis of the text, now symbolic of a literary terrain of the mind, reveals an astonishingly rigorous maintenance of symmetry: strophic, syntactic, and phonological (cf. especially the rhythmic regularity of measured pacing with a meticulous maintenance of both binary meters – iambic on the level of verse and trochaic on the level of 37 out of 38 polysyllabic lexemes).

The image *Buchengang* suggests a closely defined passage and a deliberately planted order – qualities that apply also to texts and to collections of artistic texts. Moreover the word will be shown to indicate a gallery of books, *i.e.* the literary tradition. The consciousness of such an enclosure is reiterated (lines 3-4) as the artist and his muse note the field outside the bars, but there is no intention of exiting. The threshold to non-art is something seen but never crossed ("beinah bis zum tore"). The "wir" is caged in (by choice) and the world is caged out. The symbolic discrepancy between the two *loci* is so great that the outside world exists in another temporal dimension. The "mandelbaum...im flore" is indicative of spring, whereas in the garden it is autumn ("reifen früchte").

In the second stanza, the poet and his psyche search for illuminated places of immaculate mental repose. To become artistically fruitful, these places must be devoid of shadow, *i.e.* immaculate and never disrupted by alien voices. Critical to poetic concentration, these elusive points are conveyed by George through polysemia and phonation. In a Symbolist reading, "shadow-free benches" would be a metaphor or a synecdoche: it would stand for a nonexistent name of a stringent set of conditions for fruitful inspiration. Here, the two devices – polysemia and marked phonation – help suggest the notion *(Ahnung)* as well as the feel of the expanding greater whole (see note 11). We must add that polysemia rarely causes irresolvable ambiguities. With polysemic expressions, the predominance of certain semes is determined by the semantic context surrounding the expression and by the given level of reading.

The expression *schattenfrei* is a good example of conventional usage paralleling our tri-level reading of the poem. Both members of the compound word are polysemic. With the noun part comes the literal shading of objects, the "clouding" or darkening of the mood, and the obscuring of intellectual clarity. The adjective "frei" has negative and positive meanings. First, it denotes an absence (from its preceding referent) and, if that referent ("shadow") is negatively perceived, then the compound term is a double negative. On the other hand, the notion of "liberated" carries the positive semes of relief, of being unencumbered as in "free" as a bird[23] or as an elysian shade. Denotatively, the substantive member "shadow" contributes to the corporeal picturing of "benches" into a concrete image. Although the exact image is left open to the imagination, "flitter" suggests variegated light on the benches. Alternatively, the shaded benches could be solidly dark, cool, damp, and uninviting. On the *état d'âme* level, "shadows" cast doubt, apprehension and melancholy on the subjects of emotional concern. Relieved by "frei," an untroubled tranquillity returns (cf. *sorgenfrei* or "carefree"). On this third, poetological level, *schattenfrei* means Apollonian clarity (Phoebus Apollo, the light of reason, and Apollo Musagetes, harmony and measured steps).

The same understanding of the images of shadow and light is confirmed in George's essays as metaphors for an art whose "künstliche Umformung eines Lebens" (artificial reshaping of a life) redefines the so-called separation of art and life and wards off claims of decadence and escapism. One essay, which appeared in January 1896, just months after "Wir schreiten…," states:

135

> What we in part strived for, in part made eternal, lies plainly
> before us: an art free from service:…an art that…even in what
> is violent and what is terrible ought not to obscure and *darken*
> but cheer and *brighten*: an art arising out of the joy of behold-
> ing, out of intoxication and sound and *sun*. (e.m.)[24]

The predicate "suchen nach" is an indication that this clarity is consciously sought, and the definite article "den" suggests that these illuminated points of repose are foreknown. The thus motivated strolling through the "rich" garden, then, becomes a conscious search for the most illustrious or uplifting points in the cultural tradition. (We have already noted the bearing of the persona "wir"; the etymology of *Buchengang* will be discussed shortly.) If the well-known paths represent the solid mental scaffolding on which creativity is built, then the points of intersection become platforms for turns and new departures of creative impulses.

This poem also mirrors the voiceless and shadow-free points or moments semiotically. George is explicit on the pre-eminence of form in high poetry.[25] That factor is marked in the poem by exceptional regularity. Space does not permit us to describe the entire wealth of symmetries of the syntactic, phraseological and rhythmic cadences in order to demonstrate how, on the level of minute detail, these cadences form each expressive gesture to be realized by voiced or imagined delivery. We must, however, point out one metric feature of the clausula which invariably segregates each of the twelve lines. The intensification of the rhythmic means by an identical special distribution of quantitative and accentual oppositions causes pauses between the lines; these pauses create spaces for turning, or continuing a thought, or for beginning a new one. The implementation of these breaks is seen as follows: the metric of the poem is five-foot iambs with no inverted feet and with all feminine rhymes. George's pronounced isochronism imposes a strong metronomical pulse-beat, quite in keeping with the stately pacing of the steps "back and forth."[26] That pulse mandates the addition of an extra ictus at the junctures of the constant unaccented final syllables with the invariable iambic (also unaccented) anacruses of each succeeding line. Those missing downbeats must, of course, be replaced by pauses. These voiceless gaps, caused by the invariable hypercatalectic effect, guarantee the integrity and independence of each verse line. This measured autonomy (itself expressive of solemn speech) overrides a *Parlandostil* execution of the four instances of enjambement in stanzas I and III. The symmetrical autonomies created by clausulas coexist with the other type of symmetry (which the enjambements call attention to), namely that of exact syntactic parallelisms of the two stanzas. The formal, literary voiceless rests between the lines provide the unencumbered, physically separating, but mentally illuminated places of repose.

Freedom from shadows and from alien voices equates here the two phenomena as synecdoches (respectively, visual and acoustic) of a multiform and polysemic threat of intrusion. If the garden paths are read as metaphors of the literary tradition, it is the shadows of the forebears and their formidable voices that a creator must distance himself from, by retreating toward still deeper points in one's sanctuary. With originality of one's *melos* at stake, even venerable strains become "alien voices." This second stipulation is also borne out in other, more obvious respects: George eschews the language of the "other" world – colloquial speech (*Umgangssprache*) and foreign words (*Fremdwörter*).[27] The semes of restriction, or limit (*schranke, beschränken, einschränken, umschränken*) become explicitly more dominant as the creative act is introduced at the mid-point of the poem: "...arme sich verschränken." The garden is not a zone of random artistic freedom; it is the rigorous order of self-imposed restrictions, learned from the tradition, that ultimately liberates the spirit. Within this deepening confinement, concentration seeks crystalline places in the penumbral corridors of creative thought.

From the outset of his career, George resolutely adhered to

136

classical models. His selection of his juvenalia, published as *Die Fibel* in 1901, is testimony to his apprenticeship to the tradition. Jan Aler reports that George's sonnet form was adopted from Dante, Petrarch and Graf von Platen; the hammered forms are imitations of the Parnassians; the versification prototype and the phraseological formulas stem from the German anacreontics, and a dramatic character, Titania, is patterned after Shakespeare.[28] Poetologically, all of the above-mentioned tradition-bound norms reflect a Classicist outlook.[29] George's Classicism was not an isolated streak in the Symbolist movement, and that fact is important in understanding the Modernist movement at the turn of the century. Similar norms of apprenticeship, formality, regularity, and norms of enlightenment, pomp, pathos, and piety were pursued by Valéry, Hofmannsthal, Annensky, and especially, Ivanov. Their attitude was opposed to the Romanticist approach taken by Verlaine, Rilke and Blok, or by the "Surrealist" streak initiated by Rimbaud. It must also be noted that what was properly *moderniste* in such "Classicists" and even in later George, was not manifested on the level of expression. This brand of Modernism, unlike the main "isms" around the time of the First World War and after, did not seek to exercise a radical elipticism, "nonsense" language, etc. Obfuscation of the forms of expression was never sought by George. What the "Classicists" did share with the "cloudy Impressionists" and the radical Expressionists was the supercharging of content. In semiological terms that means amassing maximal amounts of substances of content on minimal terrains of the forms of expression: hence the extensive, though varied use of polysemia on the part of all Modernists. The variant represented by George lends itself admirably to pursuing the goal of deciphering the "confused words in the forest of symbols," as commended by the first Modernist, Charles Baudelaire.

In view of the assiduously assimilated tradition, George's choice of tree species is hardly random. His neologism"buchengang" homonymically and etymologically suggests the literary tradition – literally, the path of books (*Buchgang, Büchergang*). The fagaceae, associated in antiquitity with the Roman gods, Jupiter, Bacchus and Diana, was linked in ancient Germanic folklore "with the magical art of writing, with poetry, with the graphic arts in general. This association is evident in the etymological identity in Germanic languages of 'beech' and 'book,' *Buche* and *Buch*..." possibly on the grounds that the ancient runic tablets were made from slabs of beechwood. That tree was canonized in world literature in Vergil's First Eclogue, and in German verse by Mörike ("Die

DENIS MICKIEWICZ AND ELLEN BRINKS

schöne Buche," 1842).[30] The noun *Gang* is very rich in meanings including "stroll," "passage," "process," "motion," "usage," and also "cadence of verse." Here, it would represent the chain of models on the path of George's own artistic-intellectual evolution.

It is clear on this third poetological level that the artist's progress leads him through intimidating voices – those of his Classical models. They threaten to interfere at the most intense stages of creative concentration as he passes each beech tree. In the search for his own formal boundary within the boundaries set by others, the beloved shadows with their eloquent voices must, however, recede. The poet's own "walking terrain" becomes increasingly small, but not so the space for perception and reflection. Rather, these activities increase after having had full access to the cultivated repositories of high craft, with its variegated options. From here, artists like George are sure to gain the rhythmic and intellectual momentum to launch their own transcendence.

Thus we also come to understand the *second* blooming of the almond tree on a third level. Rather than a likeness wrought on the gate, or an *état d'âme*, it is George's own original work vis-à-vis his models. The first blooming would then be the encountered stroke of genius of his forebears, "sein Vorgegebenes, das ihm etwas zu sagen hat" (Aler, *ibid.*, 17). Transcendence must, by definition, lead outside; hence we ("wir") see the bloom of their own gift for the second time beyond the canonic *Buchengang* ("aussen"). The choice of a *prunus amigdalus* of the rose family is, no doubt, of considerable weight. In the poetic tradition, since the *Aeneid* and the *Divina Commedia*, this symbol is laden with mystical connotations. Here, it stands in opposition to the native beech trees, but it is not a fantastic or a radically exotic opposition, as tropical plants or Goethe's blooming lemon trees ("Mignon") would have been. Rather, George seems to enter into a polemic with Novalis who, a century before him, rejects "des Mandelbaums Wunderöl," with alcohol and opium, in favor of mortal sleep.[31] George's celebration of life seeks neither oblivion nor a recourse to drugs and is content with the contemplation of the bloom of this *Wunderbaum*.

After the first stanza the emphasis is on light as the progenitor, and on "wir" as the attentive, receiving vessel ("wir laben," "wir fühlen," "[wir] blicken," "[wir] horchen"). The protagonist becomes a witness. In line eleven, he and the muse are confined solely ("nur") to watching and listening, and in the last line, they disappear from the scene as attention is focussed on the thud of the falling fruits. Such an *Umstellung* (a switching of places on the level of action) is in keeping with Baude-

laire's brand of the Symbolist *Weltanschauung*. Ivanov characterizes it as
the poet's call to witness and to recall his extraordinary psychic experiences, without indulging in romantic *Schwärmerei* or in fictitiousness.
(It should be noted that in line seven the persona *observes* how their
arms enfold in dreams.) Since the phenomenal language is not suitable
for describing mystical realities, Symbolism must resort to all means
available (i.e., polysemia, imagerial oppositions, phonological sugges-
tiveness) to circumvent that restriction.[32]

The refreshment or feasting on the light ("wir laben uns am
langen milden leuchten") and the "golden rain" produce a spiritual
photosynthesis, a transsubstantiation which bears special fruit.[33] The
creation or birth yields fully formed and informed art objects ("die reifen früchte"): informed because formally inscribed within the *locus poe-
sis*. The passive ("blicken nur und horchen") acknowledgement of the
artwork by the artist reveals the artist's marvel before his own rhythmi-
cally falling words. Art, as George conceived and practiced it, was for
the few celebrants and was not utilitarian: "to wish to 'say' or to 'effect'
something is not worthy of admission even to the outer court of art."[34]
In such a rarefied place, the "fruit" are perceptible only to few initiates
("wir"). The "reifen früchte" drop in intervals according to the temporal
laws of the artificial garden, i.e., artistic creativity, and are not to be
measured by the common worldly standard. They are marvels for the
creator himself as they fall to earthly ground. The image of that mysterious "cautious and muted" thud, has been further "animated" as a symbol of poetic words by Osip Mandelstam.[35] Harvesting, going to seed,
or decay cannot be assumed either because their effect (*Wirkung*) is
not even "worthy" of preliminary consideration. But their conception
(*Entstehung*) out of sensing and witnessing a fulfillment is the poetic fruit
of the recondite *état d'âme*. The falling of words worthy of marking this
quintessential moment of being is no more predictable than the soaring
of ecstasy is with any ritual.

A MULTITIERED SYMBOLIST poem brings into focus the issue of the
distinction between the real world and the projected world. All communication, all languages, must cope with this basic issue. Medieval
grammarians saw it as the distinction between *modi essendi* and *modi
intelligendi*. It is a distinction that can be traced through many works
in psychology, and linguists have also approached it: "The world as
experienced is unavoidably influenced by the nature of the unconscious
process for organizing environmental input. One cannot perceive the

139

'real world as it is'."[36] If linguistic information concerns directly only the projected world, artistic organization removes the poetic linguistic information a step further from the *modi essendi*.

George's short poem admirably embodies the notions of his Sympolist peers about the relation between an experience and its artistic transformation. In his 1903 essay which begins with the discussion of *Das Jahr der Seele*, Hugo von Hofmannsthal vehemently rejects the "absurd" notion of mistaking Symbolist poetic practice for an artificial replacement of the original facts by some other matter. The point is, precisely, to reveal the essence of things rather than to create riddles or redundant parallelisms:

> Never does poetry substitute one matter *(Sache)* for another, for it is precisely poetry which strives feverishly to define the matter itself, with a wholly different energy than does blunt everyday speech.... It never does this [substituting]. Were it to do so, one would have to stamp it out like an ugly, smoldering will-o'-the-wisp. What would poetry be seeking beside the common speech? To cause confusion? To hang paper blossoms on a live tree?[37]

A stroll in the park remains a stroll in the park, but the lyricist attaches varying significance to his perceptions of the facts. Verbal representation is by necessity synecdochical, and the best selected words reproduce only a fraction of the experience. On the other hand, polysemy, metaphoric capacity, and the semantic synergy of the words' arrangements add layers of associations to what is featured in the text. The feeling and significance of that stroll can thus be retrospectively sharpened, deepened, generalized, and raised to a higher mode of consciousness. In the struggle of retaining such a vision poets use the available rhetorical and semiotic devices, to express a single, complex *état d'âme*. As Yeats maintains in his 1901 essay:

> All sounds, all colours, all forms, either because of their preordained energies or because of long association, evoke indefinable and yet precise emotions, or, as I prefer to think, call down among us certain disembodied powers, whose footsteps over our hearts we call emotions; and when sound, and colour, and form are in a musical [Musagetian] relation, a beautiful relation to one another, they become, as it were, one sound, one colour, one form, and evoke an emotion that is made out

of their distinct evocations and yet is one emotion.[38]

The new imagerial structure *(Gefüge)* that holds this single emotion or vision and its palpable "footsteps over our hearts" may only faintly resemble the original *Urbild*. George's already cited *Vorrede* warns, therefore, against naive restoration of biographical facts "which underwent such transformation through art that [they] became unimportant [even] for the creator himself." But the focus on the generative notions is relentless and, importantly, the transformation-germination transcribes a spiral, and the resulting fruit land back on earth. "What lies plainly before us" is a "bright" and "joyous" account of an extraordinary state of mind. That ripening of a creative *modus intelligendi* is telescoped into, and reflected by, only twelve artistic lines.

141

It is the "noumenal transparency of things" (Ivanov's term) that allows poets to see through the given phenomena and construct psychic and poetological inferences on the polyvalent grounds of their signifying images. Yeats illustrates how such construction proceeds from the same source by favoring one among the available tracks of thought:

> If I watch a rushy pool in the moonlight, my emotion at its beauty is *mixed* with memories of the man that I have seen ploughing by its margin, or of the lovers I saw there a night ago; but if I look at the moon herself and remember any of her ancient names and meanings, I move among divine people, and things that have shaken off our mortality, the tower of ivory, the queen of waters, the shining stag among enchanted woods...and 'meet the Lord in the air.'

In the first instance, the moon is dissolved in the "emotional symbols [that]...come the nearer to our sympathies, although their relations with one another are too subtle to delight us fully, away from rhythm and pattern." In the second instance, Yeats effects the dissolution of the *Ur*-image in the "intellectual symbols that evoke ideas alone, or ideas mingled with emotions...where one is mixed into the shadow of God or of a goddess" (*ibid.*, 160, 162, 161, e.m.). Symbolic extension allows constructing mythological contents, as did Yeats and Ivanov, or designing entirely abstract, disembodied structures of meaning, as Mallarmé taught. Amplification or expansion of sensory or noetic effects of an original setting may require the introduction of new metaphorical names, and further filtering out of original details; but nothing is substituted, and what is given receives polysemantic or multivalent assignments.

But in 1912, defending the waning movement against the accusation of insufficiently loving this world, Ivanov writes:

> It is natural to true Symbolism to depict the earthly, rather than the celestial: what matters to it is not the force of the sound, but the force of its resonance.... True Symbolism does not tear itself away from earth; it wants to combine the roots and the stars and grows up like a stellar flower from the near, native roots. It does not substitute things and, in speaking of the sea, it means the earthly sea, and in speaking of snowy heights...it means the tops of earthly mountains.... Symbolism seeks, as an art, only the elasticity of the image, its inner vitality and extensiveness in a soul into which it falls like a seed, destined to grow and to yield an ear. Symbolism, in this sense, is the affirmation of the extensive energy of the word and of artistry.[39]

The world mirrored in "Wir schreiten..." unfolds with the sensuous and intellectual effects of a visit, or composite visits, in an autumnal park. Unlike many Modernists, George maintains the "first," realistic level *almost* intact, and his versification is ostentatiously classical (graphic peculiarities only emphasize this). The poem's capital is "the force of its resonance." The persona's ritualistic bearing sustains the oneness of the *Erlebnis* (experience) while the modes of it undergo changes. They begin with visual perceptions and end with auditory ones, as the experience becomes internalized. The syntactic parallelisms of each stanza mark three distinct narrative phases or plateaus. Each stanza-plateau begins with an anaphoric escalation: "We step...We seek...We feel...." And the last line of each stanza expresses the climax of each phase, also in an escalating order: "...a second time in flower...We feast upon... The ripe fruits drop...." The assertively orchestrated effects echo in the mind, and fill the semantic spaces among our three arbitrarily chosen levels of perception. In turn, such polyphony affirms the life-giving named and unnamed semes of a single "indefinable and yet precise" emotional procession. A Musagetian accord relates these "footsteps over the heart" to one another following the ceremonious rite of George's creative mode.

1 Manfred Gsteiger, in "Expectation and Resignation: Stefan George's Place in German and in European Symbolist Literature," *The Symbolist Movement in the Literature of European Languages*, ed. Anna Balakian (Budapest: Akadémiai Kiadó, 1984), 256, calls "*Das Jahr der Seele*...the peak of George's strictly Symbolist period"; *Kindlers Literatur Lexikon*, volume 6 (München: dtv, 1986), refers to it as "the swan song of the poet's early work"; and Johannes Klein, in "Stefan George," *Deutsche Literatur im 20. Jahrhundert. Strukturen und Gestalten*, ed. Otto Mann and Wolfgang Rothe (Bern: Francke Verlag, 1967), 25, claims that "*Das Jahr der Seele* bedeutet die erste Meisterschaft. George ist nun seiner Sprache sicher....[Er] ist um diese Zeit noch in besonderer Hinsicht Symbolist: er komponiert seine Gedichte auf ein anschauliches Symbol hin und kontrastiert dann."

2 Stefan George, *Das Jahr der Seele* (Berlin: Georg Bondi, 1930). Future line references to "Wir schreiten..." will refer to this edition and will follow in parentheses in the text. The cycle "Nach der Lese," of which "Wir schreiten..." is a part, first appeared in *Blätter für die Kunst* (Zweite Folge, V. Band), in February 1895. "Waller im Schnee" appeared in January 1896 (Dritte Folge, I. Band), and "Sieg des Sommers" in August 1896 (Dritte Folge, IV. Band), reprinted München: Küpper, 1968. These three parts which comprise the cycle were published together by Georg Bondi as *Das Jahr der Seele* in 1897.

3 With the exception of 27 "neutral" articles, prepositions and conjunctions, it is clearly evident that *all* lexemes (55 of a total of 92, or 60%) are selected and arranged to carry multiple meanings.

4 Gerhart Frommel, "Stefan George. Drei Maximen über Dichtung," *Castrum Peregrini*, LXXXIX (Amsterdam, 1969), 13-14; Gottfried Benn, "Probleme der Lyrik," *Essays. Reden. Vorträge. Gesammelte Werke in vier Bänden*, vol. I, ed. Dieter Wellershoff (Wiesbaden: Limes Verlag, 1959), 508; Gunter Grimm in *Metzler Autoren-Lexikon* contends that "als Gipfel dieser erlesenen Filigrankunst muß das 1897 erschienene Werk *Das Jahr der Seele* gelten, das Georges reinste Naturgedichte enthält" (Stuttgart: Metzler, 1986), 185.

5 Johannes Klein, "Stefan George," 24-25; Kurt Hildebrandt, *Das Werk Stefan Georges* (Hamburg: Dr. Ernst Hauswedell & Co., 1960), 93.

6 Friedrich Gundolf, *Stefan George* (Berlin: Georg Bondi, 1920), 130. See also Claude David, *Stefan George. Sein dichterisches Werk* (München: Carl Hanser, 1964), 140: "Man findet hier eine persönliche Lyrik, die dem Anlaß des Gedichtes Rechnung trägt, eine Dichtung des Herzens, für die die Gefühlsanalyse bedeutsamer ist als der Sinneseindruck oder die Idee." Paul Gerhard Klussmann concludes about the grammatical transformations of "wir" and of the extension of the authorial "I" toward a "you" that "es geht hier weniger um die Erscheinung der Parkwelt als um die Begegnung von Ich und Du." "Stefan George," *Die deutsche Lyrik*, ed. Benno von Wiese (Düsseldorf: Bagel, 1957), 273.

7 Manfred Durzak, *Zwischen Symbolismus und Expressionismus* (Stuttgart: W. Kohlhammer, 1974), 55. See also Manfred Gsteiger, "Expectation and Resignation," 259.

8 Poetic works of this type extend the natural polysemy inherent in certain words across the wording of the entire text. Such conductivity takes place when the succeeding words contain semes which echo those of previously registered words or images. Persistent instances of polysemy slice a single narrative into multiple synchronous

143

thematic layers. These tiers form themselves "between the lines," on semantic fields common among the aggregating semes, and produce their discrete messages. Such alternative readings, formally unarticulated, appear in the mind in "contrapuntal" concurrence with the main, stated, line of utterance. In concert, the tiers complement each other, and their synergy suggests the complexion of a *realiora* or "higher reality." (Mickiewicz, "Structuring the Content in Russian Avant-Garde Lyricism," *Avant Garde*, V/VI [Spring 1991], 89-107).

9 Klein, "Stefan George," 18, declares that "für die literarische Öffentlichkeit wurde George erst durch den großen Erfolg des *Jahrs der Seele* ein Begriff. Durch diesen Erfolg, der nach heutigen Begriffen erstaunlich ist, weil selbst Romane kaum noch eine Auflageziffer erreichen wie dieser Gedichtband, entstand das erwähnte Mißverständnis, daß man George unter die Impressionisten einreihen könnte." Cf. also David, *Stefan George*, 430: "Gundolf betont ebenfalls, daß *das Jahr der Seele* die Sammlung sei, die dem Durchschnittsleser am leichtesten eingehe. Er glaubt aber, daß diese Beliebtheit des *Jahrs der Seele* auf einem Mißverständnis beruhe."

10 William Butler Yeats, "The Symbolism of Poetry," *Essays and Introductions* (New York: Macmillan, 1961), 160.

11 Extensive semantic energy has been defined as "a thematic possibility for the mind to travel,…via various associations, from the primary referential point of a term to more and more noumenal spheres" (Mickiewicz, "The Acmeist Conception of the Poetic Word," *Toward a Definition of Acmeism*, special issue, *Russian Language* [Spring 1975], 60). Herein, a poetic datum seeks an ever widening set of association around a given item. As Goethe maintained, in a true symbol the particular represents the universal, not as a dream or shadow, but as a living and instantaneous revelation of the unfathomable. The presence of a greater or higher, perhaps unnameable, reality is thus reached along the chains of metonymic trajectories. Viacheslav Ivanov, the leading Russian Symbolist, founded thus his poetic theory in line with his formula: "*A realibus ad realiora. Per realia ad realiora.*" Three types of semantic energy in poetic language – "extensive," "intensive," and "fission" – are explored in Mickiewicz, 1991, *op.cit.*

12 Arthur R. Evans, "Das Antlitz Stefan Georges. Physiognomische Theorie und heroische Porträts," *Castrum Perigrini*, LXXXIX (1969), 63.

13 Arthur Symons, *The Symbolist Movement in Literature* (New York: E.F. Dutton, 1958), 71.

14 Evans, "Das Antlitz," 62. This correspondence between triumphant walking and a leonine character is presented in George's poem "Der Ringer."

15 Noteworthy in this context is Karl Bauer's portraiture of the twenty-year old George in which the sole iconographic addition is that of *Il Colleoni*, Verrocchio's equestrian statue of the 15th-century *condottiere* Bartolommeo Colleoni. See Evans, ibid., 57.

16 Ivanov, "The Precepts of Symbolism," *The Russian Symbolists. An Anthology of Critical and Theoretical Writings*, ed. and trans. Ronald E. Peterson (Ann Arbor: Ardis, 1986), 145. It was George's "absolute devotion to Holy Art, and a mystical sense for the unity of man and cosmos" that inspired Arnold Schoenberg to adopt the verse from *Das Buch der hängenden Gärten* (1904) for his exploration of the song form. Carl E. Schorske, *Fin-de-Siècle Vienna* (New York: Vintage Books, 1981), 349.

17 Cf. Werner Strodthoff's analysis of George's transition from "Seelenaristokratie" to "Seelenimperialismus" in *Stefan George. Zivilisationskritik und Eskapismus* (Bonn: Bouvier, 1976), 196-97.

144

III. THE SHAPE OF ECSTASY

18 Evans, "Das Antlitz," 56.

19 Evans, ibid., 56, 58.

20 The motifs of light and falling fruit call to mind the birth of Dionysus to Semele whom Zeus visited disguised as light. Semes sustaining a whole level of eroticism can be traced throughout the poem. In keeping with Nietzsche's conception, these semes maintain the Dionysian drive many Symbolists deemed an essential foundation for creative energy. Proximity of this poem with more overtly erotic verse such as "Entführung" (Abduction) and "Reifefreuden" (Ripeness Joys) in this same collection suggests the likelihood of George's awareness of Eros in this poem as well.

21 David, Stefan George, 161-62.

22 Gsteiger, "Expectation and Resignation," 14.

23 Philologically, vogelfrei is not a simile, but a designation for banned persons no longer protected by the law – "free game."

24 Blätter für die Kunst, Dritte Folge, I. Band. In March 1896 George equated "romanisch" with "Klarheit" and "Sonnigkeit" and regarded it as a positive influence on the "nordisch": "vom nordischen geist bleibt nicht viel zu lernen was er nicht schon besizt ohne die verzerrungen. vom romanischen jedoch die klarheit weiter sonnigkeit." Blätter für die Kunst, Dritte Folge, II. Band, 34.

25 "Den wert der dichtung entscheidet nicht der sinn ...sondern die form." Form is "durchaus nichts äusserliches [e.m.] sondern jenes tief erregende in maass und klang...." In the same essay George enlarges upon what this "maass" consists of: not solely a phonational container of meaning, "maass" is an architecture of interrelations of the parts, whether they be phonetic, rhythmic, syntactic, histrionic or semantic: "Der wert einer dichtung ist auch nicht bestimmt durch einen einzelnen wenn auch noch so glücklichen fund in zeile strofe oder grösserem abschnitt...die zusammenstellung...die notwendige folge des einen aus dem andern kennzeichnet erst die hohe dichtung," George, "Über Dichtung," Werke, I (München: Küpper, 1958), 530. Also, as Klussmann notes, since Goethe German love poetry treats nature as "free," whereas here the man-made trappings, "Gitter," "Tor," and "Bänke" are placed in the clausulas in marked, rhyming positions. The notion of "Flitter" and "Flor" as "man-made fine fabric" is thus highlighted by rhyming with "Gitter" and "Tor," "Stefan George," 270-71.

26 With minor subjective deviations, even the relative stress pattern of the five foot iamb is isochronic: - /-/-/-/-/-. The only mandatory exception is the inverted foot in line six.

27 The garden is characterized by Georg Lukács in Skizze einer Geschichte der neueren Literatur, 74, as "eine Insel des äußeren Wohlbehütetseins, wo kein Ufer der bürgerlichen Prosa zu sehen ist" [e.m.] (quoted in Strodthoff, Stefan George, 192). George's injunction against Fremdwörter appeared in March 1894: "wenn wir alle Fremdwörter auch die eingewurzelten – alle schlagworte gehören hierzu – wegließen so bliebe vieles leere ungesagt. Wenn ein satz der eines solchen wortes nicht entbehren kann fortfällt so wird weder sprache noch gesellschaft dadurch einen verlust erfahren."

28 Jan Aler, Symbol und Verkündung (München: Küpper, 1976), 27-29. The juvenalia of George was "das mühsame Werk eines spröden Anfängers, dem es vor allem um handwerkliche Sauberkeit geht" (ibid., 57). The "excessive" form consciousness of George seems to lie at the bottom of almost all of the negative criticism of George's poetry, not just of the early George.

29 George's Classicist position is apparent in his many essays. He speaks of "diese

äusserste sorge bei der feilung der gefüge; dieses ringen nach der höchsten formalen vollendung im werke; diese liebe für das Runde [das oft dasselbe wie das "kosmische" ist]; das in sich vollkommene; das nach allen seiten hin richtige; diese ablehnung des nur triebhaften skizzenhaften nicht-ganz-gekonnten; des halb überschüssigen halb unzulänglichen; das so lange ein fehler heimischer leistung war: diese liebe und diese ablehnung setzen mehr voraus als eine formel – nämlich eine geistige haltung ja eine lebensführung." *Blätter für die Kunst*, Folge IX, 1910, p. 1-2, 6-7, in *Literarische Manifeste der Jahrhundertwende 1890-1910*, ed. Erich Ruprecht and Dieter Bänsch (Stuttgart: Metzler, 1970), 253-54.

30 Eduard Mörike, *Mörikes Werke*, Harry Maync ed. (Leipzig, Vienna, n.d.), I, 75-6. "...An ironic mode lends a new dimension of meaning to a poem...the grove is idealized to the point at which it generates the numinous genius loci... the poem parallels [the Romantic] theory of landscape gardening by introducing the viewer into the spiritual landscape... Other readers stress the poetological implications...extrapolating the nature of poetic composition altogether" (Theodore Ziolkowski, "Mörike's 'Die schöne Buche': An Arboreal Meditation," *The German Quarterly*, LVI [1983], 4-13). We thank Professor Erdmann Waniek of Emory University for calling our attention to both the poem and the essay.

31 Novalis, "Hymnen an die Nacht," *Schriften*, ed. Paul Kluckhohn and Richard Samuel, vol. 1 (Stuttgart: Kohlhammer, 1960), 132, line 155. We would like to thank Professors Ann Mullaney and Maximilian Aue of Emory for calling these sources to our attention.

32 Ivanov, "The Precepts of Symbolism," in: *The Russian Symbolists. An Anthology of Critical and Theoretical Writings*, ed. and trans. Ronald E. Peterson (Ann Arbor: Ardis, 1986), 143.

33 Light as the divine power of creation (Zeus visits both Danae and Semele as light) gives rise to many Neo-Platonist echoes. It suffices to recall Dante, Arnaut Daniel, and, in our century, D'Annunzio, Ivanov, or Ezra Pound incorporating this mythical symbol.

34 George, "Über Dichtung ," 530.

35 Mandelstam thus perceives his own voice in his first extant poem (1908): *Zvuk ostorozhnyi i gluhoi / Ploda, sorvavshegosia s dreva,...* (The sound – cautious and muted – / Of a fruit that broke away from the tree). *Sobranie sochinenii*, Gleb Struve ed. (New York: Inter-language Literary Associates, 1964), I, 3.

36 Ray Jackendoff, 1983, quoted in Alan Cienki, *Spatial Cognition and the Semantics of Prepositions in English, Polish, and Russian* (München: Sagner Verlag, 1989), 1.

37 Hugo von Hofmannsthal, "Das Gespräch über Gedichte," *Gesammelte Werke in zehn Einzelbänden,* ed. Bernd Schoeller, vol. 7 (Frankfurt: Fischer, 1970), 498-99, 501.

38 Yeats, "The Symbolism of Poetry," 156-7.

39 Ivanov, "Mysli o simvolizme," *Trudy i dni*, no. 1 (1912); repr. in: *Sobranie sochinenii*, ed. Olga Shor, vol. 2 (Brussels, 1974), 611-12.

146

IV. SELF'S SHADES *and* SHADOWS

G.K. CHESTERTON'S POSSIBLE INFLUENCE on FRANZ KAFKA

BY MICHAEL O'NEAL RILEY, EMORY UNIVERSITY

In his book, *Conversations with Franz Kafka*, Gustav Janouch reports the following exchange:

> I [Janouch] was given two books by G.K. Chesterton, *Orthodoxy* and *The Man Who Was Thursday*.
>
> Kafka said, "He is so gay, that one might almost believe he had found God."
>
> "So for you laughter is a sign of religious feeling?"
>
> "Not always. But in such a godless time one must be gay. It is a duty. The ship's orchestra played to the end on the sinking *Titanic*. In that way one saps the foundations of despair."
>
> "Yet a forced gaiety is much sadder than an openly acknowledged sorrow."
>
> "Quite true. Yet sorrow has no prospects. And all that matters is prospects, hope, going forward. There is danger only in the narrow, restricted moment. Behind it lies the abyss. If one overcomes it, everything is different. Only the moment counts. It determines life."[1]

The conversations recorded in Janouch's book occurred in the period from 1920 to 1923, which was also the period of the gestation and writing of *The Castle*. It was Kafka's comments on life and art that most interested Janouch, and often he gives only the minimum of information as to what led up to those comments. Thus, any further discussion of Chesterton himself was not recorded, and only one of Kafka's statements ("He is so gay, that one might almost believe he had found God") refers directly to Chesterton. It is not even mentioned whether or not Kafka had read the two books named, but Kafka displayed a familiarity with the English writer, and Janouch was usually very careful to note when Kafka had not read a particular book that was mentioned.[2]

This familiarity raises some interesting questions. Although Franz Kafka's forty-one years (1883-1924) fell totally within the life span of Gilbert Keith Chesterton (1874-1936), and thus they existed in the world at the same time, it would be difficult to imagine two men with seemingly less in common – Chesterton the large, jovial, flamboyant, Catholic, Johnsonian man of letters, and Kafka the slender, quiet, introverted, Jewish, literary artist. However, a random sampling of thoughts from Chesterton and Kafka presents a certain similarity of outlook on several important issues. For instance, Chesterton wrote in *Orthodoxy*, "Ordinary things are more valuable than extraordinary things; nay, they are more extraordinary."[3] Kafka said, "He [Edschmid] claims that I introduce miracles into ordinary events. That is, of course, a serious error on his part. The ordinary is itself a miracle!" (Janouch, p. 74).

150 Again in *Orthodoxy*, Chesterton wrote:

> I have often had a fancy for writing a romance about an English yachtsman who slightly miscalculated his course and discovered England under the impression that it was a new island in the South Seas.... This at least seems to me the main problem for philosophers, and is the main problem of this book. How can we construe to be at once astonished at the world and yet at home in it? [pp. 9-10]

Kafka said, "Home is always different.... The old home is always new, if one lives consciously..." (Janouch, p. 104), and later, "There are some things one can only achieve by a deliberate leap in the opposite direction. One has to go abroad in order to find the home one has lost" (Janouch, p. 188). In a novel, *Manalive*, Chesterton has his hero literally flee in the opposite direction from his home until he has circled the globe in order to rediscover his home and see it in a new light.[4]

And in another conversation, Kafka commented on anarchists. He said:

> These people, who call themselves anarchists, are so nice and friendly, that one has to believe every word they say. At the same time – and by reason of the same qualities – one cannot believe that they are really such world destroyers as they claim.... They are very nice, jolly people. [Janouch, p. 86]

Kafka must have appreciated and understood Chesterton's characters in *The Man Who Was Thursday* who insisted that they were terrible anarchists, but were, in reality, "very nice, jolly people."

Similarities in thought and image; but is there more? It is becoming fairly common in studies of Chesterton, and particularly those devoted to his novel *The Man Who Was Thursday*, to make comparisons with Kafka,[5] although for Chesterton to have been influenced by Kafka was chronologically impossible.[6] But could Chesterton have been an influence on Kafka?

IT HAPPENED THAT MY first reading of Kafka's novel, *The Castle*, occurred immediately after a rereading of Chesterton's *The Man Who Was Thursday*, and I was struck by similarities in plot, structure, characters, approach, and theme between the books – similarities too numerous for me to be completely satisfied that they were all the result of coincidence. Further consideration of the two novels has convinced me that there is a real possibility that Kafka not only read *The Man Who Was Thursday* but that he was also consciously or unconsciously influenced by it when he wrote *The Castle*.

    The Man Who Was Thursday opens on a garden party in the small suburb of Saffron Park which "lay on the sunset side of London." It is beginning to get dark, and Gabriel Syme, a stranger, wanders into the party. It is never clear whether he was or was not invited. His presence is not questioned by the other guests. He introduces himself as a poet and is accepted as such, but he is really a member of the "New Detective Corps for the frustration of the great conspiracy," and had been hired by the mysterious "chief" whom he had met only in a dark room.

    As the result of an argument with Lucian Gregory, the established poet of Saffron Park, Syme is invited to a meeting of the London Branch of the General Council of the Anarchists of Europe which is being held to elect one of its members to fill a vacant position on the seven-member General Council. By a bizarre series of events, Syme manages to be elected to that position instead of Gregory and, thus, assumes another disguise. His code name is Thursday, and the six other members are named for the other days of the week. Sunday is the President of the Council.

    The first meeting of the seven takes place the next morning, and there Syme encounters the awesome and frightening figure of Sunday and the other five, evil-looking anarchists. He is shocked to find out that the objective of the group is the assassination of the French President, but probably the most terrifying moment of the meeting for him is when one of the other conspirators, Tuesday, is unmasked and revealed to be an agent of the New Detective Corps. Syme is relieved not to be the one to whom the President has been referring, but he also is made more aware of the danger of his position.

MICHAEL O'NEAL RILEY

That, however, is only the beginning, but the main body of the novel can be summarized very briefly: as the anarchists prepare for, and embark on, their journey to France, one by one, in nightmarish episodes of increasing complexity and suspense and not without touches of pure slapstick, each conspirator is revealed to be a detective in disguise – all except Sunday, that is, and all like Syme hired by the man in the dark room. There had been no plot against the French President. The detectives had been rushing to France not to assassinate him but to save him. By a kind of insane logic, what they had been trying to save him from was…themselves disguised as anarchists.

Kafka's novel is set in an unnamed village. It is late evening, and K., a stranger, enters one of the inns where some peasants are drinking beer. When accosted by a young man, K. introduces himself as the Land-Surveyor expected by the Count of the Castle. That is an obvious lie since K. had not known, until the man mentioned it, that there was a castle in that area. As if to give credence to his story, K. adds that he has two assistants who will be joining him later. The young man, whose name is Schwarzer, telephones to the Central Bureau at the Castle and is told that there is "not a trace of a land-surveyor" in their records. Before he can eject K. from the inn, the telephone rings, and Schwarzer is told that there was a mistake. For some reason, the Castle has decided to accept the story.

The next morning K. sets out to go to the Castle to meet the Count and to settle the terms of his employment, but he is strangely unable to get near it. The roads seem longer than he could have imagined, and he seems to pass the same houses again and again. Later that day two men appear and introduce themselves as the assistants he is expecting. K.'s story that he is the Land-Surveyor had been accepted, and so K. is forced to acknowledge the two men as his old assistants.

A messenger, Barnabas, then arrives with a letter from the Castle recognizing K.'s presence in the village. It is signed by Klamm, and this is the first time K. hears the name of the powerful and mysterious official whom he must go through to get in contact with the Castle. But K.'s attempts to meet with Klamm prove to be as futile as his attempts to reach the Castle, and with each attempt, his determination increases until the desire to make contact becomes an obsession.

As with *The Man Who Was Thursday*, after the exposition or introduction, the main body of *The Castle* can be briefly summarized; the rest of the novel deals with these attempts of K.'s, and the subsequent events that result from these attempts. He meets Klamm's mis-

tress, Frieda, and becomes engaged to her, but he gets no closer to
Klamm. K. is offered the job as school janitor, and to have someplace to
live, he accepts it until he can be confirmed as the Land-Surveyor. His
efforts to find out about and to reach Klamm and the Castle bring him
into contact with other people in the village, but his efforts fail and the
information he acquires is confusing and contradictory. As time passes,
he is able to make an uneasy place for himself in the village – not a
home where he feels secure and where he feels that he belongs, but
a place where he seems to be tolerated.

Kafka did not finish *The Castle*, but Thomas Mann, in his
introduction to the Schocken Books edition, summarizes the ending
as Kafka told it to some of his friends:

> K. dies – dies out of sheer exhaustion after his desperate ef-
> forts to get in touch with the Castle and be confirmed in his
> appointment. The villagers stand about the stranger's death-
> bed – when, at the very last moment, an order comes down
> from the Castle: to the effect that while K. has no legal claim
> to live in the community, yet the permission is nevertheless
> granted; not in consideration of his honest efforts, but owing
> to "certain auxiliary circumstances," it is permitted to him to
> settle in the village and work there.[7]

Chesterton, of course, did finish his novel, and the final three
chapters give the reader much the same feeling as stepping unexpected-
ly from shallow water into deep. After the six anarchists are exposed as
policemen, there is only Sunday left, and the ex-conspirators, including
Tuesday, meet in London and go to Sunday to find out who and what
he is. Sunday confuses them further by telling them that he is the man
in the dark room who hired them all. Then he eludes them and leads
them on a mad, comic chase through the city and out into the country-
side. When they do reach his lair, they find that he was literally leading
the chase because it had been his purpose to get them to that very spot.
Again the detectives realize that instead of directing their own actions,
they have had their actions directed from the outside.

The conspirators/detectives are given robes with designs on
them to correspond to the days of creation, but rather than being further disguises, the robes erase the disguises of detective and anarchist
and reveal them as what they really are, men. They are then led to seats
in a garden where Sunday, now robed as the seventh day, joins them,
and these men preside over a masquerade where the guests are dressed

like "all the common objects of field and street."

As the hour grows late and the party becomes quiet, Lucian Gregory reappears, clad completely in black, and announces that he is the "real anarchist." Syme is now able to answer him. Then, turning to Sunday, he reaches the point of understanding it all when his nightmare, or dream, or vision fades and he finds himself walking along, talking to the poet Gregory in a lane of Saffron Park. Chesterton ended the book in a garden with the ordinary, sane, and beautiful image of Gregory's sister cutting flowers "with the great unconscious gravity of a girl."

THE SIMILARITIES in the plots of *The Man Who Was Thursday* and *The Castle* are most striking in the openings. Saffron Park and the castle village are both described as they appear to Syme and to K. who are standing at far enough distances from them to have comprehensive views. Both Syme and K. are strangers. Syme enters a garden where a party is in progress, and K. enters an inn where customers are sitting and drinking; in both instances, a stranger enters an established community.

After the characters have made their entrances, they continue to follow parallel courses. Syme introduces himself as a poet, and K. introduces himself as a Land-Surveyor; both statements are lies,[8] and both lies are accepted. It is because both men are accepted at their own given identities that the later events in the novels can take place. Without Syme's disguise as a poet, he would not have been taken to the meeting of the anarchists where he assumes the further disguise of an anarchist. Without K.'s disguise as a Land-Surveyor engaged by the Count, he would have been thrown out of the inn and forced to continue his wandering.

For both men, these disguises are the source of tension, fear, and terror that each must endure. Syme feels compelled to try to defeat the plot against the French President before his impersonation is discovered, and he is haunted by the fear that Sunday knows the truth about him. K. is driven to try to legitimize his claims before his lie is made public, and he is haunted by the fear that Klamm and the Castle know he lied.

In each novel, the initial falsehood – Syme and K. presenting themselves as something they are not – performs another similar function: the falsehoods, to a great extent, rob these characters of the ability to direct their own lives. Syme must endure his terror without being able to call in outside help, and he is powerless to break from the course set by Sunday. He is like a puppet, and Sunday pulls the strings. K. is in a similar position. He dares not reject the two men (obviously spies from the Castle) who are presented to him as his assistants because to do so would be to admit that he had made up the story of having two assistants. He cannot tell anyone his secret, and like Syme, is at the mercy of the one pulling the strings.

After the main premise of each novel has been established, there are fewer similar incidents, but there are other kinds of parallels. The two novels proceed in a similar fashion – there is in each a series of nightmarish confrontations and interactions in which Syme and K. find that nothing is as it seems. In *The Man Who Was Thursday,* Syme becomes more bewildered rather than less so as each of the personifications of evil is revealed to be a detective in disguise, for those revelations do not reveal but confuse by weakening his faith in a logical world. The explanations do not explain but suggest questions even more frightening than those with which he was first confronted. As Syme hears the stories of each of the ex-conspirators, he finds that nothing adds up and that the information each of them can give him about Sunday is confusing and often contradictory.

The same process occurs in *The Castle.* K. talks to the landlord, to Frieda, to the mayor, to Olga, to the landlady, to Amalia – in fact, to almost everyone – about Klamm and the Castle, and none of his questions is satisfactorily answered. The answers contradict each other; each time he feels he is about to understand something, it slips away from him. The people he talks to speak what seem to be understandable sentences, but over and over again the end of a statement will contradict its beginning. The conversations turn around on themselves, and at the finish of one he knows no more than he did at its start. K.'s questions create more questions, and the answers he receives, like those Syme receives, suggest that there is something far larger behind it all.

Syme and K. strive for security, for stability, and for an understanding of what happens to them, and those are the things that are denied to them. They are allowed to go forward, but without any real sense of progressing. Syme solves mysteries and finds himself without a solution. K. gathers information and finds he knows nothing.

Both books are filled with such strange, convoluted logic, and made up of such shifting, quicksilver-like patterns, that it is not easy to decide just how to describe the development of the plots. The same thing happening over and over to Syme, just as the same thing happening over and over to K., does not seem to constitute any traditional plot pattern. Both novels present dreamscapes, but calling them novels or dreamscapes does not make the problem any easier, for the novel form includes a great variety of different works and the pattern of every dream can be different.

C.S. Lewis, who had a great admiration for *The Man Who Was Thursday*, wrote of *The Castle*, "I first heard the story of Kafka's *Castle* in conversation and afterwards read the book for myself. The reading added nothing. I had already received the myth, which was all that mattered."[9] Such a judgment is unfair to Kafka's art, as well as to Chesterton's, because the structures of the two novels – at least as far as Kafka completed *The Castle* – are identical. It is soon as obvious to the first-time reader of *The Man Who Was Thursday* that each anarchist will turn out to be a policeman in disguise as it is to the first-time reader of *The Castle* that K. will not reach the Castle or make contact with Klamm. The interest lies in the way each author treats each new confrontation or attempt, and the form that best fits the structure or pattern of these two novels comes from the sister-art of music.

I HAVE USED the word "development" in reference to the plots. This word, not in its usual sense of "expansion" or "growth," but in its specialized musical sense of "the exploiting of the possibilities of thematic material by means of contrapuntal elaboration, modulation, rhythmical variation, etc.,"[10] describes the pattern of these two novels accurately.

Development is important to almost all musical forms, but the one form that is almost wholly made up of development is that of the "variation," which is "the process of modifying a theme, figure or passage in such a way that the resulting product is recognizably derived from the original."[11] Within the variations, the composer can do what he or she likes with the theme – fragment it, invert it, vary the rhythm, vary the tempo, the harmony, the mood, etc. – as long as the theme is recognizable. In a series of variations, each one usually tends to increase in complexity, and the entire set can be preceded by an introduction, rounded out with a fugue, and capped with a coda. Chesterton's plot for *The Man Who Was Thursday* is in this full form.

After the introduction – that is, after Syme has arrived at the anarchists' meeting with Gregory – the theme of disguising and its inversion, revealing, is stated: Syme assumes the disguise of an anarchist. It may be argued that Syme has already assumed the disguise of

a poet at the party, but that was, I believe, no more than a preview fragment of the theme in the introduction. Syme had been a poet before he
became a policeman, and while it is entirely possible to be a poet and
a policeman, it is not possible to be a policeman and an anarchist. The
first variation is very simple: at the meeting of the seven, Sunday announces that one of the members is an impostor, and Gogol, Tuesday,
is revealed to be a detective. The second involves much terror for Syme
as he, alone, is followed by the old Professor de Worms, who turns
out to be neither old nor an anarchist. And the variations continue,
increasing in complexity, through the episode where Syme, with his
back to the sea, is confronted by an army of "anarchists," to the last
one where the six detectives/anarchists confront Sunday to find out
who he is and who they are.

As was mentioned above, at the solution of each mystery of
identity nothing is answered and larger questions are raised. This pattern follows a musical logic where each variation, although it may reach
a conclusion that is appropriate for that one variation, leads into the
next, more complex one until that point is reached where the composer
has done all that he or she can do – or wants to do – with the theme.
Then, if the composer so decides, a fugue begins, and this is exactly
what happens when the detectives/anarchists confront Sunday. He re-
solves nothing for them, but takes the theme of disguising and revealing and turns it into the great, joyful fugue of the mad dash across London. The detectives/anarchists chasing/following Sunday, and Sunday/
the man in the dark room fleeing/leading them are like the voices of a
fugue which combine with each other, change places, invert, enter in
stretto, etc. There is no set resolution to a fugue either. It also can go
on as long as the composer's inventiveness holds out, and then it stops.
Sunday's fugue stops at his house, and there, all seven of them arrayed
in the disguises that reveal, is played the great, ceremonial coda which
ends the work.

The Castle also offers an exhaustive set of variations on a
theme. Like Chesterton, Kafka, after his introduction, presents the
theme: K. will try to reach the Castle and talk to Klamm; and its inversion: K. will meet Klamm and through him reach the Castle. This
theme is also prefigured in the introduction when K. on his first morning sets out to explore the village and thinks that he might walk as far
as the Castle gate. The first variation begins when K. tries to accompany
Barnabas from the inn to the Castle and ends up at Barnabas' house
instead. The variations continue and grow in complexity. K. attempts

to meet Klamm through Frieda but acquires a fiancée instead; K. meets with the mayor to find out more about the Castle, but the result is that K. is offered the job of school janitor; and so on, as a life is built up for K. in the village without his ever achieving his purpose.

The episodes flow along in a musical way, and also very musical is Kafka's use of words in the conversations between K. and the other characters. It is difficult to discuss those conversations in terms of logic, but how easily musical expressions fit them: the changes back and forth between the major and the minor moods; the subtle modulations that transport the reader into a different key before he or she realizes what has happened; the circular, waltz-like melodies that can arrive back at the starting point, contradicting the reader's sense of a forward progression; the canon-like figurations that keep the same theme going around and around; the ensemble passages where all the characters may be talking at cross-purposes, but where all their words fit together to form a seamless whole.

Because Kafka did not finish *The Castle*, it is perhaps fruitless to speculate about what pattern the finale would have followed; the novel, as it stands, has its own unique effect, leaving the reader with the feeling that K.'s attempts and failures go on for eternity. Even without Kafka's intended ending, as related by his friends, the myth seems complete. Yet, one cannot help wondering, especially in light of Chesterton's novel, if in being denied Kafka's treatment of K.'s death scene where "the villagers stand around the stranger's deathbed" – where all the people K. had encountered during the course of the novel are gathered together in one place – we have not also been denied a fugue of convoluted logic, ambiguity, and literary brilliance that would have surpassed anything else in the novel.

Like music, then, and like dreams, these novels attempt to make their effects felt more in the subconscious than in the conscious mind. And although Chesterton is, as Kafka said, "joyous," that should not make us miss the fact that no more is resolved in *The Man Who Was Thursday* than is in *The Castle*.

ALONG WITH THE SIMILARITIES of structure and effect, it is the resemblance of K. and Klamm to Syme and Sunday that more than anything
else convinces me that Kafka not only read *The Man Who Was Thursday*,
but also remembered it when he wrote *The Castle*. Several of the ways
in which Syme and K. resemble each other have already been mentioned: both are strangers, outsiders; both enter established communities; both create false identities for themselves; both are in conflict with
some great authority; both have the illusion of making progress; both
are manipulated by forces beyond their control; and neither finds what
he thinks he is looking for. There are other similarities, of course, as
well as many differences (one of the most important being that Syme
does not fall below a certain standard of behavior or honor in his
actions – his promise to Gregory is not broken, for example – while
K. seems to resort to any kind of machination to achieve his purpose);
but probably the greatest likeness is that the most pressing problem
for both men is that of identity – "Who am I?"

159

Syme is progressively a poet, a detective, and an anarchist,
and then, what? The state of the world makes him turn from poet into
detective; to save the world, he becomes an anarchist; but each identity
is taken from him. There is no need to be an anarchist because all the
anarchists are detectives, and the world is not threatened by a conspiracy. He cannot be a detective because the man in the dark room who
made him one is also the head of the anarchists who do not exist. And
his failure as a poet had already driven him to the contemplation of
suicide. All the disguises fail and leave him with the question, "Who
am I?" During the chase across London, Dr. Bull says,

> "…we are six men going to ask one man what he means."
> "I think it is a bit queerer than that," said Syme.
> "I think it is six men going to ask one man what they mean."[12]

In *The Castle*, K. creates an identity for himself by his lie and
then spends the rest of his time trying to prove that identity. More than
telling who a person is, identity also implies a sense of belonging and
even a sense of security. K. says he is the Land-Surveyor engaged by
the Count, but the Castle neither absolutely confirms nor absolutely
denies this, and K. cannot gain his security or feeling of belonging
until it can be definitely established. Along the way, he picks up several
other identities – the fiancé of Frieda, the master of two assistants,
the school janitor – but he cannot be satisfied until the Castle tells
him who he really is.

MICHAEL O'NEAL RILEY

At Sunday's house when the six detectives put on their robes, Syme finds that those "disguises did not disguise, but reveal," and what was revealed was that Syme was a man – an ordinary man, like K., in a world beyond his comprehension; a world where no one is guaranteed security and the feeling of belonging, but where each man must make his own place and make his own compromise with an alien environment. Syme did it without realizing it. He looked at evil and found good instead. He came to feel at home because he was able to communicate with and relate to fellow creatures. The final mysteries were not revealed to him, but he was not alone in the awe and terror of them; other men, his fellow conspirators, experienced the same thing. K. also made a place without being aware of it. He never reached the Castle nor received confirmation of his right to be there, but he acquired a mate, he was given a job, and he became acquainted with people. In those ways he did become part of the village. Syme and K. were never who they thought or wished they were, but they did all that men can; they kept trying.

In the characters of Sunday and Klamm, the authors have built up entities so mysterious, contradictory, and complex that, although they admit many interpretations, they remain enigmas. Sunday and Klamm dominate their respective books as the sources of all the frustration and confusion of the main characters. Each is more talked about than seen, but their presence as incomprehensible authorities overshadows all of Syme's and K.'s actions, and in each case the question of their identity becomes tied up with Syme's and K.'s search for identity.

Apart from saying that Sunday was more a symbol of nature than of God,[13] Chesterton himself declined to explain his most mysterious creation. Sunday is introduced as the President of the General Anarchist Council of Europe, but he is also the man in the dark room who is such an important figure on the side of law and order. He is described by Syme as the personification of evil when viewed from the back and a god when from the front. He is described as a frightening individual capable of using "a voice that made men drop drawn swords," yet he is also described as looking like a "colossal urchin" and throwing nonsense notes to his pursuers in the mad chase across London.[14] Approaching his presence, Syme can feel that he is nearing "the head-quarters of hell," but in his presence, Syme can accept Sunday's statement that he is "the peace of God."

And Sunday makes a different impression on everyone who

comes in contact with him. Syme says to the other detectives,

> Each man of you finds Sunday quite different.... Bull finds
> him like the earth in spring. Gogol like the sun at noon-day.
> The Secretary is reminded of the shapeless protoplasm, and
> the Inspector of the carelessness of virgin forests. The Profes-
> sor says he is like a changing landscape. [pp. 174-75, ch. 14]

This episode parallels the various descriptions of Klamm:

> ...he's reported as having one appearance when he comes into
> the village and another on leaving it, after having his beer he
> looks different from what he does before it, when he's awake
> he's different from when he's asleep, when he's alone he's dif-
> ferent from when he's talking to people, and – what is com-
> prehensible after all that – he's almost another person up in
> the Castle. And even within the village there are considerable
> differences in accounts given of him, differences as to his
> height, his bearing, his size, and cut of his beard. [pp. 230-31,
> ch. 15]

Klamm, too, plays double roles. He is the one who recognizes K. as the
Land-Surveyor, but also the one who denies K. the confirmation in the
job. He frequents the inns in the village like an ordinary man, yet his
name is evoked like that of a god – "In the name of Klamm." His presence is felt everywhere, yet K. is unable to find him. He is described as
inspiring unceasing loyalty even though he has completely forgotten
the person. He "gives nothing of himself" (p. 103, ch. 6), but one can
have what one likes from him.

The names of these two great, dominating figures are first
spoken in almost offhanded ways. "What do you call this tremendous
President of yours?" Syme asks, and Gregory replies, "We generally call
him Sunday." K. asks, "What's his name? I couldn't read his signature,"
and Barnabas answers, "Klamm." At those inauspicious moments, Sunday and Klamm seem unimportant and easily accessible to Syme and
K., but those figures grow in authority and complexity and recede to
unimagined distances the more Syme and K. try to approach them. K.
is even told that, although he has been able to view Klamm through a
peephole and through a keyhole, Klamm will never talk to him, and
this is an inversion of Sunday in the guise of the man in the dark room
who will let Syme talk to him but not see him.

All of Syme's and K.'s attempts to penetrate the disguises of those figures and to make some logical sense of them fail because Sunday and Klamm are not in disguise. They really are the paradoxes that they appear to be because they are the mystery and the contradictions of existence.

In the puzzlement and bewilderment that beset both main characters when they confront the mysteries of Sunday and Klamm, there is a sense of the frustration that children feel when confronting the adult world: the same sense of incomprehensibility and the same sense that some gigantic joke is being played on them. And with respect to God, or to the universe, or to existence itself, Syme and K. are both children. To them it all seems confusing and arbitrary. To a child a person is either good or bad – pleasure is equated with goodness and pain with evil. It is impossible for a child's immature mind to accept that sometimes these equations may be reversed. That same feeling can be projected to man and the universe. Gogol's statement, said "with the absolute simplicity of a child," echoes this: "I wish I knew why I was hurt so much" (p. 188, ch. 15).

It seems to me that both Chesterton and Kafka took this child's view of the world and applied it to man's vision of the universe. One of the things that bothered Kafka throughout his life was the lack of understanding between himself and his father. He always battled the authority figure of his father from the point of view of his father's child. Chesterton was a late developer both physically and emotionally, and because of that, he spent more time than most among the images and perceptions of childhood. Some have speculated that the sudden development of his emotional and physical capabilities was the spark that ignited his particular trauma – the experience that drove him to a contemplation of suicide and later provided the impetus for *The Man Who Was Thursday*. Chesterton never forgot that feeling that some gigantic joke was being played on him, and he knew that the levity of God is too great for the minds of men. He ended his book *Orthodoxy* in this way: "There was some one thing that was too great for God to show us when He walked upon our earth; and I have sometimes fancied that it was His mirth" (p. 160).

Kafka, too, seemed to feel that man was being pushed and pulled about, that man's predicament was a source of amusement to some great authority – to the universe. One of the great differences between Kafka and Chesterton was how each reacted to that feeling. Chesterton recorded various reactions of different men who had come in conflict with the mystery of existence. His spokesman, Syme, says,

> I am grateful to you [Sunday], not only for wine and hospi-
> tality here, but for many a fine scamper and free fight. But
> I should like to know. My soul and heart are as happy and
> quiet here as this old garden, but my reason is still crying out.
> I would like to know. [p. 188, ch. 15]

And in a sense we recognize Kafka's position in Friday's statement: "I
am not happy...because I do not understand. You let me stray a little
too near to hell" (p. 188, ch. 15). Both reactions are those of ordinary
men to the mysteries of God and existence.

CHESTERTON, LIKE KAFKA, was fascinated by the ordinary and the commonplace. His images, metaphors, and similes are taken from the world
around him, and, although there may be many outrageous things in
The Man Who Was Thursday, there is almost nothing that could not
happen or exist in the everyday world. Kafka too, in forming his fantasies, used the ordinary things of the world with which he was most
familiar: the law; the bureaucracy of his office and his city; the dark,
medieval streets of Prague; the ordinary people with whom he came
in contact. Chesterton was more flamboyant than Kafka, but then, his
world was not a dull, bureaucracy-laden insurance company, rather the
freer, boisterous, and probably (in some ways) more common world
of Fleet Street. Their worlds may have differed, but they spun their
fantasies from their respective worlds in much the same way.

Chesterton's fantasy is made up of the light and shade of our
world. His fairyland is created by the light of Chinese lanterns in a garden or the illumination of a tree by a common lamp post. His monsters
or supernatural beings are created by the differing perceptions one has
on viewing a person from the back and from the front, or the change in
expression a pair of dark spectacles or a false beard will give a perfectly
ordinary face. Chesterton, like Kafka, was continually looking at things
from new angles, and from each perspective he viewed objects and
people with a freshness of vision as if seeing them for the first time.

Back-versus-front symbolism was important to Chesterton and
appears in many of his works. It is especially effective in *The Man Who
Was Thursday* when Syme first sees Sunday:

> I only saw his back; and when I saw his back, I knew he was
> the worst man in the world.... In fact, I had at once the revolt-
> ing fancy that this was not a man at all, but a beast dressed
> up in men's clothes.... Then I entered the hotel, and coming

round the other side of him, saw his face in the sunlight. His face frightened me, as it did everyone; but not because it was brutal, not because it was evil. On the contrary, it frightened me because it was so beautiful, because it was so good.... There was the same white hair, the same great, grey-clad shoulders that I had seen from behind. But when I saw him from behind I was certain he was an animal, and when I saw him in front I knew he was a god. [p. 175, ch. 14]

Kafka also uses shifting angles of perception, that on occasion create a back-versus-front symbolism. In the inn, K. sees a painting which may be of Klamm:

... he noticed a dark portrait in a dim frame on the wall. He had already observed it from his couch by the stove, but from that distance he had not been able to distinguish any details and *had thought that it was only a plain back to the frame.* But it was a picture after all, as now appeared, the bust portrait of a man about fifty. [p. 10, ch. 1, italics mine]

Often the shift in perception only requires really looking closely at an ordinary object, as when the landlady shows K. a photograph. K. says it is "a young man...lying on a board stretching himself and yawning." Urged to "look more carefully," he sees that it is a "young man taking a high leap" (p. 101, ch. 6). Syme had only to look closer at the man in the black spectacles who frightened him so much to see that the man was quite ordinary and that it was the spectacles that were frightening.

Because each new angle is a new vision, the world is a dream-like place of constantly shifting patterns, where things can change into their opposites, where nothing is as it seems – the most ordinary object or person can change into something of terror or of joy. Kafka had a man change into an insect; Chesterton had a beast change into a god. The end results may be radically different, but the kinds of vision that could see each transformation are, I believe, very similar.

The Man Who Was Thursday and *The Castle* both embody dream worlds – in fact, the subtitle of Chesterton's novel is "A Nightmare"; but there is no sudden tumbling down the rabbit hole as in *Alice in Wonderland* to make the reader aware of that form. The dream world in each one is entered so subtly and gradually that the reader is lulled into a false sense of security by the ordinariness of the narrative. We need only to examine the openings of the two novels to see this:

The suburb of Saffron Park lay on the sunset side of London, as red and ragged as a cloud of sunset. It was built of a bright brick throughout; its sky-line was fantastic, and even its ground plan was wild. It had been the outburst of a speculative builder, faintly tinged with art, who called its architecture sometimes Elizabethan and sometimes Queen Anne, apparently under the impression that the two sovereigns were identical.

It was late in the evening when K. arrived. The village was deep in snow. The Castle hill was hidden, veiled in mist and darkness, nor was there even a glimmer of light to show that a castle was there. On the wooden bridge leading from the main road to the village, K. stood for a long time gazing into the illusory emptiness above him.

Neither of these passages would alert a new reader that he or she, like the two strangers Syme and K., is about to enter the world of dreams. They are deceptively simple and straightforward, and, in the case of Chesterton, amiably amusing.

So too, are the two further passages, each just sentences removed from the ones already quoted. K. entered the inn and sat down on a bag of straw where "he soon fell asleep" – the very next sentence is, "But very shortly he was awakened." And in *The Man Who Was Thursday*, the description of Saffron Park continues, "The place was not only pleasant, but perfect, if once he could regard it not as a deception but rather as a dream." A stranger entering a party; a stranger entering an inn – both entering a dream world where the dream elements appear slowly and at first are not noticed, rather like a few wrong notes in a piece of music. Inexorably the wrong notes multiply until it becomes an entirely new piece of music. And in both cases the very ordinariness of the narrative has paved the way and smoothed out the transition so that one is in the midst of the nightmare before one knows it, and one wonders how one got there.

The reader is aware of it on the second and future readings when even such simple passages can be seen to be filled with clues. "Saffron Park lay on the sunset side of London" – already we have an indication of the approach of the time of dreaming or death. "Fantastic" and "wild" are used to describe the suburb's design, and it is compared to something as insubstantial and dream-like as a "cloud of sunset."

The suburb is described not as the product of a builder, but as an "outburst." And with knowledge of the remainder of the book, even the line about Queen Elizabeth and Queen Anne takes on new meaning, for in a dream the two queens might well be identical. In fact, the only way Saffron Park makes sense to Syme is "as a dream."

In Kafka's opening, it is late evening – time for dreaming – when K. arrives. The Castle – the substance of the dream – is described as hidden. K. is standing on a bridge that is the entrance to the village, and the symbolism is obvious; a bridge leads from one place to another, from one kind of existence to another. It is the entrance to a new world. From the bridge, K. stares up at the "illusory emptiness." He does not see the Castle or even know it is there. He falls asleep soon after entering the inn and almost immediately "wakes up," and it is only after that fall into sleep that the Castle becomes known and is visible to him. By such subtle means, the ordinary village of the beginning of *The Castle* is, by its end, turned into a village unlike anything in this waking world and the normal, everyday world of Gabriel Syme has literally been turned around.

Chesterton wrote in an early essay, "We find marvellous things in dreamland…. But the one thing that we never find is the thing we are looking for…. Dreams are, if I may so express it, like life only more so…. We have gratitude, but never certainty."[15] Neither Syme nor K. found what he was seeking or the answers to his questions, but both of them continued to go forward. In his conversation with Janouch Kafka said: "all that matters is prospects, hope, going forward." That sounds simple, but going forward is perhaps the most courageous thing a man can do because each step is a step into the unknown and can bring him face to face with happiness or fear, with pain or joy. And further, from what base is man to step forward when his world is always shifting and changing? Where is he to find security and home? And finally, there is the question that Gogol asked, "I wish I knew why I was hurt so much" – a question asked as far back as the Book of Job (a particular favorite of both Chesterton and Kafka), and probably asked by the first thinking human being. Is there a Being so far beyond the understanding of man to whom it all makes sense?

Syme went forward and confronted each experience with courage and honor, and what had appeared evil threw off its disguise and revealed itself as good. This is not to say that Chesterton did not believe that there is real evil in the world – his reintroduction of Gregory as the "real anarchist" makes that point clear – but he did

166

want to convey that much that seems incomprehensible and frightening is in reality not, if only it is viewed from the proper angle. K. also went forward, and he also showed great courage. Although he did not encounter the immediate kinds of terror that Syme did, he went forward in the shadow of a much greater terror: the fear that the great bureaucracy, like so much Kafka was familiar with, was merely a mask for incompetence and the lack of an intelligent authority – the fear that if he ever did reach the Castle, he might find it empty.

Ultimately, it may be just that fear – modern man's fear of an empty universe which Kafka portrayed so brilliantly – that makes Chesterton and Kafka seem, at first glance, so different. C.S. Lewis asked:

> Is the difference simply that the one is 'dated' and the other contemporary? Or is it rather that while both give a powerful picture of the loneliness and bewilderment which each one of us encounters in his (apparently) single-handed struggle with the universe, Chesterton, attributing to the universe a more complicated disguise, and admitting the exhilaration as well as the terror of the struggle, has got in rather more...?[16]

Perhaps, then, it is the differences in attitude to man's "single-handed struggle with the universe" that have kept us from realizing the great likenesses between the two men. Kafka so accurately reflects modern man's preoccupation with the oppressiveness of the struggle, but Chesterton was no less frightened by the struggle than was Kafka. He, however, recognized what few in our century have: the enjoyment, the "exhilaration," the joy to be had from "many a fine scamper and free fight."

NOTES

1   Gustav Janouch, *Conversations With Kafka*, 2nd. ed., rev. and enl., trans. Goronwy Rees (New York: A New Directions Book, 1971), pp. 94-5. I first became aware of this reference when it was quoted in a letter from John F. Maguire printed in *The Chesterton Review*, III (Fall-Winter, 1976-77), pp. 161-62.

2   *The Man Who Was Thursday* and *Orthodoxy* were both translated into German in 1909; *Heretics* in 1912; *The Innocence of Father Brown* in 1913; *Magic* in 1914; *Charles Dickens* in 1916; and *The Defendant* in 1917. Kafka also spoke and read Czech, and the Czech translations of Chesterton were: *The Man Who Was Thursday* in 1913; *Heretics* in 1915; *Orthodoxy* in 1918; *The Innocence of Father Brown* in 1918 (twice); *The Flying Inn* in 1919; and *The Napoleon of Notting Hill* in 1921. See: John Sullivan, *G.K. Chesterton: A Bibliography* (London: University of London Press, 1958), p. 180; John Sullivan, *G.K. Chesterton Continued: A Bibliographical Supplement* (London:

MICHAEL O'NEAL RILEY

University of London Press, 1968), pp. 77-78; and John Sullivan, "Chesterton Bibliography Continued," *The Chesterton Review*, IV (Spring-Summer, 1978), pp. 269-70.

Chesterton was well known in the Czech literary community in Prague. Karel Čapek, who is best known in this country for his plays *R.U.R.* and *The Makropoulous Secret*, was one of Chesterton's greatest admirers, and it is probable that Kafka read Čapek's enthusiastic review in 1920 of the Czech translation of Chesterton's *The Flying Inn*. For information about Chesterton's influence on Čapek, see: B.R. Bradbrook, "Chesterton and Karel Čapek: A Study in Personal and Literary Relationship," *The Chesterton Review*, IV (Fall-Winter, 1977-78), pp. 89-103.

3   G.K. Chesterton, *Orthodoxy* (New York: Dodd, Mead & Co., 1908; and Garden City, NY: Doubleday, Image Books, 1959), p. 46.

4   G.K. Chesterton, *Manalive* (New York: John Lane Co., 1912).

5   Some examples: "Or read again *The Man Who Was Thursday*. Compare it with another good writer, Kafka." C.S. Lewis, "Period Criticism" in *On Stories and Other Essays on Literature*, ed. Walter Hooper (New York and London: Harcourt Brace Jovanovich, 1982), p. 116.

"...*The Ball and the Cross*, and its successor, easily his finest novel, *The Man Who Was Thursday* – two novels in which he probed as effectively as Kafka, and in something of the same manner, the human predicament in a world ever more terrifying, and the relationship of man with God." Dudley Barker, *G.K. Chesterton: A Biography* (New York: Stein and Day, 1975), p. 175.

"This [*The Man Who Was Thursday*] is like a story by Kafka, in which stairs melt into crumbling sand, and horses gallop but carry one nowhere." Garry Wills, *Chesterton, Man and Mask* (New York: Sheed & Ward, 1961), p. 40.

"...Chesterton restrained himself from being Edgar Allan Poe or Franz Kafka, but something in the makeup of his personality leaned toward the nightmarish, something secret, and blind, and central." Jorge Luis Borges, "On Chesterton" in *Other Inquisitions: 1937-1952*, trans. Ruth L. C. Simms, Introduction by James E. Irby (Austin: Univ. of Texas Press, 1964), p. 84.

6   It would be interesting to be able to quote something by Chesterton about Kafka, but the admirable *Index to G.K. Chesterton*, which thoroughly covers ninety-one of his books, contains no entry for Kafka. *An Index to G.K. Chesterton*, edited, with an Introduction by Joseph W. Sprug, Preface by the Rev. James J. Kortendick, S.S., Ph.D. (Washington, D.C.: The Catholic University of America Press, 1966).

7   Franz Kafka, *The Castle*, trans. Willa and Edwin Muir, with additional materials trans. Eithne Wilkins and Ernst Kaiser, with an Homage by Thomas Mann (New York: Alfred A. Knopf, 1954; New York: Schocken Books Paperback, 1974), p. xvii.

8   Syme had been a poet before he became a detective, and K. may well have been a Land-Surveyor, but Syme's presence in Saffron Park was as a detective, and K. had not been engaged by the Count.

9   C.S. Lewis, *George MacDonald: An Anthology* (London: Geoffrey Bles; The Centenary Press, 1946), p. 16.

10   J.A. Westrup and F.Ll. Harrison, *The New College Encyclopedia of Music* (New York: W. W. Norton, 1960), p. 186.

11   *Ibid.*, p. 692.

12   G.K. Chesterton, *The Man Who Was Thursday* (New York: Dodd, Mead and Company, 1908; New York: G. P. Putnam's Sons, Capricorn Books, 1970), p. 158, ch. 13.

13 G.K. Chesterton, *Autobiography* (New York: Sheed and Ward, 1936), p. 98.

14 It is interesting that, when Janouch asked Kafka about his writings, Kafka replied, "They're only attempts, scraps of paper thrown to the winds." *Conversations with Kafka*, p. 142.

15 G.K. Chesterton, "The Meaning of Dreams" (1901) in *Lunacy and Letters*, ed. Dorothy Collins (New York: Sheed and Ward, 1958), p. 31.

16 C.S. Lewis, "Period Criticism" (see n. 5 above), pp. 116-17.

169

MICHAEL O'NEAL RILEY

VLADIMIR VOLKOFF, or the FECUNDITY of EVIL

BY JOHN M. DUNAWAY, MERCER UNIVERSITY

I n his *Crossroads: Essays on the Catholic Novelists,* Albert Sonnenfeld wrote that the sub-genre of the "Catholic novel" was a dying form. He called his book "a kaleidoscopic portrait of the major Catholic novelists of the last fifty years. The book constitutes an elegy to what I perceive as a dying form in a time of radical change for the Church and for those who saw the drama of Catholic salvation as material for modern fiction."[1] In the face of the rapidly accelerating secularization of contemporary society and even of the Church, it would be hard not to agree with Sonnenfeld. However, if one looks more closely at the contemporary literary scene, one finds evidence that, while there is nothing today to compare with the richness of the Catholic revival of the 1920s, the world of fiction writers has not been entirely abandoned to the unbeliever. In the United States, such a figure as Walker Percy commanded a significant reading public, and his work promises to have lasting importance. In France, the deaths of Bernanos and Mauriac and the slowing of the venerable Julien Green had left a yawning vacuum by the late '70s, it is true. And notwithstanding Michel Tournier's protestations to the contrary, there was no rising Christian novelist of notable stature when Vladimir Volkoff burst on the scene in 1979 with his celebrated metaphysical espionage novel, *Le retournement,* and in 1980 with his four-volume saga *Les humeurs de la mer.*

Perhaps Sonnenfeld is right in concluding that the Catholic novel in France is a thing of the past. Perhaps no one will ever again rival the spiritual/erotic drama in Julien Green's fiction, the tragic portrayal of provincial Pharisaism in Mauriac's, or the heroic struggle against evil incarnate in that of Bernanos. But if there is indeed a breath of life remaining in the sub-genre of Christian fiction in France today, it must certainly be sought in the works of Volkoff.

I

VLADIMIR VOLKOFF makes his home in the central Georgia community
of Macon. He is one of the most popular and controversial novelists in
France today. His writings have won him such distinctions as the Prix
Jules Verne (1963), the Prix Chateaubriand (1979), and the Grand Prix
du Roman awarded by the French Academy (1982). He is a highly visible member of the community of French literati, appearing often on
television talk shows, being interviewed by most major dailies and
magazines, and frequently staging dramatic productions in Paris and
Brussels.

  In view of such notoriety among French readers, Volkoff's
relative obscurity in the country where he resides is indeed puzzling.
The English translations of his novels rarely go into paperback editions.
He is never mentioned by the *New York Review of Books* or the scholarly
journals, and the coverage he has received in Macon and Atlanta newspapers has scarcely risen above the level of the "local writer makes
good" theme. These articles are often accompanied by photographs of
a short, bespectacled gentleman with a neatly trimmed beard, a formal,
military bearing, and a mischievous glint in his eye. They usually make
mention of his colorful background, his service as a French intelligence
officer in the Algerian war, his White Russian parentage (especially the
fact that he is a great-nephew of Tchaikovsky), and his hobbies of hunting, fencing, and chess.

  Who is this Vladimir Volkoff, alias Victor Duloup, alias Lavr
Divomlikoff? And what is he doing in Macon, Georgia? For one thing,
he is a journalist's dream. He always has a ready answer for any question, he possesses the histrionic flair of the actor who never needs a
script, and he takes great delight in playing the devil's advocate or coming up with the most unexpected opinions. He might have been better
prepared to respond than Jean Cocteau was when he first met Diaghilev. Cocteau tells us in his diary that the impresario's first words to him
were simply: "Etonne-moi."

  An actor himself, Volkoff organized his own French-language
theatrical troupe while living in Atlanta. Like Molière, he exemplified
the total man of the theatre: writing, directing, acting, and promoting.
The theatre remains one of his passions. Several of his recent publications are plays: *L'interrogatoire* (1986), a historical tragedy entitled *Yalta*
(1984), the comedy *L'amour tue* (1983), and *La confession du Major Popov*
(1982).

Perhaps the mischievous playfulness of this unusual writer is related to his background in military intelligence or his peculiar multicultural heritage. Many of his protagonists are spies and counterspies engaged in a bewildering maze of plots and counterplots in which the only certainty is always that things are not what they seem. The main character in *Le trêtre* (1972), Father Grigori, for example, is a KGB agent whose official mission is to infiltrate the Russian Orthodox Church. When his superiors inform him that after twenty years his assignment is ended, he finds it difficult to conclude whether he is genuinely a Communist or a Christian. *Le retournement* (1979) is the story of a Russian spy in Paris who is converted to the Christian faith. As with Saul, the Pharisaic persecutor of Christians, his conversion, or turnaround, is a stunning reversal of roles.

Born in 1932 in Paris of Russian parents, Volkoff is thoroughly multilingual. His English is elegant and betrays almost no trace of a French accent. His French prose is of a classical purity quite uncommon among contemporary writers. (Strangely enough, I might add, one of the other notable contemporary French stylists is an American citizen named Julien Green.) But his Russian is also at the native level of fluency, since he was reared in a home where Russian was spoken. This self-styled perpetual exile has written: "La France m'a appris que j'étais russe, l'Amérique que j'étais français."

The above quotation comes from Volkoff's 1981 essay *Le complexe de Procuste*,[2] which is a celebration of difference. Its author has always been a nonconformist, an avowed opponent of those who would reduce life to the drab, dull sameness of routine and habit. The cover illustration is a picture of Theseus ridding the world of Procrustes, the mythical Greek torturer whose obsession was to force everyone, by means of stretching them or chopping them off, to fit the bed to which he had strapped them. Procrustes and his modern followers would have us stamp out all distinctions of age, sex, wealth, and the like. But Volkoff has always felt himself called to defend such distinctions. Even in childhood he found himself fascinated by the differences between himself and those around him. The old-style Julian calendar, which is still observed by the Russian Orthodox Church as opposed to the reformed Gregorian calendar recognized by the rest of the Christian world, was one of the most intriguing differences to the young Volkoff, as was the variety of images portrayed on the face of playing cards.

Pour moi, prendre n'importe quelle fête, si séculaire fût-elle, pour un jour neutre, cela équivalait a préférer le dos des cartes à leur face, et, par conséquent, à les retourner dé-libérément dans le sens de l'uniformité, de l'indifférence, de l'anarchie et de la mort. [p. 22]

Holidays, like the face cards, were colorful, distinctive, more interesting and exciting. And the whole point of most card games, he discovered, had a powerfully suggestive symbolism for a White Russian whose parents had fled an egalitarian revolutionary state. Shuffling the cards introduces disorder, even anonymity. Then the players attempt to reconstruct a preestablished order or harmony.

Nul ne ressemble plus au faiseur de patience que l'artiste, qui part d'une réalité quelconque, et dont la mission consiste précisément à dégager les avances, à faire éclore les singularités, à distinguer, à mettre en place et en valeur, à éliminer les platitudes, à réordonner...la carrière en temple. [p. 17]

Naturally, such talk will be attacked as reactionary and fascist, but Volkoff claims that it is not a question of class struggle.

Je ne souhaitais pas le triomphe des figures sous prétexte qu'elles portaient des numéros supérieurs. Ce que je voyais, c'était qu'il fallait arracher toutes les cinquante-deux cartes à l'anarchie de l'indéterminé, qu'elles ne redeviendraient un orchestre et ne pourraient faire leur musique que lorsque les figures, c'est-à-dire les forces de la différence, se trouveraient en tête, tandis que les forces de l'indifférence – je l'entends au sens scientifique, état de ce qui est indifférent: un 9 diffère manifestement moins d'un 10 qu'un 10 d'un valet – seraient subjuguées. [p. 17]

It is not a matter of social justice, he insists. Social justice demands that the State protect the people from exploitation or oppression. But in so doing, modern societies have allowed the Procrustian tide to engulf them.

An anti-Procrustian must necessarily believe in nobility, and Volkoff does, although his definition of the term is, as one would expect, a bit "different." "Je propose pour la noblesse cette définition simplette: catégorie d'hommes différents" (p. 65). He goes on to observe that it is not necessarily a matter of birth, wealth, or physical appearance, but rather a difference – horizontal, not vertical – that is intuitively recognized in them, both by themselves and by others. A rather fuzzy definition, it is true, but one that conforms, after all, to the traditional "noblesse de coeur" notion.

Nobility entails privilege, and Volkoff is an avowed proponent of privilege, although, again, he notes that it is the "horizontal" privileges that he favors, those that deny no one his or her needs nor place undue burdens on any one.

> Si l'on partageait l'humanité en deux sortes d'hommes, ceux en qui le concept de privilège flatte l'imagination et ceux à qui il soulève l'estomac, je maintiens qu'on trouverait du premier côté tous les fantaisistes de bonne compagnie, tous les poètes, tous ceux qui ne confondent pas la gravité avec le sérieux et l'humour avec le comique troupier, et du second, pêle-mêle, les puritains, les grandes gueules, les hépatiques, les bidasses et les pisse-vinaigre de tout poil. [p. 51]

A particularly apt example of such privileges is that of carrying a sword. The mystique that seems to surround the sword may have something to do with its resemblance to a cross, but Volkoff is also careful to point out that "le combat à l'épée implique, entre les combattants, une certaine distance, et que la distance…est une notion sacrée" (p. 49). Here he appears to have been influenced, as in several other instances, by his readings of Simone Weil, who defines friendship as "le miracle par lequel un être humain accepte de regarder à distance et sans s'approcher l'être même qui lui est nécessaire comme une nourriture."[3] Both writers connect distance with respect, which is the most important ingredient for friendship, as well as for *agape*, or divinely infused love.

Philosophically speaking, there is every reason to emphasize the importance of difference, for, as Volkoff points out, it is the foundation of knowledge. By definition, difference refers to those qualities that distinguish one thing from another, and it is only by the differences in things that the intellect understands them. In other words, the notion of difference is essential to the most fundamental law of logic, the principle of noncontradiction. Furthermore, difference is the foundation of love, since we love someone only for his or her identity – that which is distinctive in the loved one's personality.

Finally, Volkoff aligns the Procrustians with the atheistic existentialists and leaves no doubt as to his own opinions of Jean-Paul Sartre and company.

> Je vois bien que pour croire à la différence il faut croire à un certain absolu. Il faut croire à l'être. Un existentialiste végétant

dans un monde non orienté, où rien n'a ni queue ni tête, où les
capitaines ont été dégradés par la mort de Dieu, où le 1er janvi-
er est un jour comme un autre, où Sisyphe ne roule son caillou
que par entêtement, dans une espèce de bonheur tout de même
un peu sommaire, n'a évidemment que faire de différences.
Mais aussi ce sont les existentialistes qui ont prôné le désespoir
envisagé comme une manière de vivre. Or, franchement, le désespoir ne m'intéresse pas. [*Le complexe de Procuste,* p. 156]

Volkoff ends his analysis of difference by declaring that because of the
relationship of individual human identity and the incarnation of the
logos, difference is also the love of God.

A perpetual exile with firsthand experience in espionage and
international intrigue, an actor, fencer, and chessplayer who also happens to be an Eastern Orthodox Christian in a post-Christian world
and a fierce anti-Communist Russian exile at that: such an individual
is bound to be different. He is sure to surprise us, as Diaghilev would
have had it, and one of his unique distinctions is his versatility, a versatility so remarkable that we find in his bibliography not only fiction,
theatre, biography, and essays, but science fiction as well.

If Volkoff did not think himself above writing science fiction –
witness *Métro pour l'enfer* (1963), *Le tire-bouchon du bon Dieu* (1982), *La
guerre des pieuvres* (1983) – it was because he feels at home in a world
where illusion and magic are the order of the day. "Ce sont les choses
insoupçonneés qui m'intéressent. Le monde n'est pas ce qu'il paraît
être," he says in *L'exil est ma patrie.* "J'ai horreur de ce que Dostoïevski
appelait ironiquement le palais de cristal."[4]

Thus, Volkoff provides an unusual perspective in which his
popular fiction may be understood. Rather than directly assaulting his
readers with a pompously "serious" fictional world, he prefers to catch
them unawares, to suggest the grandly heroic in the most unanticipated
ways. Like Cervantes, he is faced with the challenge of portraying a
heroism no longer credible to his cynical public. He observes that while
the modern literary public has lost the naïveté necessary to relate to a
Roland, it will always need heroic, if less naïve, protagonists. Consequently, even the most heroic of Volkoff's characters project a rather
detached air that borders on the cynical, and humor is never totally
absent. We are reminded of Quixote's famous words: "To say and write
witty and amusing things is the mark of great genius. The cleverest
character in a comedy is the clown, since he who would make himself
out to be a simpleton cannot be one."[5]

1980 MARKED THE PUBLICATION of Volkoff's masterpiece, a four-volume novel entitled *Les humeurs de la mer*. His publishers proclaimed it "l'année Volkoff." It was probably unprecedented for a four-volume novel, 1800 pages long, to be published at one time. Volkoff calls *Les humeurs de la mer* a relativistic novel in the sense of Lawrence Durrell's *Alexandria Quartet*. Each volume is a coherent unit, and they may be read in any order, although several main characters are involved in each.

Volkoff declares that, aside from Dostoevsky, he owes more to Durrell than to any other writer. It is Durrell who first understood that the theory of relativity contained the potential for rather far-reaching developments in fiction. The novel, after all, is fundamentally predicated on the notion of a time-space continuum, and since Einstein showed that the flow of time and space is not the same for two observers in two different places and moments, then the chronology of the fictional realm should reflect such an understanding. Durrell and Volkoff reject both the new novelists' technique of destroying the narrative and the surrealists' random rearrangement of the narrative. (One of the surrealists' games was to present the detached, unbound pages of a narrative, leaving it to the reader to arrange them in whatever order she wished.) Their innovation is more faithful to the essence of relativity in that they create "une continuité organisée du narré résolument différente de la continuité organique du vécu."[6] Volkoff hopes that his most lasting achievement will have been to prepare the way, along with Durrell, for what he likes to call "le classicisme de l'an 2000."[7]

The hero of the tetralogy is Colonel François Beaujeux, whose alias in the first volume (*Olduvaï*) is Frank Blok. The title of the first volume is the name of the valley in Tanzania where anthropologists found the remains of *homo habilis*, the earliest known human species, described by Robert Ardrey as an aggressive being which was advanced enough to form and wield weapons. The multiplicity of perspective in this first volume – as in two of the others – is achieved partly by the device of the work within a work. Here it is a play – also entitled "Olduvaï" – by Blok/Beaujeux that is being produced by the characters in the novel.

Most of the action of the novel, which is set in the American South during the racial unrest of the late 1960s and early '70s, is seen through the eyes of young Arnim, who incarnates the familiar Volkoffian theme of the search for the father. We are also introduced to Beaujeux's mysterious consort, Solange Bernard.

In *La leçon d'anatomie*, Beaujeux and Solange are living in Spain, and the Colonel is trying to write a screenplay – bearing the same title as the book – recounting a decisive event in his past military career. The incident, a flashback that constitutes the majority of the book, concerns an Algerian city of which he was a kind of military governor. In the context of France's impending disengagement, Beaujeux must deal with clandestine operations, his personal opposition to the widespread use of torture in interrogations, political maneuvering from all sides, and the perplexing dilemma of the Harkis.

One of his most promising officers, Lieutenant Miloslavski, a passionately idealistic young man whom the Colonel calls "l'ange bleu," sees Beaujeux increasingly as a demonic figure. The deepest theme of Volkoff's fiction is thus broached: the problem of evil. In what measure must he who governs use evil for the good of the governed? In *L'exil est ma patrie*, Volkoff says that what has fascinated him for years is not so much the existence of evil but its purpose and usefulness in the plan of God. "Dostoïevski a dit: si Dieu n'existe pas, tout est permis. Ma réponse est que si le diable n'existait pas, rien ne serait possible. Une certaine proportion de mal est essentielle à la forme du monde" (*L'exil est ma patrie*, p. 11).

If Volkoff's fiction obscures the boundaries between gravity and frivolity, the same is true of the dualisms of body and mind or of spirit and flesh. "Islam veut dire soumission," he explains in *L'exil est ma patrie*. "Eh bien, le corps est soumis et il possède une sainteté que n'ont ni l'esprit ni l'âme. Aussi je crois que l'anathème qu'on a jeté sur le corps n'est pas chrétien du tout" (pp. 22-23). This is another point on which Volkoff seems marked by Orthodox theology, which emphasizes that the believer's body is being redeemed along with the spirit.

One of Volkoff's most powerful metaphors is the intersection, the place where paths cross, the moment of encounter, which, fortuitous though it may appear, is but one of a myriad of divinely influenced appointments that combine to form the rich fabric of a providential plan.

In *Intersection*, the juxtaposition of multiple perspectives is not attributable to a text within the text but to the interplay of two different ontological orders. François and Solange are watched over in this novel by their guardian angels (Petit-Michel and Grand-Michel), who comment on the action from above and recount in flashback their respective charges' pasts. Solange is actually Svetlana Bernhardt, daughter of Stalin's unscrupulous chief of Soviet literary orthodoxy. Beaujeux, we

learn, was an actor before serving in military intelligence and has studied Gnosticism quite extensively. He believes that God intends to use
evil against Evil in his providential design.

The final volume of Volkoff's tetralogy, *Les maîtres du temps,*
finds the aging Beaujeux now composing a volume of poems in which
he seeks to renovate French metrics. Living in a windmill on a remote
island of North Africa, he and Solange receive visits from Arnim,
Miloslavski (who is about to be ordained as an Orthodox priest), and
François's three brothers. Beaujeux's writing is one attempt to master
time. Another is the belated decision to have a child through whom he
may have a continuing legacy. The problem of Solange's age leads him
to devise the scheme of using a surrogate mother, a plan whose rather
shocking implications force François to confront the real nature of his
would-be paternity and that of his relationship with Solange. The climax of the story is further complicated by the arrival of two spies who
have been sent to elicit Solange's long-guarded secret.

Les humeurs de la mer thus follows the lives and pasts of several
characters, particularly François and Solange, from the United States, to
France, Algeria, Spain, Tsarist Russia, the Soviet Union, and even into
heaven. The grand themes of love, war, time and mortality, the nature
of art, and the problem of evil are played out in a prose that is skillfully
crafted with an eye for classical elegance and simplicity.

Violence is an indispensable element in Volkoff's fictional
world. His protagonists have all come to terms with violence and
learned to harness it productively. In François Beaujeux, the most memorable and complex of his characters, we see a profoundly revealing
study of the psychology of violence. It is intimately related to the major
theme of *Les humeurs de la mer*, the fecundity of evil.

Thanks to Petit-Michel, his guardian angel, we have a particularly rich insight into Beaujeux's motives. Petit-Michel understands
François, who in earthly life was his older brother, better than he understands himself. For example, we are told that while François believes he
really loved Gisèle, his angel clearly discerns that his emotions for her
were actually compounded with his infatuation for the military life and
for Northern Africa at that moment in his life. Certain childhood memories – recounted in vivid detail – demonstrate how François was marked
by the fascination with violence. "L'incident du Visage" is a scene of precocious physical sadism perpetrated on his younger brother, albeit with
a tender touch of regret and compassion. It grows out of a similar scene
in which M. Beaujeux administers an unmerited spanking to François.

"L'incident du Maître" brings together François' gift for acting with his genius for insolence and intimidation and his ferocious sense of personal honor. It has to do with his adamant insistence upon the pronunciation of the "x" with which his last name ends ("Beaujeuks"). That the young François – about twenty years old – would cause a scene in front of a large acting class and confront and intimidate a rather imposing figure of a teacher over the pronunciation of his name indicates the seriousness of the code of honor by which he lives. It places him in an ancient tradition of French literary heroes, from Roland to Rodrigue.

As an insatiable womanizer, Beaujeux would be expected to betray some of the same sadistic *libido dominandi* toward his amorous conquests. And yet he somehow preserves intact an almost mystical respect for women, at least until a cynical feminist mistress brings out the worst in him. But his involvement in war provides for the constructive and creative channeling of his natural violence:

> Dès qu'il entra dans l'armée, la force devint son métier, et il ne put plus, à proprement parler, en abuser... Petit-Michel lui-même reconnut que, maintenant, pour François, la force était en quelque sorte exorcisée, et il se plut à voir son frère traiter les hommes avec sollicitude, l'ennemi avec humanité.[8]

Beaujeux is, then, an illustration of what Volkoff sees as the necessity to confront and come to terms with one's violence, and the epitome of man's struggle with physical violence is the mystique of chivalry.

> Moi, du moins j'avais conscience que le mal et la violence étaient présents et qu'ils faisaient partie de la nature humaine.... La chevalerie, avec tous ses défauts, était un très joli tour joué au diable, elle canalisait la violence. Et les armées traditionnelles dans la mesure où elles étaient (ou se prétendaient) chevaleresques participaient de ce tour joué au diable. [*L'exil est ma patrie*, p. 89]

Of course, the use of tactics such as torture in interrogations and the development of guerilla warfare place the modern military officer Beaujeux in a difficult position, but he repudiates such measures and prefers to outsmart his enemies whenever possible. Indeed, as an intelligence officer his refusal to allow torture is widely remarked, and he enjoys a singular reputation for subtle psychological manipulation of prisoners. For he always obtains the desired results.

JOHN M. DUNAWAY

I have made a passing reference to Beaujeux's sensuality. He is not alone in that respect among Volkoff's protagonists. Landru of *L'amour tue* goes through four successive wives, although he does – it is true – have the decency to exterminate each before taking on the next. Both Volsky and Popov in *Le retournement*, as well as Joël in *Le professeur d'histoire* and Walter de Walter in *The Underdog Appeal*, are given to sensuality. Yet, because of his intensely chivalrous attitude toward women, Volkoff himself has always held an idealistically high standard of fidelity and purity. In *L'exil est ma patrie* he says:

180

> Lorsque j'étais très jeune, j'étais profondément convaincu qu'il était indispensable que l'homme et la femme restassent absolument purs, vierges pour dire le mot, avant le mariage ou, si vous préférez, avant l'amour. Je n'avais que mépris, je dirai même: que dégoût, pour toutes ces sauteries virant en coucheries, pour toute cette vulgarité, cette puanteur de moisis des fornications oiseuses…. J'ai changé d'avis sur beaucoup de sujets, mais sur celui-là…⁹

The very courtliness of Volkoff's manner is admirably reflected in another passage from *L'exil est ma patrie*: "Il y a un sens profond à ce mythe chevaleresque selon lequel l'homme *sert* la femme: le baise-main n'a pas d'autre signification."¹⁰ But we begin to see more than courtliness in his attitude toward women when in defining love he quotes the words of John the Baptist: "He must increase, but I must decrease" (John 3:30). It is indeed a mystique of love that Volkoff's works suggest, a conception that builds on traditional Christian patterns (Christ as the bridegroom being sacrificed for his bride the Church) as well as philosophical and psychological meditations on the meaning of immortality and the body's role in it.

> Le geste d'amour est un acte d'une importance symbolique immense…. Plus nous mettrons de gravité, de religiosité, de sens du sacré, de ce que la liturgie appelle "la peur de Dieu" dans nos actes d'amour, plus il me semble que nous en recevrons de nourriture spirituelle. [*L'exil est ma patrie*, p. 177]

Why, then, the sensuality of Volkoff's fictional characters if he himself has such a Platonic notion of love? Perhaps it has to do with his focus on the fecundity of evil. Purity and angelism are to be carefully distinguished, the latter being inhuman and sterile. Perfection, like untainted happiness, is not the stuff of fiction, and Volkoff believes that part of the sacred mission of literature is to depict the unsatisfying quality of earthly life. It should remind us that the fulfillment of our deeper aspirations can come only beyond the grave.

While Volkoff believes that it is blasphemy to seek to expunge evil, he does not reject the notion of purity outright. It is a matter of distinguishing the various contexts in which purity takes on different shades of meaning. In the domain of ethics and personal conduct, the aspiration to remain perfectly pure is what Volkoff calls angelism, and in that context he cites the famous maxim of Pascal: "Qui veut faire l'ange fait la bête." Yet in the stricter sense we have seen that he emphasizes the importance of premarital chastity as well as conjugal fidelity. In aesthetic matters, one should always strive toward perfection and purity, whereas in the world of political action one must remain more modest.

> Quand vous écrivez, vous recherchez la perfection et toute votre conscience professionnelle d'écrivain, d'artiste, d'artisan, de potier, consiste à viser la perfection du pot, de la symphonie, du roman, et c'est bien, parce que l'art est du domaine de l'esprit. Dans le domaine de l'esprit, il faut viser la perfection. Tandis que dans l'ordre du politique, c'est exactement le contraire, c'est le domaine de César, celui où viser la perfection est un crime. [*L'exil est ma patrie*, pp. 194-95]

The fecundity of evil fascinates Volkoff because he believes that the most pernicious political philosophies in history have been those that have sought purity on a grand scale. He accepts the Antigones of the world as well as the Creons, but those who wish to play both roles are the most dangerous of all. "C'est abominable, c'est le jacobinisme, le fascisme, le communisme, tout ce que j'exècre: les gens qui veulent être purs et puissants" (*L'exil est ma patrie*, p. 25). Volkoff uses the parable of the wheat and the chaff, which Christ warns are not to be separated until the Last Judgment. "Si on sépare maintenant le bon grain de l'ivraie, on arrache tout.... Il faut s'occuper du monde tel qu'il est, du 'mélange mauvais' que récusaient les cathares, il faut se retrousser les manches, quoi!" (*L'exil est ma patrie*, p. 24).

For Beaujeux, living with the mixture (*vivre le mélange*) of good and evil goes even further. His study of the Gnostics leads him to conclude that in God's providential design He intends to use evil against Evil.

Le Dieu bon enchaîné par les péchés des hommes, le vrai Dieu
qui n'a jamais menti...le Dieu qui, pour finir, avait donné son
Fils à manger au monde, ce Dieu-là, auquel François se vouait
de tout son être, il n'avait pas de mal à opposer au Mal?

François se laissa secouer par un soubresaut hystérique.
Quelqu'un, au fond de lui, avait répondu: – Je veux être ce
mal. [*Intersection,* p. 429]

Thinking to himself that it would be too easy for God to be served only
by innocence, Beaujeux prays for God to make as much evil pass
through him as possible without poisoning him. The danger of that
poison, of course, is a subtle one in which mortals can be swept away.

Si être le mal de Dieu signifie qu'on extermine, en dehors
de toute proportion, comme l'a fait l'Inquisition, c'est atroce,
et il se produit alors un phénomène d'auto-intoxication
que l'on trouve dans les services secrets du monde entier,
lorsque l'action trouve en elle-même sa propre justification
comme dans les régimes totalitaires actuels. [*L'exil est ma
patrie,* pp. 203-4]

Characteristically Orthodox again in his notion of the sacred,
Volkoff finds the sacred in everything. It is not a Spinozist view, but
rather a refusal of the post-Renaissance duality of sacred and profane.
"Je crois que tout est sacré.... Je vis dans un monde médiéval où il
existe une potentialité de sacré dans tout, absolument" (*L'exil est ma patrie,* p. 268). Hence, there is no Calvinistic condemnation of the body.
In fact, Volkoff recalls having heard an Orthodox archbishop say that
man cannot be wholly evil precisely because he has a body. "Le corps
est innocent. Le diable peut être entièrement mauvais parce qu'il est
entièrement esprit: l'esprit peut être entièrement mauvais, le corps est
toujours innocent" (*L'exil est ma patrie,* p. 210).

In Canto 11 of the *Inferno,* Virgil tells Dante that the poet's art
follows the example of the Divine Artist in such a way that, by virtue of
his profession, he bears a unique relation to the Creator.

Che l'arte vostra quella, quanto pote,
segue, come 'l maestro fa 'l discente;
sì che vostr' arte a Dio quasi è nepote.

(When it can, your art would follow nature,
just as a pupil imitates his master;
so that your art is almost God's grandchild.)[11]

It is certainly no accident that this conception of the artist – shared by Dante and Volkoff, among many others – reflects and recapitulates the theme of paternity, which is at the heart of Volkoff's vision. (It is the central focus of his 1985 novel *Le professeur d'histoire.*) The father and the artist both work to master the temporal limitations of life, each seeking a kind of eternity in the creations that live on after them. Thus, they imitate God in becoming "Maîtres du temps."

Throughout Volkoff's espionage novels, there is a constant awareness of a three-tiered analogy of relationships: the interplay of reciprocal manipulation or control at the levels of the spy and the intelligence organization for which he works, the fictional character and his author, and the author and his Creator. Thus, the connections between paternity, espionage, and artistic creation all embody Volkoff's vision of man's relationship with God. And this is where the fecundity of evil holds a key to the whole problem of the Christian novelist.

Aleksandre Psar in a remarkable passage in *Le montage* thinks rather ironically of how the bizarre dissident Kournossov is being unwittingly used by the very Soviet regime that he thinks he is attacking.

> Il formerait un relais inconscient dans la propagation de ce qu'il haïssait le plus, et c'était cette haine même qui ferait de lui un relais efficace. L'influence…sait faire usage du principe d'Archimède…. Et Judas, à qui Jésus avait tendu un morceau de pain qui le désignait comme traître (non pas le dénonçait, mais le désignait, comme on désigne un homme de corvée), n'était-il pas le relais sans lequel l'opération Salut-du-monde aurait été impossible?[12]

As Psar becomes increasingly aware of the way he himself is being manipulated by his KGB superiors, the reader suspects that Volkoff is, as it were, haunted by a half-conscious notion of a Divine Intelligence network, one in which "l'ange Coïncidence," for example, plays a major role. He would, no doubt, substantially agree with Jacques Maritain's assertion that

> le roman a pour objet…la vie humaine elle-même à conduire dans une fiction, comme fait dans la réalité l'Art providentiel. C'est l'humanité elle-même à former, scruter, et gouverner comme un monde, qui est son objet de création…. A ce titre, un chrétien seul, que dis-je, un mystique, parce qu'il a quelque idée de *ce qui est dans l'homme,* peut faire un romancier complet.[13]

JOHN M. DUNAWAY

Indeed, the Volkoffian artist is engaged in fashioning and governing a fictional world of his own making, but in so doing, he is not only subject to the influence of God's purposes being lived out in his life, but his own fictional characters, if they are truly alive, have autonomy as well, and thus exert another influence on the course of events in the story. They might echo the words of Lear to Cordelia, who proposes to "take upon 's the mystery of things, As if we were God's spies" (act 5, sc. 3, lines 16-17). The role of Beaujeux, then, is not quite that of a Judas; but it seems that he is chosen (by his author and by God) to perform some permissible evil, an evil that is even essential in the providential scheme of things.

184 Volkoff points out that the most obvious contrast between the Divine Creator and the human artist is the latter's unworthiness to exercise such a sacred function. In *Le complexe de Procuste* he elaborates on the distinction between divine creation and human artistic creation by focusing on the role of light. Alluding to the divine "Fiat lux," Volkoff asserts that difference must be perceived in order to exist, and that light is a prerequisite for perception, since light is the essence of color and the symbol of all difference.

> C'est en cela que la création des artistes se différencie de celle de Dieu. Nous montrons les différences, mais elles préexistent à nous. Dieu, lui, préexiste aux différences. Il ne se contente pas de les montrer: c'est parce qu'il les voit qu'elles se mettent à exister. [*Le complexe de Procuste*, pp. 150-51]

He also recalls Mauriac's injunction to the novelist to purify the source, and says:

> Nous devrions écrire nos romans comme les peintres d'icônes peignaient les icônes. Nous devrions nous mettre en prière, jeûner, alors nous produirions probablement des oeuvres tout à fait différentes, où passerait, peut-être, le souffle de l'Esprit. Or, moi, j'ai écrit *Les humeurs de la mer,* un verre de whisky à portée de la main! Nous sommes dans le mélange.... Mais je pense que le poète, l'artiste, qui commence à se dire que ce qu'il fait est sacré en soi, file un très mauvais coton, une fois de plus nous arrivons dans le luciférisme caractérisé. [*L'exil est ma patrie,* pp. 211-12]

The Volkoffian artist, then, is aware that his craft is a high calling, a vocation in which he must seek, above all else, to serve. Having heard his family remind him all his life that he was on this earth to serve, Volkoff has understood each of his professions in that light. As a soldier, a teacher, a writer, even as a student, he knew what it was to hear the call of duty.

> Tous les matins, avant de partir en classe, je récitais une prière spéciale: "Seigneur très bon, envoie-nous la grâce de Ton Esprit qui donnera des forces à notre âme et la fortifiera, afin qu'en écoutant l'enseignement qui nous sera dispensé, nous croissions pour Ta gloire, ô notre Créateur, pour la consolation de nos parents et le bien de l'Eglise et de la patrie." Ainsi, ce n'était pas pour avoir une belle situation que l'on étudiait, mais pour servir. C'est pour cela peut-être que j'éprouve de la sympathie pour les jeunes pionniers communistes que je décris dans *Le retournement*. [*L'exil est ma patrie, p. 97*]

In a day and age when the literary establishment tends for the most part toward the political left, when the literary reviews and journals are filled with talk of feminism, Marxism, and deconstructionism, when the very fabric of French culture is being slowly but surely altered by a socialist government, Vladimir Volkoff would appear to be singularly out of place. Yet he has continued, since the big splash of *Le retournement* in 1979, to enjoy a high degree of visibility in the French media, partly because of his flair for dramatics during personal appearances, partly because his views are so strong and so boldly stated. One senses in his literary colleagues a certain patronizing scorn, as if they, too, considered him a kind of Cocteauesque dazzler with little substance. There is, however, a much deeper explanation for the important role Volkoff now plays in the French literary world.

For those who still cherish the traditional values of French culture in its (anti-Procrustian) distinctiveness and for those who recognize the manipulation of public opinion in contemporary Western society, Volkoff represents a clear prophetic voice. The White Russian émigrés who came to France with his parents and grandparents have remained faithful to the same values that were taught him from his childhood. Today they look upon him as a kind of French equivalent of Solzhenitsyn.

But most of all, he enjoys a position of prominence in French literature today as a gifted stylist who knows how to write fascinating stories with a beginning, middle, and end – stories that, while they never shy away from the gravest dilemmas of the human condition could also have pleased the demanding impresario who asked to be "étonné."

JOHN M. DUNAWAY

1   Albert Sonnenfeld, *Crossroads: Essays on the Catholic Novelists* (York, South Carolina: French Literature Publishing Company, 1982), p. xix.

2   Vladimir Volkoff, *Le complexe de Procuste* (Paris: Julliard/L'Age d'Homme, 1981), p. 22.

3   Simone Weil, *Attente de Dieu* (Paris: Fayard, 1966), p. 204.

4   Vladimir Volkoff and Jacqueline Bruller, *L'exil est ma patrie: Entretiens* (Paris: Le Centurion, 1982), p. 19.

5   Miguel de Cervantes Saavedra, *The Ingenious Gentleman, Don Quixote de la Mancha,* trans. Samuel Putnam (New York: Viking Press, 1951), p. 403.

6   Vladimir Volkoff, *Lawrence le Magnifique: Essai sur Lawrence Durrell et le roman relativiste* (Paris: Julliard/L'Age d'Homme, 1984), p. 17.

7   *Ibid.*, p. 11.

8   Vladimir Volkoff, *Intersection*, vol. 3 of *Les humeurs de la mer* (Paris: Julliard/L'Age d'Homme, 1980), p. 239.

9   *Ibid.*, p. 176 (Volkoff's ellipsis at end of citation).

10 *Ibid.*, p. 172 (Volkoff's italics).

11 Dante Alighieri, *The Divine Comedy,* trans. Allen Mandelbaum (New York: Bantam, 1980), Inf. XI, ll. 103-5, pp. 98-99.

12 Vladimir Volkoff, *Le montage* (Paris: Julliard/L'Age d'Homme, 1982), pp. 264-5.

13 Jacques Maritain, *Art et Scolastique,* 4th ed. (Paris: Desclée de Brouwer, 1965), p. 266 (Maritain's italics).

IV. SELF'S SHADES AND SHADOWS

ZWISCHEN MYSTIK und PHOTOGRAPHIE:
ZUM ERINNERUNGSBEGRIFF bei HOFMANNSTHAL

VON MAXIMILIAN AUE, EMORY UNIVERSITY

1926 SCHRIEB HUGO VON HOFMANNSTHAL an Thomas Mann: „Welch
ein merkwürdiges Wort ist wirklich dies, Erinnerung, Er-innerung,
Hineingehen in sich selber, Communion mit jener eigenen, immer da-
bleibenden tiefsten Welt."[1] Die Wiederholung des Wortes „Erinnerung"
in der die wörtliche Bedeutung betonenden Schreibweise, sowie die
folgende Definition deuten darauf hin, daß Erinnerung an dieser Stelle
vor allem als Ich-Findung im Sinn eines Zugangs zu einer zeitlosen,
unveränderlichen Sphäre gemeint ist. Angesichts der Tatsache, daß
Hofmannsthal gerade zu dieser Zeit auch intensiv damit beschäftigt
war, den kulturellen Fortbestand Europas durch Wiederbelebung
alter gesamteuropäischer Traditionen sichern zu helfen,[2] liegt aber
die Merkwürdigkeit des Wortes auch darin, daß es neben seiner
wörtlichen, weniger gebräuchlichen Bedeutung auch noch seine andere, übertragene, aber gebräuchliche hat: daß der Zugang zur zeitlosen Dimension des Ichs und der zur Vergangenheit mit demselben
Wort bezeichnet werden. Als solches wird es Hofmannsthal immer
wieder des Merkens würdig (vgl. R III 24),[3] und er setzt es in dieser
Mehrdeutigkeit immer wieder bewußt in seinem Werk ein.

187

Das Verhältnis dieser beiden Komponenten ist aber nicht sta-
tisch, sondern verändert sich je nach der Funktion der Erinnerung im
Textganzen. Im Folgenden soll versucht werden, an einzelnen Beispie-
len die Zusammensetzung der Erinnerung genauer herauszuarbeiten,
um so sowohl zu einem im Einzelnen differenzierteren Bild dieses für
Hofmannsthal so zentralen Themas zu kommen, als auch, wenigstens
in Ansätzen, die Entwicklung zu überblicken, die dieser Begriff bei ihm
durchgemacht hat.

Ein gutes Beispiel für das harmonische Zusammenwirken
der „zeitlichen" und „zeitlosen" Bedeutung von Erinnerung ist die 1907
erschienene Erzählung „Erinnerung schöner Tage." Zunächst ist sie eine
Erinnerung im doppelten Sinn: einerseits als Erinnerung an einen spe-
zifischen, dichterisch besonders produktiven Venedigaufenthalt, und
andrerseits, weil sie einen Erinnerungsprozeß (in beiden Bedeutungen)
zum Thema hat, der die Grundlage dieser Produktivität ist.

Dieser Prozeß wird nun im Detail beschrieben. Zunächst das Äußere: Ankunft, erster Spaziergang durch Venedig, der Eindruck der Piazzetta und des Markusplatzes. Sehr bald aber geht es nach innen: mit einer literarischen Erinnerung an den Anfang von Novalis' „Lehrlingen zu Sais" und mit einer Reihe von metaphorischen Einkleidungen der äußeren Eindrücke als erstem Stadium der Verinnerlichung. Dieses „metaphorische" Stadium führt zum nächsten: zwei sich einander nähernde Barken erinnern den Protagonisten an zwei Lippen, die andere „geliebte Lippen...wiederfinden"; und obwohl er noch „zu leicht auf der Oberfläche...[seines] Denkens" schwimmt und „nicht hinabtauchen [kann] um zu erfahren, an wen ich im Innersten gedacht hatte" (E 166),[4] ist hier bereits die erotische Innendimension angesprochen, die nun durch weitere Begegnungen, vor allem mit einer schönen Engländerin, die einer „antiken Statue" gleicht, weiter vertieft wird (E 168). Mit der Erwähnung der antiken Statue beginnt aber ein weiterer Bereich des Inneren, der zeitlos-mythische: zunächst noch als mythologische Einkleidung des erotischen Interesses an der Frau in der Sage von Zeus und Alkmene; dann geht es aber noch „tiefer" ins Mythologisch-Märchenhafte. Auf einem „finstre[n] Fackelwagen" fährt der Protagonist in ein Dorf im Gebirge, wo er das von einem Fisch verschluckte Licht befreien muß (E 170). Schließlich „taucht" der Protagonist noch in die eigene Kindheit, wird zum Kind, bevor er aufwacht und dann, auf Grund einer gefühlten Zugehörigkeit zum „Hier und Dort" (E 171), die Schatten seiner Träume schöpferisch-dichterisch in Gestalten verwandeln kann, die zwar seinen Wünschen gehorchen, dabei aber ihre Eigenständigkeit nicht einbüßen.[5]

Während sich also hier die Außenwelt harmonisch in den Erinnerungsprozeß einfügt, zu einem Teil davon wird, wird diese Harmonie in den fast gleichzeitig erschienenen „Briefen des Zurückgekehrten" problematisch. Hofmannsthals nach achtzehn Jahren in die Heimat Zurückgekehrtem ist diese auf unheimliche Weise fremd geworden, weil sie mit seinen Erinnerungen daran nicht mehr übereinstimmt.

Diese Erinnerungen tragen ein ganzheitliches Gepräge, das auf einer in der Jugend erlebten Einheit von Landschaft und Leben mit der in alten Dürer-Stichen enthaltenen Geschichte, ihren Landsschaftsformen und Menschentypen, beruht. Diese Einheit liegt nicht sosehr in einer Ähnlichkeit der Einzelheiten, sondern in einem grundsätzlich gleichen Verhältnis zum Leben:

188

Wieweit es Entgegenstemmen ist und wieweit Sichfügen, wo
Auflehnung hingehört und wo Ergebung, wo Gleichmut am
Platze ist und eine trockene Rede und wo Übermut und
Lustbarkeit: dies Wesentliche, dies Wirkliche hinter dem
Alltäglichen, dies was die schlichten Handlungen des Tages
aus dem Menschen heraustreibt, wie es aus dem Baum sein
Rauhes und sein Süßes hervortreibt, Rinde und Blatt und
Apfel – dies, dies hat meine Welt, wie jene Blätter es wissen,
das weiß ich heute und wußte es damals: denn es lag in mir,
daß ich das Wirkliche an etwas in mir messen mußte, und fast
bewußtlos maß ich an jener schreckhaft erhabenen schwarzen
Zauberwelt [der Dürer-Stiche] und strich alles an diesem
Probierstein, ob es Gold wäre oder ein schlechter gelblicher
Glimmer. [E 559]

189

Vor dieser erinnerten Wesenhaftigkeit, die in der Fremde immer wieder
da war, wenn ihr da etwas entsprach und die ihn, wie in dem aus zwei
„Aeneis"-Stellen ungenau zusammenerinnerten[6] „Zitat": „Argos memi-
nisse juvabat" (E 556), erfreute, können nun „das große Deutschland
und die Deutschen des heutigen Tages…nicht bestehen" (E 559). Die
immer wieder erlebte Diskrepanz zwischen den jetzigen Eindrücken
und dem inneren Urbild erschüttert die Festigkeit seiner Wahrnehmun-
gen und bewirkt ein Schwanken der Realität. Zunächst fangen die
alltäglichen Dinge an, ihre Wirklichkeit zu verlieren. Ein Krug und
ein Waschbecken in einem Hotelzimmer erscheinen „trotz ihrer unbe-
schreiblichen Gewöhnlichkeit so ganz und gar nicht wirklich, gewissermaßen gespenstisch, und zugleich provisorisch, wartend, sozusagen
vorläufig die Stelle des wirklichen Kruges, des wirklichen mit Wasser
gefüllten Waschbeckens einnehmend." Die Droschken sind „Gespenster
von Droschken," die Bäume erinnern nur an solche, sind aber für ihn
keine (E 561-62). Diese Zersetzung breitet sich aus, so daß „ich nun, ich
selber, mein inneres Leben, so unter diesem bösen Blick lag wie in den
früheren Anwandlungen jene äußeren Dinge" (E 563). Die Befreiung
davon durch das Auftauchen eines durch die heutige deutsche Wirklichkeit versagten Korrelats der inneren Wahrhaftigkeit vollzieht sich
erst in einer zufälligen Begegnung mit der Kunst, mit den Bildern van
Goghs. Die gespürte Entsprechung zwischen dem innersten Leben der
gemalten Gegenstände und dem Ich des Betrachters führt zur schlagar-
tigen Gesundung des Ichs. Sie gibt dem Zurückgekehrten mit einem
Mal „nach ungemessenem Taumel festen Boden unter den Füßen,"

den Genuß von „Außen und Innen" und sogar die Fähigkeit, in der
Welt der Geschäfte seinen Mann zu stehen und seinen Auftrag weit
über Erwarten gut auszuführen (E 566-67).

Die Rettung eines verunsicherten Ichs durch die Kunst scheint
auch in den „Augenblicken in Griechenland" vor sich zu gehen. Hier
scheinen ebenfalls die Erinnerungen an die alten Griechen angesichts
der griechischen Gegenwart zunächst zu versagen, es will sich keine
Beziehung dazwischen – und damit zwischen dem klassischen Ort
und dem Ich – ergeben. Die Erinnerungen beleben sich erst in der
Begegnung mit griechischer Kunst; erst dann kommt es zu einem tiefen
Einheitserlebnis, zu einer Vereinigung des Inneren mit einer lebenden

190 Vergangenheit. Trotz dieser Ähnlichkeit gibt es aber zwischen diesen
zeitlich nicht allzuweit auseinanderliegenden Texten wichtige Unter-
schiede, vor allem was Wesen und Funktion der Erinnerung betrifft.
Zunächst handelt es sich bei der Erinnerung an die alten Griechen
nicht um eine ganzheitliche Erinnerung, einen Prüfstein der Wirklichkeit, so wie ihn der Zurückgekehrte in der Fremde mit sich herumge-
tragen hat, sondern um angelerntes Bildungsgut, das sich auch angesichts des klassischen Schauplatzes nicht belebt:

> Da waren die Ausgrabungen auf der Agora, da war die Pnyx,
> da war der Rednerhügel, da die Tribüne; da die Spuren ihrer
> Häuser, ihre Weinpressen, da waren ihre Grabmäler an der
> eleusinischen Straße. Dies war Athen. Athen? So war dies
> Griechenland, dies die Antike. Ein Gefühl der Enttäuschung
> fiel mich an…. Diese Griechen, fragte ich in mir, wo sind sie?
> Ich versuchte mich zu erinnern, aber ich erinnerte mich nur
> an Erinnerungen, wie wenn Spiegel einander widerspiegeln,
> endlos. [E 618]

Auch das konzentrierte Bemühen um diese Erinnerungen,
der Versuch, mit Hilfe klassischer Lektüre im Schatten klassischer
Säulen die Vergangenheit zu beleben, schlägt fehl. Weder historische
Erinnerungen noch die Lektüre der Klassiker[7] können das Gefühl der
Vergänglichkeit und Labilität, jenen „grünliche[n] Schleier" beseitigen,
der sich zwischen den Protagonisten und seine Umgebung schiebt; und
er begibt sich nun in ein Museum, wo er sich von der Begegnung mit
Gegenständen „von vollkommener Schönheit," die „der Gewalt der Zeit
widerstanden" haben, „für den Augenblick wenigstens" (E 620-21) eine
Erholung von dieser Vergänglichkeit erhofft. Diese Hoffnung scheint
sich, nach der Überwindung eines seltsamen Türhüters und nach

dem Betreten eines „dritten Raum[s]" auch tatsächlich zu erfüllen. Beim Anblick der hier aufgestellten Koren verschwindet das krampfhafte Bemühen um Erinnerung und es vollzieht sich „Er-innerung":

> In diesem Augenblick geschah mir etwas: ein namenloses Erschrecken: es kam nicht von außen, sondern irgendwoher aus unmeßbaren Fernen eines inneren Abgrundes…die Augen der Statuen waren plötzlich auf mich gerichtet und in ihren Gesichtern vollzog sich ein völlig unsägliches Lächeln. Der eigentliche Inhalt dieses Augenblickes aber war in mir dies: ich verstand dieses Lächeln, weil ich wußte: ich sehe dies nicht zum erstenmal, auf irgendwelche Weise, in irgendwelcher Welt bin ich vor diesen gestanden, habe ich mit diesen irgendwelche Gemeinschaft gepflogen, und seitdem habe [sic] alles in mir auf einen solchen Schrecken gewartet, und so furchtbar mußte ich mich in mir berühren, um wieder zu werden, der ich war. [E 624]

191

So wie im Fall des Zurückgekehrten erfolgt auch hier eine schlagartige innere Beteiligung, ein sich Verlieren an das Kunstwerk; nur wird hier diese Verbindung durch eine gewissermaßen „präexistente" Gemeinschaft beider begründet, die plötzlich in ihre Rechte tritt. Das Kunsterlebnis besteht in einem Wiedererkennen „vergangener" Erlebnisse und Begegnungen, während das des Zurückgekehrten für ihn etwas Neues darstellt. Vor allem aber ist das „Endergebnis" des Kunsterlebnisses in beiden Texten verschieden. Der Zurückgekehrte hatte, bei aller Erhebung durch die Bilder, weiterhin die Außenwelt wahrgenommen, sogar ein erhöhtes Organ dafür bekommen:

> …ich…konnte fühlen, konnte wissen, konnte durchblicken, konnte genießen Abgründe und Gipfel, Außen und Innen, eins und alles im zehntausendsten Teil der Zeit, als ich da die Worte hinschreibe, und war wie doppelt, war Herr über mein Leben zugleich, Herr über meine Kräfte, meinen Verstand, fühlte die Zeit vergehen, wußte, nun bleiben nur noch zwanzig Minuten, noch zehn, noch fünf, und stand draußen, rief einen Wagen, fuhr hin [zur erfolgreichen Sitzung]. [E 566]

Diesem wachen Sinn für das Vergehen der Zeit und für seinen Sitzungstermin unter dem Eindruck der Bilder steht beim Protagonisten der „Augenblicke" ein ganz anderes Zeitempfinden gegenüber: „…nichts von den Bedingtheiten der Zeit konnte anklingen in der Hingenommenheit, an die ich mich verloren hatte; sie war dauerlos und das, wovon sie erfüllt war, trug sich außerhalb der Zeit zu" (E 624); und das Außen, das Gegenüber, an denen der Zurückgekehrte so intensiven Anteil hatte, verschwindet im Lauf des Erlebnisses vollständig. Das Kunsterlebnis führt von der Außenwelt nach innen, aber nicht mehr in die äußere Wirklichkeit zurück. In dieser Innenwelt ist das Ich freilich, wie beim Zurückgekehrten, doppelt (s. E 566); aber die beiden Aspekte vereinigen sich nicht wie beim Zurückgekehrten und lassen sich gleichzeitig beherrschen, sondern treiben immer weiter auseinander, bewegen sich unabhängig voneinander in entgegengesetzte Richtungen. Der Protagonist erlebt eine innere Reise zu einer „glorreichen Opferung," bei der er sowohl Priester als auch Opfer ist (E 625). Er weiß nicht, ob der Tumult, den er zu vernehmen glaubt, eine Bedrohung darstellt oder ob er ihm gebietet. Vor allem zeigt sich diese Gespaltenheit auch gegenüber den Statuen. Einerseits sieht er sich in vollkommener Hingabe in der Haltung der Proskynesis auf dem Fuß einer Statue ruhen; in einer Gegenbewegung aber befreit sich dann das Ich von den Statuen und wird ihnen zunächst mit Hilfe der Erinnerung ebenbürtig.

192

> Denn es ist sonderbar, daß ich sie wieder nicht eigentlich als Gegenwärtige umfasse, sondern daß ich sie mir mit beständigem Staunen irgendwoher rufe, mit einem bänglich süßen Gefühl, wie Erinnerung. In der Tat, ich erinnere mich ihrer, und in dem Maß, als ich mich dieser Erinnerung gebe, in dem Maß vermag ich meiner selbst zu vergessen. Dieses Selbstvergessen ist ein seltsames deutliches Geschehen: es ist ein grandioses Abwerfen, Teil um Teil, Hülle um Hülle, ins Dunkle. Es wäre wollüstig, wenn Wollust in so hohe Regionen reichte. Ungemessen mich abwerfend, auflösend, werde ich immer stärker: unzerstörbar bin ich im Kern. Unzerstörbar, so sind diese, mir gegenüber. Es wäre undenkbar, sich an ihre Oberfläche anschmiegen zu wollen. Diese Oberfläche ist ja gar nicht da – sie entsteht durch ein beständiges Kommen zu ihr, aus unerschöpflichen Tiefen. Sie sind da, und sind unerreichlich. So bin auch ich. Dadurch kommunizieren wir. [E 627]

Bei diesem Kommunizieren macht das Ich aber nicht halt. Seine Macht wächst bis zur völligen Dominanz, es erkennt, „als Letztes: unbedürftig bin ich auch ihrer [der Koren]. Ich brauche sie nur, wie sie mich brauchen. Sie stünden nicht vor mir, wenn ich ihnen nicht von Ewigkeit zu

Ewigkeit hülfe, sich aufbauen." Wie ambivalent diese Dominanz aber ist, wird von Hofmannsthal im letzten Absatz der „Augenblicke" hervorgehoben:

> Und indem ich mich immer stärker werden fühle und unter diesem einen Wort: Ewig, ewig! immer mehr meiner selbst verliere, schwingend wie die Säule erhitzter Luft über einer Brandstätte, frage ich mich, ausgehend wie die Lampe im völligen Licht des Tages: Wenn das Unerreichliche sich speist aus meinem Innern und das Ewige aus mir seine Ewigkeit sich aufbaut, was ist dann noch zwischen der Gottheit und mir?
> [E 628]

Hier wird zwar eine mystische Einheit mit Gott, ein Zusammenfließen mit ihm erreicht; dem steht aber der Verlust der produktiven Spannung zwischen Irdischem und Göttlichem gegenüber. Das Ich ist zwar leicht geworden und steigt in die höheren Regionen auf, aber eben wie erhitzte Luft über einer Feuersbrunst, in der das Irdische zerstört wird; und der Preis der Erlangung des „völligen Licht[s] des Tages" ist das Verlöschen des eigenen Lichtes. In letzter Konsequenz führt hier die Er-innerung zum Verlust einer wichtigen Komponente des menschlichen Lebens, zum Aufgeben der Wechselwirkung zwischen dem Ich und seiner sozialen und historisch-kulturellen Umwelt, ja ironischerweise sogar zum Selbstverlust. Daß Hofmannsthal diese Möglichkeit als Gefahr betrachtete, zeigt sich unter anderem auch in seiner um diese Zeit entstandenen Komödie „Der Schwierige," in der die Titelfigur nach Umwegen und haarscharf am Aufgehen im Unverbindlichen vorbei zu sich und in den sozialen Bereich findet – mit Hilfe einer neuen „Verwendung" der Erinnerung.

Es ist bekannt, daß Hofmannsthal in seinem Exemplar von Kierkegaards „Stadien auf dem Lebensweg" mehrmals auf den „Schwierigen" hingewiesen hat, und zwar an Stellen, die zwischen der „Erinnerung" und dem „Gedächtnis" unterscheiden. Einer solchen Notiz: „H.[ans] C.[arl] – Antoinette: Erinnerung und Gedächtnis"[8] hat man auch entnommen, daß diese als Repräsentantin des Gedächtnisses und Hans Karl als Vertreter der Erinnerung fungiert, wobei „Gedächtnis" ein unmittelbares, spontanes Sich Entsinnen darstellt, dessen Pendant das Vergessen ist, während „Erinnerung" sich nur auf das Wesentliche bezieht – aber nicht direkt, sondern auf dem Weg der Reflexion – und nicht vergessen werden kann.[9] Im Gespräch zwischen Antoinette und Hans Karl im 2. Akt des „Schwierigen" erscheint dieser Kierkegaardsche

Gegensatz in einer spezifisch Hofmannsthalschen Ausprägung.

Antoinettes eigene Aussagen scheinen zunächst zu bestätigen, daß sie, so wie Kierkegaards Mensch, der „etwas im Gedächtnis hat statt in der Erinnerung,"[10] ständig alles vergißt, nur für den Augenblick lebt. Ihr Gespräch mit Hans Karl beginnt mit der Mitteilung, sie habe ihre Briefe an ihn, die Erinnerung an ihr Verhältnis, verbrannt, denn: „Ich hab einmal nur das, was ich im Moment hab, und was ich nicht hab, will ich vergessen. Ich leb nicht in der Vergangenheit, dazu bin ich nicht alt genug" (D IV 391);[11] es endet mit der Bitte: „Sag Er mir sehr was Liebes: nur für den Moment. Der Moment ist ja alles. Ich kann nur im Moment leben. Ich hab so ein schlechtes Gedächtnis" (D IV 397); und Hans Karl setzt als Erinnerer ein: „Wenn Sie erlauben würden, so möchte ich versuchen, Sie an damals zu erinnern" (D IV 392). Schon durch die Tatsache aber, daß sich Antoinette ihrer Vergeßlichkeit bewußt ist, daß sie diese reflektiert hat, unterscheidet sie sich von den Kierkegaardschen „Gedächtnismenschen," deren automatisch eintretendes Vergessen es ihnen ermöglicht, sich das Leben „bequem" zu machen: „Ungeniert kann… [der „Gedächtnismensch"] die lächerlichsten Metamorphosen durchmachen; kann noch in vorgerücktem Alter Blindekuh spielen, sein Glück in der Lotterie des Lebens versuchen; kann alles mögliche werden nachdem… [er] schon alles mögliche gewesen [ist]."[12] Bei Antoinette ist das Vergessen dagegen eine Willenshandlung, die, wenigstens im Fall von Hans Karl, scheitert; und im Verlauf des Gesprächs mit ihm vollzieht sich eine aufschlußreiche Modifikation des Kierkegaardschen Gegensatzes, und es findet ein seltsamer Rollentausch zwischen Antoinette und Hans Karl statt. Antoinette ist es, die ihre Erinnerung an ihr zwei Jahre zurückliegendes Verhältnis mit Hans Karl nicht los wird, nicht los werden will: „Diese paar Tage damals in der Grünleiten sind das einzige wirklich Schöne in meinem ganzen Leben. Die laß ich nicht – Die Erinnerung daran laß ich mir nicht heruntersetzen" (D IV 392). Und Hans Karl erscheint als Vertreter eines unverbindlichen, gewissenlosen Ästhetentums: „Nichts ist bös. Der Augenblick ist nicht bös, nur das Festhalten-Wollen ist unerlaubt. Nur das Sich-Festkrampeln an das, was sich nicht halten läßt."

Hans Karl ist aber kein ästhetisierender Abenteurer vom Schlag eines Florindo oder Baron Weidenstamm, und er erklärt Antoinette, was er meint. Im Krieg hat er den Zufall von seiner häßlichen Seite her kennengelernt, er hat ihn als etwas erkannt, dem der Ästhet nicht gewachsen ist, was die Menschen wie Blätter

194

im Wind „zueinanderjagt und auseinanderjagt" (D IV 393). Die ihm in dieser Situation nötige Stabilität erreicht der Mensch aber nicht, indem er irgendeines der zufälligen Elemente ergreift und krampfhaft festhält. Das Zufällige muß weiterhin auf die ihm entsprechende Weise „genommen" werden, also „leicht," ohne Gewissen, mit einem Sinn für die Schönheiten, die es bringt. Dem „Grausen," das eine solche zufällige Existenz auf die Dauer mit sich bringt, kann man aber nur mit Hilfe einer gesellschaftlichen Einrichtung, der Ehe, entkommen. Diese ist zwar ein existentielles Kunststück, so wie das, sich bei seinem eigenen Schopf aus dem Sumpf herauszuziehen, also in ihren tiefsten Grundlagen paradox und gefährdet; dennoch aber macht sie „aus dem Zufälligen und Unreinen das Notwendige, das Bleibende und das Gültige" (D IV 393).

195

Man wird an dieser Stelle vielleicht einwenden, daß Hans Karls Lob der Ehe hier nicht ganz „unbefangen" ist. Schließlich hat er seinem Freund Ado Hechingen versprochen, ihn mit seiner Frau zu versöhnen, den Versuch zu machen, ihre gestörte Ehe zu retten. Diesem Aspekt der Situation trägt Hofmannsthal auch Rechnung, als er zeigt, wie sich Hans Karl bei der Beschreibung von Ados Gefühlen für Antoinette ins leicht Komisch-Pathetische hineinsteigert:

> Der hat dich lieb. Einmal und für alle Male. Der hat dich gewählt unter allen Frauen auf der Welt, und er hat dich liebbehalten und wird dich liebhaben für immer.... Für immer, gescheh dir, was da will. Einen Freund haben, der dein ganzes Wesen liebhat, für den du immer ganz schön bist, nicht nur heut und morgen, auch später, viel später, für den seine Augen den Schleier, den die Jahre, oder was kommen kann, über dein Gesicht werfen – für seine Augen ist das nicht da, du bist immer die du bist, die Schönste, die Liebste, die Eine, die Einzige.

Antoinettes trockene Replik „So hat er mich nicht gewählt. Geheiratet hat er mich halt" (D IV 394) wird schon eher der Wirklichkeit entsprechen. Durch Hans Karls übertriebenes Engagement für Hechingen, das sich sowohl in der rhetorisch überhöhten Ausdrucksweise, als auch in dem sonst bei ihm seltenen Anakoluth ausdrückt, wird aber das, was er allgemein zur Ehe zu sagen hat, nicht in seiner Bedeutung für das Stück geschmälert; denn wie an seiner Gebärdensprache von allem Anfang an klar wird, geht es ihm bei seinem Einsatz für Hechingen und auch für Stani immer unbewußt auch um seine Verbindung mit Helene; so daß er hier nicht nur nach einer Rechtfertigung für Hechingens Ehe sucht, sondern vor allem auch nach einer für seine eigene.

Trotz ihrer prekären Existenz, fährt Hans Karl fort, beruht die Ehe auf einer Notwendigkeit, die „mitten in dem Hierhin- und Dorthin- geworfenwerden" gespürt und gewußt wird. Diese Notwendigkeit „wählt uns von Augenblick zu Augenblick, die geht ganz leise, ganz dicht am Herzen vorbei und doch so schneidend scharf wie ein Schwert." Und Antoinette, die bei all ihrer Flatterhaftigkeit von Hofmannsthal mit einem gesunden Instinkt ausgestattet worden ist, bemerkt hier, was Hans Karl selbst noch nicht weiß, bzw. sich selbst noch nicht einge- standen hat: „Alles was du redst, das heißt ja gar nichts anderes, als... daß du demnächst die Helen heiraten wirst" (D IV 395); denn mit Helene verbindet Hans Karl, wie sich fast unmittelbar auf das Gespräch mit Antoinette zeigt, eine solche Notwendigkeit.

So wie das Gespräch mit Antoinette beginnt auch das mit Helene als Teil von Hans Karls „Programm" für den Abend bei Alten- wyl: er soll bei Helene als Brautwerber für seinen Neffen Stani auftre- ten; und so wie er in der Verfolgung seiner bewußten Absicht bei Antoinette keinen Erfolg gehabt hat, so auch im Gespräch mit Helene. Sie spürt die Unwahrheit seines Vorschlags, daß sie Stani heiraten soll und weist ihn förmlich und scharf zurück: „Ich möchte nicht, daß Sie so mit mir reden, Graf Bühl" (D IV 404). Damit ist aber der Weg zu der echten, aber noch immer uneingestandenen Absicht Hans Karls frei, ein Weg, der allerdings nicht direkt zum Ziel führt, sondern über Umwege, ein schwieriger Weg, dem Schwierigen angemessen, der ihn geht.

Dieser Weg führt in dem nun folgenden Gespräch mit Helene knapp am Scheitern vorbei, ja diese Unterredung scheint überhaupt das Ende der Beziehung zwischen Hans Karl und Helene zu markieren. Es endet mit einem Adieu von beiden Seiten und mit einer Gestik, die noch deutlicher auf eine „Katastrophe" hinzuweisen scheint: *Sie wollen sich die Hände geben, keine Hand findet die andere.*" In dieser direkten Anspielung auf die vorletzte Zeile von Hofmannsthals berühmtem Ge- dicht „Die Beiden" schwingt auch die letzte mit, in der der am Boden rollende dunkle Wein die verfehlte Gemeinschaft darstellt. Dennoch ist gerade in diesem Gespräch auch der Umschlag enthalten, der zur Ver- bindung mit Helene und damit zum Sozialen führt und der verhindert, daß Hans Karl seine Phrase „ich gehör eben nicht unter Menschen" (D IV 408) in die Tat umsetzt. Dieser Umschlag besteht eben darin, daß die Notwendigkeit, die Hans Karl und Helene verbindet, sichtbar wird, so- gar zur Sprache kommt; und diese Notwendigkeit ist das Produkt der Er-innerung.

Freilich beginnt ihr Gespräch eher resignativ. Helene ist eigentlich nicht überrascht, daß sich Hans Karl von ihr trennt: „...das
hab ich voraus gewußt. Daß einmal ein Moment kommen wird, wo
Sie mir so plötzlich adieu sagen werden und ein Ende machen...." Sie
hat es deswegen gewußt, weil es für sie eine Art Erinnerung ist: „Ich
glaube, ich habe alles in der Welt, was sich auf uns zwei bezieht, schon
einmal gedacht. So sind wir schon einmal gestanden, so hat eine fade
Musik gespielt, und so haben Sie mir adieu gesagt, einmal für allemal"
(D IV 405-6). Helenes Resignation kommt daher, daß auch sie, wie der
Zurückgekehrte, mit einer Art bösem Blick begabt ist, vor dem alles
Momenthafte nicht bestehen kann, auch die schönen und wichtigen
Momente nicht:

> Für mich ist ja der Moment gar nicht da, ich stehe da und
> sehe die Lampen dort brennen, und in mir sehe ich sie schon
> ausgelöscht. Und ich spreche mit Ihnen, wir sind ganz allein
> in einem Zimmer, aber in mir ist das jetzt schon vorbei: wie
> wenn irgendein gleichgültiger Mensch hereingekommen wäre
> und uns gestört hätte...und das schon vorüber wäre, daß ich
> mit Ihnen allein dagesessen bin...und Sie schon wieder ir-
> gendwo zwischen den Leuten [wären]. Und ich auch irgendwo
> zwischen den Leuten. [D IV 405]

Mit diesem Blick durchschaut sie zwar die lächerlichen Prätentionen
ihrer Gesellschaft und auch ihre eigenen, so daß sie sich nicht in Bana-
litäten verstrickt. Er verhindert aber durch seine Entwertung alles Zeit-
lich-Gesellschaftlichen auch die Möglichkeit, ins Leben zu treten. Was
der Gesellschaft als Solidität und Unbedingtheit an ihr erscheint, beruht auf einer tiefen Unsicherheit und Kontaktangst. Ihre von allen ge-
priesene „Artigkeit" ist, wie sie selbst sagt, „nur eine Art von Nervosität,
mir die Leut vom Hals zu halten" (D IV 380). Die Kehrseite ihrer Unbedingtheit ist Unverbindlichkeit, Einsamkeit, Beziehungslosigkeit; und
auch die Unfähigkeit, über irgendetwas zu staunen – und damit der
Verlust der Möglichkeit, zu einer tieferen Einsicht in die Wirklichkeit
zu kommen.[13] Helenes Dilemma ist, bezeichnenderweise, das des
„Über-ich[s]" aus „Ad me ipsum":

> Warum bemächtigt sich des Kindersinns
> So hohe Ahnung von den Lebensdingen
> Daß dann die Dinge wenn sie wirklich sind
> Nur schale Schauer des Erinnerns bringen? [R III 611]

Im „Schwierigen" wird diese Frage zwar nicht beantwortet: wohl wird aber im weiteren Gespräch das Gegenmittel gegen die „Schalheit" des Wirklichen gefunden. Es ist dies die Entdeckung, daß die in dieser Frage liegende, pauschale Entwertung aller Dinge unberechtigt ist, daß gewisse Dinge, hier das Verhältnis mit Hans Karl, auf einer tieferen Notwendigkeit beruhen, deren Gewähr die Er-innerung ist.

Daß Hans Karl diese Notwendigkeit, wenn auch mit Vorbehalt, anspricht, genügt, um Helenes Resignation in ihr Gegenteil umschlagen zu lassen. Als er davon spricht, „sehr zu jemandem [zu] gehören und doch nicht ganz zu ihm gehören [zu] dürfen," „zuckt" sie und möchte Genaueres wissen; und als sich Hans Karl rhetorisch zurückziehen möchte: „mein Gott, ja, wer könnte denn das erzählen!" beantwortet sie diese gar nicht als Frage gemeinte Frage mit einem direkten „Ja, mir. Jetzt" (D IV 406). Der Moment, der vorher für sie nicht da gewesen war, wird mit einem Mal sehr wichtig, er wird als „ausgewählte[r] Augenblick" (D IV 407) erkannt und mit aller Energie ergriffen. Vor dieser plötzlich auftauchenden Bestimmtheit versagen alle Vorbehalte, und Hans Karl erzählt ihr von seinem besonderen Augenblick beim Verschüttetwerden im Schützengraben:

> Das war nur ein Moment, dreißig Sekunden sollen es gewesen sein, aber nach innen hat das ein anderes Maß. Für mich wars eine ganze Lebenszeit, die ich gelebt hab, und in diesem Stück Leben, da waren Sie meine Frau. Ist das nicht spaßig?… Nicht meine zukünftige Frau. Das ist das Sonderbare. Meine Frau ganz einfach. Als ein fait accompli. Das Ganze hat eher etwas Vergangenes gehabt als etwas Zukünftiges. [D IV 406]

Mit dieser Er-innerung ist aber die notwendige Verbindung zwischen Hans Karl und Helene ausgesprochen, die Verbindung, die nicht auf einer zufälligen Konstellation von Umständen beruht, nicht durch den Moment geschaffen wird, sondern durch einen besonderen Moment als zeitunabhängige und wesentliche enthüllt wird, so „wie im Hohenbühler Teich, wenn man im Herbst das Wasser abgelassen hat, auf einmal die Karpfen und die Schweife von den steinernen Tritonen da waren, die man früher kaum gesehen hat" (D IV 372).[14] Freilich wird diese Verbindung von Hans Karl im Einklang mit seinem schwierigen Temperament sowohl nach dem Erlebnis selbst, als auch nach der Erzählung dieses Erlebnisses zensuriert; anstatt das Erlebnis einfach zu sehen, anstatt die logische Folge daraus zu ziehen, nennt er es zuerst eine „Anekdote ohne Pointe," konstruiert aber gleich darauf eine „Lek-

tion" daraus, die seine Vision in ihr Gegenteil verkehrt und das Er-
wünschte verhindert: „Es hat mir in einem ausgewählten Augenblick
ganz eingeprägt werden sollen, wie das Glück ausschaut, das ich mir
verscherzt habe.... Indem ich halt, solange noch Zeit war, nicht erkannt habe, worin das Einzige liegen könnte, worauf es ankäm. Und
daß ich das nicht erkannt habe, das war eben die Schwäche meiner
Natur. Und so habe ich diese Prüfung nicht bestanden" (D IV 407). Daß
er vorher nicht erkannt habe, worauf es ankommt, muß also als Grund
herhalten, daß er jetzt, nachdem er es erkannt hat, nicht die richtigen
Konsequenzen zieht: die seltsame Logik dieses Gedankengangs entlarvt
ihn als Ausflucht, schlimmer noch, also Selbstbestrafungsneurose.
Aus einer angeblichen Schwäche seines Erkenntnisvermögens wird
eine nicht bestandene Prüfung, auf Grund derer er jetzt sozusagen im
Leben durchgefallen ist; womit sein Wunsch, sich aus dem sozialen
Bereich zurückzuziehen, eine komplizierte Rechtfertigung erfährt.

199

Wie stark die Abwehr der sich für ihn aus dieser Er-innerung
ergebenden, sozialen Konsequenzen ist, sieht man auch daran, daß
er sich selbst nachträglich aus der ursprünglichen Vision seiner Ehe
ausblendet. Als er während seiner Genesung darüber nachdenkt, ist
es nicht mehr „meine Ehe, die ganz ungerufen die Mitte von diesem
Denken war...sondern es war Ihre [Helenes] Ehe" (D IV 407). Seine
wirklichen Wünsche zeigen sich allerdings an der Vehemenz, mit der
er seine Distanz von der vorgestellten Eheschließung Helenes betont:
„...sogar das Ja-Wort hab ich gehört...ganz von weitem, denn ich war
doch natürlich nicht dabei, ich war doch nicht dabei! – Wie käm ich
als ein Außenstehender zu der Zeremonie..." (D IV 408).

Diese starke Zensur, auf Grund derer er sich fast um sein
Glück bringt, kann aber nicht verhindern, daß Helene aus seiner
Er-innerung die Konsequenzen zieht. Für sie ist nicht, wie Antoinette
bemerkt hat, ein Wort entscheidend, sondern das, was hinter den
Worten steht. Und deswegen fragt sie Hans Karl bei den krampfhaften
„Erklärungsversuchen" seines Erlebnisses immer wieder, ob es wirklich
das ist, was er ihr hat sagen wollen (D IV 407). Für sie gibt es eben
unter den „tausend Erinnerungen," die Hans Karl „in so einem Ab-
schiedsmoment...durcheinander[-kommen]," nur *eine* wirkliche
Er-innerung. Die anderen durchschaut sie als Abwehrmanöver, als
Ausdruck dessen, daß sich Hans Karl, wie er selber sagt, wirklich
nicht „beisammen" hat (D IV 408).

Wie bekannt, erreicht Helene dieses „Beisammensein" Hans
Karls (und auch ihr eigenes) durch ein Opfer und zwar durch ein dop-

peltes. Sie setzt einerseits, durch ihren Entschluß Hans Karl nachzuge-
hen und dann durch ihre unkonventionell-direkte Liebeserklärung,
ihren Ruf als „artige Frau" aufs Spiel; vor allem aber gibt sie ihre Unverbindlichkeit auf und die Möglichkeit, sich hinter diese zurückzuziehen.
Dadurch, daß sie vom Leben Hans Karls „ihren Teil" (D IV 429) einfor-
dert, verliert sie ihre Distanz vom Sozialen und damit einen Teil ihrer
Freiheit, ihrer „Unbefangenheit" (D IV 428). Sie tritt damit aber auch aus
dem „quasi-Gestorbensein" (R III 599) in die Existenz. Die Stärke dieses
Entschlusses, der auf der Erkenntnis einer Er-innerung unter den
„schalen Schaudern des Erinnerns" beruht, ist es, die auch Hans Karl
zu sich selbst und unter die Menschen bringt.

Bevor sie allerdings Hans Karl gegenübertritt, um ihn mit
seiner Erinnerung in Einklang zu bringen, vergewissert sie sich selbst
noch einer anderen Art von Erinnerung: nachdem sie vom Kammerdiener erfahren hat, daß Hans Karl weggegangen ist, ohne eine Nach-
richt zu hinterlassen, daß also das irrige Adieu im Begriff steht, Wirklichkeit zu werden und daß daher ihre Tat, ihr Opfer nötig sind, gibt
sie dem Kammerdiener den Befehl, ihrem Vater, nachdem sie ausgegan-
gen ist, im richtigen Augenblick einen Brief zu übergeben. Dann stockt
sie und fragt: „Wie alt war ich, Wenzel, wie Sie hier ins Haus gekommen sind?" Und auf die Auskunft „Fünf Jahre altes Mäderl waren Kom-
tesse" antwortet sie: „Es ist gut, Wenzel, ich danke Ihnen..." (D IV 416).
Diese letzte, zum Klischee erstarrte Formel, die normalerweise ein
Gespräch zwischen Herrschaft und Diener beendet, wird hier bedeut-
sam vertieft. Bevor sich Helene aus dem Schutz der gesellschaftlichen
Bindungen begibt, appelliert sie an die Erinnerung des Kammerdieners
und an die historisch-gesellschaftliche Kontinuität, die darin liegt.
Obwohl sie im Begriff ist, eben diese zu verlassen, ja sie durch ihren
Entschluß in Frage zu stellen, ist es trotzdem „gut," daß es sie gibt und
Helene ist Wenzel wirklich dafür dankbar, daß er sie daran erinnert.
Denn letzlich drückt die Er-innerung Hans Karls seine wesenhafte
Verbundenheit mit Helene in gesellschaftlicher Form aus und verlangt
daher von ihm, daß er auch die gesellschaftlichen Konsequenzen zieht,
die sich für ihn daraus ergeben. Eben diese hat Hans Karl aber ver-
drängt, Helene muß sie ihm in Erinnerung rufen, selbst auf die Gefahr
hin, dabei gewisse gesellschaftliche Konventionen zu verletzen. Helene
drückt damit auch aus, daß es nach einschneidenden Katastrophen wie
dem ersten Weltkrieg ganz ausgeschlossen ist, die gesellschaftlichen
Konventionen in ihrer Gesamtheit herüberzuretten; gleichzeitig aber
auch, daß es eine soziale Kontinuität geben muß, daß auf höherer

Notwendigkeit beruhende Verhältnisse weiterhin einen gesellschaftlichen Ausdruck finden müssen. Die Erinnerung des Kammerdieners, der nicht unsonst den böhmischen Namen Wenzel hat, stellt für Helene diese grundsätzliche Kontinuität her und wird damit zum äußeren Korrelat der inneren Sicherheit, mit der sie kurz darauf Hans Karl die wahre Bedeutung seiner Erinnerung klarmacht.

Ganz in der Tradition des Lustspiels kommt es auch im „Schwierigen" nicht zum Äußersten, wird dieses Äußerste nur als Möglichkeit, als potentielle Bedrohung gezeigt. Helenes Bereitschaft zum äußersten Schritt wird nur symbolisch durch das Abwerfen und Fallenlassen ihres Mantels ausgedrückt. Durch die Rückkehr Hans Karls erübrigt sich der tatsächliche Bruch gesellschaftlichen Anstands.

201

Diese Rückkehr und das darauffolgende, entscheidende Gespräch sind nun auf verschiedene Weise mit der Erinnerung verbunden. Auf der bewußten Ebene werden sie durch die Erinnerung an das vorangegangene Gespräch mit Helene motiviert; die peinliche Erinnerung, daß er sich so wenig in der Hand hat, hat ihn zurückgetrieben, sagt Hans Karl. Er will sich für die Erwähnung der Er-innerung entschuldigen, die in Helene einen so entscheidenden Umschwung bewirkt hat: „Man kann das Vergangene nicht herzitieren, wie die Polizei einen vor das Kommissariat zitiert. Das Vergangene ist vergangen. Niemand hat das Recht, es in eine Konversation, die sich auf die Gegenwart bezieht, einzuflechten" (D IV 427). Die damit ausgesprochene Infragestellung der praktischen Funktion und Berechtigung der Erinnerung und die Postulierung eines in seine Atome aufgelösten Zeitverständnisses, sowie die daraus hervorgehende Wiederherstellung der „Unbefangenheit" (D IV 428) Helenes sind aber, wie Helene richtig erkennt und ihm auch zu erkennen gibt, das genaue Gegenteil dessen, was er wirklich meint. Hinter der vordergründigen Herabsetzung der Erinnerung liegt die Wichtigkeit verborgen, die sie in ihm einnimmt. „Hart sind nicht solche Abschiede für Sie," sagt sie ihm, „aber hart ist manchmal, was dann in Ihnen vorgeht, wenn Sie mit sich allein sind" (D IV 428). Denn dann tritt die Er-innerung in ihre Rechte, die Vision der Verbindung mit Helene, und bewirkt die Rückkehr, die durch Helenes Einsatz schließlich auch zu einer Umkehr wird, am sterilen Ästhetentum vorbei zu sich selbst und ins Soziale zurück.[15]

Der Ausgang des Lustspiels ist eine Verlobung, durch die sich Helene und Hans Karl auch in gesellschaftlicher Form binden. Es wird aber damit von Hofmannsthal nichts über das Fortbestehen der Gesellschaft als ganzer gesagt, der die beiden Schwierigen entstammen.

Ihre Verlobung steht nicht für das Weiterbestehen dieser Gesellschaft, sondern drückt nur die erkannte Notwendigkeit einer Fortsetzung des Sozialen im Allgemeinen aus. In welchen Formen es sich fortsetzen soll, darüber sagt Hofmannsthal hier nichts Konkretes aus; nur daß es nicht die überkommenen sein werden, wird am Ende des Lustspiels klar, an dem die konventionelle Umarmung des verlobten Paars von Stellvertretern vollzogen werden muß. Auch bleibt die Wirkung dieser Verlobung auf die Gesellschaft sehr in der Schwebe. Obwohl Neuhoff dadurch in gewisser Hinsicht besiegt wird, ist die Bedrohung, die er durch sein in Gewalttätigkeit umschlagendes Willensmenschentum für diese Gesellschaft darstellt, keineswegs aufgehoben. Wie aus Hofmannsthals nächstem Lustspiel, „Der Unbestechliche," hervorgeht, machte er sich in dieser Hinsicht wenig Illusionen; und noch weniger, was die einheitsstiftenden Kräfte der Erinnerung betrifft, die im „Schwierigen" zum letzten Mal im dichterischen Werk auftauchen.

Zunächst scheint es zwar, daß im „Unbestechlichen" mit Hilfe der Erinnerung ein traditionelles, soziales Gefüge erhalten wird. Dem Diener Theodor gelingt es, die beiden ehegefährdenden Freundinnen des Grafen Jaromir mit Hilfe seines peinlich genauen Gedächtnisses zu vertreiben – im Fall von einer sogar dadurch, daß er eine andere Form der Erinnerung, nämlich die indiskreten Aufzeichnungen Jaromirs, wirkungsvoll einsetzt. Jaromir wird von seinen Abschweifungen geheilt, kehrt zu seiner Frau zurück und macht, ohne sein Wissen von Theodor dazu veranlaßt, endgültig mit seiner lockeren Vergangenheit Schluß, indem er sich von dem sie enthaltenden Manuskript lossagt: „…ich brauche es nicht," sagt er zu seiner Frau,

> Ich will es nicht. Nie wieder, das ist alles nur eine eitle, unwahre Grimasse! Ein abscheuliches Überbleibsel aus meiner zu langen Junggesellenzeit! Das brauch ich nicht.
> [Küßt sie.]
> Das will ich nicht haben. Dich will ich haben, dich! [D IV 520]

Hier geht es aber nicht mehr, wie im „Schwierigen," um Erinnerung, weder im Sinn von Er-innerung, noch in dem von einem Wissen um historisch-soziale Kontinuität, sondern nur noch um Gedächtnis. In Theodors „nichtvergessender Herzkammer" sind „alle diese…Weibergeschichten und Schlechtigkeiten abphotographiert… bis in die kleinsten und niederträchtigsten Zärtlichkeiten und Meineide" (D IV 470). Und dieses alles photographisch festhaltende Gedächtnis wird systematisch und erpresserisch gegen die beiden Freundinnen

Jaromirs eingesetzt. Auf Grund dieses Einsatzes besteht zwar die alte Ordnung weiter. Sie erscheint aber durch die Art und Weise, wie sie gerettet wird, und durch die Person ihres Retters in einem sehr zweifelhaften Licht. Die Kompliziertheit der Intrige, mit deren Hilfe das Ganze bewerkstelligt wird, die dazu eingesetzten Lügen und Brutalitäten und dann die Machtergreifung und -ausübung Theodors, der einerseits als Erlöserfigur, andrerseits als präfaschistischer Diktator auftritt, zeigen die Ausgeliefertheit und prekäre Existenz der alten Ordnung, die in den ambivalenten Schlußworten Theodors deutlich zum Ausdruck kommt:

> Es sind Euer Gnaden die irdischen Dinge sehr gebrechlich. Es kann auch eine sehr starke Hand keine Schutzmauer aufbauen für ewige Zeiten um ihre anbefohlenen Schützlinge. Aber ich hoffe, solange ich hier die Aufsicht über das Ganze in Händen behalte, wird demgemäß alles in schönster Ordnung sein!
> [D IV 525]

203

Während Hofmannsthal 1919, bei der Fertigstellung des „Schwierigen," vielleicht noch hoffen konnte, daß die Er-innerung dem sozialen und geistigen Zerfall der Nachkriegszeit wenigstens bedingt würde widerstehen können, glaubte er das 1922, als er den „Unbestechlichen" schrieb, nicht mehr. In einer von Neuhoffs beherrschten Welt regiert nur noch das Gedächtnis, dessen Inhalt ohne Rücksicht auf die Zwecke, zu denen es eingesetzt wird, jederzeit abrufbar ist im Dienst der Macht. In einer solchen Welt hat die Er-innerung Einzelner kaum noch Funktion oder Wirkung, und Hofmannsthal wendet sich, wie schon anfangs erwähnt, gesamteuropäischen Kulturerinnerungen zu: um die in ihnen enthaltenen, verbindenden und verbindlichen Werte über den Bruch des Ersten Weltkriegs herüberzuretten und zu aktualisieren und um so der politischen und ideologischen Zersplitterung Europas entgegenzuwirken – in dem selbst einen solchen Wert darstellenden, „von Geschlecht zu Geschlecht" überlieferten Glauben, „daß sich Nationen verstehen, ihre Kultur mit wechselseitiger Sympathie umfassen und über ihr nationales Dasein hinaus sich in einer höheren Einheit zusammenfinden sollen und können" (R III 20).

ANMERKUNGEN

1   Zitiert bei: Richard Exner, „Erinnerung – Welch ein merkwürdiges Wort: Gedanken zur autobiographischen Prosadichtung Hugo von Hofmannsthals," *Modern Austrian Literature,* 7 (1974), 170.

2   Arthur R. Evans Jr., „Ernst Robert Curtius," *On Four Modern Humanists: Hofmannsthal, Gundolf, Curtius, Kantorowicz*, hsg. v. Arthur R. Evans Jr. (Princeton: Princeton University Press, 1970), 106. Evans erwähnt hier in diesem Zusammenhang Hofmannsthals Rückgriff auf Calderóns *„comedias"* und *„autos sacramentales."* Die mit Richard Strauß und Max Reinhardt ins Leben gerufenen Salzburger Festspiele, sowie auch seine Tätigkeit innerhalb der europäischen Kulturverbände legen davon weiteres Zeugnis ab.

3   Die Signatur *R* bezieht sich jeweils auf Bandnummer und Seitenzahl der Bände „Reden und Aufsätze" in: Hugo von Hofmannsthal, *Gesammelte Werke in zehn Einzelbänden* (Frankfurt/Main: Fischer, 1979-80).

4   Die Signatur *E* bezieht sich auf die Seitenzahl des Bandes „Erzählungen; erfundene Gespräche und Briefe; Reisen" in: Hugo von Hofmannsthal, *Gesammelte Werke in zehn Einzelbänden* (Frankfurt/Main: Fischer, 1979-80).

5   In gewisser Hinsicht veranschaulicht diese Erzählung, daß Mnemosyne die Mutter der Musen ist (Evans, 140).

6   Für die Hinweise auf die beiden Stellen (*Aeneis* I, 203 bzw. X, 782) bin ich meinen Kollegen Herbert W. Benario und Robert A. Bauslaugh sehr dankbar.

7   Neben Sophokles, der als Lektüre des Protagonisten direkt erwähnt wird, erscheinen noch weitere Vertreter der Literatur, allerdings Klassiker anderer Art. Sie erscheinen nicht so direkt wie Sophokles, sondern in der Form literarischer Erinnerungen und Anspielungen. Stefan George erscheint als ein „Vorübergehender" – eine Anspielung auf Hofmannsthals Gedicht an ihn – auch wenn er sich ebenfalls als Platon entpuppt (E 619); der Kustode des kleinen Museums, in dem die Koren stehen, ist eine Erinnerung an die in verschiedenen Gestalten auftretende dämonische Figur aus Thomas Manns „Tod in Venedig" (E 622-23); und an Novalis' „Lehrlinge zu Sais" erinnert die Reflexion über die Aufhebung des Schleiers, um „in den ewigen lebenden Tempel" einzutreten (E 626).

8   Michael Hamburger, „Hofmannsthals Bibliothek," *Euphorion,* 55 (1961), 71; zitiert bei: David H. Miles, *Hofmannsthal's Novel* Andreas: *Memory and Self* (Princeton: Princeton University Press, 1972), 94.

9   Sören Kierkegaard, „Stadien auf dem Lebensweg," *Gesammelte Werke,* Bd. 4 (Jena: Diederichs, 1914), 11-12; Miles, 94.

10 Kierkeggard, 11.

11 Die Signatur *D* bezieht sich jeweils auf Bandnummer und Seitenzahl der Bände „Dramen" in: Hugo von Hofmannsthal, *Gesammelte Werke in zehn Einzelbänden* (Frankfurt/Main: Fischer, 1979-80).

12 Kierkegaard, 11.

13 Auf Platons Gedanken beruhend, daß das Staunen der Anfang der Philosophie sei.

14 Dieses Bild der Er-innerung ist selber wieder eine Kindheitserinnerung Hans Karls und zeigt im Kleinen das Zusammenfallen der beiden Bedeutungen von Erinnerung.

15 Eine frühe Version dieser Stelle lautet: „Hart sind nicht Deine Abschiede aber hart ist, was ihnen vorhergeht, wenn du allein bist" (D IV 450). Der Gegensatz zwischen den beiden Stellen weist darauf hin, daß die Wichtigkeit der Erinnerung in der endgültigen Version hervorgehoben wurde.

V . THE ELUSIVE HUNT

IN SEARCH of ADORNO *IN SEARCH of WAGNER**

BY JAMES F. JONES, JR., SOUTHERN METHODIST UNIVERSITY

Each sentence of Kafka's says "interpret me."[1]

Couched within the debates on the nature of criticism in our time
lies a rudimentary issue more often than not obscured by the
sometimes trenchant taking-of-sides endemic to the debates
themselves. This issue – the "ontological" status of critical discourse –
is of all issues the most basic, for at stake is the feasibility, present and
future, of communicating about art, whether the particular manifestation be musical, literary, pictorial, or multi-media. Like any form of
communication, critical discourse by definition involves the transmission of a message, to borrow the idiom of Roman Jakobson's famous
axis, encoded by a sender (the "author," "emitter," or "encoder") and
then subsequently decoded by a receiver (the "reader," "recipient," or
"decoder").[2] The message being communicated, then, has a referent
whose meaning is possibly transferable from one pole of the axis to
the other, and whose reception is rendered theoretically conceivable
by dint of the message's position, hanging, as it were, suspended like
Rabelais' "paroles gelées" (*Quart Livre*, chapters 55-56) to be thawed
and digested by those individuals who wish, for whatever reason, to
note the message's innate potentiality of significance. We may be too
close ourselves, historically considered, to the front lines of the debate
to determine with any certainty whether the current battle over critical
methodology is just another facet of the seemingly eternal one between
the Ancients and Moderns, the Conservatives and Liberals, Rubenistes
and Poussinistes, Good Guys and Bad Guys.[3] But that a battle is now
being waged cannot be disputed.

One crucial distinction remains, however, between the arguments of the past and those of our day. Formerly, critical discourse
found its employ in the discussion of subjects exterior to itself, as
Matthew Arnold's mid-nineteenth-century essay, "The Function of
Criticism at the Present Time," so clearly sets forth. Whatever scholarly
arguments arose concerned differences in interpreting the subjects of

207

* I should like to thank J. Thomas Rimer III, for his suggestions for the improvement
of this essay, an earlier version of which was first delivered at a Washington University
Faculty Seminar, directed by William Gass.

that discourse. Thus art critics in the eighteenth century, Diderot for example, could join in the mêlée between the partisans of line and the partisans of color. Music commentators in the nineteenth century, like Liszt, could take positions on the question of Wagnerian opera's ascendancy over bel canto. Literary critics could trace themes in literature or discuss numerous sorts of developments in certain works. Such criticism had precedents and traditions to emulate, gradually becoming so established and fixed within our cultural and intellectual heritage that René Wellek could sketch the history of literary criticism from the middle of the eighteenth century to the middle of the twentieth.[4]

208   Yet now criticism's "ontological" status is going through a radical metamorphosis characterized by the ever-increasing number of works that deal specifically with critical discourse itself and not with the traditional material of literary discourse. How else may we explain the current plethora of titles demonstrating not always successful attempts to gloss structuralism, semiotics, Marxist theory, post-structuralism, hermeneutics, or *Rezeptionstheorie*, in the manner of so many Monarch Notes? A second, equally telling characteristic in the modern evolution of criticism's "ontological" status would be the charge of intended obfuscation and obscurantism launched at some of the most often cited figures in the scholarly world today. Harold Bloom, Geoffrey Hartman, J. Hillis Miller, the late Paul de Man, and above all Jacques Derrida have been cited as proponents of what Leo Bersani once called a still undefined and amorphous trend of "difficult thinking" that may be contrasted to "optimistic humanism" and to what "cultural conservatives" have long been wont to effect.[5] How significant the shift in criticism has become is evident when one compares the goal of those studies included in Wellek's multi-volumed history, a goal which was without exception to illuminate or explain some aspect of a particular work or movement, both with the host of present titles that seek to explain a specific critical discourse and with the ubiquitous charge that, whereas critical discourse traditionally has sought to elucidate, many of its tendencies now seek only to obfuscate.[6]

It is into this last category – that of representatives of Bersani's "difficult thinking" with its attendant role in the changing status of critical discourse – that we may place Theodor Adorno the music critic, for he shares the distinction of being accused of deliberate unintelligibility along with the above-named individuals who are perhaps more notorious at the moment in certain American intellectual circles than he. The charge of deliberate unintelligibility against Adorno turns his own comment about Kafka, cited in the exergue to this essay, upon itself. We are accustomed to reading such statements about any number of writers, painters, or musicians, especially those of more "modernist" persuasions. Critics (like the Adorno of *Prisms* or of the *Noten zur Literatur*) are intermediaries, deciphering for those less versed what is "difficult," ferreting out "meanings." But when one posits that "[e]very page of *Adorno* says 'interpret me'," the issue becomes one of substance pertaining not to the subject of the critical discourse but specifically to the critical discourse itself. Robert Craft's diatribes against Adorno proceed from this presumed fault of ubiquitous uninterpretability,[7] and Craft on Adorno is not dissimilar to Graff on Bloom, Donoghue on Hartman, or Crews on Derrida. To cite "obscurantist" tactics on the part of the practitioners of "difficult thinking" did indeed become something of an intellectual commonplace in the late seventies and early eighties. When Craft accuses Adorno of upholding "the highest standards of obfuscation,"[8] he foreshadows by five years Graff's equally caustic accusations against what is often erroneously labelled the "Yale School" and its rapport with the philosophy of Jacques Derrida.[9]

As a representative of the diverse group of German intellectuals who fled Nazism, Adorno seems peculiarly isolated insofar as indictments of unintelligibility are concerned. Consider as an appositely contrasting figure Ernst Robert Curtius. Seven years older than Adorno, Curtius came under the sway of the poet Stefan George, along with Friedrich Gundolf and any number of young German intellectuals in the early 1920s. Witness to the same historical chaos of the 1930s and 1940s, physically and emotionally affected by that chaos in much the same way (flight from National Socialism, eventual and uneasy association with an American culture in many respects the antithesis of the European with which he was obviously more at ease), Curtius experienced that identical, acute sense of a decaying world order that is found in every one of Adorno's major works. Yet Curtius' ultimate reaction to that decay was the opposite of Adorno's. Perhaps nothing can better demonstrate that truth than a passage from the author's foreword to the English translation of *Europäische Literatur und lateinisches Mittelalter*, Curtius' study which was first published in 1948:

> What I have said will have made it clear that my book is not the product of purely scholarly interests, that it grew out of

concern for the preservation of Western culture. It seeks to serve an understanding of the Western cultural tradition in so far as it is manifested in literature... In the intellectual chaos of the present it has become necessary, and happily not impossible, to demonstrate that unity....[10]

As George had proposed in theory and as the art historians Aby Warburg, Fritz Saxl, and Erwin Panofsky had repeatedly sought to show in practice, European culture was one indivisible phenomenon of Western civilization, and according to Curtius that *sense* of cultural unity had to be recovered from the tatters of two world wars and from the barbarism of the Nazis. Curtius' method (the famous *Toposforschung* that purposefully sweeps across languages, national boundaries and, most importantly, across time) was as clear as were his goals.[11] Leo Spitzer, Erich Auerbach, Ernst Kantorowicz, and several others equally gifted shared to a remarkable degree this same humanistic proclivity which may well be viewed as the polar opposite of Adorno's pessimism.[12] By writing in German and by frequently repeating their contention that the cultural heritage of Europe was one, these individuals sought to refurbish that which had been so widely blighted by the Third Reich's ascendancy, to evidence not only by the subject of their critical discourse but also by their critical discourse itself that German was the language of Goethe (the key figure in Curtius' intellectual conceptualization of Western culture) before it became the ignominious language of Hitler and Goebbels.

Although Adorno may well have experienced this same instinctive compulsion to restore to the German language the dignity it once had enjoyed before history thrust myriad connotations upon it, any comparison with the representatives of the German "universalist school" of cultural historians ceases there. Indeed a marked cleavage exists between Adorno and the "universalists" despite the fact that he, like they, chose to continue to write in German (even though most if not all were fluent in several other languages) at a time when it might have been easier to be published in a language other than German, and despite their common intellectual roots going back to George and his eminent circle. The German of Auerbach and Curtius is rich and learned to be sure, yet by no means is it hopelessly convoluted, generally lending itself to translation. Willard Trask, who skillfully rendered into English both *Mimesis* and *Europäische Literatur*, never found it necessary to make a comment even remotely similar to that found at the end of the "Translators' Introduction" to Adorno's *Philosophy of Modern Music*:

> The difficulty of Adorno's German is a matter of legend to
> those familiar with his works in the original language. The in-
> tensity of his thought results in a hard-wrought syntax, often
> of esoteric vocabulary, which at times defies comprehension
> upon first sight and makes translation seem impossible. A neg-
> ative view of this particular type of idiom might well employ a
> term used by Adorno to characterize the language of others:
> jargon. Adorno is often guilty of falling into a jargon which is
> detrimental to whatever he would hope to express. In so do-
> ing, he takes a place in a long, though not necessarily enviable
> or admirable, German tradition.[13]

This citation finds its mirror image in translators' prefaces
for each of the works by Jacques Derrida, all of which announce that
Derrida cannot really be translated, that such an enterprise is at best
"an exercise in violent approximation."[14] From this perspective the
author's syntax, word-choice, and tortuously involuted style pointedly
undergird the density of Derrida's "message,"[15] just as they do in Adorno (the "intensity of his thought results in a hard-wrought syntax...").
Within Adorno's works, as elsewhere in our present intellectual environment, the transmission of the "message" assumes hermetic properties. The movement between the two poles of Jakobson's axis of communication appears skittish if not purposely detained altogether.
As in the case of Derrida, Adorno's very untranslatability, so widely
proclaimed, tends to present itself as an intention. Rabelais' "paroles
gelées" here would wait endlessly to be thawed so that they can be
properly digested. *Forme et fond* are thus indigenous in each other,
establishing an unbreakable bond between the innate difficulty of
"difficult thinking" and the difficulty of its critical discourse. Yet once
again, the issue does not center on the hermetic *artist* who apparently
requires glossing in order to be "understood," but rather on the hermetic *critic*. And are we therefore blithely to accept Harold Bloom's
assertion that criticism's changing "ontological" status now demands
that it be considered an art ("la critique pour la critique") on a par
with that same art it formerly sought to discuss and elucidate?[16] If
so, we return to an intellectual sphere that antedates the conventional
seventeenth-century argument over the *faculté créatrice* and the *faculté
critique*. The former's primacy over the latter becomes fixed in the
history of criticism between the seventeenth century and the last

JAMES F. JONES, JR.

decades of the twentieth, at which time a compelling modification occurs in whose throes we find ourselves today.[17]

In his foreword to the 1968 edition of *Introduction to the Sociology of Music*, Adorno writes of his own efforts, referring to himself in that characteristically German third-person singular that when literally translated into English has a hollow, distant ring to it as if one could ever truly be witness to one's own actions: "In general, the author tends not so much to say what he is doing and how, but to do it. This is the consequence of a theory which does not adopt the accepted separation of matter and method and is suspicious of abstract methodology."[18] While this statement may in fact be pointedly accurate for his Sociology, it is equally valid for Adorno's earlier *In Search of Wagner*. There is no "abstract methodology" that governs the study of Wagner, no guiding principle or group of axioms set forth at the outset, then methodically substantiated by subsequent discussion. We may safely assume that Adorno wished his book to bear no resemblance to those "...popular biographies, this latest offspring of culture industry which feasts parasitically on the success of famous men and cashes in on their established names rather than furthering an insight into the significance of their work and their existence."[19]

From one superficial perspective, *In Search of Wagner* is a modified *vie et oeuvre* but certainly not in the sense of the biographies Adorno belittles in his review of Newman. We have the obligatory introduction (the chapter entitled "Social Characters") and the customary analysis of individual works; but the result – the Wagner for whom Adorno outwardly searches here – is not readily accessible, refusing to spring out as it were from the critic's pages fully formed like Athena from Zeus' head. And insofar as this one specific work from the Adorno canon is concerned, the reason for this fact stems precisely from the density of the study's style. Historical, biographical fact intersects with psychological commentary, which itself intersects with intense stylistic analysis of particular musical passages, alternating with Marxist sociological terminology, quasi-universalist references to artistic milieux outside music, and containing not a few attempts to promote a psychoanalytical reading. There are, in short, many widely varying aspects of Wagner the subject that provide the material for Adorno the critic, who takes them all on at the same time.

One of the primary unifying factors in Adorno's book would by necessity be the Wagner whose historical position in the nineteenth century is viewed here as an eminently central one. That such a Wagner would appear prominently in Adorno's commentary should come as no surprise, given Adorno's long attachment to the Frankfurt School with its philosophically Marxist presuppositions concerning the decaying order of bourgeois society. Thus we find passages such as the following:

> ...Wagner's oeuvre comes close to the consumer goods of the nineteenth century which knew no greater ambition than to conceal every sign of the work that went into them, perhaps because any such traces reminded people too vehemently of the appropriation of the labour of others, of an injustice that could still be felt. A contradiction of all autonomous art is the concealment of the labour that went into it but in high capitalism, with the complete hegemony of exchange-value and with the contradictions arising out of that hegemony, autonomous art becomes both problematic and programmatic at the same time.... To make works of art into magical objects means that men worship their own labour because they are unable to recognize it as such.[20]

Wagner's case conforms to the traditional theory of Marxist critical doctrine. The codes that Adorno the Marxist sociologist uses are ones with which we have been familiar since the inception of such ideologically grounded criticism. "Appropriation of labor," "hegemony of exchange-value," and other such turns-of-phrase are intrinsically vital supports of the metalanguage of a specific, recognized critical discourse. Their presence here exemplifies the straightforward, connotative strategy of theory and example (decay of nineteenth-century bourgeois culture and its vibrant manifestation in Wagner's works).[21] It is perhaps not unfair to Adorno to wonder why, as he does on any number of other occasions in *Wagner*, he does not at such a point immediately shift perspectives from the exterior world to its rapport with Wagner's own psychological constitution. Adorno abruptly ends his discussion, and for that matter the chapter which lasts only a few more sentences, with no reference to the most obvious extension of his proposition that to "make works of art into magical objects means that men worship their own labour because they are unable to recognize it as such": Wagner's own obsession with the idea of Bayreuth.[22] In Wagner's mind Bayreuth was indeed a magical kingdom, an external work of art where his operas would at long last receive the quality performances they merited. To a large degree the illusion Bayreuth came to encompass for Wagner did represent something semi-religious which hid his own intense labors as well as those of the musicians and the supporting personnel required for performances. That Bayreuth eventually did evolve into a shrine, a place of ardent pilgrimage like Mecca or Jerusalem with an absent god and idolizing congregations of the faithful, is an historical fact.[23]

Closely related to Adorno the sociologist's depiction of Wagner's oeuvre as representative of the tensions of class-consciousness and the ultimate inner decay of bourgeois society are the passages interspersed throughout this book in which another Adorno appears to address the notion that the mystical analogues to ideas receive, in Wagner, musical interpretation. Throughout such passages, Adorno the historical musicologist tries to link the societal influences of Wagner's music to the music's innate referentiality, and in an important part of the eighth chapter ("Myth"), Adorno uses an example from *Lohengrin* that underscores his intention:

> ...Wagner's work allows itself to be appropriated by bourgeois ideology. Myth becomes mythologizing.... The links connecting bourgeois ideology to myth can be seen at their clearest in *Lohengrin* where the establishment of a sacrosanct sphere inviolable by any profane tampering coincides directly with the transfiguration of bourgeois arrangements. In line with the authentic spirit of ideology, the subjugation of women in marriage is dressed up as humility, as the achievement of a pure love.... The man who "fights" for his means of existence out in the world becomes a hero, and after Wagner there were doubtless countless women who thought of their husbands as Lohengrins. [*Wagner*, p. 127]

Here Adorno the Marxist sociologist joins Adorno the historical musicologist whose goal would be to trace how this referentiality occurs between idea (mythical "wedding" as epitomized by *Lohengrin*) and actions in the "real" world (actual weddings in bourgeois society). The appropriation of Wagner by bourgeois ideology is indeed particularly evidenced by *Lohengrin*'s critical fortunes, and in this instance Adorno has intuitively sensed a fact that can be – perhaps crudely – demonstrated by asking a randomly picked clerk in an American music store for the "wedding music." The "Bridal Chorus" from the third act of *Lohengrin* (Scene 1) has been for some decades now part of a "traditional" bourgeois wedding in America, as intrinsic to the ceremony itself as the repetition of vows.[24] It should be remembered, in support of

214

Adorno's notion, that Lévi-Strauss once called Wagner "the unquestionable father of the structural analysis of myths" ("le père irrécusable de l'analyse structurale des mythes"), saying that it was indeed revealing that such analysis first came to exist through the "language" of music.[25]

Adorno the Marxist sociologist and historical musicologist sometimes bases his evidence upon comments made by Adorno the nascent semiotician. In view of the last example from *Lohengrin*, consider how the following remarks support what would be the critic's later contention in *Wagner*:

> What specifically characterizes Wagnerian expression is its intentionality: the motiv is a sign that transmits a particle of congealed meaning. For all its intensity and emphasis, Wagner's music is as script is to words.... Wagner's leitmotivs stand revealed as allegories that come into being when something purely external...is appropriated by meanings and made to represent them, a process in which signifiers and signified are interchangeable. [*Wagner*, p. 44 f.]

215

The brief eight measures from *Lohengrin* that define what succeeding generations will come to speak of simply as "the Wedding March" (Act III, Scene 1, measures 5-12) have demonstrated time and again the validity of Adorno's assertion. In his commentary Adorno uses the now traditional, binary opposition, borrowed from an unnamed Ferdinand de Saussure, between the two components of the communicative sign: the signifier and the signified. That Adorno has again reached a telling conclusion is borne out by the undeniable interchangeability of this one particular musical leitmotiv and the idea which this same leitmotiv has historically come to represent in bourgeois ideology. Today schoolchildren invent rhymes that parody "Here Comes the Bride" (the adopted English "text" for Wagner's leitmotiv), a fact that betrays the extent to which Adorno's observation is correct. This motiv – undoubtedly more so than any other from Wagner's oeuvre – has long entered bourgeois consciousness.

The possibility of tradition's summarily "lifting" such motivs from Wagner's oeuvre apparently disturbed Adorno, although no such claim could be made about the later author of the *Philosophy* or the *Sociology*.[26] Providing examples such as "The Ride of the Valkyries," the "Liebestod," and the "Good Friday music," Adorno decries that the "... music had been torn out of [its] context, re-arranged and become popular...[t]he disintegration into fragments sheds light on the fragmentariness of the whole" (*Wagner*, p. 106). Here is a telling instance of Adorno's thinking prior to the four postulates announced in his 1945 "Social Critique of Radio Music." In opposition, however, to Adorno's stated position, one might well note that Wagner's music is no more fragmentary than any other composer's in the modern technological and post-technological world. It is the transmission of music that has radically changed. As Adorno himself later wrote when considering the then critically important and growing role of the radio in twentieth-century society, "Are not the stations...bringing the masses in contact with something totally different from [what is] intended?"[27]

216   The unlimited and uncontrolled (mis)use of music in a media-oriented society points directly to the fact that all "serious" music can suffer the same fate at any given moment. With the exception of "Préludes," Liszt's symphonic poems, for instance, rarely appear on American concert programs. Yet how many individuals came into *weekly* contact with the last section of that piece in movie theatres after the Depression as they watched Flash Gordon's matchbox spaceship (suspended on a sometimes visible string) blast off, wafted into space by – of all things – Liszt's musical rendering of Lamartine's *Nouvelles Méditations poétiques*? A like phenomenon occurred during the early days of American commercial television in the fifties. The opening bars of the overture to *William Tell* are surely more associated with the Lone Ranger by most Americans today than they are with Rossini or the chaotic state of Italian opera in 1820. Had Adorno not returned to Europe and had he remained in America, perhaps his indictment of Wagner on the grounds of what he calls the music's self-defeating "fragmentariness" would have evolved into a sociological study of the fragmentary reality of any music which most people encounter through electronic media rather than through attendance at a concert or opera.

Besides Adorno the sociologist, the musicologist, the semiotician, and the social commentator, another Adorno appears in *Wagner*, this one concerned with the composer's psychic development, its rapport with exterior reality, and with the manifestations of the composer's inner conflicts as found within his musical creations. Adorno here falls back into the time-honored critical stance of a nineteenth-century intentional reading coupled with more modern twentieth-century Freudian trends of interpretation. Subconscious aspects of Wagner's psyche thus reveal themselves openly in his work. According to Adorno, Wagner sometimes was conscious of just how his musical creations came from within himself and sometimes not. (Adorno's

assessments in these instances border on the psycho-histories published at the start of the 1980s.) Utilizing the various sources, such as
Hildebrandt, Glasenapp, and the ever-present Paul Bekker, Adorno
discusses the difference between the Wagner of the later operas and
the Wagner of the middle-period, noting the composer's own recognition of two principles which were at best contradictory and whose synthesis explained the "'harmony between the two tendencies'..., namely
unrestrained sexuality and an ideal of asceticism" (*Wagner*, p. 14).

This sort of commentary then leads to two different yet concomitantly presented areas of inquiry. On the one hand, such comment
enables Adorno to discuss Wagner and Nietzsche and then Wagner
and Schopenhauer. On the other, especially from the point of view of
Tannhäuser and *Siegfried*, Adorno can attempt a purely Freudian analysis of his subject. In the first case, Adorno observes, for example, that
Nietzsche's own contradictory relationship with Wagner finds its nexus
in the fact that Nietzsche understood Wagner better than the composer
understood himself and that Nietzsche erred grievously in giving names
to Wagner's phobias ("Nietzsche knew the secret of Wagner's idiosyncrasies and broke their spell by naming them," *Wagner*, p. 25). What
Adorno calls idiosyncrasies reveals the violent antisemitism found in
those grotesque operatic figures Mime and Alberich. Yet this is not all,
for Adorno in a moment of psycho-historical analysis then suggests that
"Wagner recoiled with shock from the similarity between Mime and
himself" (*Wagner*, p. 24), ultimately cutting from the score of *Siegfried*
a set of specific directions for the character whose ultimate portrayal
pointedly resembled Wagner himself. (The picture of the composer on
the jacket of the NLB translation was not, one might assume, chosen
by chance from the many that exist.) Adorno's point here is that when
Wagner brutally caricatured the Jew in his operas, he was brutally cari-
caturing himself on a subliminal level, a notion borne out by the composer's sadistic humiliation of Hermann Levi, the brilliantly talented
conductor who was to conduct *Parsifal* (*Wagner*, pp. 18-20). Adorno
systematically returned later, it should be added, to Wagner's demonic
playing with the whole notion of Jewishness in "Wagner, Nietzsche,
and Hitler."

What is absent in Adorno's attempting a perhaps somewhat
"amateurish" Freudian analysis of Wagner through the medium of the
latter's works is the choice of highly technical, psychoanalytic terms
that one finds throughout the later *Philosophy*. In *Wagner* passages do
occur that deal, for example, with the death-wish: "the kingdom of

death" is defined as "the ideal of Wagnerian music" (*Wagner*, p. 60) toward which in Adorno's view all the composer's music strives. Adorno does not write in *Wagner*, however, sentences such as "[u]niversal necrophilia is the last perversity of style" (*Philosophy*, p. 204) or "[t]he impossibility of the aesthetic program [in Stravinsky] is a stratagem of reason over hebephrenia" (*Philosophy*, p. 176).[28] This tendency on Adorno's part to uncover psychoanalytical explanations for events in Wagner's life and for the unconscious manifestations of Wagner's psyche in his oeuvre appears at various intervals throughout *Wagner*, and his growing desire to provide such a reading of Wagner is here more than apparent.

218

Finally, there appears Adorno the "universalist" who adds in *Wagner* an occasional allusion to literature in order to bolster whatever argument he may be trying at the particular moment to sustain.[29] Such literary allusions tend on the surface of the critical discourse to provide concrete authority to an idea otherwise solely supported by musical evidence. Attempting to show the utter accuracy of Nietzsche's statement that Wagner was – despite the claims of radical modernity – "a man out of key with his time" (*Wagner*, p. 64) and thus an authoritative classicist, Adorno notes the "self-righteousness in the author of *Tristan*, the idol of the Paris symbolists down to Mallarmé" (*ibid.*). When discussing the romantic ambiguity of altered chord structure, Adorno writes that it was precisely this ambiguity "that excited Baudelaire, the most advanced musical consciousness of his day" (*Wagner*, p. 44). In his pages linking the Impressionist movement and Wagner's notion of a "total art work," Adorno states that we must remember "that the credo of universal symbolism to which all his technical achievements subscribe is that of Puvis de Chavannes and not Monet's" (*Wagner*, p. 50).

Such allusions, however, are not always as convincing and supportive as Adorno must have intended them to be. Mallarmé had not heard a note of Wagner when he wrote the prose poem for the 1885 number of the *Revue Wagnérienne* which attacked the idolatry of the numerous Wagnerian partisans in Paris at the time.[30] Baudelaire's knowledge of music was at best quite limited, judging from the few comments in his various "Salons." His one critical essay, *Richard Wagner et Tannhäuser à Paris*, appeared in the *Revue européenne* for April 1, 1861, after the mêlée in Paris over the performance of *Tannhäuser* there. It is therefore quite misleading to label Baudelaire "the most advanced musical consciousness of his day" on the basis of those scant pages. And as for Puvis de Chavannes, the comparison is simply not clear.

Puvis de Chavannes was a severe classicist, as "L'enfant prodigue," "Le repos," and the frescoes for the Boston Library pointedly attest. With these and many other similar allusions, Adorno strains for breadth and sometimes fails at the effort.

With some of the short pieces from the *Moments musicaux* and his book on Kierkegaard's aesthetics, *In Search of Wagner* belongs to Adorno's earliest published works. The Kierkegaard study dates from 1933 and *Wagner*, portions of which had already been published in the *Zeitschrift für Sozialforschung*, from 1937 and 1938. Already in this first attempt to tackle a major figure from music we have the Adorno who will later take on Schoenberg, Stravinsky, Mahler, and Berg. And here in *Wagner* exists the very cacophony of Adornos for which Adorno will become so celebrated, and why, ultimately, he would justifiably earn pride-of-place in Bersani's "difficult thinking" category of critical endeavors in our time. As perhaps no other musical commentator before him, Adorno sought to incorporate in his writing any number of established critical discourses: the history of ideas, psychoanalysis, Marxism, sociology, "European highbrow criticism of culture,"[31] biography. *Wagner* points directly to the 1960 study of Mahler and, especially, to those exceedingly "difficult" pages of *Philosophy,* in large measure because Adorno's synoptic vision of his chosen subject categorically insists that the perspectives applied be applied concomitantly. This fact might explain why one Adorno runs directly into another Adorno, why his critical discourse alternates among discourses that are otherwise more traditionally grounded, as it seeks a "method," for want of another term, that would permit language to convey what Adorno wishes to convey, to let his "message" move from the *destinateur* pole of Jakobson's axis to the *destinataire* pole, to allow Adorno's conception of Wagner or Stravinsky or Berg to be transferable from his mind to that of his reader via the printed word.

The density, then, of his thought *is*, as his translators have noted, directly reflected in the density of his style, intricately one (as in Derrida) and incapable of being dissected. To try – as this short essay has – to explicate a few of the Adornos in Adorno's *Wagner* in the end is by definition an act of dismemberment, for the synopsis of voices cannot be disassociated from the synoptic, all-inclusive, and all-explaining totality that is Adorno's vision of his subject. *Versuch über Wagner* implies far more than the title for the English translation indicates. "Versuch" indeed means something more closely associated with "testing" and "experimenting" than with "searching." *Wagner* portrays an Adorno who seeks a critical discourse appropriate both to his subject and to his own desire to communicate about the subject, a discourse markedly unlike those which preceded his own and one which surely allows his own voice to join those others in our time that question the very assumptions of critical discourse itself. Walter Benjamin, writing in French to Gershom Scholem in January of 1930, remarked, "Se faire une situation dans la critique, cela, au fond, veut dire: la recréer comme genre."[32] In this attempt on the part of one of Benjamin's most celebrated friends, Theodor Adorno, we may witness a concerted experiment to forge a new discourse, to found, as it were, a new criticism. It is, therefore, not merely Wagner who is the subject of Adorno's *Wagner*; it is at the same time Adorno who is also the work's subject. In the final analysis, each page of Adorno does indeed say "interpret me."

NOTES

1 Theodor Adorno, "Notes on Kafka," in *Prisms*, trans. S. and S. Weber (London: Spearman, 1967), p. 246.

2 Roman Jakobson, *Essais de linguistique générale* (Paris: Editions de Minuit, 1963), pp. 213-14.

3 Cf. Marcel Proust's satirical remark that each generation of critics does nothing but limit itself to proposing "truths" diametrically opposed to those which had been trenchantly adhered to by its predecessors. See *A la recherche du temps perdu* (Paris: Gallimard, Bibliothèque de la Pléiade, 1954), II, 469.

4 René Wellek, *A History of Modern Criticism: 1750-1950* (New Haven: Yale University Press, 1955 ff.).

5 Leo Bersani, review of Marshall Berman's *All That Is Solid Melts Into Air, The Experience of Modernity*, in *The New York Times Book Review* (February 14, 1982), p. 29.

6 See among many others the following early studies for various aspects of the debate: Geoffrey Hartman, "Literary Criticism and Its Discontents," *Critical Inquiry*, II, 2 (Winter 1976), 203-20; Frank Lentricchia, *After The New Criticism* (Chicago: The University of Chicago Press, 1980), especially part I, chapter 5 "History or the Abyss: Poststructuralism," pp. 156-210; part III, chapter 8 "Paul de Man: The Rhetoric of Authority," 282-317; part III, chapter 9 "Harold Bloom: The Spirit of Revenge," pp. 318-346; Jonathan Culler, *The Pursuit of Signs, Semiotics, Literature, Deconstruction* (Ithaca: Cornell University Press, 1981); Gerald Graff, *Literature Against Itself: Literary Ideas in Modern Society* (Chicago and London: The University of Chicago Press, 1979); Denis Donoghue, *Ferocious Alphabets* (New York: Little, Brown, 1981); and "Deconstructing Deconstructions," *New York Review of Books* (January 2, 1980), pp. 37-40; Frederick Crews, "Criticism Without Constraint," *Commentary*, LXXIII, no. 1 (January 1982), 65-71.

7 Robert Craft, *Prejudices in Disguise* (New York: Alfred Knopf, 1974), pp. 92 ff. Craft, of course, had enjoyed a long period of co-operation with Stravinsky that ultimately resulted in a number of coauthored books: *Themes and Episodes* (New York: Alfred Knopf, 1966), *Expositions and Developments* (New York: Doubleday, 1962), *Conversations with Igor Stravinsky* (Garden City: Doubleday, 1959), etc. Thus Adorno's own frequent and often embittered attacks upon the man with whom Craft had worked and whom Craft had greatly admired may well have played more than an inconsequential role in Craft's position against Adorno himself.

8 Craft, *Prejudices*, p. 92.

9 See, besides *Literature Against Itself* cited in note 6, especially Gerald Graff, "Fear and Trembling at Yale," *The American Scholar,* XLVI (Autumn, 1977), 467-78.

10 Ernst Robert Curtius, *European Literature and the Latin Middle Ages,* trans. Willard R. Trask (New York: The Bollingen Foundation, 1953), p. viii. Cf. Serenus Zeitblom's autobiographical pages which poignantly mirror this very theme (chapter II) in the 1947 *Doktor Faustus* by Thomas Mann, who consulted with Adorno on the music chapters.

11 See Arthur R. Evans, Jr., "Ernst Robert Curtius," chapter 3 of *On Four Modern Humanists,* ed. Evans (Princeton: Princeton University Press, 1970), pp. 85-145.

12 See in this regard Harry Levin, "Two *Romanisten* in America: Spitzer and Auerbach," in *The Intellectual Migration, Europe and America*, 1930-1960, eds. Donald Fleming and Bernard Bailyn (Cambridge, Mass.: Harvard University Press, 1969), pp. 463-84, and Edward Said, *Orientalism* (New York: Pantheon Books, 1978), pp. 258-62.

13 Anne G. Mitchell and Wesley V. Blomster, "Translators' Introduction" to *Philosophy of Modern Music* by Theodor Adorno (New York: The Seabury Press, 1980), p. x. This work is hereafter referred to as *Philosophy*.

14 Barbara Johnson, "Translator's Introduction" to *Dissemination* by Jacques Derrida (Chicago: The University of Chicago Press, 1981), p. xviii. See also Alan Bass, introductions to Derrida's *Writing and Difference* (Chicago: University of Chicago Press, 1978) and *Positions* (Chicago: University of Chicago Press, 1981) and especially Gayatri Chakravorty Spivak's introduction to *Of Grammatology* (Baltimore: The Johns Hopkins University Press, 1976), pp. lxxxv-lxxxvii.

15 Johnson, *ibid.*

16 In a pastiche of Archibald MacLeish's often cited "Poetry should not mean but be," the last line of his "Ars Poetica," and as a rebuttal to Bloom's notion, Graff once speciously quipped, "Criticism should not mean but be." See "Fear and Trembling at Yale," p. 470.

17 In what is one of the most literate and unpretentious commentaries on the debates over literary theory, Terry Eagleton has observed that there "...is no clear division for post-structuralism between 'criticism' and 'creation': both modes are subsumed into 'writing' as such." See his *Literary Theory, An Introduction* (Minneapolis: University of Minnesota Press, 1983), p. 139.

18 Theodor Adorno, *Introduction to the Sociology of Music*, trans. E.B. Ashton (New York: The Seabury Press, 1976), p. vii. This work is hereafter referred to as *Sociology*.

19 Theodor Adorno, "Wagner, Nietzsche, and Hitler," review of the fourth volume of Ernest Newman, *The Life of Richard Wagner*, in *Kenyon Review*, XI, no. 1 (1947), p. 155. Adorno does absolve Newman's monumental study, it should be noted parenthetically, of any complicity with the "trend" in biography Adorno was then

221

decrying so emphatically.

20 Theodor Adorno, *In Search of Wagner*, trans. Rodney Livingstone (Troubridge and Esher: NLB, 1981), p. 83. This work is hereafter referred to as *Wagner*.

21 For Adorno on this point in his study of Wagner, see Fredric Jameson, *Marxism and Form* (Princeton: Princeton University Press, 1971), pp. 15-18 and p. 21.

22 Ernest Newman, *The Life of Richard Wagner* (New York: Alfred Knopf, 1942), vol. II, p. 321: "...even Bayreuth, which was in theory a withdrawal from the world, was in reality the creation of a kingdom in which he [Wagner] could at last gratify his passion for despotic power." See also vol. III, p. 74 and especially p. 254.

23 Thomas Mann would categorically refuse in the late 1940s to be officially associated with Bayreuth precisely because of the fascist "worship" of Wagner that in his view had so tainted the place during Hitler's regime. Marcel Proust captures in devastatingly exquisite detail the whole phenomenon of Bayreuth when he has Odette ("...she who was incapable of distinguishing between Bach and Clapisson") insist on taking a house there for the season so that she at long last would have a "proper" setting in which to entertain the Verdurins. See *Du côté de chez Swann* in *A la recherche du temps perdu*, vol. 1, pp. 300-301.

24 Oddly enough, the section of *Lohengrin* that is now referred to as the "Wedding March" and about which Adorno writes comes in the opera after Elsa and Lohengrin are already married. The familiar strains heard in church wedding processions today actually accompany the operatic characters to their bridal chamber ("Treulich geführt ziehet dahin..."), a fact which alludes to the pointed distinction between the eventual status of mythical analogy and its possible sources in cultural history.

25 Claude Lévi-Strauss, *Le cru et le cuit* (Paris: Plon, 1964), p. 23.

26 Note, for examples, the absence of this idea when Adorno discusses the "collective pretense" and the "monumentality" of Stravinsky (*Philosophy*, p. 211), *Wozzeck*, p. 31), and especially the twelve-tone "unity" of Schoenberg (pp. 40 ff.).

27 Theodor Adorno, "A Social Critique of Radio Music," *Kenyon Review*, VII, no. 2 (1945), p. 209.

28 The "hebephrenia" section in *Philosophy* is particularly singled out in Craft's mockery of Adorno's style. See *Prejudices in Disguise*, pp. 94-95.

29 George Steiner, who arrives from a different perspective at an acute cultural pessimism similar to that of Adorno, has long been accustomed to the reverse strategy: that is, adding musical allusions to critiques based otherwise upon literary evidence. See the discussion of *Don Giovanni*, for one example, in *After Babel, Aspects of Language and Translation* (New York and London: Oxford University Press, 1975), p. 45.

30 See Lucy Beckett, "Wagner and His Critics," in *The Wagner Companion*, eds. Peter Trowbridge and Richard Sutton (London: Faber and Faber, 1979), p. 368.

31 The phrase is Langdon Winter's in "Roland Barthes Meets the Sex Pistols," a review of Simon Frith's *Youth, Leisure, and the Politics of Rock 'n' Roll*, in *The New York Times Book Review* (February 7, 1982), p. 14.

32 Walter Benjamin, *Briefe* (Frankfurt a.M.: Suhrkamp Verlag, 1966), vol. II, p. 505.

222

SOME PROBLEMS of (A)TYPICALITY in LITERATURE, as SEEN by a GENERALIST

BY YAKOV MALKIEL, UNIVERSITY OF CALIFORNIA AT BERKELEY

Typicality and its opposite, atypicality, may mean various things to a student of literature*; for instance, in reference to the transmission of medieval texts, we may view the situation as atypical, or at least as less than typical, if a work independently known to have been rather influential has been preserved only in a few copies; or if, assuming that only a single partial copy is extant, the part available to us is neither the beginning, nor the end but, through a strange coincidence, the midriff, as it were; or if, where successive translations are involved, the link in the given chain that one would have expected to be particularly strong turns out to be missing, as when scholars have at their disposal a clearly derivative saint's life in a medieval vernacular of the West as well as its distant source in Church Greek, while the intermediate stage posited on internal evidence and in probabilistic terms, namely a version composed in Church Latin, happens to be nonexis-tent (or, at least, unavailable). Within the context of today's meeting I shall confine myself, however, to just one class of atypicality – namely, that category which is closely connected with genres – so that we can eliminate from further consideration all and any anomalies bearing on the accidents of textual transmission, on the vicissitudes of the author's or presumed author's life, etc.

Whoever says genre, conjures up the phantom of definition, whereas in other varieties of literary research the watchword, or key concept, is, instead, reconstruction. Now, definitional terrain, which has for ages been the favorite playground of logicians and mathematicians, is full of traps for the unwary humanist. On the other hand, definitional analysis is very much in tune with the general cultural pattern of our present-day society. Most of you must have noticed an article in a recent issue of a metropolitan weekly, a piece provoked by a trial that took place in Boston late last year and that involved several hundred Wampanog Indians who live on Cape Cod. The question that went before

223

---

* This paper, originally designed for oral presentation alone, was read at one of the meetings of the 1987 convention of the Modern Language Association. Its wording has profited from careful critical comments by several medievalists, including Dr. Barbara N. Sargent-Baur, who chaired the meeting and had issued the invitation. It has been deemed appropriate to preserve the original informal flavor of the piece, rather than try to squeeze it into a rigid monographic mould.

the jury was: what is the definition of a legally constituted tribe?

By asking ourselves similar questions about medieval genres of varying degrees of typicality we shall thus not at all step out of order, as regards the preferences of society at large. Neither are we apt to offend the narrower circle of our fellow workers, because in this particular decade the issue of the genre seems to have eclipsed various other problems, which also lend themselves to, even invite, definitional analysis and which excited previous generations, such as: How far back can one push a current worthy to be called "pre-Renaissance"? What is "the Baroque" or "Romanticism"? Where does one draw the line between utilitarian literature and pure art? Do the realms of *Literatur* and *Dichtung* overlap? and many others, similarly slanted.

I must apologize for the abundance of interrogative sentences, which may seem unwarranted to you. Yet consider this state of affairs: in highly specialized fields, in which the onrush of events – new books, new articles, new symposia, new jargons – keeps the real experts on their toes and not infrequently out of breath (yes, the delimitation of genres along the axis of typicality is, I dare say, one such field), what right does the generalist have to cut into the discussion? He constantly runs the risk of betraying his naïveté or, equally damaging, of showing that he is behind the times. Let me forego the ritual of further self-deprecation and declare that, though seldom able to enlighten specialists on details possibly overlooked, the generalist may nevertheless, with a measure of luck, be in a position to ask a few sharply formulated questions. And so, assuming the role of an immensely curious observer eager, at intervals, to smuggle in a question or to draw a remote parallel, I shall leap *in medias res* and place on record my surprise that after over two millennia of critical legislation and discussions, the issue of genres should still bedevil scholars (be they structural analysts or historians) and creative writers as well, although they are likely to be less articulate about their doubts.

To a small extent this incessant restlessness may be due to a fact which requires no ponderous documentation: ever-new genres are created in our midst through cross-breeding, deft exploitation of previously unknown media, etc. A more profound reason is, I feel, the circumstance that the literary genre, from the outset, was defined in part formally and in part topically. As a matter of fact, over the last decades a third definitional axis has been added: the manner of communication between, on the one hand, the author (or, as the author's local representative, the actor, reciter, juggler, etc.) and, on the other, the reader or auditor. It is this third axis that has, of late, assumed crucial importance. If the theorist demands that a work of a sizable length written in dialogue form qualify for the status of a drama only on condition that it was composed for the sole or primary purpose of being actually performed on a stage, then *La Celestina* at once ceases to be a *comedia* and must be transferred to some such marginal category as *novela dialogada*. But if the critic can be persuaded to waive this demand, then *La Celestina* reverts to one of the two classes to which Fernando de Rojas assigned it at two different stages of elaboration, calling it, first, a *comedia* and, at a later date, a *tragicomedia*.

At this point, two major complications deserve mention. To some extent, at least at the initial stage of his inquiry, the present-day explorer, in groping for the most appropriate classificatory label, is guided by the original title the author, a copyist, a translator, a reviser, or an early printer may have given to the text at issue. Thus, the fact that Russia's most celebrated medieval epic, the Igor Song, or, more accurately, the "Song about Igor's Host," or "Igor's Campaign," is known as *Slovo o Polku Igoreve*, is due to the circumstance that the lexical unit *slovo*, which at present means solely 'word,' once upon a time referred to a narrative song, i.e., a special lyrico-epic genre. Yet what is one to do if tradition provides no incontrovertibly clear title?

As is well-known, the Old Spanish Cid epic has been preserved in a single manuscript, which, as if to complicate the situation, was so truncated as to leave the start, rather than the end of the text, undecipherable. After ten years of intensive research, the great Menéndez Pidal, in his monumental edition of that text, entitled it *Cantar de mio Cid*; a few years later, paying closer attention to the embarrassing fact that each of the three major sections of the venerable text was also tagged "cantar," he bethought himself and, by 1914, adopted for the epic as a whole the new title *Poema*. Did the switch from *Cantar* to *Poema* carry with it any implications for the genre? Finally, the real title of a fully transmitted medieval text, instead of being proudly displayed at the start, may be hidden away in one of the first stanzas, as if to tease the reader or the listener; this is what happened to Juan Ruiz's uniquely structured poem, with the result that the title now assumed to have been correctly reconstructed, namely *Libro de buen amor*, was unknown until Menéndez Pidal, in a pithy comment, advocated it; the late-eighteenth-century discoverer of the text, Tomás Antonio Sanches, and all nineteenth-century scholars spoke in unison of *Cantares que hizo Juan Ruiz*....

The second complication consists in that the same word used

as a label, to set off a genre, need not mean the same thing in different cultures. Take the tag "tragicomedy": it is usually traced to Plautus, who applied it to just one of the plays attributed to him, namely *Amphitryo*. Now it is not implausible to conjecture that Plautus used *tragicomedia* semifacetiously; even the formation of this compound, which involves a violent, unexpected haplological contraction, from *tragico-comoedia*, points in this direction. (I refer you for details to the late Anna Granville Hatcher's probably most provocative and, at the same time, solid book, on copulative compounds [1951], and to its stimulating discussion by Émile Benveniste.) But when Rojas, over seventeen hundred years later, resuscitated the word, to affix it to the definitive version of his play about Calisto and Melibea, any trace of the jocular connotation had long since evaporated; an air of dead-seriousness surrounds, as you remember, the Celestina play. Something similar may have happened to the term *sirventes* in Old Provençal. Judging by its etymology, the word contains as its nucleus the lexical kernel 'servant' plus a suffixal element suggestive of 'manner, fashion, way of speaking,' very similar to the facetious -ese of modern English 'journal-ese,' 'legal-ese,' 'official-ese.' Literally, then, *sirventes* meant "in the manner of servants' speech," and thus contrasted effectively with the more refined aristocratic genres. Before long, however, the primary allusion to the folksy level of talk of low-born speakers was effaced, and the emphasis was shifted to the initally secondary element of satire and derision.

As we face up to the problem of (a)typicality in literary genres, it seems essential to introduce a dichotomy (and this is the central point of today's message), determined by the beholder's choice either of the static or of the dynamic perspective. The static or descriptive approach, which has, almost from time immemorial, been the standard *modus operandi*, describes a genre already in existence along the three aformentioned axes of form, content, and manner of communication. Where a certain freedom of variation exists, the analyst is at liberty to break down a genre into a limited number of subgenres. Thus, the Spaniards have been uncompromising about the basic octosyllabicity of any line of their ballads, the *romances*, so no further subdivision along the axis of form, with special reference to meter, immediately suggests itself.

On the other hand, it is easy to subdivide the corpus of popular ballads from Spain, on topical grounds, into certain recurrent more narrowly delimited genres, the familiar *romances fronterizos, carolingios, moriscos,* etc., with the ever-present possibility of contamination and also of further specification, on the basis of length, the ratio of dialogue to narrative parts, and similar criteria. With all of these features clearly engraved in his mind, the analyst can neatly contrast a Luso-Hispanic romance with, say, a traditional Russian *bylina*. Where a few practitioners of a widely acknowledged genre have infringed a commonly accepted norm, we make bold to speak of an exception or an anomaly. Since a sonnet, cross-culturally and by definition as it were, runs to fourteen lines, we set aside the rare representative of this class that exceeds this expected quota as a monstrosity – as a sonnet with a tail attached to it, a *sonetto caudato*. Lines 9 to 14 are differently arranged, so far as rhymes and stanzaic configuration are concerned, in an Italian Petrarchan and English Elizabethan sonnet; here we prefer to invoke two rival subgenres. The transition from exception, atypicality, to alternative typicality is, then, co-determined by the factor of frequency.

    The static classification of genres is so familiar and has been, for generations, so thoroughly explored, with respect to individual nationally bounded literatures and also across the board, as it were, that I deem it advisable to dwell somewhat longer on its counterpart, the dynamic classification, which looks more like a task reserved for the future. In this context "dynamic" is taken as a near-synonym of "evolutionary" or "developmental." Suppose one observes that in a given national tradition early epics, at a certain stage of their growth, are discontinued and thenceforth tend to be transmuted either into pithy ballads or into short narrative accounts couched in prose and absorbed into chronicles. Or imagine saints' lives originally written in verse and – after some turning point, some change in literary fashion – prosed; or short stories expanded into novels; or one-act farces so consolidated as to form three-act comedies, etc. One need not hesitate to call such metamorphoses, or mere adaptations, normal or typical, as long as they assume the shape of sweeping, cataclysmic changes, almost (if not entirely) predictable, in terms of probabilistic rather than absolute prediction, of course. Now, if such a well-nigh certain mutation fails to occur and if one witnesses instead either an anachronistic preservation of the older genre, far beyond the limits of its life expectancy, or its transformation in an unseen direction, then it seems legitimate to speak of atypicality in dynamic terms. It is even conceivable (though it may seem a shade far-fetched) that, in a certain place and at a certain time, a Genre X, traceable to an older Genre Y, is perfectly normal, while an example of the same Genre X serving to perpetuate a theme initially presented in stray specimens of Genre Z may be something of an oddity. To a synchronist all that really matters is the typicality, the vogue of X at a chosen time level. The diachronist may find this approach simplistic and will argue that, counter to first impressions, X extracted from Y and X echoing Z involve totally different situations.

The distinction between synchrony and diachrony here postulated may yet stand us in good stead as we concern ourselves further with (a)typicality. In a not very experimental or morbidly self-conscious age – that is, one very much unlike our own – writers are least likely to be sensitized to the existence of transitional genres and of genres best described as blends. These two generic categories must be carefully distinguished. As Genre X is on its way to giving rise to an autonomous Genre Y – through addition, subtraction, or modification of a vitally important feature – a sort of short-lived, intermediate subgenre may assert itself for a while, still maintaining that characteristic feature normally peculiar to X alone but already exhibiting the innovation idiosyncratic to Y (as we know through hindsight). Let us label it X'. A blend, or merger, or crossing, or compromise, or contamination is something different; in this instance, X and Y must be assumed to have led their independent existences sometime ago (whether or not, in the last analysis, they stem from the same source), but occasional interbreeding between them, with happy or disastrous results on the aesthetic scale, is still possible. The difference between the two states of affairs (of which only the second involves genuine hybridism) is, then, temporal or, at least, developmental. Typologically, amalgams of genres can be likened to blends of ballads in folk tradition, in which the history of the Hispanic *romance(i)ro* abounds.

My guess is that it is easier to mix – more or less deliberately – two genres already fully developed than to start, from a single point of departure, a slow, gradual movement in a single generic direction. But only on rare occasions shall we be in a position to demonstrate the "anatomy" of a blend and so much as to raise the issue of its purposefulness. Thus, it has been averred that the Old French narrative in verse, *Aye d'Avignon*, is a deft combination of two genres, epic and romance, and Ellen Rose Woods, in her 1977 Stanford dissertation, went one step farther by contending (p. 64) that romance has here been incorporated into a pre-existent epic structure rather than the reverse, inasmuch as love – a characteristic trait of medieval romances – briefly offers a challenge to the dominant ideology of a typical epic, a scheme which – in the given unique cultural context – aligns Christians against pagans in a string of military confrontations. That is to say, the hierarchically dominant pattern in the end remains immune to change. So far so good; but we still do not know, and probably shall never ascertain, whether this remarka-

228

ble variation on a neatly designed epic is traceable to a search for novelty on the part of the anonymous author or initially represented a kind of miscarriage.

If we are prospecting for something unmistakably medieval in the domain of generic atypicality, not a few disappointments are in store for us. First and foremost, we must reckon with the possibility that the generic uniqueness of a work – the *Cantilène de Sainte Eulalie*, say – may be due to the chance survival of a single representative. In addition, medieval culture, unlike our own, did not – except for certain islets such as Provence – encourage an attitude of planned experimentation with new forms. In other words, we are unlikely to encounter many examples of variation for variation's sake. A medieval writer, to be sure, was apt to chance upon an innovation and then, if he was sufficiently analytical, quickly to recognize its worth and to add it to his inherited tool kit; but his mind was not haunted by the irresistible appeal of an *écart* as such, to use Paul Valéry's favorite term.

229

The ingredient of chance, as if by compensation, was substantially heavier in the Middle Ages than in later periods. Take, to begin with, all sorts of hazards (including those fraught with eventual luck and happiness) in connection with the hard facts of manuscript transmission. The oft-cited circumstance that writing material was scarce and expensive prompted scribes, as no medievalist needs to be reminded in tedious detail, to use the same piece of parchment – and even the same side – for radically different purposes. Not all consequences of that practice had a direct bearing on genres. Scholars continue, for instance, to be at loggerheads, after over a half-century of discussions, as to whether all twenty-two of the secular lyrical poems (love songs) composed in medieval Latin and copied on three pages of a tenth-century *Liber glossarum* from Ripoll really belong together. Whatever the outcome of the controversy at some future point, the canon of medieval genres is unlikely to be affected by it.

The situation is entirely different with the archaic Spanish *Razón de amor*, a delicately worded, intensely sensuous, richly suggestive amorous poem – half narrative, half dialogic – appended to which, in the sole manuscript that has preserved it, one is shocked to discover a coarsely comical debate between personifications of water and wine. Either part, at first glance, boasts a style utterly unreconcilable with that of the other. Patient study, as conducted by Margaret Van Antwerp, has led to the following conclusion, which takes off from the discovery that in several representative selections of Old Spanish lyric the respective anthologists have found a niche only for the court poem: "[Their] separation of the court poem from the *Denuestos* (that is, the vilifications) is certainly justifiable. Comical in tone and traceable to medieval sources, the debate between wine and water cannot be properly said to belong to the same genre or tradition as the lyrical love poem."

And yet, the separation of the two constituents cannot be definitive, because wine and water each turn out to play a pivotal, if symbolic, role in the love poems also. Sheer coincidence? Or can one dare to argue that the sentimental and the burlesque treatments of, basically, the same theme for once constitute two sides of the same coin – a single complexly structured genre appealing to two sides of every prospective auditor or reader? Leo Spitzer, in a rather unorthodox, slightly sensational paper published at mid-century, affirmed the essential indivisibility, hence unity, of the poem at issue, a bipartite pattern which purported to evoke the two sides of profane, human love. One is reminded, let me say on my own, of Shakespeare's clowns, who are wont to make their noisy appearances at very pathetic or poignant junctures.

Even if we reject this interpretation as too far-fetched and, overriding the recurrence in leitmotiv fashion of wine and water, prefer to separate the amorous tryst from the ensuing exchange of insults – by "separate" I mean 'keep them apart both genetically and generically' – there still remains a loophole for some sort of cross-connection. Granted that the adjacency of the two discrepant poems on the same manuscript folio was the result of mere chance, one cannot cavalierly discard the possibility, however remote, that subsequent copyists could have taken a liking to this sort of clashing, self-contradictory pattern and have thus contributed to propagating it, at first through a rash of copies, later through increasingly free imitations. In that event the conjecture Spitzer tossed off could be so modified as to explain not so much the genesis of the two poems as the continued or increased popularity of a bifocal genre newly created practically by accident. Needless to say, we are here referring to a strictly conjectural situation, which actually failed to materialize.

It is hardly idle to raise the question whether, numerically, prose genres or verse genres predominate in a given culture, during a segment along the time axis selected by the observer. If we turn our attention to the literary landscape of medieval Provence, at the peak of its unparalleled spontaneous growth, we shall at once be struck not only by the parsimoniousness of its best-remembered prose genres, but also, with the possible exception of the biographical sketches of the trouba-

dours (called *razos* and *vidas*), by the lack of any true originality among
them: the same didactic treatises, sermons, saints' lives, historical
accounts, etc., that one finds in any typical Western literature of the
period, the same heavy dosage of *déjà vu, déjà lu, déjà entendu*. One further
exception – not unimportant – should probably be made in favor of
certain didactic genres – not those bearing on the technique of falconry,
but rather diversified grammatical, rhetorical, metric, lexicographic
writings – which were, in all likelihood, not only more vigorously
developed and, indisputably, launched at a distinctly earlier date here
than elsewhere, but may also have been more finely nuanced as to
generic classification.

    In poetry, however, the exuberant wealth of the isolatable genres   231
will at once strike even a neophyte; every beginner is aware of the sharply
profiled characteristics of the *alba*, the *cansó*, the *estribot*, the *planh* (including a sort of moral *planh*), the *tenso*, the *ensenhamen*, the polyglottal
descort. There are also on record transitional or composite forms, e.g. the
sirvantes-cansó, conceivably devised by Piere Vidal ("mos cors s'alegr' e
s'esjau," as J.H. Marshall has shown – see *Romance Philology, XXXII*, p. 28),
later imitated by Piere Cardenal ("Un decret fa drechurier"). This extraordinary, unprecedented proliferation of genres in medieval Provence – the
topic of a recent book-length investigation – cannot, in my opinion, be
effectively isolated from other manifestations of a certain delight, traceable
to a *l'art pour l'art* attitude long before Théophile Gautier, taken in all sorts
of variations on inherited forms, often carried out in a playful mood.
Thus, one cannot very well scrutinize Old Provençal genres in strict isolation from an equally austere and elaborate study of metrical units, especially the configuration of stanzas and, indissolubly connected with it,
the rhyme patterns. To put it differently: the same bent that pushed the
troubadours toward experimenting with *coblas unissonans, coblas singulars,*
"mots refrains," *coblas doblas, coblas capcaudadas, coblas capfinidas,* and
other refinements, comparable in level of sophistication (practices which
in certain privileged instances can be securely traced to the inventiveness
of a particular troubadour, not necessarily one of major stature, a virtuoso
more than an inspired poet, e.g. Aimeric de Peguilhan) – that bent for
metrical playfulness may also account for the rapid proliferation and
ephemeral blossoming of certain aberrant genres and, significantly, coin-
cides with a high degree of artistic self-consciousness. Such self-awareness
in turn explains the fact that Occitan poets, more than their counterparts
and contemporaries in other European countries, would often turn to
theory, either as a stimulant or as an afterthought, as when Raimon Vidal

composed his *Razos de trobar*. We cannot, then, self-confidently isolate the study of the accumulation of genres, some of them erratic, from a broader concern with parallel manifestations of the same deep-seated attitude toward poetic, or even poetico-musical, form.

To a certain extent, the number of unclassifiable or hard-to-classify works of literature one is bound to encounter depends on the beholder's own attitude rather than on the available corpus. Like any other attempt at generalization, the setting-up of genres involves an appeal to definition, and this is a dangerous game: the analyst can easily become entrapped in an edifice of his own making. In certain contexts a milder, less stringent form of classing, namely characterization, may emerge as the preferable procedure. The risk consists in this: the more neatly you individuate a genre, the fewer will be such representatives as meet all your conditions. In a finely-honed and attractively-phrased introduction to his English translation of the *Song of Roland*, Frederick Goldin, in circumscribing the domain of an Old French epic, reaffirms what has long before been known and stated, as distinctive features of an Old French epic, namely the primacy of religious self-assertion, the historical core, the determination of the hero's motives by the action rather than by individual moral experiences, the mandatory presence of a sizable audience (at least an implied one), etc. But beyond this Goldin deftly champions the acceptance of a new feature, namely, that the world of a typical epic is ruled by conditional rather than absolute necessity. The unpredictable present and the un-alterable past, Goldin goes on, "thus wonderfully coincide"; and he discerns a subtle interplay of the two forces of free human will and transcendental historic purpose. All this is doubtless true so far as the *Roland* is concerned and enables us to draw a razor-sharp line between the epic at its best and the romance at its best in medieval France, to the extent that we can declare pointless certain issues raised by earlier, more näive generations of scholars. But is it not true that we run the risk of too closely identifying the characteristics of a single masterpiece with a whole genre, a peccadillo of which the pioneers Kerr and Comfort were, not unfairly, accused by their successors? And is it not, further, a fact that by a too close definition of, let us say, the Old French epic we needlessly complicate the task of finding a classificatory formula that might equally well fit the Old Germanic, or any other, epic?

Thus, concern with abnormality of artistic genres, even if it originally stems from a sort of morbid teratological curiosity, bids fair, as long as we are level-headed, to lead eventually to new and potentially important insights.

T. S. ELIOT as CHRISTIAN READER

BY ERASMO LEIVA-MERIKAKIS, UNIVERSITY OF SAN FRANCISCO

I

The interplay among aesthetic and moral criteria in T.S. Eliot's criticism has not always been fully appreciated. One source of antagonism against Eliot is the misunderstanding which attributes to his position a claim to universality and monolithic exclusiveness, an intolerant and arrogant imposing of personal standards. Eliot explains that

233

> literary criticism should be completed by criticism from a definite ethical and theological standpoint.... In ages like our own, in which there is no...common agreement [on ethical and theological matters], it is the more necessary for Christian readers to scrutinize their reading, especially of works of the imagination, with explicit ethical and theological standards. The "greatness" of literature cannot be determined solely by literary standards; though we must remember that whether it is literature or not can be determined solely by literary standards. [*SE*, 343][1]

It is important for us, in order to focus our concerns properly, to notice in what manner Eliot is here imposing limitations on himself. Not only does he distinguish between ethical and aesthetic criteria, but he specifically announces that his are to be *Christian* standards of judgment. He can no more understand the substitution of aesthetic for ethical criteria, or vice versa, than he can comprehend the attitude of those who call themselves Christians and yet do not see the connection between their Christianity and their critical judgments on literature. "There are definite positions to be taken, and...now and then one must actually reject something and select something else" (*SE*, 14). Such a statement begins to define for us the content of Eliot's position as moral realist even in aesthetic matters.

Eliot clearly reacts against contemporary trends of philosophy and criticism which, in the name of liberation, strive to debunk all objective criteria of judgment and proclaim that each individual mind is henceforth to be its own legislator. This attitude, Eliot holds, has consistently yielded a maelstrom of ethical and philosophical relativisms whose repercussion in the field of literary criticism has, for one, been the idealistic conviction that art is a revolt against reality, that this reality must be scorned as mediocre, and that art creates a superior world because the creative imagination is supremely autonomous and, in fact, *creates* truth. It is the confounding of real differences that provoked Eliot's conservative reaction. On a philosophical plane, this confusion must be traced to an abandonment of the transcendental imagination which seeks the unification (not the fusing or con-fusing) on a metaphysical level of whatever is good, true, and beautiful. We will return to the question of the unity of the three transcendentals in the third part of this essay.

It is basically the collapsing of distinctions that Eliot deplores, both on a philosophical and a literary plane. "The whole of modern literature is corrupted by what I call Secularism,...it is simply unaware of, simply cannot understand the meaning of, the primacy of the supernatural over the natural life: of something I assume to be our primary concern" (*SE*, 352). Secularism is a chief instance of the collapsing of vital distinctions. Eliot wishes to alert those who supposedly should be "aware" of the existence of a supernatural order to the fact that most modern literature implicitly gives the lie to this aspect of the Judeo-Christian tradition. Unless Christianity is to be reinterpreted beyond recognition, those who call themselves Christians must take note of this event and its implications. With the disappearance of a supernatural vision, the natural world assumes primacy and an ominous homogeneity comes to dominate a whole culture's mentality. Under the sign of this *homogeneity* all feasible substitutions and interchanges of values and entities become possible, so that a dire relativism throws the collective conscience into chaos. By comparison, Eliot's manner of seeing reality remains thoroughly *relational*, which is not to say relativistic: "I am concerned with what should be the relation between Religion and Literature" (*SE*, 346). A seemingly casual statement such as this actually conceals a concern for the vital and intimate relation between what is true and what claims to be beautiful.

II

WE WILL SHORTLY REVIEW the specifically literary criteria which Eliot made his own. But in order to understand Eliot's position as moral critic of literature we must first briefly survey the spiritual and philosophical pilgrimage which took him finally to a position of enlightened orthodoxy. The term "enlightened" here refers to the fact that Eliot's orthodoxy was not something given him ready-made by a group to which he belonged. Eliot's final position as orthodox Christian came as the result of a long and painful struggle for liberation from subjectivistic idealism. His intellectual career is marked by turnings on all levels: politically he turned from individualism to belief in a traditional, organic society; philosophically he worked his way out of Kantian idealism to a position of Christian realism; aesthetically, in addition to intensifying his lyric voice, the mature Eliot ventured into the classical objectivity of dramatic poetry; historically he gave up the strictly literary seeking for an ideal pattern in literature for a vision of the real pattern of history as an objective manifestation of God's work. All of these "turnings" could perhaps be best summarized as concrete applications of a basic metaphysical turning from the ideal to the real.

235

It is important to understand Eliot's subjective-idealistic beginnings in order to fully appreciate the import of his orthodoxy. His idealism was never of the passive sort, but rather of the critical brand of a Heine. Irony lies at the base of all his early poems, and, with a knowledge of Eliot's later course, we can see in this irony an embryonic form of his mature realism. J. Hillis Miller gives us a good definition of Eliot's use of irony at this early stage. It was "a synthesis which, bringing things together, recognizes their separateness. The disparate remains disparate, the fragments fragmented, and unity emerges from a clash of these which affirms the ideal and at the same time admits the unattainability of the ideal."[2] In this Eliot's sensibility is radically modern; the tormenting dichotomy that exists between the interior ideal and the external "reality" (in the pejorative sense) has come to be a characteristic of the modern crisis.

The typically ironic tone of Eliot's earlier poems manifests a deep-seated dissatisfaction not only with the shabby "reality" of the exterior world, but also with the purely ideal processes of the human mind. To say that Eliot evolved a position of realism is to say that he staunchly opposed any tendency towards nominalism. Language for him has a positive character; it really manifests to us the identity and differences of things. Thus, "nothing in this world or the next is a substitute for anything else; and if you find that you must do without something, such as religious faith or philosophical belief, then you must just do without it" (UP, 113).[3] A chair is not a table and a man is not an angel, even though you might fancifully switch their names. The fact is that there exist basic differences between things – whether physical or spiritual – and these ontological levels of existence are not interchangeable among themselves. Strange as this may seem, Eliot's realism or anti-nominalism is not a rationally worked out scholastic position, but an existential intuition: by changing goals and objects of belief, "I can persuade myself that it is the same desires that are satisfied, or that I have in effect the same thing under a different name" (UP, 114).

236

Another aspect of Eliot's realism is his conviction of man's *duty to be*. In his essay on Baudelaire he carries the expediency of concrete existence to an extreme reminiscent of Christ's warning that "the luke-warm I will spew forth from my mouth": "So far as we are human, what we do must be either evil or good...and it is better, in a paradoxical way, to do evil than to do nothing: at least, we exist.... The worst that can be said of most of our malefactors, from statesmen to thieves, is that they are not men enough for damnation" (SE, 380). I have called Eliot a *Christian* realist, and the extremity of these statements is a direct manifestation of the Christian character of his realism. For the Christian the turning from subjectivism to realism necessarily implies forsaking Idea for Incarnation.

The reasons for Eliot's turning to Christianity and hence to specifically Christian criticism spring from his own experience of the desolation wrought by idealistic subjectivism and by cultural fragmentation. For him the dogma of the Incarnation, foundation-stone of the Christian faith, is the deliverance out of a subjectivistic imprisonment within the self, that dissociation of sensibility begun in the Renaissance and culminating with Rousseau and Romanticism. The cultural heritage of Europe, on the other hand, is seen as the historical precipitation of vital Christianity, that is, a Christianity that still believes in and *feels* in its bones the truth of the Incarnation. Thus the interior awareness of personal insufficiency and fragmentation concurs with the realization of the need for cultural integrity. Miller remarks that "only when he [Eliot] sees the emptiness of collective subjectivism [cf. 'The Hollow Men'] can he find the humility [cf. 'Ash Wednesday'] to see that existence is outside himself and not the same as his understanding of it."[4] We may conjecture that thoughts like these constituted the "powerful and concurrent reasons" which made Eliot, like John Henry Newman before him, convert to (Anglo-)Catholic Christianity. The genuineness and whole-hearted character of Eliot's commitment to Christian faith and Christian culture inevitably led him to formulate a specifically Christian criticism of literature, a criticism which cannot evade the moral repercussions of aesthetic considerations.

Subjective idealism may be seen from the Christian perspective as the modern version of the ancient and ever-recurring Docetist heresy, which denied substantial reality to Christ's body, and asserted that it was an illusion used by God to lead men to a purely spiritual existence. Docetism is, in fact, a rejection of the dogma of the Incarnation. Miller excellently describes the intimate relationship between belief in the Incarnation and the position of realist that Eliot ultimately attained: "Eliot represents a specifically Christian version of the recovery of immanence, a version which may be defined as a reaffirmation of the Incarnation. It is loss of belief in incarnation which turns Christianity into idealism, and Eliot can only become a Christian when the Incarnation is a reality for him."[5] "Incarnation," of course, refers here not only to the particular dogma of God's taking on a human nature; from this belief flows also the affirmation of self as incarnate and world as incarnate: the body of the self and the body of the world have real, objective existence, independent of mental constructs. Miller concludes: "Another [form of incarnation] is that social form of embodiment which is a man's acceptance of a limited role in his community."[6]

A paramount consequence of belief in the Incarnation is the objective character of truth. Truth lies at a point outside the mind of any individual man: men relate to the truth and do not invent it. It must be understood that the objectivity in question refers to the autonomy and independence of the truth and, as such, objectivity bestows upon truth a dynamic quality. Eliot's objective truth has nothing to do with the scientific "objectivity" of extended matter. It is a metaphysical and not an empirical objectivity. The Germans have the two words *Gegenständlichkeit* and *Objektivität* to distinguish between the different concepts. The first connotes the quality of a material or spiritual object being independent and recognized as such by a subject. The other word refers to the objectivity of the scientific method. On the basis of the *Gegenständlichkeit* of the truth Eliot attacks the liberal-democratic idea of truth: "These liberals are convinced that only by what is called unrestrained individualism will truth ever emerge. Ideas, views of life, they think, issue distinct from independent heads, and in consequence

237

of their knocking violently against each other, the fittest survive, and truth rises triumphant" (*SE*, 351).

The conviction that the truth, if it is to be worthwhile, must be more than a purely human creation, leads Eliot ultimately to a rejection of humanism in the style of Irving Babbitt: "My objection is that the humanist makes use, in his separation of the 'human' from the 'natural,' of that 'supernatural' which he denies. For I am convinced that if this 'supernatural' is suppressed…, the *dualism* of man and nature collapses at once. Man is man because he can recognize supernatural realities, not because he can invent them" (*SE*, 433). Indiscriminate experimentation with the "truth" finally results in the deprivation of all content. The process becomes its own end, and an unending solipsism gains ascendancy: "What is the higher will to *will*, if there is nothing either 'anterior, exterior, or superior' to the individual? If this will is to have anything on which to operate, it must be in relation to external objects and to objective values" (*SE*, 425).

Morality, if it is to be something more than mere conformity to an arbitrary code of dos and don'ts, must mediate between the thoughts and actions of an individual and the objective truth. Morality for morality's sake is a masochistic absurdity: "I cannot understand a system of morals which seems to be founded on nothing but itself – which exists, I suspect, only by illicit relations with either psychology or religion or both, according to the bias of mind of the individual humanist" (*SE*, 432). It is possible to be moral in a negative way, as in the case of Baudelaire. To Baudelaire's aphorism, "La volupté unique et suprême de l'amour gît dans la certitude de faire le mal," Eliot gives the following commentary:

> Baudelaire has perceived that what distinguishes the relations of man and woman from the copulation of beasts is the knowledge of Good and Evil (of *moral* Good and Evil which are not natural Good and Bad or puritan Right and Wrong). Having an imperfect, vague Romantic conception of Good, he was at least able to understand that the sexual act as evil is more dignified, less boring, than as the natural 'life-giving,' cheery automatism of the modern world. For Baudelaire, sexual operation is at least something not analogous to Kruschen Salts. [*SE*, 380]

The truth, then, is outside of man in the sense that man does not invent or invest it. This duality results in the radical imperfection and dependency of man. On this point the influence of T.E. Hulme on

Eliot was decisive: "It is to the immense credit of Hulme that he found out for himself that there is an *absolute* to which man can *never* attain" (*SE*, 437). The main flaw of modern humanism is "the refusal to believe any longer in the radical imperfection of either Man or Nature" (*SE*, 437). This insight is obviously a re-statement of the dogma of Original Sin, rediscovered existentially in the debate with the humanists. Quoting Hulme, Eliot proclaims quite clearly the key to his anthropology: "Man is in no sense perfect, but a wretched creature, who can yet apprehend perfection" (*SE*, 438). It is in this context of the tension resulting from the imperfection of the individual and his ability to apprehend the truth that we will consider Eliot's concept of tradition.

One can speak at length about the primacy of objective truth and draw all sorts of logical conclusions from it – such as the radical imperfection of man *vis à vis* the fullness of truth. But for Eliot the truth is no disembodied entity. Again as a consequence of the dogma of the Incarnation, the truth has taken flesh in human history and is to be found among us, not, to be sure, in any one of us, but in the Judeo-Christian tradition as a whole. This tradition is the mediator of the truth and provides forms by which to relate to it.

In order to focus more clearly Eliot's concept of tradition it is best to state beforehand what tradition is *not* for him. Eliot's "tradition" is a decisively living and dynamic idea. One instance of false traditionalism is "the conservatism which springs from lack of faith, and the zeal for reform which springs from dislike of change" (*UP*, 119). It is dangerous "to associate tradition with the immovable; to think of it as something hostile to all change; to aim to return to some previous condition which we imagine as having been capable of preservation in perpetuity, instead of aiming to stimulate the life which produced that condition in its time" (*ASG*, 19).[7] "Not only is it possible to conceive of a tradition being definitely bad; a good tradition might, in changing circumstances, become out of date. Tradition has not the means to criticise itself; it may perpetuate much that is trivial or of transient significance as well as what is vital and permanent" (*ASG*, 31).

Positively, Eliot defines tradition as "a way of feeling and acting that characterises a group throughout generations" (*ASG*, 31), that "involves all those habitual actions, habits and customs, from the most significant religious rite to our conventional way of greeting a stranger, which represent the blood kinship of 'the same people living in the same place'" (*ASG*, 18). Tradition is important as a sociological entity, as a vessel which is secondary but indispensable to the contents it is

239

charged with conveying from generation to generation.

> Tradition by itself is not enough; it must be perpetually criti-
> cised and brought up to date under the supervision of what
> I call orthodoxy; and for lack of this supervision it is now the
> sentimental tenuity that we find it. Most 'defenders of tradi-
> tion' are mere conservatives, unable to distinguish between
> the permanent and the temporary, the essential and the acci-
> dental. [*ASG,* 67]

Whereas the living of a tradition is, for the most part, unconscious,
"the maintenance of orthodoxy is a matter which calls for the exercise
of all our conscious intelligence" (*ASG,* 31). Thus, tradition and orthodoxy complement each other and correspond at the level of a culture
to the unconscious and conscious processes of the individual. "In the
co-operation of both is the reconciliation of thought and feeling" (*ASG,*
31). It is of paramount importance that, for Eliot, "tradition" and "orthodoxy," far from being synonymous or inseparable, are in fact in
tension with one another.

Just as on a philosophical plane the polarity was established
between subjective idealism and Christian realism, so too here, on a
cultural plane, the concept of a vital tradition constantly revised and
criticized by orthodox thinking is opposed to the cult of originality and
personality. Remarking on the increasing trend towards individualism
in nineteenth-century novelists, culminating with Hardy, Eliot writes:

> When morals cease to be a matter of tradition and orthodoxy –
> that is, of the habits of the community formulated, corrected,
> and elevated by the continuous thought and direction of the
> Church – and when each man is to elaborate his own, then
> personality becomes a thing of alarming importance. [ASG, 58]

The dissociation of the individual from criteria external to himself
results in "an exaggerated novelty, a novelty usually of a trifling kind,
which conceals from the uncritical reader a fundamental commonplace-
ness" (*ASG,* 24).

Insertion in the living tradition, however, does not imply the
levelling of personality, rather the efficacious activating of personality
in relation to what many generations have agreed to be true. Eliot dis-
cards the type of contemporary literature "which attempts to do what
has already been done perfectly,... [the] superfluous kind of writing
[to which] the word 'traditional' is commonly applied: *mis*-applied, for

the word itself implies a movement" (*ASG*, 24). As an illustration of the difference between a living and an obsolete sense of tradition, I would offer the relationship between Eliot's own poetry and his critical criteria. It seems that not sufficient attention has been paid to the apparent contradiction that exists between Eliot's critical position (presumably one of classical orthodoxy) and the actual form of his aesthetic productions. The same man who judges works of literature with such criteria as "eccentricity" and "orthodoxy," conformity and non-conformity to the Christian tradition, became the most avant-garde poet writing in English in his day. The discrepancy remains only if we misunderstand Eliot's concept of tradition. Eliot writes paradoxically that for a new work of art "to conform merely [with the existing monuments of literature] would be for [it] not really to conform at all; it would not be new, and would not be a work of art" (*SE*, 5). The point is that, while the truth remains the same, cultural manifestations of the truth change according to circumstance. If it is not to be a pious lie, the expression of orthodoxy may at times, in fact, *demand* that the aesthetic form of a work of art assume unheard-of shapes. As an aesthetic form, *The Waste Land,* for instance, tells us that it simply will not do to express oneself, say, in stately Alexandrine verses in the face of social and cultural cataclysm.

241

The opposite of "orthodoxy" is, of course, "heresy" or, in more meaningful terminology, eccentricity – "being off-center." *Eccentricity* is treating one's inevitably private center (microcosm) as if it were *the* Center. No one man, or group of men, has insight into the whole truth. The closest we can come to it, Eliot would say, is in a valid tradition, criticized from within by the orthodox mind, the fruit and composite of what many generations have experienced to be the best mode of life and belief. Hence the value of the *fragment* as a philosophical or literary form. The fragment reveals the truth by acknowledging the inability to communicate it completely. Heresy is a usurpation or synthetic forgery of the truth: passing off a part as if it were the whole. The aphorism "The fear of the Lord is the beginning of wisdom" is such a fragment. Fear in this case is the realization of one's personal insufficiency and the need to rely on an Other. Orientation beyond the self is the beginning of salvation; the merely self-assertive personality the path to perdition.

J. Hillis Miller describes accurately, if somewhat unsympathetically, what it means for Eliot to acknowledge a center outside himself: "For [Eliot] the divine center exists, but is seemingly at an infinite distance. In Eliot this leads to an inability to believe in the significance of any isolated person or thing. Only as a nexus of relations importing meaning from without can any man or object be of value."[8] To say that for Eliot the "divine center" is far removed is another way of saying that he continually refuses either to fabricate a divine center within himself or indeed to identify himself as such a divine center, an action which constitutes the "heresy" of D.H. Lawrence. For a man to realize his alienation from the center is, in theological terms, his awareness of the need for grace. It is, therefore, his conversion from self and the beginning of salvation. Such an awareness of alienation from the divine center is the moral application of T.E. Hulme's philosophical distinctions between realms of existence. Hulme, in turn, is but reformulating or discovering for himself an orthodox and essential Christian tenet.

In conclusion, let us remember that the radical imperfection of man has as a corollary the impossibility of any man's being perfectly orthodox, perfectly in tune with the truth. One may be fully orthodox in the negative sense of *realizing* that the center of truth lies outside oneself; but this does not mean that one is automatically in possession of the whole truth. The moral and metaphysical distance between the truth and the self is never fully bridged, hence the necessity of constantly *seeking* for the truth. Only one man may be wholly identified with the truth, and in this sense only he is fully orthodox: the God-Man Jesus Christ, who is "the way, the truth, and the life." Eliot's concept of orthodoxy is of necessity self-critical. Eliot presumably includes himself when he refers to "the small number of writers in this or any other period who are worth taking seriously" (*ASG*, 68). Of these he says that he is "very far from asserting that any of [them] is wholly 'orthodox' or even that it would be relevant to rank them according to degrees of orthodoxy...[because] most of us are heretical in one way or another" (*ASG*, 68).

III

THE CHRISTIAN-REALISTIC awareness of man's radical imperfection lies at the root of Eliot's criticism. Over and over Eliot makes his point, in the most diverse contexts. "Our lives are mostly a constant evasion of ourselves," he writes, "and an evasion of the visible and sensible world" (*UP*, 155). Elsewhere he says that the "*unregenerate* personality [is] capable of much good or great mischief according to the natural goodness or impurity of the man: and we are all, naturally, impure" (*ASG*, 68).

The poet or novelist is an imperfect man writing for imperfect men, and some third criterion is essential to stabilize their relationship.

The negative insight of man's imperfection has a counterpart in the positive belief in the transforming capacity of literature. Literature affects people. "The author of a work of imagination is trying to affect us wholly, as human beings, whether he knows it or not; and we are affected by it, as human beings, whether we intend to be or not" (SE, 348). Here we have the simplest and most basic instance of the continuity between the two derived transcendentals – the *bonum* and the *pulchrum* – humanly manifested as work of art and its moral effect. The effect of poetry is manifold: "[Poetry] may effect revolutions in sensibility such as are periodically needed" by helping "to break up the conventional modes of perception which are perpetually forming and make people see the world afresh" (UP, 155). "In expressing what other people feel, [the poet] is also changing the feeling by making it more conscious; he is making people more aware of what they feel already, and therefore teaching them something about themselves" (OPP, 9).[9] Moreover, Eliot even sees a connection between the private and public arenas, and hence between lyric poetry and politics: "[Poetry and the arts] give the spiritual aspect of problems the material aspect of which is the concern of politics" (OPP, 15).

It must remain clear that Eliot is neither a theoretician of poetry, one trying to establish its natural laws (see UP, 15), nor a dogmatist who requires that poetry should be made subservient to and used as propaganda for a particular religious persuasion. On these grounds he criticizes the Abbé Brémond and the theory that would make poetry a mouthpiece of the mystical experience (UP, 139). In the case of Matthew Arnold, Eliot deplores "the moral and religious effects of confusing poetry and morals in the attempt to find a substitute for religious faith" (UP, 116). On this point Eliot cites Jacques Maritain, to him a leading Catholic representative of "enlightened" orthodoxy: "By showing us where moral truth and the genuine supernatural are situate, religion saves poetry from the absurdity of believing itself destined to transform ethics and life" (UP, 137). Most religious verse, likewise, is judged to be a "pious insincerity," the product of poets that write "as they want to feel, rather than as they do feel" (ASG, 30). No statement in all of Eliot's writings could make it clearer that orthodoxy does not consist for him in the hackneyed and propagandist repetition of traditional formulas of belief. The pious insincerity of much religious verse is at best an irrelevant, because purely formal, expression of orthodoxy. At worst it could

243

be a subtle form of immorality.

Eliot is everywhere concerned with the effect of literature on the reader's sensibility, and "insincere" religious verse might well have the adverse effect of immunizing or deadening people's sensibilities against the real and dire needs of the times. The poet not only "expresses himself," but in creating a work of art he is performing both an aesthetic and a moral act in that he is responsible to his readers for the effect such a work might have on them. There is no so-called pure "aesthetic" enjoyment which does not in fact imply a *moral* effect upon the receptor of the literature in question. "'Pure' artistic appreciation is to my thinking only an ideal, when not merely a figment, and must be, so long as the appreciation of art is an affair of limited and transient human beings existing in space and time. Both artist and audience are limited" (UP, 109). Eliot's position is obviously a reaction against the modern (Faustian) tendency that would deify the artist. Aesthetic creation should not effect the apotheosis of the artist as creator of perfection, but should be a sensitive expression of the truth of a situation: "The essential advantage for a poet is not to have a beautiful world with which to deal: it is to be able to see beneath both beauty and ugliness; to see the boredom, and the horror, and the glory" (UP, 106).

In the greatest poets Eliot discovers the unity and continuity of aesthetic and moral concerns, which is to say that in his art the genuine artist is seeking for truth. The transcendental triad of the True, the Good, and the Beautiful is the metaphysical understructure that lends the artistic product credibility, coherence, and relevance. A case in point is Wordsworth, whose social interests "inspire[d] his own novelty of form in verse, and back[ed] up his explicit remarks upon poetic diction; and it is really this social interest which (consciously or not) the fuss is all about" (UP, 74). By the same token, Eliot is of the opinion that "the true claim of Baudelaire as an artist is not that he found a superficial form, but that he was searching for a form of life" (SE, 375). Aesthetic phenomena, if probed to their origins, will always be shown to be the formal manifestations of an existential, and hence also ethical, crisis. If an artist is sincere he will avow the deep organic unity of all areas of his life: "I cannot, in practice, wholly separate my poetic appreciation from my personal beliefs.... It would appear that 'literary appreciation' is an abstraction, and pure poetry a phantom; and that both in creation and enjoyment much always enters which is, from the point of view of 'Art,' irrelevant" (SE, 231).

We must admire the manner in which Eliot rediscovers and

formulates on an existential plane the implications of the metaphysical distinction and unity of the transcendentals: "All human affairs are involved with each other, consequently all history involves abstraction, and in attempting to win a full understanding of the poetry of a period you are led to the consideration of subjects which at first sight appear to have little bearing upon poetry" (*UP*, 76). In my opinion such an attitude amounts to the rehabilitation and almost the rediscovery of the concept of poetry at a very dynamic level.

For this reason – because relevant poetry and relevant art should be sources of social dynamism – the artist has a rather awesome responsibility. While poetic "inspiration" may have its roots in emotion, a poem is never a direct transferring of an emotion into language (which would in any event be an impossibility by definition). The poet brings his intellect to bear upon the emotion, and the result is a "formed" or "poetic" emotion which bears the stamp of many choices on the part of the poet's will. While no emotion is censurable in itself, its form of expression is indeed subject to criteria of moral judgment. "The poet has, not a 'personality' to express, but a particular medium, which is only a medium and not a personality" (*SE*, 9). The work of art results from a conscious and, therefore, responsible creative act.

Artistic responsibility again brings us to the concept of eccentricity. In this case artistic genuineness and integrity correspond to the idea of orthodoxy. "The difference between the writer who is merely eccentric or mad and the genuine poet: the former may have feelings which are unique but which cannot be shared, and are therefore useless; the latter discovers new variations of sensibility which can be appropriated by others" (*OPP*, 9). Artistic responsibility imposes upon the writer a peculiar form of *ascesis*: that of renouncing the invention of self-indulgent nonsense for the sake of plumbing the inexhaustible depths of human nature, with all its horrors and causes for exultation. "One error of eccentricity in poetry is to seek for new human emotions to express; and in this search for novelty in the wrong place it discovers the perverse" (*SE*, 10).

The ascetic renunciation which the artist's responsibility calls for (here I am combining Eliot's early aesthetic theory of impersonalism in art with his moral stance of orthodoxy, one being the anticipation of the other) is "a continual self-surrender of himself as he is at the moment to something which is more valuable. The progress of an artist is a continual self-sacrifice, a continual extinction of personality" (*SE*, 6f.). In an essay on William Blake, Eliot makes it clear that this process

ERASMO LEIVA-MERIKAKIS

of depersonalization in art, a true form of *ascesis*, actually liberates the personality to a higher level of existence, and has nothing to do with the modern phenomenon of the levelling or destruction of the personality by the lethal anonymity of mass man: "[The artist's] education is one that is hindered rather than helped by the ordinary processes of society which constitute education for the ordinary man. For these processes consist largely in the acquisition of impersonal ideas which obscure what we really are and feel, what we really want, and what really excites our interest" (*SW*, 277).[10]

When Eliot speaks of orthodoxy, and of artistic responsibility as measured by it, he does not primarily imply that such and such a writer is going to "lead us into error." The truth of the matter is much less melodramatic than that and also much more serious. In his *Primer of Modern Heresy* Eliot takes the theological concept of Original Sin and shows quite convincingly, I think, how its disappearance from most modern literature results in the irresponsible picture of human nature which is a lie, an illusion, and, above all, a bore:

> With the disappearance of the idea of Original Sin, with the disappearance of the idea of intense moral struggle, the human beings presented to us both in poetry and in prose fiction to-day, and more patently among the serious writers than in the underworld of letters, tend to become less and less real. It is in fact in moments of moral and spiritual struggle depending upon spiritual sanctions, rather than in those "bewildering moments" in which we are all very much alike, that men and women come nearest to being real. If you do away with this struggle, and maintain that by tolerance, benevolence, inoffensiveness and a redistribution or increase of purchasing power, combined with a devotion, on the part of an elite, to Art, the world will be as good as anyone could require, then you must expect human beings to become more and more vaporous. [*ASG*, 45]

The literary end-product of writers who have debunked, and been "liberated" from, the Christian tradition becomes a truth-test for the relevancy of ancient dogma. The experience of reading these works directly reveals to us the fact that sinless characters who express a glorious life-urge in whatever they do are actually far less real than sinful ones. Aesthetic dissatisfaction does in at least this rare instance become a check for the credibility of dogma. Ancient Christian teach-ings such as the doctrine of the Incarnation or of Original Sin are far more than mere ecclesiastical jargon. They tell us something concerning the very nature of things.

Acceptance of the dogma of the Incarnation liberated Eliot from the paralysis of subjectivistic idealism by opening up to him the complex nexus of natural and supernatural realities. The first result of being free from idealism is the ability to make real distinctions where they exist, fundamental distinctions such as between God and man, time and eternity, the reality of sin and of redemption, the uniqueness of individuals and their dependence on the community for ultimate significance, and, finally, the supernatural goal of man and his consequent character of pilgrim in his present life. These are not matters for merely religious conjecture and elaboration. Or rather, authentic religious conviction necessarily involves the application of its criteria to every aspect of human activity, not the least of them being the criticism of imaginative literature.

247

IV

IN ELIOT'S DEFINITION the essential function of criticism is to "promote the understanding and enjoyment of literature" (OPP, 127-28). However, because "the critic must be the whole man, a man with convictions and principles, and of knowledge and experience of life" (OPP, 130), the task of promoting understanding and enjoyment of literature is not as simple or as univocal as it might at first glance appear. For "understanding" demands far more than a grasp of the formal inner workings of a novel or poem, and "enjoyment" implies far more than intellectual hedonism.

> For literary judgment we need to be acutely aware of two things at once: of 'what we like,' and of 'what we ought to like'.... The first means knowing what we really feel....
> The second involves understanding our shortcomings; for we do not really know what we ought to like unless we also know why we ought to like it, which involves knowing why we don't yet like it. [SE, 353]

Behind this playful phraseology concerning taste lies a serious concern for moral values, and the word "moral" here refers very basically to the fact that a person may be rightly or wrongly influenced to make right or wrong choices: that what we experience, whether in literature or in life, actually *makes a difference* in the substance of who we are. Eliot

criticizes most modern criticism, not for lack of thoroughness of research or for the irrelevancy of its findings, but rather for its lack of
direction and for its being unaware of the connection between literature
and life: "I wonder whether the weakness of modern criticism is not an
uncertainty as to what criticism is for? As to what benefit it is to bring,
and to whom? Its very richness and variety have perhaps obscured its
ultimate purpose" (OPP, 116). Now, lack of concern for an ultimate
purpose is the chief symptom of a mentality which has reduced all of
experience to the aesthetic dimension and has forgotten the organic
ties of the aesthetic to the ethical and the sapiential.

248 Trying to "complete" aesthetic criticism by restoring its unity
with the other transcendentals, Eliot makes it his task to judge representative novelists and poets according to a holistic conception of man,
his present condition, and his final goals. I will now examine those
instances which have seemed to me to be the most relevant and paradigmatic.

Throughout his career the writer whom Eliot has most consistently offered as an instance of the totally unified artist is Dante. Dante's
analogical vision of reality everywhere keeps him from isolating any
one character, emotion, or situation, and exploiting it for its own sake.
This would constitute the decadent fallacy. Dante's aesthetic design
is the symbolic equivalent or sensual manifestation of the invisible
analogue. No part can be fully understood without the whole; and yet
each part has a poetic beauty of its own, heightened by its being or-
dered to the final end. The grandiose breadth of this vision is made
possible only by Dante's intellectual lucidity, tempering and shaping
his aesthetic medium. It presumably constitutes Dante's claim to universality. Universality of appeal, too, is the result of Dante's masterly
fusion of personality and the objective means of expression. "[Dante's]
private belief becomes a different thing in becoming poetry" (SE, 219).
Personal lyricism is combined with epic objectivity. The former gains
in solidity and the latter remains vital. "No emotion is contemplated
by Dante purely in and for itself. The emotion of the person, or the
emotion with which our attitude appropriately invests the person, is
never lost or diminished, is always preserved entire, but is modified
by the position assigned to the person in the eternal schema" (SW, 167).
If Dante is able to accomplish such consistency it is because he never
abandons the continuity between thought and art. "In Dante, philosophy is essential to the structure and the structure is essential to the
poetic beauty of the parts" (SW, 160).

Not every form of philosophical thought, however, is relevant or desirable. The reason is that it is *art* that is created and not *truth*. This is the ground of Eliot's criticism of William Blake. By accepting and acting within a living traditional framework, the poet is liberated to work out specifically artistic problems. Through no fault of his own, Blake lacked such a framework and was handicapped by its absence. "The concentration resulting from a framework of mythology and theology and philosophy is one of the reasons why Dante is a classic and Blake only a poet of genius" (SW, 280). What is at stake here is the concentration of creative energy, an energy which modern writers regularly squander through the fabrication of eccentric points of view. Eliot offers an aesthetic "check" as manifestation of this squandering of energies: Blake's over-individualism makes him an eccentric poet inclined to aesthetic formlessness. His marriage of philosophy and poetry is not considered "felicitous" by Eliot since, in the process, the two disciplines are confused (see SW, 277). Philosophy should be a meditation on the ontological nature of reality. The attempt to create a philosophy at the same time as fashioning a poem results in eccentricity of contents and meanness of form.

In Eliot's opinion the great poet of the modern world is Charles Baudelaire. Baudelaire is the negative counterpart of Dante, perhaps the only Dante possible in our time. The relation between Eliot's judgment of Baudelaire and his criticism of Hopkins is to my mind the best and clearest statement of Eliot's concept of a vital orthodoxy. His relegation of Hopkins to the category of devotional and therefore minor poet comes as something of a surprise. The distinction between the religious and the devotional poet is, in fact, for Eliot, the difference between Baudelaire and Hopkins. The devotional poet "is not a poet who is treating the whole subject matter of poetry in a religious spirit, but a poet who is dealing with a confined part of this subject matter: who is leaving out what men consider their major passions, and thereby confessing his ignorance of them" (SE, 345). Examples of great Christian religious poets in this sense are Dante, Corneille, Racine, Villon, and – case in point – Baudelaire. By contrast, Vaughan, Southwell, Crashaw and Hopkins are considered minor, "devotional" poets (see SE, 345).

In what sense, then, is Baudelaire a religious poet, which for Eliot means: In what sense is Baudelaire's work an example of relevant orthodoxy in art? In the first place, there is the fundamental matter of artistic sincerity, as opposed to the "pious insincerity" we have dis-

cussed. A genuine and great poet naturally exhibits a moral attachment to his own time. If he is honest, he will feel a part of the human
community and its destiny, whatever that might be. Only by being a
part of it in a deep, spiritual sense will he be able to speak to it. This
authentic participation in the tragedy of an age does not, of course,
have anything to do with fashionable dilettantism. "A poet in a Romantic age," Eliot writes, "cannot be a 'classical' poet except in tendency.
If he is sincere, he must express with individual differences the general
state of mind – not as a duty, but simply because he cannot help
participating in it" (SE, 376). One cannot help thinking here of Eliot's
own *The Waste Land.*

Baudelaire participates intensely in his age both as an heir of
the Romantic mentality and as a dissenter in the aftermath of Romanticism. In the poem "Le balcon" there is initially all the Romantic sensibility of love, but also a correcting of its excesses and a going beyond
it, "the reaching out towards something which cannot be had *in*, but
which may be partly had *through*, personal relations." Baudelaire sees
through the sadness of much Romantic poetry resulting from "the exploitation of the fact that no human relations are adequate to human
desires" and from "the disbelief in any further object for human desires
than that which, being human, fails to satisfy them" (SE, 379). Eliot
would agree with the statement that the end of the Romantic age in
France, for which Baudelaire is directly responsible, is probably due
to a great extent to Baudelaire's orthodoxy of sensibility that enabled
him to expose many Romantic "lies." Orthodoxy of sensibility in this
instance may be summarized as the realization that what really matters
is Sin and Redemption.

Eliot interprets Baudelaire's penchant for blasphemy in the
light of this awareness. Blasphemy may have been the only form of
faith available to Baudelaire and as such it expresses radically the extent
of his moral honesty. By blaspheming, Baudelaire hurled his reproach
at an age in which blasphemy was not only unfashionable but practically impossible:

> To a mind observant of the post-Voltaire France…the recog-
> nition of the reality of Sin is a New Life; and the possibility
> of damnation is so immense a relief in a world of electoral
> reform, plebiscites, sex reform and dress reform, that damna-
> tion itself is an immediate form of salvation – of salvation
> from the ennui of modern life, because it at least gives some

250

significance to living. [*SE*, 378-79]

As with Wordsworth, and unlike Hopkins, the formal innovations introduced by Baudelaire into French versification are judged to proceed by inner necessity from the moral stance. "Baudelaire is indeed the greatest exemplar of *modern* poetry in any language, for his verse and language is the nearest thing to a complete renovation that we have experienced. But his renovation of and attitude towards life is no less radical and no less important" (*SE*, 377-78). Once again the emphasis falls on the continuity and coincidence of the aesthetic and the moral.

Baudelaire is "orthodox" because of his belief in Hulme's disparate realms of existence – the natural, the human, and the supernatu- ral. Baudelaire's anguish is a result of his anti-naturalism, his refusing to compromise with this truth: "In his way of suffering is already a kind of presence of the supernatural.... He rejects always the purely natural and the purely human; in other words, he is neither 'naturalist' nor 'humanist'" (*SE*, 374-75). For Eliot, as for the tradition, the "purely human" is by definition already inhuman because it seeks to collapse the distinction of realms of existence. In his essay on Irving Babbitt, Eliot presents this penetrating critique of humanitarianism and of humanism, both claiming that the "purely human" is enough: "The humanitarian has suppressed the properly human, and is left with the animal; the humanist has suppressed the divine, and is left with a human element which may quickly descend again to the animal from which he has sought to raise it" (*SE*, 420-21). This judgment is not the expression of mere anti-liberal conservatism. The controversial Russian philosopher Nicolas Berdiaev, for instance, who could by no means be considered either a conservative or an "orthodox" thinker in any ecclesiastical sense, could write in the same vein as Eliot:

> I have often dealt with the crisis of European humanism...,
> with the inner dialectic of humanism by which humanism
> transforms itself into anti-humanism. The affirmation that man
> is enough for himself changes into a negation of man, ends up
> in the decomposition of the properly human, in a conception
> which pretends to surpass the human: the 'super-man.' [11]

Nor is the absence of the supernatural the only thing that Eliot deplores. To be lamented, too, is the absence of the properly human, which is always in relation to the properly divine. D.H. Lawrence and Thomas Hardy present instances of writers who create characters who are so devoid of any objective attachment to reality, of any submission to a belief in something besides their own "life-force" or personality, that in the end they evaporate into nebulous caricatures of human beings. In these instances, Berdiaev's principle of the super-human turning into the in-human is graphically illustrated. The super-human is unmasked as the demonic. As a result of the monistic character of his metaphysics, which does not respect the distinction between realms of existence, Hardy creates a world of pure Evil in which his characters are helpless and only come alive in their emotional paroxysms (see *ASG*, 3). Lawrence, on the other hand, sins through the irresponsibility of a quasi-Nietzschean over-spiritualization of man, which likewise transforms itself finally into inhumanity. "[Lawrence] had no guidance except the Inner Light, the most untrustworthy and deceitful guide that ever offered itself to wandering humanity.... It would seem that for Lawrence any spiritual force was good, and that evil resided only in the absence of spirituality.... The man's vision is spiritual, but spiritually sick" (*ASG*, 64-5). The undiscriminating and exclusive emphasis on "spiritual instinct" results in the lack of responsibility and conscience in Lawrence's characters, and they therefore fail ultimately as portrayals of real human beings with obligations.

W.B. Yeats, elsewhere praised for his poetic freedom from compulsion and the integrity of his art (see *OPP*, 307), is likewise censured for living in the "wrong supernatural world." "It was not a world of spiritual significance, not a world of real Good and Evil, of holiness or sin, but a highly sophisticated lower mythology summoned, like a physician, to supply the fading pulse of poetry with some transient stimulant so that the dying may utter his last words" (*ASG*, 50).

V

I HAVE CONCERNED MYSELF in this essay with the exposition, and not the critique, of Eliot's standards of moral judgment in literature. It seemed necessary to spend considerable space outlining the philosophical convictions and spiritual pilgrimage which brought Eliot to his position of Christian realist. It is hoped that an understanding of the roots of Eliot's stance will at least modulate the intransigency of which he is accused in some circles.

I am quite aware, also, of the numerous shortcomings of his "method," if it may be called that. One of them is the fact that it cannot easily be applied to a single work of an author, but rather addresses itself to the meaning of his or her whole production. To this objection I would respond, not only that other highly regarded methodologies, such as the phenomenological, suffer the same limitation, but more importantly that Eliot never suggested that moral criticism should substitute for aesthetic or formal criticism. Moral criticism is intended to *complete* aesthetic criticism, since it is primarily concerned with meaning rather than with *form*.

Another possible objection is that Eliot, in his concern – some would say "compulsion" – to see a given author's work *sub specie aeternitatis,* shows no appreciation for the originality and uniqueness of that author. It seems to me that Eliot is not insensitive to originality and even demands authentic originality as a criterion for relevant orthodoxy. But Eliot censures novelty for novelty's sake and in any event is concerned with the integration of literature into the whole of life. In this precisely consists the *moral* sense of his criticism.

The reference to Nicolas Berdiaev above in part served to illustrate the fact that Eliot was not alone in his fight against religious and critical liberalism. Other illustrious examples could be drawn from all quarters of intellectual and political activity in the earlier part of the twentieth century: in England, G.K. Chesterton, Christopher Dawson, and Evelyn Waugh, to name but three; on the Continent, Jacques Maritain, Karl Barth, Henri de Lubac, and Hans Urs von Balthasar, to name but four others. The most important thing is that these thinkers were combating ignorance or oblivion concerning the perennial distinctions of the Judeo-Christian tradition – were opposing the wholesale and uncritical confusion of the animal, the human, and the divine. T.S. Eliot is original in that he worked out the specifically literary strategy of the battle.

NOTES

1   The letters *SE* refer to Eliot's *Selected Essays* (New York: Harcourt, Brace & World, 1964), and are followed by page references.
2   J. Hillis Miller, *Poets of Reality: Six Twentieth-Century Writers* (New York: Atheneum, 1969), 154.
3   The letters *UP* refer to Eliot's *The Use of Poetry and the Use of Criticism* (London: Faber and Faber, 1948), and are followed by page references.
4   Miller, 180.
5   *Ibid.*

6   *Ibid.*, 185.

7   The letters *ASG* refer to Eliot's *After Strange Gods: A Primer of Modern Heresy* (New York: Harcourt, Brace & Co., 1934), and are followed by page references.

8   Miller, 167-68.

9   The letters *OPP* refer to Eliot's *On Poetry and Poets* (New York: The Noonday Press, 1961), and are followed by page references.

10 The letters *SW* refer to Eliot's *The Sacred Wood: Essays on Poetry and Criticism* (London: Methuen & Co., 1948), and are followed by page references.

11 Nicolas Berdiaev, *Essai d'autobiographie spirituelle* (Paris: Edition Buchet Chastel Corrêa, 1958), 272. My translation.

254

CLEVERNESS: THREE VERSIONS of a FOLKTALE

BY ERDMANN WANIEK AND CRISTINA DE LA TORRE, EMORY UNIVERSITY

L'acqua ch'io prendo già mai non si corse.
(*Paradiso*, II.7)

FAUST. Wohin der Weg?
MEPHISTOPHELES. Kein Weg! Ins Unbetretene,
Nicht zu Betretende; ein Weg ans Unerbetene,
Nicht zu Erbittende. Bist Du bereit?   255
(Faust beim Gang zu den Müttern; *Faust* II, Act One, 6222-25)

I

Children exercise an almost boundless curiosity that is on occasion curbed by fear of darkness. At that age we are intimidated more by the dark void of unexplored space than by the figurative one of the future, of time yet to come. As we grow up this curiosity about and fear of the unknown level off for most of us. We settle into a routine and are active within comfortable limits. Residual anxiety, now about an always uncertain tomorrow, we assuage as best as we can and often not convincingly: we take out life insurance. It is the rare person whose curiosity does not flag and atrophy with age and complacency, whose daily worries and unconquered fears of the unknown do not shrink his world to a familiar environment.

We may call that person an explorer, either of the inner or outer world. In a sense, the explorer not only maps out space, but also masters and manipulates time by anticipating the future. What did not exist yesterday becomes reality today, whether it is a region of (still) private experience or a matter of public usefulness. Our society, "hooked" on change, values the active, inquisitive attitude that shapes an amorphous future into a present different from the past. In holding in high regard those that aggressively cross the boundaries into tomorrow our technological age may have reached new and dubious heights, but such public esteem is not without precedent or risk. The prophet, the soothsayer, and the astrologer have much in common with the explorer or inventor: they describe the particularities of new areas of time and space and share the burden of public scrutiny. Their tales may be ignored or dismissed as improbable – perhaps Marco Polo needed a rhetoric of persuasion more than the Roman augurs.[1] In any case, the reported or projected reality is subject to time: will it become and remain a living present, or sink again into renewed darkness, namely that of forgetting?

There are no blank spots left on the globe for the proverbially intrepid adventurer, so this age has invented another frontier and pursues the exploration of outer space. At the same time, more planet-bound academics and researchers continue to fill the never-ending gaps in our knowledge of ourselves and of the world surrounding us. Even though the natural sciences are increasingly dominating this effort, in the human sciences we may yet find another kind of explorer, readers of the past who try to keep the blank spots on the map of our memory from spreading too rapidly. In 1969 – a year after the walls in Paris proclaimed "l'art est mort" – J.H. Plumb diagnosed *The Death of the Past*. Among other things this implies the end of historicism but, to be sure, not due to an act of present life revolting against the tyranny of the past as Nietzsche advocated over a century ago in his "Vom Nutzen und Nachteil der Historie für das Leben" (1874). There is a difference between the nineteenth-century tendency to succumb to a dead past, which Nietz-sche pinpoints and so vehemently rejects, and the attempt by the historical mind to appropriate the past. The latter attitude is expressed in Friedrich Schlegel's bon mot that the historian is "ein rückwärts gekehrter Prophet." Though the historians' task appears to be more and more difficult and fundamentally changing in a world of instant legends, their efforts are still needed for comprehensive syntheses in the manner of Herder, Toynbee, or Spengler, or in the mode of Fernand Braudel and William H. McNeill. On a different, and no less important, scale – "der liebe Gott steckt im Detail"[2] – historians also help in mediating our daily encounters with the scattered fragments of a receding past. Only exact knowledge that neither overlooks nor flounders in specific details allows us access to the past, regardless of how alive it will be in the consciousness of coming generations.

Identification of quotes, for example, is not a matter of gratuitous pedantry; it rather establishes their context and possible meanings. The motto for this essay owes its attribution to Arthur Evans. The "io" of the motto is Dante, who sees his writing as a nautical voyage, fraught with the dangers of getting lost. The image of poetry as a journey is well documented,[3] and it fits with the notion of the poet as an explorer, a notion that applies not only to the designers of utopias, or to seers from Klopstock to George, or to poets, before Freud, of our subconscious. In a sense, all story-tellers are explorers who invite their audience into unknown waters. This metaphor, and the image of the wanderer on which it is based, are perhaps best and earliest fused in the figure of Ulysses, the *Musterbild* of the wily voyager whom Athena praises: "of all men now alive you are the best in plots and story-telling."[4] His reputation has been rather mixed. In Canto XXVI of the *Inferno* Dante attests to Ulysses' noble if extreme disposition. No memory of home can extinguish his desire for experience, and he succeeds in persuading his companions to join him in an ultimately frivolous attempt to transgress the human limits as set by Hercules, by reminding them of man's destiny and nature. We are made "per seguir virtute e canoscenza" (120).[5] Nonetheless, this journey – "il varco folle d'Ulisee" (*Paradiso*, XXVII.82-83) – into the unknown, triggered by boundless curiosity indeed, is madness that engulfs and finally kills Ulysses. Dante's figure of Ulysses deviates from tradition. In the Greek epic Ulysses becomes an explorer by default. He is yearning to return home when he is made to navigate the primordial obstacle course, an odyssey that takes him to the entrance of Hades' realm. In the end he does reach Ithaca and, though his homecoming is for our sensibilities severely tainted by cruelty, this final success vindicates the "great tactician," whose "life is all adversity."[6] He subdues any fears of unknown space and time, and proceeds trusting his divine helper, the foresight of Tiresias, and his own ingenuity. Ulysses is one *Urtyp* not included in Theophrastus, but succinctly characterized by Goethe in this way: "Wenn er handeln soll, greift er grad das an, was jetzt nötig ist."[7] Goethe, who believed that the English practiced this attitude especially well, raised it to a well-known commandment for psychological health: "Was aber ist deine Pflicht? Die Forderung des Tages."[8] If we often appear to be doing justice to this tenet, then perhaps it is only because our daily ventures require little effort beyond the routine established over time. Rarely do our lives blossom into a true odyssey, or at best only in the highly diluted, figurative sense of every life's journey being one.[9] We are not heroes on a perilous voyage in search of the Golden Fleece. There are buffers, insurances, the path is known, and, with very notable exceptions, the world, moving ahead on a course of enlightenment since the eighteenth century promoted progress and declared it virtually inevitable, until recently seemed increasingly familiar and bright. Late in this century, we are no longer so sanguine about progress and our future.

257

Homer, Dante, and Goethe open up vast perspectives on the ever more overcast predictions for this planet. Here they are meant as a frame for appropriating one sample of our collective memory, namely three folktales from Germany, Ireland, and Italy. They belong to Aarne-Thompson's type number 1450: "Distress over imagined troubles of an unborn child."[10]

II

FOLKTALES, JUST AS PROVERBS and fairy tales, provide a limited, distilled record of human endeavors, prejudices, and anxieties. The straightforward Aarne-Thompson formulation of the motif common to all versions is strangely neutral. Brief by necessity, it indicates neither possible reactions to such distress, nor probable resolutions, let alone evaluations. Yet even imagined troubles need to be resolved, and the different versions of the tale do suggest different options.

FIRST VERSION: *DIE KLUGE ELSE*

Es war ein Mann, der hatte eine Tochter, die hieß die kluge Else. Als sie nun erwachsen war, sprach der Vater 'wir wollen sie heiraten lassen.' 'Ja,' sagte die Mutter, 'wenn nur einer käme, der sie haben wollte.' Endlich kam von weither einer, der hieß Hans, und hielt um sie an, er machte aber die Bedingung, daß die kluge Else auch recht gescheit wäre. 'O,' sprach der Vater, 'die hat Zwirn im Kopf,' und die Mutter sagte 'ach, die sieht den Wind auf der Gasse laufen und hört die Fliegen husten.' 'Ja,' sprach der Hans, 'wenn sie nicht recht gescheit ist, so nehm ich sie nicht.' Als sie nun zu Tisch saßen und gegessen hatten, sprach die Mutter 'Else, geh in den Keller und hol Bier.' Da nahm die kluge Else den Krug von der Wand, ging in den Keller und klappte unterwegs brav mit dem Dekkel, damit ihr die Zeit ja nicht lang würde. Als sie unten war, holte sie ein Stühlchen und stellte es vors Faß, damit sie sich nicht zu bücken brauchte und ihrem Rücken etwa nicht wehe täte und unverhofften Schaden nähme. Dann stellte sie die Kanne vor sich und drehte den Hahn auf, und während der Zeit, daß das Bier hineinlief, wollte sie doch ihre Augen nicht müßig lassen, sah oben an die Wand hinauf und erblickte nach vielem Hin- und Herschauen eine Kreuzhacke gerade über sich, welche die Maurer da aus Versehen hatten stecken lassen. Da fing die kluge Else an zu weinen und sprach 'wenn ich den Hans kriege, und wir kriegen ein Kind, und das ist groß, und wir schicken das Kind in den Keller, daß es hier soll Bier zapfen, so fällt ihm die Kreuzhacke auf den Kopf und schlägts tot.' Da saß sie und weinte und schrie aus Leibeskräften über das bevorstehende Unglück. Die oben warteten auf den Trank, aber die kluge Else kam immer nicht. Da sprach die Frau zur Magd 'geh doch hinunter in den Keller und sieh, wo die Else bleibt.' Die Magd ging und fand sie vor dem Fasse sitzend und laut schreiend. 'Else, was weinst du?' fragte die Magd. 'Ach,' antwortete sie, 'soll ich nicht weinen? wenn ich den Hans kriege, und wir kriegen ein Kind, und das ist groß, und soll hier Trinken zapfen, so fällt ihm vielleicht die Kreuzhacke auf den Kopf und schlägt es tot.' Da sprach die Magd 'was haben wir für eine kluge Else!' setzte sich zu ihr und fing auch an über das Unglück zu weinen. Über eine Weile, als die Magd nicht wiederkam, und die droben durstig nach dem Trank waren, sprach der Mann zum Knecht 'geh doch hinunter in den Keller und sieh, wo die Else und die Magd bleibt.' Der Knecht ging hinab, da saß die kluge Else und die Magd, und weinten beide zusammen. Da fragte er 'was weint ihr denn?' 'Ach,' sprach die Else, 'soll ich nicht weinen? wenn ich den Hans kriege, und wir kriegen ein Kind, und das ist groß, und soll hier Trinken zapfen, so fällt ihm die Kreuzhacke auf den Kopf und schlägts tot.' Da sprach der Knecht 'was haben wir für eine kluge Else!' setzte sich zu ihr und fing auch an laut zu heulen. Oben warteten sie auf den Knecht, als er aber immer nicht kam, sprach der Mann zur Frau 'geh doch hinunter in den Keller und sieh, wo die Else bleibt.' Die Frau ging hinab und fand alle drei in Wehklagen, und fragte nach der Ursache, da erzählte ihr die Else auch, daß ihr zukünftiges Kind wohl würde von der Kreuzhacke totgeschlagen werden, wenn es erst groß wäre, und Bier zapfen sollte, und die Kreuzhacke fiele herab. Da sprach die Mutter gleichfalls 'ach, was haben wir für eine kluge Else!' setzte sich hin und weinte mit. Der Mann oben wartete noch ein Weilchen, als aber seine Frau nicht wiederkam und sein Durst immer stärker ward, sprach er 'ich muß nur selber in den Keller gehn und sehen, wo die Else bleibt.' Als er aber in den Keller kam, und alle da beieinander saßen und weinten, und er die Ursache hörte, daß das Kind der Else schuld wäre, das sie vielleicht einmal zur Welt brächte und von der Kreuzhacke könnte totgeschlagen werden, wenn es gerade zur Zeit, wo sie herabfiele, darunter säße, Bier zu zapfen: da rief er 'was für eine kluge Else!' setzte sich und weinte auch mit. Der Bräutigam blieb lange oben allein, da niemand wiederkommen wollte, dachte er 'sie werden unten auf dich warten, du mußt auch hingehen und sehen, was sie vorhaben.' Als er hinabkam, saßen da fünfe und schrien und jammerten ganz erbärmlich, einer immer besser als der andere. 'Was für ein Unglück ist denn geschehen?' fragte er. 'Ach, lieber Hans,' sprach die Else, 'wann wir einander heiraten und haben ein Kind, und es ist groß, und wir schickens vielleicht hierher, Trinken zu zapfen, da kann ihm ja die Kreuzhacke, die da oben ist stecken geblieben, wenn sie herabfallen sollte, den Kopf zerschlagen, daß es liegen bleibt; sollen wir da nicht weinen?' 'Nun,' sprach Hans, 'mehr Verstand ist für meinen Haushalt nicht nötig; weil du so eine kluge Else bist, so will ich dich haben,' packte sie bei der Hand und nahm sie mit hinauf und hielt Hochzeit mit ihr.

Als sie den Hans eine Weile hatte, sprach er 'Frau, ich will ausgehen arbeiten und uns Geld verdienen, geh du ins Feld und schneid das Korn, daß wir Brot haben.' 'Ja, mein lieber Hans, das will ich tun.' Nachdem der Hans fort war, kochte sie sich einen guten Brei und nahm ihn mit ins Feld. Als sie vor den Acker kam, sprach sie zu sich selbst 'was tu ich? schneid ich ehr? oder eß ich ehr? hei, ich will erst essen.' Nun aß sie ihren Topf mit Brei aus und als sie dick satt war, sprach sie wieder 'Was tu ich? schneid ich ehr, oder schlaf ich ehr? hei, ich will erst schlafen.' Da legte sie sich ins Korn und schlief ein. Der Hans war längst zu Haus, aber die Else wollte nicht kommen, da sprach er 'was hab ich für eine kluge Else, die ist so fleißig, das sie nicht einmal nach Haus kommt und ißt.' Als sie aber noch immer ausblieb und es Abend ward, ging der Hans hinaus und wollte sehen, was sie geschnitten hätte: aber es war nichts geschnitten, sondern sie lag im Korn und schlief. Da eilte Hans geschwind heim, und holte ein Vogelgarn mit kleinen Schellen und hängte es um sie herum; und sie schlief noch immer fort. Dann lief er heim, schloß die

Haustüre zu und setzte sich auf seinen Stuhl und arbeitete. Endlich, als es schon ganz dunkel war, erwachte die kluge Else, und als sie aufstand, rappelte es um sie herum, und die Schellen klingelten bei jedem Schritte, den sie tat. Da erschrak sie, ward irre, ob sie auch wirklich die kluge Else wäre, und sprach 'bin ichs, oder bin ichs nicht?' Sie wußte aber nicht, was sie darauf antworten sollte, und stand eine Zeitlang zweifelhaft: endlich dachte sie 'ich will nach Haus gehen und fragen, ob ichs bin oder ob ichs nicht bin, die werdens ja wissen.' Sie lief vor ihre Haustüre, aber die war verschlossen: da klopfte sie an das Fenster und rief 'Hans, ist die Else drinnen?' 'Ja,' antwortete Hans, 'sie ist drinnen.' Da erschrak sie und sprach 'ach Gott, dann bin ichs nicht,' und ging vor eine andere Tür; als aber die Leute das Klingeln der Schellen hörten, wollten sie nicht aufmachen, und sie konnte nirgends unterkommen. Da lief sie fort zum Dorfe hinaus, und niemand hat sie wieder gesehen.

261

One glance at the Grimms' tale number 34, "Die kluge Else," perhaps the best-known example of the type, is sufficient to determine that this is not a fairy-tale in the vein of "Snow White and the Seven Dwarfs." It is a folk-tale with sharp, hostile undertones and a remarkable portion of didacticism. The central motif, the (anticipated) experience of loss, is drawn out at length. Clever Else engages in a lament. To be sure, it is a rudimentary form of lament but the decisive characteristic is fully delineated. Else gives expression to an incapacitating sense of personal loss which she successfully imparts to the members of the household. They mourn the loss of a young life. If, for the time being, we take Else's wailing at face value, we can hear it as an echo across centuries and genres. Antigone is Else's remote and seriously threatened ancestor, Antigone, who bewails her fate of a life cut short: "Unwept, no wedding-song, unfriended, now I go, / the road laid down for me."[11] Else, of course, has no immediate reason for her fully self-induced lament; the future that she outlines is not irrevocably imminent but tenuously predicated on a sequence of "ifs." She indulges her imagination. No one forces her to accept the tomb as her marriage chamber (*Antigone*, 891); she is not herself facing the descent "to the hollow chambers of the dead" (*Antigone*, 920); still unwed, she is mourning the imagined fate of an unborn child. For a brief moment, and without any irreversible cause in reality, Clever Else exiles *herself* "from our life on earth" (*Antigone*, 890). In her descent we perceive the faded outline of a mythic pattern, which we can read as an unintentional travesty of a most venerable tradition, established by *The Odyssey*, elaborately treated in Virgil's *Aeneid*, Book 6, and central to Goethe's *Faust*.

The "road laid down for" Else is simple and commonplace. Her mother tells her: "geh in den Keller und hol Bier." As the story progresses all the members of the household congregate in the cellar where the imagined child meets his/her imagined death. Nowadays, as in the tale, "cellar" or "Keller," both derived from late Latin *cellarium*, have a primary connotation of an underground location, and its use as a symbol for hell is documented by Grimm, *Deutsches Wörterbuch,* for the sixteenth century. The Latin, however, and until the sixteenth century also its English derivation, lacked this aspect. The predominant feature of such a potentially ambiguous cellar is its supply of beer or wine. This storage space holds provisions to nourish the family and the guests. It is not necessarily *"the dark entity* of the house,"[12] let alone a place of death threatening in the pursuit of rare spirits, as in Poe's "The Cask of Amontillado." To be true, in German folklore basements are thought to hold a threat for a pregnant woman and her unborn baby, but no such superstition surfaces in "Die kluge Else." Instead, this basement could be the well-spring of merriment and satisfaction.

Occasion and lament are deeply incongruous. The result is more the ridicule of the protagonist than a travesty of the form of lament, or the motif of descent. Actually the whole household is held up to laughter since they react to Else's story as if it were inexorably bound to happen, indeed as if the child were already dead. Else cries over "das bevorstehende Unglück," but the maid breaks into tears over "das Unglück," and while the father's reaction is phrased in the subjunctive and softened by a "vielleicht," the bridegroom, assuming that we cry after an accident, not in anticipation of it, asks: "Was für ein Unglück ist denn geschehen?"

Typically, the true prophet is not listened to in his own house or country. But Else's foresight is not the often obscure one of a prophet; she is not a late disciple of Cassandra's. We may psychologize the moment, the *Augenblick* of her seeing the pickax, as the crystallization and release of latent fears which she pours into not unlikely conclusions. Yet her "if...then" logic of observation and prediction is too clever by far, and in any case her premise is not at all inescapable. The pickax can be removed. Though death *is* ever-threatening, the distance between Else's current situation and the envisioned future calamity,

mirrored in the length of her "if... then" sequence, invalidates her un-
timely grief. It seems especially out of place given the fact that the
whole household is gathered under the instrument of death without a
thought to their own welfare.

The episode, although not specifically intended as a marriage
test, is firmly cast within such a traditional frame. In fairy-tales this test
is often a seemingly impossible task. Else's sisters-in-trouble extricate
themselves in works such as "Die kluge Gretel" (which Carl Orff turned into an opera, *Die Kluge*), or in fairy-tales about spinning, such as
"Rumpelstilzchen" or "Die drei Spinnerinnen."[13] Beyond all differences
these tales share a basic feature: they show women spinning with limited resources. Else does not transform rooms of flax into thread; un-   263
asked she spins her yarn of the future with only the slightest supply
of material. Yet in the fairy-tales the women prove themselves against
the greatest odds. At the end of our folktale Else has failed without any
obstacle in her path.

The outcome of the tale does not surprise us. From the outset,
when we hear the parents' talk about Else, we know that something is
askew. The father's comment that Else has "Zwirn im Kopf," prepares
us for her story-telling talents and for her cleverness;[14] but the mother's
bragging about her daughter's heightened perception raises our suspi-
cion about her kind of cleverness. To our astonishment Hans, the prospective bridegroom who at the beginning of the tale clearly states his
expectations regarding his future wife's cleverness, concludes after the
basement scene that Else has passed the test. Her surplus of ingenuity,
as it were, is taken as sufficient proof of her ability to master less demanding situations. With this most questionable judgement Hans
seems a spouse fit for Clever Else. However, in the second part of the
tale Hans reverses his original judgement. If the first part is a test of
Else's cleverness, with the bridegroom's condition and conclusion
framing it, then the second, much shorter part, is the test of the bridegroom's conclusion. It should be noted that Hans bases both his initial
approval of Else and his subsequent rejection on the very same kind
of behavior – namely, Else's inability to stay in the present, to follow
the sensible sequence of events. Once married, she anticipates pleasure
the way she had anticipated pain before, and eats and sleeps before she
works.

Going beyond the confines of the tale, Heinz Rölleke has suggested a specific, contemporary gist for its satiric component: "Die Verbindung von Kettenmärchen und Schwank mutet vor allem eingangs

wie eine Parodie auf das zeitgenössische Schicksalsdrama an."[15] The
tale has a broader application than that of a literary parody. All imagination is fed but not fettered by the immediate surroundings which it
leaves behind to chart new worlds. *If on a winter's night a traveler* is the
fetching title of one of Italo Calvino's books. This incomplete conditional clause points to, and the book exploits, the process of all fictions:
an "if" releases the imagination, and it unfolds on the strength of "and
then" (E.M. Forster). Clever Else is no exception. Her fiction germinates
in the marriage of her keen observation of a potential threat from the
pickax with a fruitful "if": "Wenn ich den Hans kriege...." The "Zwirn"
that she spins from this condition is a tearful tale, as the audience's
reaction demonstrates. One after the other, as they come in search of
her and the beer, they surrender, and cry. Such a strong participatory
response strikes us as an exception; here it is the result of confusing
fiction with reality, to which the storyteller herself succumbs first and
foremost. Once Else inserts a "vielleicht" into her fiction, but it is as
if the repetition has the power to make the projection so real for Else
and her listeners that it both completely usurps the open future and
displaces the present. There is, and can be, no liberating power to her
fabulazione: a strangely disembodied, calculated performance of self-
stimulation, it lures her and most of her audience into the straightjacket
of worry, of *Sorge.*

A revisionist reading of "Clever Else" as the story of a woman
resisting expectations, going her own way and carving out an inner
sanctum of grief over inescapable death while preserving against the
pressures of labor a deep, bodily appreciation of the moment – a reading that has her warning us against our own blindness toward death,
and against our preoccupation with work – runs counter to the ironic
tone of this folktale and to the gist of folktales in general, namely, the
reinforcement of prevailing social values. Her heightened perception
(in her mother's praise of her) is not a metaphor for unusual powers
to be honored and appreciated. Even escapist folktales look rather
askance at such abilities – Else perceives what is not the case, i.e. the
future. A positive reading of Else becomes fully implausible in view of
the ending. There her inability to interpret a situation and respond appropriately reaches a painful climax as her temporary exile from reality
becomes permanent. Her husband enacts her separation from accepted
modes of behavior by identifying her with the "Vogelgarn mit kleinen
Schellen" as a fool. We may be strongly dismayed by the seeming dis-
proportion between Else's mild misdemeanor and her husband's exag-

264

gerated reaction, but the folktale has strains of the *exemplum* in it. Else
after all succumbs to the deadly sin of *acedia*, and the second part of
the tale is as little an indictment of the husband as the first one is an
endorsement of Clever Else. Else cannot shake off the net of her own
foolishness, and, reiterating the motif of loss, the story culminates in
her doubting her identity and losing her place in society.

The German version of the neutrally labelled category "Distress…" is a satiric story about the dire effects of "Zwirn im Kopf."
In combination with slothfulness it is Else's undoing. In this sense
she loses herself.[16]

SECOND VERSION: *A LEGEND OF CLEVER WOMEN*

Before Joan was married all her people had a high opinion of
her. When Darby came to woo her, her mother told him in
confidence that she could see the wind, and hear the flies
when they coughed. Well, when they were at dinner the beer
came short, and Joanna went down to the cellar to draw a
gallon-full. She stayed awhile, and then her mother went to
see what was keeping her. She wasn't coming back, and the
father's and Darby's thirst was getting more troublesome; so
the old man went after the rest. As he forgot to return, the
bridegroom thought fit at last to try what had become of his
new relations, and when he got inside the cellar, he found
the whole of them sobbing and crying. "What in the world
has happened, dear friends?" said he. "Oh nothing," says the
mother,"but something terrible might happen only for the
cleverness of my poor Joan. Do you see that loose stone in
the vault just over the spigot? When my poor child was filling
the gallon, that stone caught her eye, and she thought what a
heartscald it would be when the little boy, that God will please
to send to herself and yourself, would be filling a vessel, maybe when he'd be ten years old or so, and that stone tumble
down and kill him dead. So how could she help clapping her
hands an' roarin' an' bawlin' when the thought came into her
head? and I'm sure her father an' meself would have the hard
hearts not to feel for her." "Well, well," says Darby, "I'll soon
put it out of the stone's power to do mischief." So he got on
a stillion, and pulled it away, and they all dried their eyes and
returned to their dinner.

ERDMANN WANIEK AND CRISTINA DE LA TORRE

Well, when they were living by themselves, Darby
says one morning to his wife after breakfast, "You'll have my
dinner ready at half-past twelve to the minute. You know I
have to go to the town after it." "Never fear, Darby," says she;
and sure enough she had a big black pudding hissing in the
pan about ten minutes before she expected him. While she
was watching it, the thought came into her mind that it would
be a good thing to be drawing the beer while the pudding was
frying. But while she was watching the beer falling into the
jug, she heard them cry out, "The dog is running away with
the pudding!" Out she flew like a racer, and after the dog with
her; but when she had chased him two fields he was a whole
field ahead of her, and she thought she might as well go back.

Poor Joan! when she came to the cellar door, the
floor was covered three inches deep with beer, the barrel was
empty, but the jug was full any way. "We must make the best
of a bad market," says she. "Darby would be vexed to see
the cellar this way, and I must get out his drink whatever happens." So she emptied a sack of meal on the pool, and was
delighted to see it was almost all sucked up. Then she laid
the sack across to the barrel, and hardly wet her pumps, and
would have had the full jug coming back only for a kick she
happened to give it. Poor Darby had a poor dinner, but Joan
was so heated, and so proud of her good management, that he
hadn't the heart to scold her. She showed him how nicely all
would have happened, and what a comfortable dinner she
might have ready for him, only for the roguery of the dog
when he found the door open, and how could she spare time
to turn the cock when she heard the shout? Darby, however,
began to suspect that she was not so clever as her father and
mother had said she was.

A week after he had to go into the town, and says he,
just as he was setting out, "Joan, you must mind what I say to
you. *Shan na Mo* (Jack of the Cows) will be apt to call while
I'm away, for Browny, and Blacky, and Brackedy. He agreed to
pay thirty pounds for them, but he's rather tricky; so don't let
him get a hoof of one of them without paying the money on
the nail." "I'll be careful," says Joan. Darby came back in the
evening. "Well, Joan my darling, how did you succeed?" "Oh,
nicely. You'll never say after this that I wasn't clever. I think

Shan is just as tricky as you say he was, but he didn't circumvent me." "Them cows," says he, "is dear enough, but I'll take
'em; what's a man but his word?" and he was driving them out
at the bawn gate. "Oh stop!" says I, "You didn't give me thirty
pounds." "Didn't I," says he, "Well, what a memory I have!
and bedad," says he, rummaging his pockets, "I left the rowl of
notes on the dresser coming out. Now I'll have the trouble of
going for them. Ah! I wish my wife was as clever as you, Joan.
I'd be a thousand pounds richer to-day. Happy is the man that
owns you! Oh, this is what we can do, and save trouble. These
three cows are mine. I'll leave you one in pledge till I send you
the money this evening or to-morrow morning." "Well, see my
cleverness! I kept the smallest because she'd eat the least till
he'll send the money. Now what do you say to me, Darby?"
"Indeed, I'll say this to you. You are such a fool that I'll never
lie a night by your side, till I find some other woman more
foolish;" and he turned his back, and to the road with him.

267

The first foolish woman he found had no window
to her mud-wall cabin, and the door was turned to the north.
She was running with a sieve in her hands in and out, crying
"I have it now," and "I haven't it now," till Darby asked her
what she was doing. "And ain't I striving to carry the sunshine
into the cabin, and I can never get it inside the door?" "Have
you got a pick-axe in the way?" "Yes, to be sure." "Well, I'll
soon bring it in to you." He went to the wall next to the sun,
gave two or three strokes, and a grey streak was soon coming
in, and a splash of light on the floor. "Oh, fortunate was the
wind that drove you in my road! what will I be giving you
for this good job?" "Ah, my good woman, all you're worth
wouldn't be enough; I'll take nothing;" and he went on, saying to himself, "She is not more foolish than Joan."

He was going by a cabin and such roaring and bawl-
ing as was coming out through the door! In he ran, and there
was a man sitting on a chair, with a clean linen sack on his
head and his shoulders, and his wife with a beetle, coming
down on his head with the hammers of death, and he roaring
like fifty bulls. "What are you doing, you wicked woman?"
says Darby. "Do you want to kill the poor man?" "Indeed, an'
I don't, but I want to make a hole in this divel of a shirt to let
his head and face up through it!" "Have you a scissors about

you?" "To be sure; I'd be a purty housewife if I hadn't." Darby made a cut in the top of the bag, and the poor bruised head came out. "Oh, mush, wasn't it good fortune that drove you into the cabin! What'll we be giving you for your trouble?" "All that you're worth wouldn't be enough; so I'll take nothing; *banacht lath!* I don't think she's worse than Joan. I'll go on."

The next adventure he met was in a widow-woman's barn, where herself and a few neighbours were striving to lift up a big cow to the eaves of the cabin, and the poor animal kicking off their hats, and tearing their clothes with her hoofs. "God bless the men and their work!" says Darby. "God save you kindly," says they. "What are yous doing with the poor baste?" says he. "An' sure we're striving to get her up on the *tatch*," says the widow, "'till she makes a meal on all that fine grass that's growing on itself, and the scraws at the top." "Let her down," says he, "and may be we'll come on an easier plan. Give us a reaping-hook, if you have the like." So he got a ladder, and was soon down again with an armfull of the grass. "Well to be sure!" says the poor widow, "nothing bates the wit of man barring the bees. It was a good wind," &c. &c. "I don't think," says Darby, "she's a bit worse than Joan. My journey is not over."

Just as night fell, he went into a farm-house and put up for the night. The owner was a widow-woman that was after burying her third husband. The first two were such crooked disciples that she married a third to get the taste of them off her mouth, as she said. "Where do you come from, honest man?" says she to Darby, after supper. "I am from the *Gairdheen*" (Garden, the name of his farm.) "Oh, and are you from the GARDEN in earnest?" "Faith I am so; what do you admire about it?" "Oh, and may be you are acquainted with my poor husband, the last I mean, the others I'm sure never had the grace to get there." Darby now smelled a rat. "And what sort of a man was your last, and what was the name was on him?" "An' wasn't he poor Jack Miskella, the innocentest and little-good-for-est man that ever drew on a stocking? A child of three years old would buy and sell him any day he ever got up." "I know the man you mean, and have a message to you from him. He have no means of earning his bread, and his clothes is nearly worn out. So he does be begging at the good

Christians' doors, and he bid me tell you, if you'd send him a comfortable suit of clothes, not forgetting a pair of double-soled brogues, you'd make a man of him; and if he had an ass or a small garran to carry him from one charitable house to another, he'd be as happy as a king, it 'ud be such an ease to his poor legs." "Ah, an' them's the very things he must have, my poor Jack! I suppose you'd like to be off early to him. The ass will be ready bridled and saddled in the stable, and the full suit will be laid out here on the kitchen table; and if you think they'd be of any use, there'll be a few guinea notes in the pockets." "Never mind the notes; every family does everything for itself in that country."

"I think," says Darby to himself next morning, "I've found a woman rather more foolish than poor Joan; so I'll go back to her." He did so, and they led such a life that whenever a loving couple are seen going together to Mass or market, every one says, "There goes Darby and Joan."

The Irish version is the longest, least didactic, and most embellished one. The basic difference from the German version is signalled in the title, "A Legend of Clever Women," obviously with the same ironic intent but now extended to a gallery of women, as if the tale, instead of presenting a single case of dubious cleverness, were meant to illustrate and settle with a wealth of cases the long and lively debate (by men) about the irreconcilable contradiction between brains and the female sex. Consequently the first part, the wooing and the scene in the basement, is condensed and summarized. Nonetheless, all the features are present, from the mother's bragging about her daughter, with the very same two formulas used in the Grimms' version, to everyone crying with the daughter because they "feel for her." But the lament, so prominently repeated in the German version, is given only once. In this tale the Aarne-Thompson motif is one episode among many. The accumulation of episodes decisively alters the tone and twist of the tale.

As the specific story of one woman "Clever Else" does not display a misogynist stance.[17] In contrast, the Irish version seems intended to ridicule women since it strings together several incidents of foolish behavior by women, incidents that exist in other types of tales but are ascribed to men.[18] The women are portrayed as thoroughly dumbfounded in situations that Darby, the bridegroom and later husband, solves swiftly and easily. Time after time he acts decisively, laconically deflating women's problems: "I'll soon put it out of the stone's power to do mischief," something the German Hans does not think of. Darby gives commands and knows what he is about. Corresponding to the women's foolishness, the man's role as a judge is enlarged in this version. More so than the German tale the Irish one tells of a community characterized by barter and cunning, and imbued with an atmosphere of inequality between man and woman. Though the cow-dealer is not to be trusted, his choice of verb seems singularly apt when he distracts Joan with flattery: "Happy is the man that owns you!" Acting with foresight and decisiveness the woman is supposed to be the circumspect housekeeper. Joan thinks she does justice to this expectation, so she boasts of being clever after having been cheated, and is proud of her "good management" after wasting a dinner, and a sizable supply of beer and flour.

"Good management," among other things, means control. Joan and all the other women fret over one mishap after the other; it is only the male protagonist who exercises "good management." In gauging the degree of female foolishness he is not heartless, but even rather sympathetic, helpful, and acting according to common sense. At the end Darby in fact returns to his wife, presumably because it is best to be loving and happy within the given limits if there is no choice. However, the joviality and good humor of the story, and especially its ending are a veneer. While on the story level the tale seems to leave the conceptual frame of the marriage test, it actually broadens it to include all women. Since they all fall short of common sense, Darby's happy return to matrimonial bliss amounts in fact to a sarcastic claim that all women are dim-witted. It is another compliment to the man who recognizes that dead end and makes the best of it.

THIRD VERSION: *CICCO PETRILLO*

C'era una volta moglie e marito che avevano una figlia femmina, e avevano trovato a maritarla. Il giorno delle nozze avevano invitato tutti i parenti e dopo lo sposalizio si misero a tavola. Sul piú bello del pranzo, venne a mancare il vino. Il padre disse alla figlia sposa: – Va' giú in cantina a prendere il vino.

La sposa va in cantina, mette la bottiglia sotto la botte, apre la spina e aspetta che la bottiglia si riempia. Intanto che aspetta, cominciò a pensare: «Oggi mi sono accasata, di qui a nove mesi mi nascerà un figlio, gli metterò nome Cicco Petrillo, lo vestirò, lo calzerò, diventerà grandicello...e se Cicco Petrillo poi mi muore? Ah! Povero figlio mio!» e sbottò in un pianto, un pianto da non dirsi.

La spina intanto era sempre aperta, e il vino correva giú per la cantina. Quelli a pranzo, aspetta la sposa, aspetta la sposa, ma la sposa non ricompariva. Il padre disse a sua moglie: – Va' un po' in cantina a vedere se quella là si fosse addormentata, alle volte!

La madre andò in cantina e trovò la figlia che piangeva da non poterne piú. – Che hai fatto, figlia? Cosa t'è successo?

Ah, mamma mia, stavo pensando che oggi mi sono maritata, tra nove mesi farò un figlio e gli metterò nome Cicco Petrillo; e se Cicco Petrillo poi mi muore?

Ah! Povero mio nipote!

Ah! Povero figlio mio!

E le due donne sbottarono a piangere tutte e due.

La cantina, intanto, s'empiva di vino. Quelli che erano rimasti a tavola, aspetta il vino, aspetta il vino, il vino non veniva. Disse il padre – Gli sarà preso un colpo a tutt'e due. Bisognerà che vada a darci un'occhiata.

Andò in cantina e trovò le due donne che piangevano come due creature. Disse: – E che diavolo v'è successo?

Ah! Marito mio, sapessi! Stiamo pensando che ora questa figlia nostra s'è maritata, e presto presto ci farà un figlio, e a questo figlio gli metteremo nome Cicco Petrillo; e se Cicco Petrillo se ne muore?

Ah! – gridò il padre. – Povero Cicco Petrillo nostro!

E si misero a piangere tutti e tre, in mezzo al vino.

Lo sposo, non vedendo tornar piú su nessuno, disse: – Ma che accidente staranno a fare giú in cantina? Fatemici andare un po' a vedere, – e scese giú.

A sentire quel piagnisteo: – Che diavolo v'è sceso, che piangete?

E la sposa: – Ah! Marito mio! Stiamo pensando che noi ora ci siamo sposati, e faremo un figlio e gli metteremo nome Cicco Petrillo; e se Cicco Petrillo nostro se ne muore?

Lo sposo dapprincipio stette a vedere se facevano per scherzo, poi quando capí che facevano sul serio, gli saltarono le paturnie e cominciò a urlare: – Che eravate un po' tonti, – dice, – me l'immaginavo, ma fino a questo punto, – dice, – non me l'aspettavo proprio –. Dice: – E adresso mi toccherà perdere il mio tempo con questi mammalucchi! – Dice: – Ma manco per sogno! Me ne vado per il mondo! – Dice: – Sissignore! E tu cara mia, datti l'anima in pace che non mi vedi piú. A meno che girando il mondo non trovassi tre matti peggio di voi! – Dice, e va via. Uscí di casa e non si voltò nemmeno indietro.

Camminò fino a un fiume, e c'era un uomo che voleva levare delle nocciole da una barca con la forca.

Che fate, buon uomo, con codesta forca?

È un pezzo che ci provo, ma non riesco a levarne nemmeno una.

Sfido! Ma perché non provate con la pala?

Con la pala? To', non ci avevo pensato.

«È uno! – disse lo sposo. – Questo qui è piú bestia ancora di tutta la famiglia di mia moglie.»

Camminò, finché non arrivò a un altro fiume. C'era un contadino che s'affannava ad abbeverare due buoi col cucchiaio.

Ma che fate?

Sono qui da tre ore e non sono buono a cavar la sete a queste bestie!

E perché non gli lasciate mettere il muso nell'acqua?

Il muso? Eh, dite bene: non ci avevo pensato.

«È due!» disse lo sposo, e andò avanti.

Cammina cammina, in cima a un gelso vide una donna che teneva in mano un paio di brache.

Che fate lassú, buona donna?

Oh, se sapeste! – gli disse quella. – Il mio uomo è morto, e il prete m'ha detto che se n'è salito in Paradiso. Io sto ad aspettare che torni giú e rientri nelle sue brache.

«È tre! – pensò lo sposo. – Mi pare che non s'incontra che gente piú tonta di mia moglie. È meglio che me ne torni a casa mia!»

Cosí fece e si trovò contento, perché si dice che il peggio non è mai morto.

In the German and Irish versions the spilled beverage is beer, in the Italian version it is predictably wine. This is only one of a number of obvious differences. The Italian version is not clearly within the tradition of a marriage-test preceding the wedding. The setting is the wedding itself, and altogether the tale is more joyous and concentrated than either the German or the Irish one. The parents do not brag about their daughter, and she does not engage in clever predictions. The bride simply spells out the inevitable, almost foreordained sequence of events: nine months after the wedding everybody expects a child, and even her certainty that it will be a boy is less prediction than cultural pressure. Significantly, and in contrast to both German and Irish tales, the cause for the child's possible death is not identified. The creative moment of idleness is distinctly different in the three versions. Clever Else, intent on not letting her eyes be "müßig," searches for something to keep them and her mind busy. Joan's eye is "caught" by the threatening stone, but the Italian bride simply "cominciò a pensare" while she is waiting for the jug to fill up. She does not fall asleep, as her father suspects, but alone in the basement her idle mind gives birth to a Freudian *Tagtraum* with happy prospects of the future, until it derails for no apparent reason. We may not follow Gaston Bachelard in assuming that when we dream in the cellar, "we are in harmony with the irrationality of the depths" (*Poetics of Space*, p. 18), yet what wells up in the bride's tears is an intimation of human vulnerability, an unmotivated recognition of unpredictable, ever present death "mitten im Leben" (Rilke). The German version has the heroine give a clever demonstration of seemingly iron-clad, deductive reasoning, whereas the bride in the Italian version is overcome by her awareness of the limits of all motherly care: "…e se Cicco Petrillo poi mi muore?"

273

All these differences add up and are reflected again in the title, "Cicco Petrillo," which does not proclaim any ironic distancing from the bride and putative mother, let alone from clever women in general. The irony in this title is made gentle by the fact that the choice of a boy's name acknowledges a justified attitude: for this bride and her family the baby is the consummation of the wedding. The husband is needed to turn the imagined future, at least the good part of it, into reality. The choice of the boy's name over the mother's affirms the anticipatory power of the imagination as much as it questions its disruptive intrusion into daily life. This is borne out by the way the story ends: the German version destroys the possibility of a future child, the Italian version allows for it. It is as if the future with its child-bringing potential overrode the present, as if the trust in life triumphed over the fear of stupidity and death.

"Cicco Petrillo" does comment on the wine being wasted, but it is not developed as a mistake in good management. Different from the wedding at Cana, this wedding party does not need a miracle of water turning into wine. Rather, the bride lets the wine spill, and instead of following the dictates of practical action and taking care of her duties as a hostess, she is literally inundated by a fantasy that drowns out the present. Yet in the Italian version with its considerably muted lament and no pretensions to logic, it seems appropriate that the bride should extend this fragile moment of withdrawing from the wedding, this midpoint of a life, to incorporate its endpoints, birth and death. What appears a silly lack of presence of mind contains an aspect that requires our respect. Surely overburdening the moment and the occasion, the bride nevertheless experiences an oblique kind of epiphany.

274

The groom, however, is not at all affected by it. Unlike duped Hans, and practical Darby, this groom speaks with the rash voice of haughty reason and, seeing his bride and her family caught in the web of future calamities, he turns his back on them. In the middle of the wedding he leaves for a quest which serves as a retroactive test of the bride's behavior. Thus the marriage trial, though postponed and transformed into a comparison, has not been abandoned. The rules of the *Kettenschwank*, with its repetition of similar episodes, almost dictate that the Italian groom find what he searches for. What is unexpected is the husband's changed basis and goal: he judges his wife's whole family dumb and with a certain fairness goes to find three persons dumber than his wife and her relatives. His first two encounters especially are interesting in our context because they involve men. Their behavior, just as the bride's, goes against common sense. However, the man who wants to pick up hazelnuts with a pitchfork and the one who wants to water his oxen with a spoon fail to master practical problems of everyday life not because of an excess in imagination leading to dreamy neglect. Rather, they are too narrow in their use of their imaginative faculties.

This pattern reverses the progression in the German version, where the husband is led to the conclusion that his wife is beyond help and of no use in mastering daily tasks. That is to say the German tale, full of cruel mirth about the characters' follies, presents the story of a man's mistake, of his awakening and of his ridding himself of his wife. Darby's sampling in the Irish version yields a result that seems less cruel on an individual basis, namely that the grass is not greener on the other side, but more objectionable in its stance to women, namely that

Joan is at best as dumb as other women and not quite as foolish as some. The Italian version, too, disabuses the husband of his, in this instance immediate, conclusion. He learns to value what he has: home is better than the rest of the world that he meets. Like its title, the last sentence of the Italian story is bathed in a benign, ironic ambiguity.[19] Nevertheless, the Italian version, which gives the most even development both in detail repetition and variation, and in the relation between the two parts of the tale, tries for a delicate balance. Neither the Irish nor the German versions leave any doubts about the priorities: daily tasks govern our lives and require common sense; imagination only interferes and distracts; it arises from and leads to slothfulness. The Italian version keeps the pattern of a two-part story, but assigns the first half to the woman, and the second half to the man, with a considerable shift in the emphasis between the parts. For all his quick perception it is the husband who learns of his lack of perspective. As he gets to know the world, his bride and her use of imagination are vindicated, a turn of the tale not within the compass of the other versions. The Italian version is conciliatory rather than vengeful, and of course the conciliatory version is needed for life to go on, for Cicco Petrillo to be born. By not making death the matter of a freak accident, the Italian version acknowledges death most straightforwardly, and then transcends it with a gesture of hope.

275

III

WE CANNOT AGREE with Italo Calvino's note to "Cicco Petrillo" in which he claims that this story about the boundlessness of human stupidity is the same the world over. The differences go well beyond the dramatizations. The infinite repetition suggested by the abstracted and neutrally formulated Aarne-Thompson type that is the thread common to these stories unravels towards an equally remarkable diversity. The Aarne-Thompson classification is quite correct, yet it neither registers nor prepares us for the varied portrayals of the prospective mother, of the imagination and the distress, of the husband and his reactions. What might account for these differences is a thorny problem without any clear answers in sight. What does it mean, for example, that, according to Calvino, Italian folktales were mostly told by women? Were Irish ones mostly told by men? In our context it is more fruitful to ask whether the stories, in their distinct elaboration of the simplified motif, share a kernel of didactic intent, characteristic of this kind of folktale.

After all, the Aarne-Thompson type 1450 identifies at best the beginning part of these stories. Yet their *basso continuo* is indeed the same throughout, even though they execute and embellish it in distinct, not to say incompatible ways. If, in Calvino's words, folktales offer "il catalogo dei destini che possono darsi a un uomo e a una donna" (p. xx), then these tales internalize this most general theme as the protagonist's concern. The women in the Aarne-Thompson type 1450 exercise their curiosity about the future, and, in so doing, they come face to face with death, the certain uncertainty that will end our lives. Such an attitude, thus formulated, touches on the heroic. These women, however, are not only victimized by the adult's version of the child's fear of darkness, namely the fear of death; their preoccupation with death is uncalled for. In the end, the Aarne-Thompson type 1450 is only implicitly about our stance towards the future and death, and that, in the Irish version, it can be grouped so seamlessly with other anecdotes hints at the actual theme also of type 1450. At times even the realization that death is inescapable can be trite and foolish. These funny stories all chide a blindness to the needs of the moment, and castigate idle worries and futile toil.[20] The stories expose the foolishness of tackling tasks with inappropriate means and procedures. Their common concern is "good management."

Living in and for the moment has its limits, and good management does look to the future, as the proverb asserts: "Der kluge Mann baut vor." The husband in the Irish version anticipates the cow dealer's slyness and warns his wife. The drastic retaliation of the husband in the German version is plausible when we see in it the apprehension that, although Clever Else can speculate about the future she, like another idle creature and singer, namely the cricket in the very first of de la Fontaine's fables, will not prepare for it. The point of good management is central to all the incidents in all versions, but it is most unforgivingly made in "Clever Else" in the opposition between developing an idle, pointless scenario, and the need to provide for a tomorrow, between the vain success in story-telling, and the failure to act and work when needed, between the "Zwirn im Kopf" and "good management." That our imagination easily outshines reality is a blessing only if it stimulates us to change this reality. The down-spiraling version of the "what… if" cleverness breeds fatalistic paralysis.

Though the level and the range of implications differ, the insistence of these folktales on "good management" converges with Goethe's admonition to face the "Forderung des Tages." It would be a mistake to interpret this "Forderung" narrowly. Goethe is neither denigrating imagination and its good uses – "Das wirkliche Leben verliert oft dergestalt seinen Glanz, daß man es manchmal mit dem Firnis der Fiktion wieder auffrischen muß" (*Dichtung und Wahrheit; HA* 9:366) – nor is he advocating blinders towards tomorrow – "Müßig und träumerisch, weil ihm keine Gegenwart genügte, fand er das, was ihm abging, in einer Freundin, die, indem sie fürs ganze Jahr lebte, nur für den Augenblick zu leben schien" (*HA* 9:543). This concentration on the moment, in keeping with Goethe's conviction "daß der Mensch eigentlich nur berufen ist, in der Gegenwart zu wirken" (*HA* 9:447), is also not to be confused with routine and its pitfalls of stagnation. Goethe certainly equated "Gewöhnung" with "Wohlbehagen,"[21] but only of a never changing Arcadia can it be stated: "Hier ist das Wohlbehagen erblich" (*Faust* II, Act III, 9550). In our world change rules and is necessary.[22] We are unable to determine that change fully; as a matter of fact a certain blindness is helpful as we walk into the dark future. It is an insight that Goethe captures magnificently in the grand and unresolved irony of Faust's last moments. Blind but guided by an inner light shining all the more brightly, Faust mistakes the noise caused by the digging of his grave as an indication that his utopian plans are being executed. Perhaps it is not quite knowing the future in all its details, or the path with all its obstacles, that allows room for curiosity and for "un salto a freddo, come tuffarmi da un trampolino in un mare."[23]

"Man geht nie weiter, als wenn man nicht mehr weiß, wohin man geht."
(Goethe, *HA* 12:547)

«Dice: – Tutto è inutile, se l'ultimo approdo non può essere che la città infernale, ed è là in fondo che, in una spirale sempre più stretta, ci risucchia la corrente.
E Polo: – L'inferno dei viventi non è qualcosa che sarà; se ce n'è uno, è quello che è già qui, l'inferno che abitiamo tutti i giorni, che formiamo stando insieme. Due modi ci sono per non soffrirne. Il primo riesce facile a molti: accettare l'inferno e diventarne parte fino al punto di non vederlo più. Il secondo è rischioso ed esige attenzione e apprendimento continui: cercare e saper riconoscere chi e cosa, in mezzo all'inferno, non è inferno, e farlo durare, e dargli spazio.»
(Calvino, *Le città invisibili,* 170)

"It's over, and can't be helped, and that's one consolation,
as they alvays says in Turkey, ven they cuts the wrong man's
head off."

(Sam Weller in *The Pickwick Papers*, ch. 23)

NOTES

1   Italo Calvino's Marco Polo (*Le città invisibili*, Torino, 1972) does not use or need any,
    although the musings begin with this sentence: "Non è detto che Kublai Kan creda a
    tutto quel che dice Marco Polo...." Later on the great Khan compares Marco Polo's
    tales with those by his ambassadors and asks him: "Torni da paesi altrettanto lontani e
    tutto quello che sai dirmi sono i pensieri che vengono a chi prende il fresco la sera se-
    duto sulla soglia di casa. A che ti serve, allora, tanto viaggiare?" (p. 33).

2   Arthur Evans, in his essay on E.R. Curtius, attributes this quotation to Aby Warburg.
    See *On Four Modern Humanists* (Princeton, 1970), 139.

3   See E.R. Curtius, *Europäische Literatur und lateinisches Mittelalter* (Bern, 1948), 138-
    41. See, with a wider frame of reference, Hans Blumenberg, *Schiffbruch mit Zuschauer.
    Paradigma einer Daseinsmetapher* (Frankfurt, 1979), who places his study under this
    motto from Pascal: "Vous êtes embarqué."

4   Homer, *The Odyssey*, trans. Robert Fitzgerald (New York, 1961), 13.295-6.

5   Ulysses wants to follow the sun – " di retro al sol" (XXVI.117) – , an image which is
    partly derived from the Icarus myth, recurs in Marlowe's *Doctor Faustus*, in Goethe's
    Faust (1074-75) – " O daß kein Flügel mich vom Boden hebt, / Ihr nach und immer
    nach zu streben!" – and in Grabbe's *Don Juan und Faust*.

6   *The Odyssey*, 11.356,486.

7   Goethe, *Tagebücher* (Zürich, 1964), 81; 14. Juli 1779. Otherwise, Goethe is quoted
    from the *Hamburger Ausgabe* (Hamburg, 1949ff.), abbreviated *HA*.

8   *Wilhelm Meisters Wanderjahre*, *HA* 8:283; see also the advice of the *Landgeistlicher* in
    Lehrjahre, *HA* 7:346ff., in connection with Goethe's general concept of *Tätigkeit*.

9   Italo Calvino concludes with such a general notion in his essay "The Odysseys Within
    the *Odyssey*," in *The Uses of Literature* (New York, 1986).

10 Antti Aarne and Stith Thompson, *The Types of the Folktale* (Helsinki, 1961). It is motif
    J2063 in Stith Thompson, *Motif Index of Folk-Literature* (Bloomington, Indiana, 1951).
    The motif is found in India, in Jewish lore, as well as in Jamaica, and the versions
    listed by Bolte/Polivka in their annotation to Grimm range from Finnish to Ukrainian
    and Bulgarian. We use versions from the following editions: Brüder Grimm, *Kinder-
    und Hausmärchen* (Darmstadt, 1971); *Fiabe italiane*, ed. Italo Calvino (Torino, 1956);
    Patrick Kennedy, *The Fireside Stories of Ireland* (1870; reprint, Norwood Editions,
    1975).

11 Sophocles, *Antigone*, trans. Elizabeth Wyckoff (Chicago, 1954), lines 878-79. Further
    line references are given in the text.

12 Gaston Bachelard, *The Poetics of Space* (Boston, 1969), 18.

13 Marianne Rumpf, "Spinnerinnen und Spinnen. Märchendeutungen aus kulturhistori-
    scher Sicht," *Die Frau im Märchen*, ed. Sigrid Früh and Rainer Wehse (Kassel, 1985),
    59-72. See also Maria Tatar, *The Hard Facts of the Grimms' Fairy Tales* (Princeton,

1987), chap. 5: "Spinning Tales: The Distaff Side," 106-33.

14 See "Zwirn" in Lutz Röhrich, *Lexikon der sprichwörtlichen Redensarten* (Freiburg, 1973).

15 *Kinder- und Hausmärchen gesammelt durch die Brüder Grimm*, ed. Heinz Rölleke (Frankfurt/Main, 1985), 1212.

16 The search for or the loss of one's identity is another widespread motif in folktales. The latter seems to be always the result of laziness. Following Rölleke's tempting example one might draw far-fetched connections either to stories about the Romantic artist, and read the tale as a warning against the excesses of an idle imagination that has lost touch with immediate reality, or as a comment on the Romantic philosophy of the *Ich*.

17 A remarkable equality between the sexes in fairy tales is noted by Verena Kast, *Mann und Frau im Märchen* (Olten, 1983). A different reading of the Grimm collection is provided by Ruth B. Bottigheimer, *Grimms' Bad Girls and Bold Boys. The Moral and Social Vision of the 'Tales'* (New Haven, 1987), esp. chap. 8.

18 In his note to the story Patrick Kennedy lists some of those tales but he deflects from the implication by inflating the application of the story: "The original compiler of this tale probably intended to question the wisdom of folks who delight in working out simple ends by complicated and difficult processes, such as that of promoting the happiness of a country by getting five-eighths of its able-bodied men killed in battle, or by the ordinary hardships of warfare" (163). It is correct that there is also one remarkably dense-headed male accomplice in the story, but the spotlight is on women.

19 See the variant to the concluding sentiment in Calvino's *Se una notte d'inverno un viaggiatore* (Torino, 1979), 4: "Tu sai che il meglio che ci si può aspettare è di evitare il peggio."

20 The inappropriateness of any anticipation of the future is most clearly emphasized in the version of type 1450, "Die Belehrung," recorded in *Der Born Judas*, coll. M.J. bin Gorion, vol. 4, 2. rev. ed. (Leipzig: n.d.), 55-58. Two German proverbs come to mind in this context: "Vorfreude ist die beste Freude," which implies a warning against such anticipation, and "Müßiggang ist aller Laster Anfang," "Laster" here being the dream of a future perhaps never to be.

21 See, for example: "in der Gewohnheit ruht das einzige Behagen des Menschen; selbst das Unangenehme, woran wir uns gewöhnten, vermissen wir ungern" (HA 8:38-39). See also Goethe's comments on Werther in *Dichtung und Wahrheit*. For Goethe's concept and experience of the "Augenblick," interesting also within a history of reverie, see Gerhard Neumann, "Wissen und Liebe. Der auratische Augenblick im Werk Goethes," *Augenblick und Zeitpunkt*, ed. Christian W. Thomsen and Hans Holländer (Darmstadt, 1984).

22 See Goethe's poem and famous formula "Dauer im Wechsel." For his views in the historical realm, see his remarks as recorded by Eckermann for January 4, 1824.

23 These are the phrases with which Calvino (p. xvii) describes the beginning of his venture to collect and edit Italian folktales. The English translation turns it into a "leap into the dark, a plunge into an unknown sea." Dante Della Terza, in Sara Maria Adler, *Calvino: The Writer as Fablemaker* (Madrid, 1979), i, xvi, calls Calvino a "literary adventurer" whose "hazardous and perilous journey was one and the same thing with his character's perilous adventure toward the unknown."

279

VI. THROUGH *the* MAGIC MIRROR

Collage
by Mollie Michala

Fig. 1

HIERONYMUS BOSCH
*The Temptation
of Saint Anthony*
(detail of the central
panel including the
"mouserider").
Lisbon, Museu Nacional
de Arte Antigua.

BOSCH'S MOUSERIDER in
THE TEMPTATION of ST. ANTHONY

BY DOROTHY JOINER, WEST GEORGIA COLLEGE

F aced with a poem or a painting that resistantly withholds its
meaning, the commentator must with caution modify his critical
approach. Literary interpreters in the twenties, for example,
established "New Criticism" largely to explicate nineteenth-century
Symbolist poetry, which, until then, had been inadequately understood. So, too, must new techniques – or rather altered versions of
older ones – be devised to explain Hieronymus Bosch.

285

Bosch demands such a reformulation because traditional
procedures have so far only partially elucidated his bizarre imagery.
With considerable understatement, James Snyder terms Bosch scholarship "vast" and "very controversial."[1] More graphically, Gregory
Martin calls Bosch criticism "a nightmare of confusing interpretations
of abstruse significance."[2] And, of course, even Erwin Panofsky[3]
demurred at interpreting the Netherlandisher.

Bosch is so little understood because his works are generally
enigmatic and dreamlike. Let us look at *The Temptation of St. Anthony*
(Lisbon, Museu Nacional de Arte Antigua). Space prevents my describing the work in detail, but even the most cursory glance confirms how
bizarre is its imagery. Let me focus on one of Bosch's strange figures,
the woman riding a mouse on the central panel [fig. 1].

This blue-faced figure is encased in wood, clutches her
swaddled child in twig-like hands, and sits in an elaborate, pearl-lined
side saddle. Her mermaid tail, disjointed from her body and tinged
with the same blue as her face, sweeps downward, its tip trailing in
the water. A luxurious red cloth drapes over the mouse-mount's rump.
Nearby, a second child with no arms balances a bowl and spoon on
his head.

Commentary on this figure represents a microcosm of Bosch
scholarship. Clement Wertheim sees the woman and infant as "the
rigidified virgin of the stars and her wasted child, materialism."[4]
Wilhelm Fraenger, who customarily offers in-depth interpretations,
settles in this case for a denigrating description: "She clutches…[the
infant] to her bark-covered bosom with withered twig fingers, though
she at least refrains from pressing it to her gray, wasted, melancholy
face and tight-lipped mouth."[5] For Dirk Bax, the woman is a mendi-

Fig. 2

MELCHIOR BROEDERLAM
The Flight into Egypt,
1394-1399.
Musée des Beaux-Arts, Dijon.

cant, the prime evidence of her poverty being her beggar child (the one standing in the water), who has "spent his begged penny on eats."[6] It is difficult, however, to accept the woman's state as penurious when pearls line her saddle and a rich cloth drapes over her mount. Bax's final comment, on the other hand, is apposite. He perceives "the correspondence between this group and depictions of Mary and the Infant Jesus together with Joseph on the flight to Egypt,"[7] and compares Bosch's image to Melchior Broederlam's version of this conventional theme [fig. 2]. I will return to Bax's idea shortly.

Yet, since none of these readings plumbs the richness of Bosch's image, I propose a modest alteration of art-historical technique in order to understand the image more fully. For this alteration, I will borrow from Panofsky's methodology and from Freud's commentary on dream interpretation.

Let us first look briefly at classic art-historical procedure as Panofsky outlines it. In "Iconography and Iconology: An Introduction to the Study of Renaissance Art," Panofsky distinguishes three "strata" of meaning in a work of art. The first is "primary subject matter" or "pure forms," which bear, he says, "natural meanings." To clarify these "artistic motifs," Panofsky prescribes a "pre-iconographical description of the work of art." The second stratum, that of "conventional subject matter," is specifically the domain of iconography. Interpretation at this level requires a knowledge of the cultural tradition and relies heavily on information gleaned from literary sources. Recognizing, for example, that a certain configuration is a man belongs to the first level of interpretation whereas identifying that same man as St. Bartholomew because he bears a knife, belongs to the second. Commentary on the third stratum of meaning, Panofsky continues, is the province of iconology. Here the art historian must delineate "underlying principles which reveal the basic attitude of a nation, a period, a class, a religious or philosophical persuasion – qualified by one personality and condensed in one work." For instance, interpreting the artist's personality or some aspect of High Renaissance culture from Leonardo's *Last Supper* is an iconological pursuit. The "symbolical" values present in this third stratum of meaning – here Panofsky borrows Ernst Cassirer's term – are frequently unperceived by the artist himself and may even diverge from his conscious aims.[8]

A superb vehicle in numberless instances, Panofsky's method, as the master himself recognized, is inadequate to unfold the complexities of many Boschian images such as the mouserider. Though one can without difficulty identify elements of the figure in a "pre-iconographical description" – the wooden body suit, the squamous tail, the pearl-encrusted side saddle, the swaddled child she holds – one is thwarted at the second level of interpretation, that of iconography. No model in literature or in art fully explains the genesis of this strange creature. And, except for Bax's recognition of an inverted *Flight into Egypt*, commentary on the figure is arbitrary and unconvincing.

I propose that Bosch's wooden lady, like most of the strange imagery of the *Lisbon Triptych*, is a dreamlike configuration and can be fully understood only as one understands a dream. As an interpretive tool, therefore, I add to Panofsky's approach certain techniques from Freud's analysis of dream structure.

Freud's description of what he terms the "dream-work" derives from his theories concerning the fundamental antagonism within the human mind. The unconscious, regulated by the "pleasure principle," Freud believes, is essentially at odds with the conscious mind, governed as it is by the "reality principle." The latter, often called by Freud the "censor," represents, in other words, the forces of repression. A dream, he says, is a means of satisfying unconscious desires and at the same time slipping past the "censor." The "latent content" of dreams, also known as the "dream-thoughts," is that nexus of unconscious wishes repressed by consciousness. The "manifest content" is the specific symbolic structure created by the unconscious for approval of the "censor." The dream, then, is a symbolic manipulation of the "latent content," rendered almost unrecognizable by "condensation," "displacement," and the representation of a thing by its opposite. By "condensation," the "dream-thoughts" are compressed into brief, meager, and laconic images, and some are omitted altogether. By "displacement," the unconscious transfers "psychical intensities" from some images to others: "…the fragments [of the dream-thoughts]," Freud says, "are turned about, broken up and compacted, somewhat like drifting ice." It is as though the two contents, latent and manifest, speak two distinct languages. For understanding, therefore, the dream symbols must be "translated" into a discursive expression comprehensible to the rational mind. It is the burden of interpretation, according to Freud, "to restore the coherence which the dream-work has destroyed."[9]

Bosch's wooden lady, an image oneiric in its strangeness and complexity, illustrates superbly this deliberate, dreamlike scrambling of elements which are seemingly disparate but actually akin. Almost all aspects of the woman – her dress, her mermaid tail, the color of her face, her half-closed eyes, the pearls lining her saddle – can be traced to the wisdom figure in Kabbalah and in Gnosticism, the two major occult mystical traditions, or to one of the multitudinous versions of the fairy-tale character, Cinderella, who is a popularization of the occult *Sophia*.

The most notable evidence of Bosch's borrowing from the Cinderella legacy is the figure's wooden body suit; this garment recalls the legendary Maria Wood, whose aliases include Maria Wainscot and Princess Woodencloak. All of these variants of Cinderella wear wooden clothes, either a wooden sheath or a petticoat made from a hollow log.[10] In almost all forms of the tale, Cinderella's wardrobe is focal. Sometimes she wears her garments one over the other in envelope fashion, a nondescript outer garment, such as the wood, hiding her shining heavenly garb within. After she has been restored to her royal status, Cinderella reveals her miraculous inner clothes, bedazzling those who had previously scorned her. As a princess she wears robes "woven from the stars of heaven," or from "moonbeams," from "sunbeams," or from pearls "without slit or seam." In other accounts, she has "a diamond robe"; sometimes hers is a wonderful scintillating dress "of splendour passing description." One story compares Cinderella's robe to "the curling of a stream in the sun."[11] Cinderella's putting on humble garments that signify her exile parallels the same basic paradigm in esoteric lore. In Kabbalah, the Jewish mystical system, the female element in God, named the *Shekhinah*, or wisdom, is exiled from her masculine counterpart; evil *kelippoth* (translated "bark" or "shells") hold her captive in the material world, hiding her divine splendor. The exiled *Shekhinah* is sometimes termed the "tree of death," overcome as she is by the demonic *kelippoth*.[12]

The kelippoth must be understood in the light of Kabbalah's emanationist concept of creation, usually illustrated in two analogous pictographs: the nut image and the Tree of Life. Both of these representations involve ten *sephiroth* (singular, *sephirah*), or spheres, each symbolizing a step in the emanation of the world from "En-Soph," the unknowable God. The nut pictograph arranges the *sephiroth* in concentric circles, expressing the idea that the universe is composed of interlocking orders of reality, analogous to a series of shells and kernels. The Tree of Life groups the *sephiroth* in inverted arboreal form, with the roots in the Godhead and the tip in matter. Kabbalists superimpose three columns on the tree, representing the forces flowing out of God: masculine on the right, feminine on the left, and the central column balancing these polarities. The Satanic *kelippoth*, "bark" of the Tree

289

of Life or "shell" of the nut, are frequently spoken of as a kind of waste product of cosmic processes.[13] (One must remember that Kabbalah is a mythic-mystical system, not a philosophical one. Its symbolic "explanation" of reality baffles the logical mind at the same time that it compels the intuitive faculties.) Since in Kabbalah, as in many mystical systems, man is a microcosm, manifesting universal principles, he too is formed according to the "shell" principle. His lower faculties encase his higher faculties. In this conception, man's vegetable soul is the "shell" of his animal soul, which is the "shell" of his rational soul, which is the "shell" of his intellectual soul.[14]

The *Shekhinah's* counterpart in the Gnostic tradition is *Sophia*, or Wisdom, a name which Hans Jonas terms "paradoxical… in view of the history of folly of which she is made the protagonist." *Sophia*, sometimes called the "fallible aspect of God," was actually co-agent of the Divine in the world's creation. Though co-creative and co-existent with God, Wisdom came to earth and was there enmeshed in matter, exiled, like the *Shekhinah*, from her true home. *Sophia's* guilt caused her great suffering: "She repented and wept violently and, moving to and fro in the darkness of ignorance, she was ashamed of herself and dared not return."[15] As the *kelippoth* bind *Shekhinah*, the "chains," "rings," or "shells" of the universe imprison *Sophia*. These images of evil derive from the Gnostic idea that the universe is a prison, with the earth its innermost "dungeon," encircled by "concentric enclosing shells." These demonic "shell" forces serve to bind the *Sophia* in the material realm and to distance her from God.[16]

As in Kabbalah, "shells" are basic not only to cosmic structure, but also to man's make-up. During its "falling" into matter, the soul acquires integument-like, negative appendages from each planet ("the torpor of Saturn," "the wrathfulness of Mars," etc.). Thought of as coverings for the "acosmic principle" in man, that transcendent element of his being, these planetary accretions are called variously "corruptions," "garments," or "envelopes" of the soul.[17]

Returning to Bosch's wooden lady, we can now appreciate her multiple associations with both the popular and the esoteric strains of the wisdom tradition: the woman recalls Maria Wood and her several aliases, as well as the Kabbalistic *Shekhinah* and the Gnostic *Sophia*. Her wooden garment suggests at once Maria Wood's dress, the evil "bark" from Kabbalah, and the Gnostic material "garment" of the body.[18] Structurally, Bosch's image is comparable to Freud's dream symbol; it is "laconic" in that it condenses into a single image multiple meanings from both popular and occult sources.

Images related to the wooden body-suit are the metal rings: one is affixed to the saddle; and a second, part of a chain, is strung over the shoulder on the man behind the mouserider. Both images reflect literal Gnostic imagery, which likens the imprisoning integuments of the material world to "rings" and "chains."[19] Bosch has again made concrete a metaphorical concept from hermeticism.

The mermaid tail, awkwardly disjoined from her torso, is another component of the configuration which allies Bosch's lady with the Cinderella-*Sophia* tradition. Often Cinderella's mother is a mermaid who dwells in a pearl in a coral grotto; the daughter, moreover, is almost always said to be identical to her beautiful mother.[20] As before, this aspect of the legend can be related to esoteric sources: water, a mermaid's customary habitat, is an important Gnostic symbol for the material world "into which the divine has sunk."[21] Using a technique comparable to the "displacement" of dreams, Bosch, as it were, "dislocates" the mermaid tail from its usual role in the tradition.

The blue of the wooden lady's face is also significant. It is a color often associated in a positive manner with Cinderella. Her dress is sometimes "blue like the sky," "the colors of the noonday sky," or is "dark blue covered with golden embroidery." Elsewhere, her garment is "like the waves of the sea" or "like the sea with fishes swimming in it."[22] But to understand the valuation which Bosch places on the color in his figure, we must examine how he uses it in other images. The pig-headed cleric standing in the water at the central platform's edge, for example, wears a blue garment ripped open to uncover his inner corruption. Also blue is the cloak of the witch-like hag near Anthony's temptress. Similarly, in other works, Bosch uses the color for negative figures. One of the most notable examples is the blue-bodied, devouring demon on the hell panel of *The Garden of Earthly Delights* (Madrid, Prado). But in *The Haywain* (Madrid, Prado), the evidence is ambivalent; atop the central mound of hay, both the monster and the angel are blue. These latter images suggest that Bosch associates blue with the immaterial, both positive and negative. I propose that the wooden lady's blue face implies her status as a spiritual entity.

A further reflection of the complex Cinderella-*Sophia* tradition can be found in the wooden lady's apparent dimsightedness. Cinderella, saddened by her miserable state, wept by the fire. The Gnostic *Sophia*, too, was grief-stricken according to the Naassene "Psalm of the Soul": "She now…is plunged into misery and weeps." And in the twelfth-century Kabbalistic treatise, the *Zohar*, the *Shekhinah* is said to weep for her children. Misunderstanding the *Zohar*, subsequent Kabbalists called her "the beauty who no longer has eyes," so blinded is she by her lamentations.[23] The slit-like eyes of Bosch's figure may be swollen from weeping. But she bends close over her child in a posture suggestive of one who cannot see, in which case Bosch has followed the mistaken reading from Kabbalah.

The pearls lining the lady's sidesaddle further link her to the popular and esoteric branches of the wisdom tradition. Cinderella's garment, as I have mentioned, is sometimes woven from pearls. In Gnosticism, the pearl represents a fragment of the divinity dispersed in matter. In the Gnostic "Hymn of the Pearl," a prince is sent by his parents to retrieve the lost treasure, a pearl, located in the sea and protected by a dragon. Although he almost fails in his mission because he succumbs to the soporific influences of the material world, the prince is finally awakened by a letter from his parents. Jonas interprets this tale as a parable of the ambiguous Gnostic savior, who himself becomes one in need of salvation.[24] Thus, the pearls on Bosch's image suggest esoteric sources, especially when associated with the Gnostic savior, the child standing in the water nearby. (Space, however, prevents my exploring this last identification.) As with the mermaid tail, Bosch has "displaced" the pearl from its normal role in the tradition, in a manner analogous to the "displacement" of dreams.

In the mouse-mount, we can find a further correspondence between Bosch's lady and the Cinderella tales, though not, as far as I can determine, with the esoteric tradition. It is well known that Cinderella's horses turn into mice at midnight, the hour of her humiliation. And, less frequently, she hides her sunbeam raiment under a lowly mouse- or ass-skin mantle because of humility.[25] Harold Bayley maintains that in antiquity, the mouse was an emblem of humility. Apollo's epithet in the *Iliad*, Smintheus, the "mouse god," derives, according to Bayley, from the humble position Apollo assumed when guarding the flocks of Admetus and when serving as hireling for Laomedon. As symbols of humility, in memory of the god's virtue, mice were sometimes kept in temples dedicated to Apollo.[26]

The virtue of humility associated with the mouse becomes important as I return now to Bax's recognition that the wooden lady, together with the swaddled child and the man behind her, represents an inverted *Flight into Egypt*. In the light of the wisdom tradition, we can understand Bosch's inversion more fully. Not a mere "beggar-woman" as Bax maintains, the wooden lady has rather a "royal" ancestry. As an amalgam of the *Shekhinah-Sophia* figure and the Cinderella character, she becomes a quasi-divine female element stranded in the material world, grieving over her tragic exile. In the context of Bax's inversion, I refer again to the artist's dreamlike technique. A conventional *Flight into Egypt* pictures Mary seated on a female ass. Bosch's substitution of a mouse (indicative of humility in antiquity) for the customary ass (also linked with humility in the Christian tradition) illustrates particularly well how his technique is analogous to that which the unconscious employs when forming a dream. A dream, Freud says, frequently substitutes one thing for another when the two have a common quality.[27] Has not Bosch done much the same thing? The common quality sparking his transfer is humility. In other ways, too, Bosch's method resembles that of a dream. Most obviously, his inversion of a conventional theme parallels the practice in dreams whereby a thing is often represented by its opposite.

293

Consequently, when we add Freud's technique to Panofsky's strategies, we are able to derive further meaning from Bosch's strange imagery. In constructing his wooden mouserider, Bosch has drawn from Kabbalah, from Gnosticism, as well as from popularizations of these mystical traditions. But he has, in a sense, disguised his borrowed elements by an associative technique much like that of a dream. With a kind of Freudian "condensation," Bosch fuses symbols from Kabbalah and from Gnosticism with Cinderella's wooden clothes to form his lady's bark-like garment. Moreover, in what Freud would call a "displacement," the artist dislocates the mermaid tail and the pearls from their usual roles in the tradition. And on the basis of their common association with humility, he has substituted a mouse for the ass of a conventional *Flight into Egypt*. And, finally, this inversion of a well-known theme is akin to the reversals of dreams.

I have not here gone beyond Panofsky's second stratum of interpretation, that of iconography; nor have I established the "logical ties" – to borrow Freud's term – between the mouserider and other images in the work. Such is the burden of further commentary.

1 James Snyder (ed.), Preface to *Bosch in Perspective* (Englewood Cliffs: Prentice Hall, 1973), p. ix.

2 Gregory Martin, Introduction to *The Complete Paintings of Bosch*, Notes and Catalogue by Mia Cinotti (New York: Harry N. Abrams, 1966), p. 5.

3 Panofsky terms Bosch "an island in the stream of...his tradition" and borrows doggerel – now a cliché among those who know Bosch studies – from a frustrated sixteenth-century translator of Marsilio Ficino: "This too high for my wit, / I prefer to omit." Erwin Panofsky, *Early Netherlandish Painting*, vol. 1 (Cambridge, Mass.: Harvard Univ. Press, 1966), pp. 357-58.

4 Clement A. Wertheim-Aymes, *The Pictorial Language of Hieronymus Bosch* (Horsham, Sussex: New Knowledge Books, 1975), p. 73.

5 Wilhelm Fraenger, *Hieronymus Bosch* (New York: G.P. Putnam's Sons, 1983), p. 391.

6 Dirk Bax, *Hieronymus Bosch, His Picture-Writing Deciphered* (Rotterdam: A.A. Balkems, 1979), p. 110.

7 Bax, p. 113.

8 Erwin Panofsky, "Iconography and Iconology: An Introduction to the Study of Renaissance Art," in *Meaning in the Visual Arts* (Garden City, N.Y.: Doubleday Anchor Books, 1955), pp. 26-32.

9 Sigmund Freud, *The Interpretation of Dreams* (New York: Macmillan, 1913), pp. 289-309.

10 Harold Bayley, *The Lost Language of Symbolism* (New York: Barnes and Noble, 1952), vol. 1, p. 229.

11 Bayley, pp. 222-23.

12 Gershom Scholem, *On the Kabbalah and Its Symbolism* (New York: Schocken, 1965), pp. 114-16; Isaac Myers, *Qabbalah* (New York: Samuel Weiser, Inc., 1972), p. 126.

13 Gershom Scholem, *Major Trends in Jewish Mysticism* (New York: Schocken, 1941), p. 238.

14 Alexander Altmann, "The Motif of the 'Shells' (Qelipoth) in Azril of Gerona," in *Journal of Jewish Studies*, 9 (1958), p. 78.

15 Hans Jonas, *The Gnostic Religion* (Boston: Beacon Press, 1970), pp. 109, 176-77, 202.

16 Jonas, pp. 43, 156.

17 Jonas, p. 158.

18 Since wood is one of Gnosticism's many symbols for the world, the suit on Bosch's lady bears even further esoteric meaning. In *The Great Mother* (Princeton: Princeton Univ. Press, 1955), pp. 49-50, Erich Neumann says that "in all gnosticizing religions from Christianity to Islam the symbol *hylé*, wood, becomes inert, negatively demonized 'matter,' as opposed to the divine-spirit aspect of the male *nous*."

19 The Gnostic universe imprisons man both spatially and temporally. Jonas says (p. 43) that, according to the Gnostics "the universe, the domain of the archons, is like a vast prison whose innermost dungeon is the earth, the scene of man's life. Around and above it the cosmic spheres are ranged like concentric enclosing shells." Sometimes these spheres are said to form "rings." Time also incarcerates man. "No less demonized," according to Jonas (p. 53), "is the time dimension of life's cosmic existence, which also is represented as an order of quasi-personal powers, e.g., the 'Aeons....' Thus the way of salvation leads through the temporal order of the 'generations':

294

through chains of un-numbered generations...." The term "chain of emanations" is frequent in Gnostic terminology (p. 181).

20 Bayley, p. 197.
21 Jonas, p. 117: "*Sea* or *Waters* is a standing Gnostic symbol for the world of matter or of darkness into which the divine has sunk. Thus, the Naassenes interpreted Ps. 29.3 and 10, about God's inhabiting the abyss and His voice ringing out over the waters, as follows: The many waters is the multifarious world of moral degeneration into which the God Man has sunk and out of whose depth he cries up to the supreme God, the Primal Man, his unfallen original (Hippol. v. 8.15)."
22 Bayley, p. 212.
23 Jonas, p.67 (Hippol. v. 10.2); Scholem, *Major Trends,* p. 230. Scholem does not specify exactly when what he terms this "magnificent misinterpretation" of the *Zohar* takes place.
24 Jonas, pp. 119-20.
25 In vol. 1, p. 48, Bayley writes: "The symbol of humility and patient endurance was the ass...." On p. 225 of the same volume, he states: "Not only does Cinderella cloak herself under a mantle of mouseskin, but among her disguises is the hide of an ass. The ass on which Christ rode into Jerusalem is proverbially the emblem of humility; and the ass-skin mantle may be identified as the cloak of humility."
26 Bayley, vol. 1, pp. 224-55; vol. 2, p. 46.
27 Freud, pp. 310-11.

295

PICASSO and TELEMACHUS

BY CARLOS ROJAS, EMORY UNIVERSITY

P ablo Picasso painted *Science and Charity* between 1896 and 1897, when he was fifteen years old. His father, don José Ruiz Blasco, not only conceived the general composition but also posed for the figure of the doctor, who takes the dying woman's pulse and eyes his watch in the presence of death. Salvador Dalí would say many years later that from that moment Picasso's art was, consciously or unconsciously, a desperate race with death.

The canvas made the adolescent Picasso very proud because it was awarded an honorary mention at the National Exhibit of Fine Arts in Madrid and, the following year, a gold medal at Málaga's Provincial Fair of Art. Nevertheless, more than ninety years later the painter Carlos Planell still clings to the unshakable conviction that *Science and Charity* was the work of don José Ruiz Blasco, and that the son – no matter how precocious – had little or nothing to do with the work.

BORN IN 1839, don José Ruiz Blasco was nearly sixty when Picasso painted *Science and Charity*, under his father's obvious guidance. A photograph of don José in his youth shows us a dapper dandy perhaps too self-conscious of his natural elegance in the very last days of Romanticism. Born in Málaga, from a family of remote Castilian ancestry – "with all members exempted from taxation because of their chivalry" – in later years don José would be described by his famous son as "English-looking" because he was very tall, blue-eyed, and fair.

In Málaga it is said that as a very young man, almost an adolescent, don José Ruiz Blasco underwent a drastic and dramatic change with the death of his sweetheart with whom he was very much in love. In any case, many years later, in the fall of 1878, don José was about to be married to María Picasso López. She was the only child of a certain Francisco Picasso Guardeño, a very prosperous gentleman who sailed to Cuba on a business voyage and probably forgot his family, because he disappeared forever, without a trace. Another sudden death, that of Canon Pablo Ruiz Blasco who was supposed to bless the wedding of his brother José and María Picasso, made don José postpone the marriage no less than two full years. We may also add that the same year in which don José was to marry María (fourteen years younger than he), the phylloxera ruined her vineyards. It would be obvious to conclude that don José had intended to marry María without much or any love and possibly only for her lands. With the vineyards gone, two years later he did finally make her his bride, perhaps out of sheer fatigue and boredom.

When the phylloxera ruined María's vineyards, don José was unemployed and had no known source of income. He seemed determined to live on his wife's fortune. When it vanished, don José started working as a teacher of drawing and painting at the Municipal School of Fine Arts. As soon as the children started coming – Pablo in 1881, Lola in 1884, and Conchita in 1889 – don José even moonlighted as assistant director of Málaga's museum. In fact, until his marriage, don José was a bohemian painter of little prestige but with such a passionate obsession for painting doves that he received the nickname El Palomero.

In December 1890 the city government did away with don José's position at the museum in a budget readjustment after a bad year. Now the father of three children, aged nine, six, and three, don José desperately hunted for another job, and three months later found a position as drawing instructor with the School of Da Guarda in Corunna. He signed his contract on April 4, 1891. In the fall of the same year and after a long, stormy voyage that did not inspire much hope for the future, the Ruiz Picasso family landed in Corunna and don José began his teaching duties.

From that day until his death in Barcelona in 1913, Picasso's father was a finished man. Afflicted with bouts of melancholy and interminable depressions, far away from the sunshine of Málaga, the friendly gatherings at the Café de las Chinitas and the bullfights, he spent entire Sundays watching the rain – the eternal rain of Corunna – from his bedroom window. To make life more unbearable and to bury don José deeper in sadness, Conchita, the youngest child and the only one who resembled don José's "British" countenance, died from whooping cough in January 1895. In the fall of that year don José got a better job with a higher salary at the School of Fine Arts in Barcelona. Some time by the end of September the whole family arrived in Barcelona, a city which from then on Picasso would regard as his home.

Pablo and Lola, the surviving children, shared with their mother her short, strong, and somehow plebeian figure. By capricious irony of the genes they also inherited the large, black eyes of all of the Ruiz family – except don José, that is, who had tiny, narrow, clear, and very blue eyes. In July, 1896, when his family was vacationing in Málaga, Picasso painted the portrait of his aunt Pepa, his father's older sister, who posed for him all covered with furs and jewels on the sweltering beach of Málaga. In the portrait, the old woman's black, shiny eyes are identical to those of her nephew. It is as though Picasso portrayed his own eyes when painting hers, as if this almost insane woman and this fourteen-year-old boy were to meet at a crossroads of art and blood, very far from the serene sadness of don José. Many years later Eduardo Cirlot would state that Picasso's portrait of his aunt Pepa is one of the greatest portraits in the history of Spanish painting. Patrick O'Brian believes that Cirlot's statement is not as grotesque as it sounds, considering that here a child invents expressionism for his own use twenty years before the official birth of expressionism, only to abandon it a few months later when he painted *Science and Charity* in a far more conservative style and under the instructions of his father.

298

A year before, and soon after the Ruiz Picassos landed in Barcelona, a classmate of Picasso at the School of Fine Arts – Ramón Riu Doria – had taken a photograph of his friend Pablo. It was autumn and Picasso's hair was beginning to grow back after his head had been shaved for the summer, as was customary in Spain in those days. Ironically, a few weeks later, Picasso painted a self portrait (unfinished, like so many of his other later works, both major and minor) in which he stares at us, as if trying to see himself in our eyes as in a mirror. His expression is solemn. His lips are thick and sensual. An air of strength and determination seems to mark his features. If we compare this self-portrait to the picture taken by Riu Doria, we immediately realize the change which has taken place in this adolescent. In other words, in Barcelona and at the age of fourteen, Picasso has become a man. Even though the fact may be of little importance here, let us remember that many years later, and when asked at what age he had started visiting the brothels of Barcelona, Picasso would smile and reply that he was still very, very young when introduced to those dubious pleasures. In fact Picasso's change here concerns the appearance more than the content, for if the genius is he who retains part of his childhood in the expression of his talent – as some Freudians would put it – all the marks of Picasso's artistic singularity are already present in this childhood which abruptly ends here and in Barcelona. Perhaps the nostalgia for this childhood – that lost Arcadia with more vivid memories for the genius than for anyone else – made Picasso say that his paintings and drawings from the period of Corunna were better than those he did in

Barcelona. "When I was a child I could draw like Michelangelo," he said, "later on, I had to learn to draw like a child."

Also in Corunna, according to Picasso himself, his father made him the most remarkable gift, don José's own brushes and palette, saying: "Son, there is nothing I can teach you any more. From now on, I renounce painting." Don José's unexpected abandonment of his art has been compared to Verrocchio's giving up painting when confronted with the mastery of his young student, Leonardo. *Mutatis mutandis*, the comparison is apt if we consider the affection and respect Picasso always showed to his father's memory, even though he refused to attend his funeral for some very dark and complex reasons of his own. Finally, I may also add that, on the evidence of several drawings whose subject is don José at his easel or getting ready to paint, dated by Picasso at Corunna, I am inclined to believe that Picasso's father gave up his art works after moving to Barcelona.

On several occasions don José's renunciation – his *gran rifiuto*, as Dante would put it – has been compared to a symbolic act of self-castration. It goes without saying that the deliberate abandonment of painting by an artist is a clear metaphor for self-inflicted blindness. John Berger wonders whether, in circumstances when a father kills his vocation to make his son fulfill his own, the adolescent son will not tend to attribute his later success to magical powers. In fact, it may be said that, in a hidden sort of way, the son had wished for the father's abdication. Whatever the case, Picasso would always keep a dark, guilt-laden memory of don José's renunciation, not very different in fact from the absurd way in which he later would make himself responsible for the death of his little sister, Conchita, much to the amazement of his mistress, Françoise Gilot.

Even though don José freely abandoned painting, he did not renounce guiding the career of his son, who was still little more than a child, no matter how gifted. In Barcelona don José registered Picasso in an advanced course of Classical Art and Still-Life Painting, after talking his colleagues into exempting the child from two of three entrance exams and after making him challenge the human figure examination which was the hardest one to pass. Not yet fourteen, Picasso passed the exam with flying colors and became the pet student of all his teachers, although he would soon tire of their methods and would stay at the School of Fine Arts for only two years.

In fact, *Science and Charity* is little more than a trivial illustration, though don José probably regarded it as his son's test of artistic manhood. Perhaps more interesting than the painting itself is the subsequent fate of the canvas. Even nowadays, at the Picasso Museum in Barcelona, *Science and Charity* delights semi-illiterate medical doctors who honestly wonder how a child of fifteen could have painted that masterpiece and sadly regret that Picasso would eventually go badly astray and ruin his talent. Perhaps moved by such feelings one not very bright doctor, Picasso's uncle Salvador, originally admired *Science and Charity* and either bought the painting or gladly received it as a gift from his nephew. Uncle Salvador, don José's younger brother, was the family's Good Samaritan and the only well-to-do member of the Ruiz clan. He drew an excellent salary as head of the Health and Welfare Services at the Port of Málaga and was married to an extremely wealthy woman, the Countess of Casa Loring.

300

Many years later Picasso would tell Antonina Vallentin that he nearly died at birth in the early morning of October 25, 1881. Although the baby seemed well-formed and vigorous, the doctors had begun to despair when uncle Salvador, who was present at the delivery, rescued his nephew from the grip of death. "My uncle," he explained, "used to smoke those old, big cigars, which were favored by doctors in those days. He blew the smoke in my face and I started crying."

When giving *Science and Charity* to uncle Salvador, in a way Picasso also gave him back the life he had owed him since the moment of his birth. If the true life of a painter is his art, and if Picasso had proven his artistic coming of age in that canvas, as don José probably believed, the payment of one life as the price for the other becomes self-evident. At the same time *Science and Charity* became an inverted metaphor of the events of October 25, 1881. That morning uncle Salvador had rescued Picasso from the clutches of death. In the painting don José plays the part of another doctor, who happens to be helpless in the face of death. We will never know if don José's abdication as a painter took place in Corunna or in Barcelona, but we can be certain that he gave up his vocation before Picasso had painted *Science and Charity*. The dying woman, whose life literally slips away between don José's fingers, is nothing but the true image of that art he never completely mastered and which he eventually abandoned.

"Son, there is nothing I can teach you anymore. From now on, I renounce painting." There is no logical sequence between the two statements. Don José could have admitted his son's superior talent without giving up his own vocation as an artist. Also, the Oedipal interpretation that Ernst Gombrich attaches to the event seems to be rather

far-fetched, though traces of an Oedipal complex are evident throughout Picasso's life. We may also parenthetically add that Picasso is the
man who "destroyed" representative thematic painting, the only kind
of art with which don José identified himself before he ceased to be a
painter. Nevertheless, I believe we could define here a different kind
of human complex which, although the opposite of the Oedipal one,
would not necessarily deny it. I am thinking of an unconscious form of
conduct, constantly exposed by myth from Homer's *Odyssey* to Joyce's
Ulysses, and also expressed by religion when Christianity makes it its
cornerstone. I am referring to what I could call here the Telemachus
complex, because Odysseus' son illustrates it better than any other
hero. Picasso does not seem to recover from his trauma as a result of   301
don José's renunciation. At the very moment when don José abandons
art, he destroys Picasso's artistic identity. Up until then the child has
been the son of an "artist and painter," as the expression goes at the
turn of the century. Artistically speaking, now he is the son of No One,
in other words, he becomes the archetypal figure of the eternal bas-
tard without roots or family past. From that moment, and according
to his own phrase, Picasso turns that art that had been so dear to his
father into a "storehouse of destruction." Ironically, also from that
moment and until the end of his long life, Picasso would never stop
searching for his father's image throughout his painting.

On his long way back to his father, Picasso had to assume that
don José started dying at the moment he renounced both painting and
his artistic paternity. The son's answer to his father's symbolic suicide
was a life-long creative outpouring which could amply cover the work
of two painters: Picasso and don José. Through more than eighty years
of incredible, endless creation, Picasso kept on going back to don José's
specter to complete his identity and return to the sources of his existence.

In occupied Paris, in the winter of 1942, the French-Rumanian
photographer Brassaï asked Picasso why the slender figure of a middle-
aged, sad-looking gentleman with a long face and an even longer beard
appeared and reappeared so many times throughout his painting and
his graphic work. We may also add that in 1942 Picasso was going
through the most somber period of his existence. He was an outcast
because the Nazis had banned his work and had even prohibited the
press from writing about it. Depressed and defenseless, he dropped his
usual circumspection and candidly answered: "For a long time, I didn't
even know who that man was. Now I know that every time I sketched

him I was inadvertently thinking of my father. To me don José will always be the double archetype of the father and the man. He would display a long beard as long as I remember and I see his features in every bearded man I paint or draw."

Forty years before his confession to Brassaï, when just before Christmas 1902 Picasso and Max Jacob were nearly starving to death in Paris, the mistletoe vendors – the *porte-bonheurs* as they call them in France – attract Picasso's attention. He draws a bearded old man, slender and stylized like an El Greco, with a derby hat and a white scarf, holding a pole on his shoulder with mistletoe hanging from both ends. In the foreground and next to the man there is a child on whose back the mistletoe vendor places a long, guiding hand. A blue wash on paper renders the final version of that composition, with a few changes that seem to be of great consequence in retrospect. More El Greco-like than ever, the mistletoe vendor has aged considerably as the child has been transformed into a little boy. In other words, those who previously appeared as father and son now seem to be a grandfather and a grandchild. That is to say they are a man who is "twice" a father and a child who is "twice" a son. Consequently, the old man is much taller than he was in the original sketch and the child shrinks into a white, vulnerable, and delicate creature who barely comes up to the man's waist.

The blue wash is a magic metaphor of Picasso for his father. In fact, it is magic in two different senses. According to James Frazier's first law of the primitive magic mentality, the appearance tends to be transformed into the reality. Thus, the Parisian mistletoe vendor and his child become don José Ruiz Blasco and his son through the medium of painting. Also and according to another law of magical manifestations as stated by Frazier, those who were separated in time and in space – as Picasso and his father happened to be – are reunited here in the ambit of art.

In the wash the old man kindly leads the child with the palm of his hand. His grandson seems to walk in a daze, as though he trusted only the old vendor to help him find the light and the way out of his darkness. Many years later Picasso would tell Françoise Gilot that in his youth he had contracted a venereal disease in the brothels of Barcelona, but that he was cured by the time he married Olga Koklova in 1918. Remembering the many blind men who appear in Picasso's work, John Berger concludes that, during his blue period, Picasso was afraid of losing his eyesight because of a venereal illness. We may also add that by the time Picasso paints his wash, a year has passed almost to the day since he desperately cabled his father for money at Christmastide 1901. He cannot forget that don José sent him enough to pay for his trip back to Barcelona, but now, when his poverty is even more appalling, he refuses to ask for his father's help again.

Another blind man is *The Old Guitar Player*, now at the Art Institute in Chicago and one of the masterpieces of the blue period. Cirici Pellicer and Phoebe Pool think that the *Man of Sorrows* by Hans Holbein could be a possible precedent for *The Old Guitar Player*. In fact, Picasso's brand of mannerism comes from El Greco and the guitar player is a new transformation of José Ruiz Blasco in the style and the manner of an artist, El Greco, whom don José wholeheartedly detested. We may also remember in passing that there can be no more terminally castrating blindness than that of a painter incapable of understanding his son's art, after having abandoned his own painting to favor the child's.

Precisely because he had always heard his father cynically stating that truth is nothing but a glorified lie, Picasso kept on searching for truth in the labyrinth of blindness. Thus, he confessed to having painted *The Old Jew*, now at the Pushkin Museum in Moscow, in the winter of 1903 and at his father's house in Barcelona. In this sketch the old beggar and his grandson were a transformation of the mistletoe vendor and his grandchild, just as the latter had been a metamorphosis of don José Ruiz Blasco and his child Pablo. Also, as the "Old Guitar Player" had done, the "Blind Jew" begs with his back to a wall, whilst the big, black eyes of the child are obviously Picasso's.

Many years later, between March and May 1933, Picasso turned out a series of forty-six etchings and dry points of a strong-looking, bearded sculptor, who shares the studio with a naked model. The woman's features and build immediately evoke Marie-Thérèse Walter, the young mistress of Picasso at that time and the mother of his daughter María de la Concepción – in other words, Conchita – nicknamed Maïa since the moment she was born. We would tend to identify the sculptor with Zeus, the father of the gods, if Picasso had not said to Brassaï that consciously or unconsciously he had thought of his father every time he painted or designed a bearded man. Also the look in the sculptor's eyes – halfway between pensive sadness and deep introspection – is clearly don José's. This is the countenance and the mood he had shown in *Science and Charity* and in so many portraits of his father that Picasso made in Barcelona. Nevertheless, from the neck down, the sculptor's vigorous appearance is closer to Picasso's than

303

to don José's. Consequently, and according to this human symbiosis, Picasso shares his mistress and his success with his father. Finally, we have to point out that unlike don José – the man who freely abandoned painting – this sculptor looks at his work and seems to find it satisfactory.

The transformation of the bearded sculptor into the minotaur in another series of eleven etchings of May, 1933, seems almost inevitable in retrospect. Naked, the monster and the model are relaxing on large pillows in front of a window. The minotaur raises his glass of champagne as though he were celebrating the very existence of life. Curiously enough, the lovers do not look at each other, and Marie-Thérèse's glance seems lost in the void. The minotaur's eyes bear the same introverted expression we have already seen in the sculptor.

Four engravings entitled *The Blind Minotaur* are far more interesting than the two previous series, where I find the extreme correctness of the design terribly monotonous. The first three engravings of *The Blind Minotaur* date from September or October, 1934. The last one, undated in the original, seems to have been done around the beginning of 1935. In this plate a starry night is set above a calm ocean. A little girl holding a dove leads the blind minotaur. Two fishermen look at the monster without fear or amazement, as though they have known him from long ago. An adolescent boy thoughtfully observes the girl and the minotaur, as if he were silently debating with himself rather serious and complex matters.

"Blinded like Oedipus, the monster proclaims the crimes that are his fate," writes Roland Penrose about the minotaur. Perhaps this is true, but the demeanor of that boy, his apparent judge, doesn't seem to indicate that the full responsibility of those crimes lies exclusively with the minotaur. In fact, Penrose himself has identified the minotaur with the bearded sculptor of the previous series of etchings. Without the shadow of a doubt, the minotaur is nothing more than a new transformation of the sculptor. And here I quote Roland Penrose once again: "There is an innocent gentleness in [the minotaur's] eyes that is belied by the strength of his muscles and the horns that crown his head. The human beast or the horned god, in spite of his excesses, is accepted as one of the family. The patriarchal head of the artist becomes interchangeable with that of the demi-god, as if they both wore masks." If Picasso and his father had converged in the sculptor's physical appearance, don José Ruiz Blasco and his son will be reincarnated together in the minotaur. In his series *Sculptor and Model,* Picasso makes his father share his art and his sensual pleasures. In *The Blind Minotaur,* the identities of father and son blend together in the monster, but at the same time Picasso transforms himself into the pensive adolescent who is about to pass judgment on the minotaur at the threshold of heaven.

The reason for the minotaur's blindness becomes self-evident when we see in the monster the partial reincarnation of don José. The loss of eyesight is a symbol of castration and Picasso never forgave his father for having metaphorically destroyed his creative powers, when he abandoned art and therefore put out his painter's eyes. The deadliest sin of the minotaur – the sin which he is now confessing to the adolescent – is his refusal to believe in himself, thus denying his son an identity as an artist after having given him human life. Now the son is getting ready to judge his father, transformed into the demi-god. As a judge, the boy doesn't seem to be motivated by a desire for vengeance, but his thoughtful severity is also unquestionable.

Under the bright stars and above the calm ocean, the night in the engraving is somewhat unreal. It is not the dark night of the soul because it is death, pure and simple. Thus, the beach becomes a clear symbol of the Styx, which in a painting by Patinir, seen by the young Picasso at the Prado, is flat and still as though made of onyx. The fishermen remain in that small boat, which the monster and the little girl seem to have just left. The fishermen are a probable double avatar of Charon, the mythical demon who ferries the souls of the condemned across the Styx in Dante's *Inferno*. Still alive among the dead, and in a surprise descent into the kingdom of Hades, Picasso disguises himself as the adolescent he was when don José gave up painting, and prepares himself to judge his father, now monstrous and blind.

Telemachus enters the realm of death and there he finds Odysseus, disguised as the minotaur. Nevertheless, night will fall in Hades leaving their plight unresolved and Telemachus still undecided about pardoning his father for having forsaken him. Also, the monster exhibits a notable change in attitude between the first and last engravings of this series. At the beginning the minotaur gropes in the dark, as though desperately trying to reach the adolescent without the boy's making the slightest move to approach the minotaur. In the end, when Picasso's muscular body has been more closely blended with don José's slender figure, the minotaur does not beg for compassion but seems to make accusing statements holding his cane on the ground. The expression of his son and judge remains uncompromising and emotionless.

Not even in death has the time come for the final reconciliation between Telemachus and Odysseus. At the same time we cannot

305

thoroughly explain the plate without identifying the little girl who leads the minotaur. If here the ocean is the Styx and the time is eternal death, the child with the unkempt hair and delicate appearance guiding the minotaur would be Picasso's sister Conchita, the youngest daughter of don José, who had died in Corunna forty years before.

In fact, this new Antigone does not look any older than seven years, Conchita's age when she passed away. When we see the child holding a dove, the identification is even more obvious both in the light of the Oedipal myth and in don José's personal history. As we know, the dove was don José's favorite bird before he symbolically blinded himself by forsaking painting. As dead as don José himself, Conchita takes her father to Picasso in a vain attempt to resolve their differences and without realizing that the time of pardon cannot be anticipated. Besides, as we have already pointed out, María de la Concepción, that is to say Conchita, is the name Picasso and Marie-Thérèse gave their own daughter – nicknamed Maïa – when she was born and registered in Paris as *enfant adultérin*, literally "child born of adultery," on October 5, 1935.

Also, in 1935, the year of Maïa's birth and of Conchita's symbolic resurrection, Picasso engraved an etching, named *Minotauromachy*, which he would eventually donate to Barcelona. Curiously enough both *Minotauromachy* and *Guernica* have nine protagonists. Once again there we see the minotaur coming from the sea, as a boat sails away on the horizon. In front of the minotaur flees a terrified horse carrying a fainting *señorita-torera*, or young lady bullfighter, as they used to be called at that time. The girl's breast shows through her open jacket and she still holds a sword at the end of her outstretched and rigid arm.

Almost inevitably the woman's profile is that of Marie-Thérèse. But more interesting than their resemblance is the return of the little girl who in *The Blind Minotaur* was leading the monster; now she confronts the minotaur, holding a bunch of flowers in one hand and some sort of Bengal light in the other. We immediately identify her as a new metamorphosis of Conchita, here disguised with a flat hat and some kind of school uniform. If we remember that on October 5 of that year a new María de la Concepción, or Conchita, was born to Picasso, the little girl's double identification with the artist's sister and daughter imposes itself.

Behind the girl, climbing a ladder that seems to lead nowhere, flees a tall, almost naked, bearded man. Leaning out of a window and totally ignorant of the drama on the beach, we see two more girls with a pair of doves. Perhaps contrasting with the clarity of the sky and ocean, this somber world beneath their window could be the realm of art, where the living and the dead share the same ambit and keep transforming one into the other as images do in dreams. Here, at the margin of time and next to an ocean, which traditionally is the symbol of eternity, the minotaur rages and charges with his eyes widely opened. He has been seen before as a cross between Picasso and don José Ruiz Blasco, both in his physical appearance and in his blindness. Now the minotaur is the metamorphosis of only Picasso. Let us add that the artist doesn't seem to be ready to pardon his father for the sin of artistically alienating himself. If Picasso is the minotaur, the tall and almost naked bearded man who flees from the monster is none other than don José. He is easily identifiable through his figure and his beard. To his humiliation and further discredit, Picasso's father – the man who fancied himself a model of natural elegance – here has to escape from his own son, barefoot and naked.

307

In his escape, don José is protected by the same little girl who once acted as the minotaur's guide but is now stopping that monstrous chimera in its tracks with a Bengal light or candle. Here the minotaur encounters this girl – Conchita or Maïa – whom Picasso has registered as the daughter of an unknown father, though he has volunteered to be her godfather at her christening. Here he has to recognize her, as she shows him the shameful humiliation of don José. Finally, Picasso seems to consider don José as one of his innocent victims, although until now he has consistently and ironically refused to pardon him. In other words, don José Ruiz Blasco did not deny his paternity when he relinquished painting, after having begotten Picasso as his legitimate son and heir. It was Picasso himself – as he seems to admit in *Minotauromachy* and in his transformation into the minotaur – who inadvertently forced his father to give up painting and therefore to blind and kill himself as an artist.

Finally, we see here the woman who had fainted and whom the horse carries off after having probably been gored by the minotaur. Now Marie-Thérèse is a broken, defeated human being as Conchita-Maïa shows her to the monster. Fate made her come across Picasso when she was barely sixteen and they bumped into each other as she was stepping out of the Paris subway. "Mademoiselle, please do come with me," said the artist, who was already in his fifties, "I have the feeling we are going to do great things together. I am Picasso." The story goes that she timidly asked him at that point, "And who on earth is

Picasso?" She was not trying to be facetious; she had never heard the name before in her life. Two years later she gave Picasso a daughter he could not legally recognize because he was a married man whose wife would not grant him a divorce. In fact, and even though she was terribly ignorant and not very intelligent, Marie-Thérèse knew that fate condemned her to an almost clandestine existence with hidden encounters with her lover on some holidays and on every Thursday afternoon. The fact that Picasso called her "the best of all women" – and he probably meant it in all honesty – is totally irrelevant. Little by little the Thursday visits by "the monster," as Pierre Cabanne called Picasso, would be fewer and farther between as Conchita-Maïa grew up. Inevitably there would come a time when Picasso would never visit at all. For a young girl like Marie-Thérèse was incapable of transforming her affair with Picasso into an intellectual adventure, as Fernande Olivier did and Françoise Gilot or Geneviève Laporte would do. The first encounter with the artist was the beginning of a very tragic and tormented life. Her long agony would end only four years to the day after Picasso's death when Marie-Thérèse Walter would hang herself in 1977.

In May, 1968, the Picasso Museum in Barcelona received a large donation from the artist himself, a series of paintings named *Las meninas* (The Ladies in Waiting), which he did between August and October, 1957. Apparently that creative storm, much too hasty and rather unpolished, found its source of inspiration in a large black-and-white photograph of Velázquez's *Ladies in Waiting*, which Jaime Sabartés, Picasso's secretary and life-long friend, had purchased for his own living room. Of Picasso's many approaches to *The Ladies in Waiting*, the most interesting is the first one, painted in black and white as was *Guernica*. In reference to that canvas, Jean Southerland Boggs remembers a confession that Picasso made to Françoise Gilot: "I want to push the inadvertent human mind through unaccustomed paths and suddenly wake it up." Nevertheless, Picasso's interpretation disappoints Southerland Boggs, because instead of trying to solve Velázquez's mystery in modern terms, Picasso only adds irrelevant enigmas to the vast metaphysical and plastic questions presented by the seventeenth-century master.

All that may be very true, but John Berger takes a more relevant approach to Picasso's *Ladies in Waiting*. In this black-and-white interpretation of the celebrated painting, Picasso's Velázquez appears so gigantic and so full of his own identity that he can only be seen as the archetype of the *father figure*. At the same time we have here Picasso

himself, transformed into another universal symbol which is both biblical in its origin and guilt-ridden. That is to say, the artist has assumed
the image of the *prodigal son*. Let us never forget that Picasso created his
version of *The Ladies in Waiting* precisely after Velázquez, who is the
father of Spanish painting. In other words, and quoting Picasso himself,
"Velázquez only needed to be Velázquez to be forever unique." Thus,
through Velázquez as a father figure, Picasso gave back to don José the
palette and the brushes he relinquished in Barcelona. Moreover, Picasso's
donation of the entire series of *Las meninas* to Barcelona, the city where
don José renounced his identity as a painter, would underscore Picasso's purpose when creating his own *Ladies in Waiting*, a purpose which
seems to be both obvious and very conscious on the part of the artist.   309

Moreover, the other don José (or don José Nieto Velázquez, as
fate named the royal majordomo who appears on the threshold of the
back door in Velázquez's *Las meninas*) moves into the painter's studio
in Picasso's version and becomes the tiny shadow of Velázquez/don
José Ruiz Blasco. Thus, the painting takes a progressive geometric perspective, from the background to the foreground and from the past to
the present in order to project the titanic figure of a *father painter*, who
is as tall as the canvas that Picasso is recreating is high.

On the other side of the studio, precisely in confrontation with
the painter we called Velázquez/don José Ruiz Blasco, we have the last
transformation of Velázquez's royal buffoon as we saw him in the seventeenth-century canvas. We even know the buffoon's name, Nicolasito
Pertusato. In real life he was a well-formed midget and therefore was
also a man with the perennial appearance of a child. Here, in Picasso's
painting, he becomes a sort of phantom, sketched out with five thick
black lines around a white background. In other words, he is the tenta-
tive project of a human figure which could eventually become any man.
To understand his presence as a child, and also as a reincarnation of Nicolasito Pertusato, we have to consider the dog at his feet as another relevant clue. Also barely sketched by Picasso with a few lines and painted
all white, this dog is the simplified caricature of Lump, the affectionate
dachshund the American photographer David Duncan gave Picasso in
1957. Therefore, Picasso not only transformed himself into the midget
of his *Ladies in Waiting*, but he also shared the buffoon's appearance as
a child, here accompanied by the pet he owned as an old man.

In this manner not only the Picasso the world knows, but also
Picasso as the child he was when his father gave him his palette and
brushes, fuse into each other. They merge in this tiny clown of the

Baroque Age with the sole purpose of rendering homage to don José. Incidentally, this homage in *The Ladies in Waiting* could not become more paradoxical, because here one of the greatest geniuses art has ever had – Velázquez – blends himself with a defeated painter – Picasso's father – while another painter of renown comparable to that of Velázquez – Picasso himself – contemplates their symbiosis, when transformed into Velázquez's buffoon and his father's infant child.

While all these transformations are taking place before our eyes, Picasso wreaks havoc in Velázquez's studio. In a similar manner, half a century before, cubism broke away from an artistic tradition which counted Velázquez as one of its geniuses and which also had in don José Ruiz Blasco – Velázquez's paradoxical alter ego – a very mediocre follower.

310

Picasso turned ninety in apparently excellent health and, as usual, working through the evening, the night, and part of the next morning. Nevertheless, the man who had always been terrified of death now seemed to assume the fact that his old age was slowly coming to an end and pushing him into eternity. At times, he seemed to have returned to Corunna or to Málaga, when he still was his father's pupil before don José relinquished painting. He constantly interrupted the conversations around him with such phrases as: "Well, look, I'm sure that my father would have said at this point that –"; or, "As my father once told me and I will never forget –"; or, "Here my father would have been of another opinion"; or, "If I may quote my father." Ironically, it seems that poor don José had become an oracle and treasurer of wisdom, some sort of sage whom his son kept alive with his citations. One day he startled the printer Piero Crommelinck, the son of Fernand Crommelinck, author of the *Magnificent Cuckold*. "Please," he exclaimed, "wait a second and be very still here, showing me your profile against the window. My God, how you do resemble my father! It's simply incredible!"

Around that time the American photographer David Duncan was spending a few days with Picasso and his second wife, Jacqueline Roque. One evening they were having dinner when a visitor was announced. He happened to be an art collector from Málaga who offered Picasso a small canvas with some doves, painted by don José Ruiz Blasco in another century. David Duncan kept his thoughts to himself, but found the painting nothing short of horrible in its ridiculous handling and poor use of color. Nevertheless, Picasso seemed to be very moved and was almost incapable of finding words to express his gratitude for the precious gift. Then he started quoting don José once again: "Well, looking at the doves and remembering what my father used to say –."

A year and a half before his death Picasso painted one of his last self-portraits, posthumously exhibited at the Palace of the Popes in Avignon. Ironically this was not the first time that the face of Christ had appeared in a painting by a professed atheist such as Picasso. Throughout his life, and with very different meanings and intentions, he had produced a large variety of canvases and drawings with a religious theme. Nevertheless, and for the first time, Christ here took on a very personal significance for the artist. The long, bearded features that religious iconography attributes to Jesus Christ bear an inevitable resemblance to those of don José Ruiz Blasco in this painting. On the other hand, the eyes are not don José's but those of all the Ruiz – including his children's – except for don José himself. In other words, Picasso gave his own eyes to his father in order to replace the narrow, blue pupils don José had symbolically put out when he blinded himself by abandoning painting. Likewise, and with the twofold intention of rescuing his own origins and finding the man who begot him, Telemachus started his quest for Odysseus in order to return him to his palace. He was determined to bring his father back even from the kingdom of Hades, if necessary, because at that time everybody believed that Odysseus was dead.

311

Perhaps we should add that also everybody believed don José dead, or ignored him as if he had never existed, when Picasso desperately attempted to resurrect his memory. If strangers had overtaken Odysseus' place during his long absence, his son, Telemachus, knew that sooner or later Odysseus would be back to avenge himself and to complete his child's identity with his return. Also Picasso kept reminding the world of don José with his quotations. Finally, in order to convince the world with a painting – since the world seemed to be determined not to listen to his words – he turned out a portrait where he and his father were one and the same man. Nevertheless, by now it was too late and the portrait would be exhibited only after Picasso's death. Incidentally, on this occasion it was stolen from the Palace of the Popes and disappeared into thin air.

In Picasso's last interpretation of Jesus Christ's face, there coincide God, the eternal Father, and the Eternal, Immortal Son of Saint Joseph (san José), as well as don José Ruiz Blasco. In the last instance, as Norman Brown would put it, there is no healing without completing oneself from two opposite halves. Through Eros and in response to

Thanatos, which is always separation, man returns to his essential unity. In his long way back to his father, Picasso began his quest by assuming his alienation from the day that don José had renounced being a painter. Picasso's response to this symbolic suicide would be that creative outpouring that sufficed for the two of them, his father and himself. At the same time, through the labyrinth of his complex creative work, Picasso's quest took him to his own interpretation of his father as the mistletoe vendor, the minotaur, and finally Jesus Christ himself at the hour when don José's time for resurrection had finally come in virtue of the eternal miracle of painting.

312

WORKS OF ART CITED

I. Works by Picasso:
Science and Charity (Ciencia y caridad), 1897; Museo Picasso, Barcelona.
Portrait of Aunt Pepa (Tía Pepa), 1896; Museo Picasso, Barcelona.
Self-Portrait, 1896; Museo Picasso, Barcelona.
The Mistletoe Sellers, 1902; private collection, Paris.
The Old Guitar Player, 1903; Art Institute, Chicago.
The Old Jew, 1903; Pushkin Museum, Moscow.
Etchings and dry points of the so-called Vollard suite, named for the collector Ambroise Vollard, who acquired the plates by 1937 and had them printed by the master printer Roger Lacourière. These include the prints of Sculptor and Model, the Minotaur prints from May, 1933, and the eleven Blind Minotaur images from 1934-35.
Minotauromachy, Spring, 1935; the Musée Picasso in Paris has as series of states.
Guernica, 1937; Museo Reina Sofía, Madrid.
Variations on Velázquez's Las meninas, 1957, including several in the Museo Picasso, Barcelona.
Self-portrait, c. 1971; exhibited posthumously in Avignon (lost).

II. Works by others:
Hans Holbein, Man of Sorrows, 1519-20; Öffentliche Sammlung, Basel.
Patinir, Landscape with Charon's Boat, c. 1520; Prado, Madrid.
Velázquez, Las meninas, 1656; Prado, Madrid.

REMEMBERING the MEMORABILIA
in MALRAUX'S *MUSÉE IMAGINAIRE*

BY THOMAS LYMAN, EMORY UNIVERSITY

Now that reception theory is firmly in place, I look back to 1949 and try to remember what I fancied to be the audience André Malraux had in mind, other than me, for the essays he had just published under the title *La psychologie de l'art.* Did it occur to me that his tours de force may not have been addressed to me at all but to some world of sophisticates I might have imagined on the basis of those Paris vernissages where the postwar perpetuators of Van Dongen's world made small talk about the decline of the Paris School? Duly warned that I was out of my element, I persisted nevertheless for months on end, following the darting arrow of Malraux's allusions back and forth across time and natural boundaries, from Ajanta to the Faubourg Saint-Honoré, convinced that his errant missile had my number on it. The warning came from Père Couturier during one of his surprise visits to our studio. Living in the Faubourg himself, the open-minded priest (who was responsible for persuading non-believing modern artists to decorate churches) knew well the *mentalité* of those first visitors to the chapel in Vence who saw Matisse's image of St. Dominic (for which Couturier ironically served as model) not as the founder of an order of preaching inquisitors but as a sign of the transcendence of art over history. *Man's Fate* had by then been transferred in Malraux's imagination to the Quixotic hand of the artist from the trigger finger of the soldier of fortune. Existentialism had spilled beyond Saint-Germain-des-Prés to art schools everywhere, and other American expatriates like the action painter, Sam Francis, fully shared my indulgence for what we called "Malravian art history."

Since then, I admit to having mistaken students of art history often for the audience Malraux had in mind. What misguided me was not so much his flair for aphorisms but his assurance that a cavalier comparison between art objects from one end of history to the other would somehow fall on imaginations fertile enough to get the point. This miscalculation began soon after returning to Chicago from France to teach what I thought was art history without pay in an evening school. Was I not a little dismayed when the dean allowed as how the immigrants for whom the classes were offered gratis might not know or care what André Malraux said about art? I probably even emulated his style when projecting Oceanic masks alongside paintings by Jackson Pollack while referring knowingly, and without taking a breath, to Irish illuminations and Louis Sullivan. I was, in effect, guilty of what Malraux in his 1928 novel, *Les conquérants*, had already noticed in Americans by the time I was born:

> [Les Américains cultivés] pensent que la culture américaine est une des cultures nationales de l'Occident, qu'il n'y a pas plus de différence entre la haute culture américaine et la haute culture française, qu'entre celle-ci et la culture anglaise, ou ce que fut la haute culture allemande.

I went a step beyond that and, in my democratic way, assumed that everyone in my classes was privy to high culture, or had a right to it by virtue of the universal message and power of art. Without ever having read *Les conquérants* I spoke as if I intuited another passage where Malraux ascribes to Americans an openness to culture that would eventually qualify them as the ideal audience for his "musée imaginaire":

> On considère que l'Amérique est un pays sans racines, que c'est un pays citadin: un pays qui ignore cette vieille et profonde relation avec les arbres et les pierres ou s'unissent les plus vieux génies de la Chine et les plus vieux génies de l'Occident. Un pays qui a sur nous l'avantage de pouvoir et de vouloir accueillir d'un coeur égal tous les héritages du monde, et dont tel musée principal montre, dans la même salle, les statues romanes qui regardent au loin notre Occident, et les statues T'ang qui regardent au loin la civilisation chinoise.

What is more, as if to reciprocate this early tribute, wasn't it an American audience who, with Edmund Wilson, hailed *La psychologie de l'art* as "one of the really great books of our time"? Small wonder I would catch myself projecting a slide on the screen in mute wonderment, trusting in my audience to summon up all of the relevant comparisons and oppositions Malraux might have offered to put the work into a cosmic perspective beyond mere words. Indeed, that same year, my occasional lapses into silence were vindicated by the French editors who, to the general satisfacion of art critics, changed the title of *La psychologie de l'art* to *Les voix du silence*.

Everyone had already pointed out, of course, that *La psychologie de l'art* was not about art history, much less psychology. Even its detractors admitted that it was a very literary way of taking stock of the modern taste, acquired through travel and photography, for a heterogeneous array of objects from which history had somehow been drained. One might also have noted that it was a timely way of reinvesting them with meaning in an age of anxiety not only about the future but also about the past. The bomb had recently gone off twice – at human expense – like double exclamation points at the end of a century during which modernists had declared open war on the burden of European historicism. Malraux was hardly the first to remark that our perception of past art had become a function of our detachment from, not to mention our ignorance of, its original context. Although he later wrote as if he knew exactly what psychological needs brought certain works into existence, his conviction that only the present can give meaning to past works of art was stated in "L'oeuvre d'art" (1934), his first essay on the subject:

315

> Every work of art is created to satisfy a need, a need which is sufficiently urgent to give it birth. Then the need withdraws itself from the work as the blood drains from a body and the work begins its mysterious transfiguration. It passes into the realm of shadows. Only our own proper need, our own passion can call it forth. Until that time it will remain like a great statue with sightless eyes before which passes a long procession of the blind. And the same necessity which obliges one of the blind to approach the statue opens simultaneously the eyes of both...

Thus quoted by his most ardent champion in the American press, J.B. Hodin, as a repudiation of art for art's sake and as an existential reclamation of man's sense of greatness, the statement also posits the nexus of genius in the eyes of the beholder before whom art, like the dormant God of the existentialists, has "need of our passion, need of our desire, need of our will." Displaced artworks, and even photos of the smallest part of them, are like pawns in a cosmic game, the secret rules of which can be discerned through heroic and passionate engagement. The absolute is not to be found in patterns of continuity needed by the historian in order to string histories together but in the uncommon coin of creativity, whose head, free of its conventionalized "tale," is at once comparable and yet unlike anything else before or since, except for that quintessential truth imbedded in individual style. History, in this perpective, is insignificant alongside that transcendent moment willed into being, along with the greatest human experiences worth having, in the act of reanimating the blind statue which, in its own time, was willed to mankind, in the fullest sense of the word, by an artist.

Malraux's central idea was recapitulated in the essay that introduced the sequel to his *Voices of Silence*, a series of three volumes that enriched even further the extensive panoply of his artistic memorabilia. Entitled *Le musée imaginaire de la sculpture mondiale*, it comprised one volume spanning all of history and two others that expanded on the message of those two statues facing East and West which had epitomized America's openness to the "univers des formes" (to coin a phrase from the title of another collection of art books he sponsored later when he was French Minister of Culture and which continues to be expanded today): *Des bas-reliefs aux grottes sacrées* which treated religious art from ancient Mesopotamia across Asia to Oceania, pre-Columbian America, and Africa, was followed, some time later, as if by dint of a superhuman effort, by *Le monde chrétien*. That essay begins with a nocturnal *rêverie* that took place alongside the Campo Santo at Pisa, an appropriate setting for his message about sculpture's role in man's fateful confrontation with destiny. There, he reflects on juxtaposed heads that stand out from shop pieces, one left unfinished in the workshop of Giovanni Pisano and the other by an anonymous artist of the Haniwa culture in ancient Japan. They bear an uncanny resemblance one to the other, but that is not his point. About the Pisan head he asks, "Comment en preciser l'accent, parent de celui de tels arts parmi les plus anciens ou les plus sauvages, et auquel nous donnons parfois le nom de génie?" Together, they evoke a rejoinder: "Leur question se projetait sur toute l'histoire; elles suggéraient d'abord que maints chefs-d'oeuvre sont loin de s'unir, aussi étroitement que l'affirment les histoires de l'art, à la production des civilisations où ils sont nés." Contemplating the chasm he perceives between "production et création," he sees artistic production as the stuff of history, of that history of continuities without consequence alongside those rare statements of genius that defy time.

A sample of his language gives us a glimpse of Malraux's notion of how the history of art flows unforeseeably from its mysterious sources around a few time-defying peaks into oblivion:

> Comment ne pas distinguer, de Senlis à Naumbourg, une coulée semblable à celle qui va de l'Acropole d'Athènes à Pergame, et comment ne pas la distinguer de ce qu'elle dépose sur ses bords? Le sculpteur de l'Adam et de l'Eve de Bamberg, celui de

la comtesse Uta de Naumbourg, continuent imprévisiblement la coulée gothique qui meurt dans la Sainte Anne, comme le génie égyptien retrouve le génie antérieur après les cataclysmes, comme la Victoire de Samothrace retrouvant le drapé des Parques.

What the sculpture at Senlis has in common with that of Naumburg or whether the drapery mentioned in the last instance falls from the knees of the three "Muses," the "Fates" ("les Parques," as one might expect him to call the female statues from the east pediment of the Parthenon transplanted by Lord Elgin from the Acropolis to the British Museum) or the "Three Goddesses" (as they are identified by art historians) is secondary to the expression of Malraux's weariness with the art historian's futile search for sources and influences when compared with the ability given to all mankind to distinguish creativity from artistic production of even the highest quality. All that is required to discover the genius from a photoengraved detail of works, whether created by an anonymous potter or the assistant of a highly regarded harbinger of the Italian Renaissance, is a special act of the will.

I ask myself again in retrospect how much these last three volumes may have contributed to my decision, and that of many other romantically inclined American colleagues, to study sculpture rather than painting when the time came to write a dissertation. Was it perhaps unconsciously because of what he also said in the first sentence of that introductory essay:

> Depuis la mort de Miche-Ange jusqu'à l'art moderne, la sculpture, sans excepter Rodin, devient un dialogue avec le passé. La peinture est notre art, et la sculpture celui que nous avons ressuscité; c'est pourquoi celle-ci semble parfois l'âme impérieuse de la plus lointaine histoire, le symbole du vieil Homme interrogateur des astres…

Was it André Malraux who gave me the excuse to take refuge in the anonymity of a poorly documented art form so I could have my own private dialogue with the past, unfettered by the rigors of scientific art history? My original intention was to write a thesis at the Sorbonne on artistic freedom in the nineteenth century. Was I giving vent to that very American infatuation shared by Frenchmen with the notion of "la liberté" when I went to France, a copy of John Mundy's *Liberty and Political Power in Toulouse* in hand, as if driven by the need to find the statue whose eyes I might open along with my own? In what must be one of the most recondite undertakings of the structuralist era, *Le dictionnaire des idées dans l'oeuvre d'André Malraux,* I looked up "liberté" and found that it was cited only once in connection with France, and in the very same novel where Americans were characterized as free of the burdensome past and therefore as open to a Romanesque as to a T'ang statue: "Nous voulons rendre à la France le rôle qu'elle a tenu déjà à plusieurs reprises, aux époques romane et gothique comme au XIXe siècle, et qui a imposé son accent à l'Europe quand il était à la fois celui de l'audace et celui de la liberté." Had my fate been sealed when *Les conquérants* was written in 1928, or was it blind audacity that led me to France and then turned me from the nineteenth century toward another, darker age of liberty?

318

I HAVE RARELY had occasion to regret that decision, at least not until a few years ago when a colleague asked me if I would help write a catalogue for an exhibition of medieval art in Canadian collections. It wasn't that I minded writing the essay; it gave me an occasion to explain how romantic Americans were the ultimate beneficiaries of those nineteenth-century Frenchmen who felt free to savage Romanesque buildings in the interest of progress, an ideal occasion to dwell on "la liberté" in two great moments of French history. But writing the catalogue entries for the Romanesque sculpture became an odious if not impossible task because the Canadian government could not afford to bring me to Toronto to see the objects themselves. Writing an exhibition catalogue involves reinserting stray elements of a dismembered past into a fabricated history, a task that can be done only by looking long and hard at the lineaments of each fragment against a background comprising the sum total of the connoisseur's remembered repertory of images. For want of data about provenance, a history of the sundry collected objects began as a history instead of their dispersal, of the dismemberment of authentic monuments and of their replacement by copies or, worse, what Malraux dismissed as works of production. I refrained from commenting on the individual works and let the museums furnish their own measurements of works I knew only from photographs and which for me were at best a part of *my* "musée imaginaire."

However, by the time I was to talk at a meeting of medievalists about the collection, I learned that most of the sculptures had been acquired originally by a Frenchman during the 1950s. It was then that another history emerged from my drawer full of closeup views of volute masks, of human heads, of featureless cranial armatures, of jack-o'-lantern faces, gaping mouths, nostrils and eyeless sockets – strangely like those of the Haniwa heads. In contrast with the several foliate capitals – more or less debased "production" versions of svelte, inhabited vinescroll capitals and therefore subject to classifying historically – those with anguished human physiognomies seemed to me clearly to have belonged to someone who had been both looking at and listening to *Les voix du silence* and who, with its author, had recognized in the transcendent genius of anonymous Romanesque carvers a mute howl of defiance in the face of destiny. Once at the podium, I found myself addressing the projected images as if my audience knew exactly what I meant when, with reference to those gaping masks, I evoked Malraux's "musée imaginaire." It was my only way of lending some semblance of history to those grotesque heads without regressing to autobiography.

There are moments, in retrospect, when I have been tempted to think that the only authentic history is autobiography and that what each of us carries around in his or her head is the sum total of what matters. But the fallacy in that notion was brought home to me again soon after I began to think about this essay for Art's sake. Malraux's "musée imaginaire" is evidently an important part of my own, and of my sense of history. Yet, if history is the content of our memory, how could I have completed an eight-year long effort to recall everything that has ever been written about Romanesque sculpture in France, in the form of an annotated bibliography, and yet have completely forgotten about André Malraux who once meant so much to me? Still stumbling over the memorabilia in the attic of his "musée imaginaire," I often forget, too, that his idiosyncratic preference for details, a taste that came to influence a generation of editors at *Vogue* as well as Harry Abrams, Inc., brought forth more than mere illustrations of what he saw when he closed his eyes and communed with world genius. They touched many of us deeply. We are perhaps no less arrogant than then with respect to what we think can be known about the past and how we go about explaining it. However, if I had paid closer attention at the time, I might have noticed that some art historians were as indulgent as I had been with Malraux's disdain for fact and his penchant for overstatement. They realized then that he was offering a substitute for a kind of history repudiated by modernism, one that puts the present in touch not with a theoretical past but with a transcendent present buoyed in those days by the internationalism of the postwar period. The most generous minds of the next generation of Americans – with Arthur Evans notable among them – felt free to will into existence a far broader world because of what Malraux offered as the saving grace of "la condition humaine."

THOMAS LYMAN

VII. RECALLING *the* PRESENT

OF TIME and WALTER CRONKITE

BY EUGENE J. McCARTHY

T ime is not easy to handle. It is tough and evasive and many other things. Philosophers, theologians, poets, watchmakers and the people – all have tried, without success, to comprehend it. Failing in that, they have tried to control it through definition or measurement.

The philosophers have been most concerned about time, and have tried harder than the others to understand and explain it. One of the earliest and best efforts was that of Aristotle. Time, said he, is not "itself movement." But, "neither does time exist without change. Time is neither movement nor independent of movement." Moreover, although he held that a continuous quantity is divisible, and that "time, past, present and future, forms a continuous whole," he said that time seemed to be an "indivisible instant." How about that? 323

Saint Augustine, as a philosopher struggling with the same problems, said that what we call the present has "no extent or duration," and that only past and future time could be called "long or short." Past and future time have duration, he held, but in what sense, he asked, "can that which does not exist be long or short? The past no longer is; the future is not yet." This position is challenged by George Allen, the longtime and successful coach of the Washington Redskins. In his player selection and game strategy, he follows his theory that "the future is now."

Back to Augustine again. His last position on time was that, if no one asked him what time was, he knew, but if he asked, he did not know. He left the issue, more or less, at that "point in time," hoping, I assume, that no one would ever ask him about time, and that he would go on knowing what time was or is.

George Berkeley, of eighteenth-century intellectual fame, after considering all human knowledge, concluded that our troubles with time were probably of our own making. Albert Einstein simply avoided the issue by making time into another dimension in his four-dimensional space-time continuum.

Theologians have been troubled less and less by time than have philosophers. Theologians have accepted, essentially on faith, that since God created the world, He must have created time; or that time came with creation and was, therefore, concomitant to that act or an instant consequence of it. "There is no time before the world," wrote Augustine, writing as a theologian, not as a philosopher.

Generally, theologians are and have been less interested than philosophers in the beginning of time, and more concerned about the manner of its ending and what comes after that. For St. Thomas Aquinas, time existed in God or with Him, although it was not particularly important until the creation of the world and the division of the work of creation into seven days. St. Thomas tried to sort time out by defining two "nows" – the eternal "now" and a first "now" from which time begins.

God, insofar as the record can be traced, did not meddle much with time, once it began or once He began it. He did stop the sun in the heavens, a kind of first daylight-saving time, to help Joshua fight the battle of Jericho, but he did not lengthen the day, only the time of light. Politicians have done the same with modern daylight-saving time, although critics of that change have charged them with meddling with God's time, and dairy farmers have protested that the change has affected the flow of milk from their cows.

Poets have been less patient with time than have philosophers and theologians. They have resented it, denounced it, challenged it, made the best of it or ignored it. Shakespeare, the master, played the whole range. He surrendered to it in one sonnet:

> Ruin hath taught me thus to ruminate
> That time will come and take my love away.

In another, he struck back in challenge:

> Do thy worst, old Time, despite thy wrong
> My love shall in my verse ever live young.

Milton appeared to be unafraid. He challenged time, in time, asserting that he would, in eternity, get even. Thus, he wrote:

> ... glut thyself with what thy womb devours,
> Which is no more than what is false and vain,
> And merely mortal dross...
> So little is our loss
> So little is thy gain.
> For when as each thing bad thou hast entomb'd,
> And last of all thy greedy self consum'd,
> Then long Eternity shall greet our bliss

324

With an individual kiss...
Then all this Earthly grossness quit,
Attir'd with Stars, we shall forever sit,
Triumphing over Death and Chance, and thee,
O Time.

Lesser poets have been more ready to compromise, suggesting
that we make the best of time. One wrote:

Be a gleaner of time.
Claim what runs through the hour glass
When no one watches
Claim what is counted by clocks, ticking
When no one listens.
Save remnants
From the cutting room of day
End pieces from the loom of night
Brand and hold
Unmarked, maverick minutes
Salvage time left derelict
By those who despair of light
Yet fear the dark
Steal only from sleep
And from eternity
Of which time, no one dares ask
What? or Where?

The poets, having had their turn, the clockmakers and watchmakers, the measurers, took theirs. They gave up trying to understand
time. They undertook to measure, harness, dominate, and control time,
even though they didn't know what it was, where it had come from,
or where it was going. Try anything, was their theory: drops of water,
sand in an hourglass, notched wheels with weights or wheels moved by
springs, impulses and ions. The appearance, rather than the reality, of
controlling time was something they found marketable in every society.
Among primitives, along with an English bicycle and an American
fountain pen, a watch – preferably Swiss (but Japanese makes would
do) – became a sure mark of upward mobility. As in more advanced
civilizations, the possessor could at least appear to have achieved some
mastery over time. He could set his watch backward or forward. He
could look at the dial as though he were supposed to be where he was,

325

or at some other place.

In early modern civilizations (roughly 1950 to 1975), watchmakers attacked time even more subtly. Primitive watches had to be wound. The self-winding watch was introduced to free the busy man or woman from that distressing demand. But even the fact that the winding was a by-product of other physical motions by the wearer was a limitation. Newer watches drew their power from more mysterious, scientific, non-human sources. Ions were in. At the same time that the power source was changing, so was the face of the dial. The lower classes might have to watch hours, minutes and even seconds. But the movers and the shakers, and those just below them, budgeted time in larger lots. The second hand was first to go. Numerals began to disappear, until only four markers divided the day and the night. And then there were no markers. The next emancipation, the "in" thing, was to wear no watch at all, thus defying time, saying in effect what the philosophers suggested, that "I will measure the now by my changing, and my changing by the now," and making a theological assertion that "I shall measure, as I have been measured."

What of the people and time? The general historical record is that people are rather accepting of time, not trying too hard to understand or control it. They tried to get along with it, occasionally hanging an adjective on it in passing, or subjecting it to a verb of some usefulness. Most of the adjectives applied to time have been uncomplimentary – "devouring," "bloody," "avenging," "threatening," "demanding," "relentless," "deceiving," "greedy," or somewhat obvious like "past and present," "early and late," and "good and bad," with no real attempt to penetrate meaning or assert control. The verbs have been like the adjectives. Time is wasted and saved. It is lost and found, released and regained. It is served. Some time is taken out and then declared in again. There is free time and borrowed time.

Then came radio and television and their new treatment of time. For the first time in history, time was offered for sale. If time was to be offered for sale, it had to be graded. The old time categories were cast out. Time came to be classified as "prime," "choice," and "good." These grade designations, incidentally, are the same used for grading beef. The classifications for cattle continue through "common," "canner," and "cutter," three grades which could also, with a little imagination, be applied to some time allowed for television programs.

The new radio-television treatment of time is not limited to commercial transactions. The media have attacked the philosophical and theological conceptions as well. Although some philosophers have said that no moment of time is like any other moment, radio and television say, "Not so." They claim that there is such a thing as "equal time." Whereas other philosophers have said that every moment of time, except for the incidentals that pass through those measured units, is like every other moment of time, radio and television say, "Not so." They say that there is unique time, not equal to or like any other time. Thus, there are "Maud's time," "Mary Tyler Moore's time," "Roseanne's time," and "Kojak time," marked forever and unsaleable, because if sold, "equal time" provisions of the law would, by some inherent, metaphysical fact, be violated. Radio-television has introduced other conceptions of time, new categories like "shared time," and "pooled time," as well as "time slots."

Radio-television has even asserted a control over time which the theologians have denied to God, at least until the world ends. Television interviewers, without apology to God, regularly say, "We are out of time." This does not always happen. Television, for example, can be out of sound without being out of time. Thus, in the 1976 Ford-Carter debate, time continued to run although the sound had failed. Commentators were moved very quickly to tell us, when the twenty-eight minutes of silence on the part of the candidates began, that the candidates had not stopped to think or been struck dumb, as the audience might have suspected, but rather that radio-television had lost their sound. They still had their time.

All of which brings us to the ultimate period: the time between the light and dark, by Longfellow called "The Children's Hour," in the age of faith set aside for Vespers, and then distinguished as "Cronkite Time," which ended when Cronkite said what philosophers and theologians believe God cannot say while time runs on: "That's the way it is." To which we can only add, "Amen."

DELUDING the PUBLIC: THE "MICROBE KILLERS"[1]

BY JAMES HARVEY YOUNG, EMORY UNIVERSITY

An end-of-the-eighteenth-century London flyer, recently acquired by the History of Medicine Division of the National Library of Medicine, touted the extensive therapeutic powers possessed by J. Barton's "Vital Wine."[2] Orthodox physicians of the age went in for expansive theorizing, and Barton aped them. "Vital Air" he held to be "the direct exclusive principle in nature, which gives power to all the active energies of animal life," for without air all die. To use Vital Air as a medicine, it is more efficiently administered to the stomach than to the lungs, for the "whole system; the blood, the brain, and nerves, are all acted upon by the stomach." Barton had "discovered a method of combining Vital Air in liquid form…a pleasing and nutritious wine." Even infants of the earliest age might use it safely. Vital Wine eradicated venereal diseases, even when mercury had failed. In fevers it was "superior to every other medicine," for scrofula an "absolute specific." In Barton's brochure the indications for Vital Wine's healing use ran on and on.

In such panaceas – and there have been many– infectious diseases appeared along with other ailments within the purview of the healing potion. When quacks sought to adjust to epidemic conditions, a sense of specificity surfaced. Yellow fever serves as an example. A few years after Barton published his pamphlet, another London promoter issued a circular for the eyes of travelers departing for the "West Indies, America, [and] the Mediterranean."[3] He offered them powders "to prevent and cure the yellow fever," his claims buttressed by glowing testimonials. During the devastating Philadelphia epidemic of 1793, "dozens of quacks and empirics plied their various trades."[4] One Samuel Correy, for example, vended his speedy cure for yellow spotted fever, as well as a prescription by which those who nursed the stricken could keep themselves immune. This remedy consisted of gin, honey, and mercury.

During these years of the great northern epidemics, it is not surprising that both the first health device and the first drug patented under the authority given to Congress by the new Constitution, both in 1796, should include yellow fever within the compass of their purported healing power.[5] Samuel Lee, Jr., of Windham, Connecticut, patented the drug, which he called Bilious Pills. The specifications for his reme-

328

dy were burned in a patent office fire. A later dispensatory assumed
the ingredients to be gamboge, aloes, soap, and nitrate of potassa.

Elisha Perkins patented the medical device.[6] A Connecticut
physician who knew of Franklin's and Galvani's experiments with electricity, Perkins came to believe that this powerful force of nature caused
disease. If he could remove the bad electricity, he could produce a cure.
He devised metallic tractors, small pointed rods, to draw the bad electricity out when pulled across the body, points downward, from the
center out. One was a gold-colored alloy, the other silver. Having
members of Congress, Supreme Court Chief Justice Oliver Ellsworth,
and President George Washington interested in his invention, Perkins
precipitated a national mania of cure by tractoration. In 1799, armed
with his device, he went to New York City, where yellow fever raged,
hoping to help. Perkins himself contracted the fever, died, and was
buried in what is now the site of Washington Square.

In the South, where yellow fever persisted, so did the promise
by patent medicine promoters to prevent and cure the saffron scourge.[7]
During epidemic seasons, even before New Orleans newspapers had
begun to discuss the fever editorially, Yankee nostrums would be ad-
vertised with their preposterous claims: Brandreth's Vegetable Universal
Pills, Radway's Relief, Duffy's Pure Malt Whiskey, "A Scientific Remedy,
Not a Beverage."

In Pensacola in the 1880s, a dubious doctor named Bosso sold
Bosso's Blessing for Mankind as a yellow fever preventive.[8] He himself,
contracting the disease, sought a pledge from his attending physician
that, should he die, the doctor would sign a certificate attributing death
to some other cause. "If I die of yellow fever," Bosso explained, "people
will not buy my medicine any more!" Bosso did die. The doctor did not
yield to Bosso's plea, but gave the accurate cause of death on the certificate. Nonetheless, Bosso's heirs kept his Blessing profitably on the market through the city's last epidemic early in this century.

Indeed, after the mosquito-vector mode of yellow fever transmission became known, other nostrums for the yellow peril besides
Bosso's Blessing continued.[9] "Disinfective," a soap which "opens and
searches the pores – destroys and removes germs," was guaranteed to
heal mosquito bites and thus prevent yellow fever. So too did G.H.
Tichenor's Antiseptic. A 1905 advertisement read: "Mosquito Bites
Rendered Harmless...Rub in Well." Tichenor's label bore a Confederate
battle flag.[10]

What happened with yellow fever happened with cholera.

Those who could, Charles Rosenberg has noted, fled the inexorable advance of the mid-nineteenth-century cholera epidemics. "Those who stayed stocked up, if they could afford to, on the cholera specifics which were being hurriedly concocted, bottled, and labeled by apothecaries and free-lance quacks."[11] One remedy was heralded as made from a formula recorded in hieroglyphics on a papyrus scroll found under the mummified head of an Egyptian Pharaoh.[12] Another was alleged to be a famous Near Eastern Recipe which had wrought wondrous cures in Bethlehem and Jerusalem, in Sodom and Gomorrah.

Many Americans got their first inkling of the germ theory of disease from patent medicine advertising. Even before most American physicians became persuaded of the theory's truth, germ-eradicating nostrums assailed the mass market. The ubiquity of germs was an awesome and frightening concept, and popular periodicals made the most of it. "Let no man," warned a *New York Tribune* editorial of 1881, "call himself happy over his spring lamb and mint sauce; they are only wolves in disguise; typhus may hide its pallid face in an ice, or smallpox lie perdu in a strawberry."[13] The next year in *Harper's Weekly* Epps Cocoa was presented as a breakfast beverage which helped consumers resist disease. "Hundreds of subtle maladies," the text read, "are floating around us ready to attack wherever there is a weak point. We may well escape many a fatal shaft by keeping ourselves well fortified by pure blood and a properly nourished frame."[14]

The inescapable omnipresence of hostile germs too tiny to see provided the rationale for a new category of nostrums which may be called, after one of the first of them, the Microbe Killers.[15] Microbes posed a universal threat. Babies drew them in with their first breath, even if they had not already inherited them from their mother's womb. Germs ran rampant in barns and museums. They congregated in homes. They proliferated in hospitals. They infested the sky and the sea. A quarter of a million of the tiny demons could cluster on an inch of surface. There was absolutely no escape.

Slowly and laboriously, titans of natural science, like Koch and Pasteur, had learned that a few diseases were caused by bacteria. But these inquirers, decided a Texas gardener named William Radam, had been halting and short-sighted, more intent on theories than on facts.[16] The significant conclusion had evaded them, that "A microbe is a microbe," that all disease is in the end the same, that killing all microbes will cure all disease. Doctors, therefore, would no longer be needed, even for diagnosis, because Radam, who deemed killing germs in the body just like killing bugs on plants, had devised a total cure, a universal Microbe Killer.

Radam had patented his invention in 1886 under a description that disguised his true intent, "a New and Improved Fumigating Composition for Preserving and Purifying Purposes." His trademark conveyed his purpose better, depicting a determined man in a business suit wielding a huge club labeled "Microbe Killer" against a skeleton, its arms raised futilely in final defense. Radam's profits moved him from his Texas acres to a New York mansion overlooking Central Park. There he sat, microscope at the ready, through which he made photographs to frighten laymen into buying his potion. Evil-looking dots and blobs, his promotional pictures bore such titles as "Microbes in stale meat," "Fungus on a ripe strawberry," and the germs of piles, cancer, and uterine catarrh.

A Department of Agriculture chemist put the amount of water in Radam's pinkish liquid at 99.381 percent. As for the rest – what rest there was – a critical physician suggested that a product identical with the Microbe Killer could be made for less than five cents a gallon by adding to a gallon of well water an ounce of red wine, a dram of hydrochloric acid, and four drams of sulfuric acid.

Exposure of ingredients did little to slow Radam's booming market, and no regulatory laws yet existed to say him nay. The ex-gardener had long departed this life, and the 1906 Federal Food and Drugs Act was seven years old, when a shipment of 539 wooden boxes and 322 pasteboard cartons of the Microbe Killer was seized in Minnesota.[17] After an extensive trial, a jury, finding the label claims false and fraudulent, condemned the seized nostrum to destruction. "It was taken from the warehouse," a food and drug inspector in St. Paul wrote, "the cases broken open and the bottles and jugs smashed and the cases and cartons...burned."

Meanwhile microbe-phobia had spawned many similar nostrums. Red Raven was promoted as "absolute death to germs."[18] Hydrozone not only prevented yellow fever but conquered all germ-generated diseases.[19] When Samuel Hopkins Adams undertook to debunk the patent medicine business as "The Great American Fraud" in a famous series of articles for Collier's in 1905, he devoted a chapter to another universal germ-slayer.[20] "[F]rom the ashes of" the Microbe Killer's "glories," Adams wrote, "has risen a mightier successor, Liquozone."

This slightly acid water could cure, according to its advertising, "all diseases that begin with fever – all inflammations – all catarrh –

all contagious diseases – all the results of impure or poisoned blood." Promoted by bogus or distorted medical testimonials, by advertisements fashioned by one of the pioneer geniuses of the nascent advertising profession, and by false linkages to famous organizations – Hull House denied that it was one of the "Chicago Institutions which Constantly Employ Liquozone" – this nostrum flourished for a time, then went its way. Yet fear of germs, and in time, of viruses, retained the power to push people to unwise choices in health matters.

When a major epidemic of poliomyelitis broke out in 1916, the Bureau of Chemistry of the Department of Agriculture, charged with enforcing the 1906 law, issued special instructions to its inspectors to be on the alert for fraudulent remedies.[21] Experience had taught enforcement officials that "whenever a serious epidemic exists, unscrupulous dealers prey upon the fear or ignorance of the public by flooding the market with worthless, hastily prepared concoctions, for which they assert curative properties which have no foundation whatever in fact." A few such mixtures were quickly found. In New York City, the Health Department secured jail sentences for two exploiters.[22] One vended a polio preventive consisting of a cotton bag containing cedar shavings to be worn around the neck. The other sold as a cure for infantile paralysis a fusion of capsicum, sassafras, and alcohol.

Today's frightening epidemic, of course, is AIDS, acquired immuno-deficiency syndrome, caused by a newly discovered retrovirus. Each new announcement by the experts expands the predicted spread of AIDS, within the nation and within the world. The mortality of those afflicted seems certain, medications now in use only slowing somewhat the pace of the dread disease. Scientists seeking preventive vaccines and effective therapies express guarded optimism about long-range prospects but caution against hope for swift success. These circumstances open a broad door for the hyping of alternative options to the afflicted. So too does the existence of a preliminary stage, AIDS-related complex, that can be tested for, and that may or may not develop into the full-blown disease. So too does the knowledge that the nature of one's sexual experience, or of one's drug habits, or of one's history of blood transfusions, may well have brought exposure to the virus. Therefore, a range of products and treatments offered as preventives or as cures has pandered to the panicked. "Indeed," asserts a business periodical, "AIDS may already have created a multibillion-dollar market."[23]

In the diagnostic category, hair analysts have promised to detect oncoming AIDS.[24] And from Baton Rouge the worried may order by mail, for $99.95 plus $9 for shipment, The Home Aids Test Kit, to learn the worst in the privacy of one's own dwelling.[25]

For prevention, a room deodorizer has been promoted to cleanse the air of the AIDS virus.[26] A drug approved by the Food and Drug Administration as a spermicide has been vended both in a cream and in a condom lubricant.[27] Some studies have shown this drug to kill the AIDS virus *in vitro*, but the implication of *in vivo* efficacy is at present too bold. Another drug, the Anti-AIDS Pill ZPG-1, containing zinc compounds, may be used as "an oral lozenge, or as an anal or vaginal suppository."[28] However employed, the pill's promoter suggests: "Safe Sex May Now Be Possible!"

333

Two figures long prominent in the promotion of Laetrile, the disproven anti-cancer drug, Robert Bradford and Mike Culbert, now operate American Biologics, a firm with headquarters in San Francisco and a treatment center in Tijuana.[29] Here the proprietors have used live cell therapy in treating AIDS, the implantation in the human body of embryonic cellular extractions from calves, although sheep and goats, it is said, would also serve. Similar cell therapy, the cells secured from unborn donor animals, has been announced as one facet of a complex regimen of AIDS treatment – although "full-blown bed-ridden AIDS cases" are not accepted – provided at The Phoenix International Health Care Center of Coral Gables.[30] Other parts of the program include diet reformation, megadoses of intravenous vitamins, and "rectal implantation of ozone."

Across the country another complex therapeutic system may be resorted to by AIDS patients, at the Institute for Thermobaric Studies at Berkeley.[31] Here patients may hope to have their immunity competence restored by bathing, taking breathing and stretching exercises, eating a diet centered on organically grown vegetables, wearing nothing synthetic, and drinking some three gallons of ionized water a day.

At a clinic in Mexico, perfusion of ozone is employed as an AIDS treatment.[32] In a closed system, blood is withdrawn from the body, saturated with ozone, then reintroduced. Less physiologically intrusive, psychic treatments, sometimes broadcast on television, have been reported as having cured sufferers nearing death from AIDS.[33]

In Mexico an émigré German metallurgical engineer named Ewald Grass provides a bottled liquid containing medical herbs called Elixir Eubiotic which, he says, reduces AIDS symptoms within days.[34] Grass hopes he soon will have a device to treat stubborn cases, employing ultra-high-frequency impulses to reopen the "chakras" in patients' bodies. "Chakra" is a yoga designation for a center of spiritual power.

The botanical folk tradition has also been brought into play in Florida. In Pensacola, an untutored healer added AIDS to the long list of ailments his assortment of remedies could cure.[35] The sign on his store read: "The Old Path: God's Herbal Blessing to Mankind." This simple entrepreneur obviously hoped that the Old Path would cause patients to beat a new path to his door.

The macrobiotic diet, a decades-old regimen stressing whole grains, vegetables, soybeans, fish, and seaweed, has been pushed as a mode of restoring the shattered immunity in AIDS patients.[36] Still another major element in the alternative therapy arena with respect to AIDS is Vitamin C. In an article in *Medical Hypotheses*, a California orthopedic surgeon, Rogert F. Cathcart, III, reported his activities and his results.[37] "My previous experience," Cathcart stated in his abstract, "with the utilization of ascorbic acid in the treatment of viral diseases led me to hypothesize that ascorbate would be of value in the treatment of AIDS.... Preliminary clinical evidence is that massive doses of ascorbate (50-200 grams per 24 hours) can suppress the symptoms of the disease and can markedly reduce the tendency for secondary infections."

Before long Dr. Cathcart moved his message into the pages of a book for the masses, Michael Weiner's *Maximum Immunity*, with its long and cheering subtitle: *How to Fortify Your Natural Defenses Against Cancer, AIDS, Arthritis, Allergies – Even the Common Cold – and Free Yourself from Unnecessary Worry for Life!*[38] Here again Cathcart prescribes huge doses of ascorbate. "Patients are titrated to bowel tolerance (the amount that almost but not quite causes diarrhea)." Intravenous ascorbate may be needed to supplement the oral dosage in order "to scavenge all of the free radicals created by AIDS and the various secondary infections...." "With this protocol," Dr. Cathcart assures, "...a large percentage of patients will slowly go into clinical remission."

Nutritional scientists who have been skeptical of the value of megadose Vitamin C for other ailments may be expected to remain dubious of its use for AIDS.

As has long been true of assorted unorthodox cancer therapies, now the leading unproven AIDS therapies may be readily secured in Tijuana. Traffic across the border has been heavy, patients buying from drugstores without prescriptions the two drugs with the reigning reputation for treating AIDS.[39] Patients can pay several hundred dollars a month to secure sufficient tablets to meet the customarily prescribed dosages, and drugstore supplies occasionally are exhausted.[40] In October 1985 the Food and Drug Administration and the Customs Office announced that they would allow Americans to bring these drugs back across the border, so long as they are intended for their own personal use.[41] Larger quantities have been smuggled in for sale. A San Francisco Bay area AIDS group called the "Tooth Fairies" was active in this way.

The two drugs are ribavirin and isoprinosine, the first an anti-viral agent, the second an immune system booster. Sometimes the two are used in tandem. West coast physicians estimate that 25 to 30 percent of the AIDS patients they see have tried one or both drugs.[42] Neither has been approved by FDA for use in AIDS, although both drugs continue in clinical trials. Physicians have reported severe adverse reactions to the use of ribavirin, especially anemia and liver damage.[43]

Isoprinosine has gained the reputation of being "a cure looking for a disease." The California company that makes the drug has through the years sought approval from FDA to market it for a variety of ailments, without success.[44] Other nations have approved isoprinosine for various forms of anti-viral use, but FDA so far has not found evidence submitted by the manufacturer persuasive. On the same grounds, in February 1986 FDA turned down the company's New Drug Application to market isoprinosine for treating AIDS.[45] The agency also publicly scolded the firm's officials for holding a press conference at which false claims were made about the drug's utility in AIDS. Research in hand, FDA asserted, did not warrant the statement that the drug's use had restored basic immunity deficient in patients with AIDS-related complex. Nor had there been "a 50 percent reduction in the rate of progression to full scale AIDS among the same patients." Nor did the evidence justify the company claim that among AIDS patients receiving isoprinosine, with FDA permission, in compassionate treatment centers, 80 percent had derived clinical benefit. FDA would consider additional evidence from further trials, and the results of research continued to be reported in the literature, some of it with hopeful implications.[46] Journalistic observers, however, have expressed doubt that evidence of efficacy will ever be sufficient to convince FDA scientists to allow isoprinosine into the American marketplace as a treatment for AIDS.[47] Reporters also have doubted that, should such a negative decision occur, it would stop the fearful and the desperate from seeking out and using the drug.

Centers for Disease Control scientists point out that the use of

335

unproven drugs can hasten the death of AIDS victims.[48] Particularly the reliance on such drugs during a treatable attack of such an opportunistic infection as pneumonia, to which AIDS sufferers are prone, can be a fatal decision.

The AIDS crisis has even broader repercussions in the wonderland of alternative therapies. AIDS has stimulated a fearful fixation upon immunity. In commenting on these trends, Stephen Barrett cites a health food newspaper: "there is now a growing public recognition that AIDS, cancer, arthritis, even colds – very nearly the whole spectrum of infections and degenerative diseases – become manifest dangers only when the immune system is depressed. Strengthening the immune system... is clearly emerging as a health priority."[49] According to another health food journal, another factor besides AIDS has been at work. The discovery that President Ronald Reagan had developed cancer forced the public "to admit the possibility that large numbers of Americans are being stripped of their ability to resist infections, and...that no one, not even the President, was beyond the reach of many diseases."[50]

Michael Weiner's book, *Maximum Immunity*, seems obviously aimed at these popular perceptions, as does an earlier book, Stuart Berger's *Dr. Berger's Immune Power Diet*.[51] The dietary changes and vitamin and mineral supplementation required to "rebuild your immune system" have already brought a boom to health food stores.[52] The editor of the *Harvard Medical School Health Letter*, William Bennett, says of Berger, who studied at the Harvard School of Public Health, that his book should be considered fiction for it "is selling...a collection of quack ideas about food allergies that have been around for decades."[53] Jean Mayer, the nutritionist president of Tufts, where Berger received his medical degree, stated in a review of Berger's volume: "It is my hope that no future graduate of the Tufts medical school will exhibit as little knowledge of nutrition as does Dr. Berger in this book."[54]

This expansion of the immunity pitch represents one facet of the most significant trend in alternative medicine in the past few years. The proponents of assorted isms and ologies, having combined forces for lobbying state legislatures and the national Congress, have gone further.[55] Under the umbrella of holistic medicine, they have sought to create a paradigm for alternative therapies to pose against that of scientific medicine and to persuade the public that this alternative paradigm is just as philosophically respectable and therapeutically valuable as the medicine of modern science.

Two philosophers, Clark Glymour and Douglas Stalker, pointed to this campaign in an article entitled "Engineers, Cranks, Physicians, Magicians," in the *New England Journal of Medicine*.[56] They and other critics whom they have assembled expose the illogic of the alternative paradigm and its constituent strands in a book published in 1985 entitled *Examining Holistic Medicine*.[57] William Osler once suggested that no physician should be surprised to find a case of Warner's Safe Cure in the bedroom of his best patient.[58] In our own day, when observers of the phenomenon suggest that $26 billion a year may be expended on health fraud,[59] the need for keen scrutiny of commercial claims for health products and the necessity for vigorous enforcement of regulatory laws is apparent.

337

NOTES

1 In its original form, this paper was presented at a symposium arranged by Robert J.T. Joy on "Managing the Infected Patient: A Historical Perspective" at Suburban Hospital, Bethesda, Maryland, on May 30, 1986.

2 J. Barton, *Remarks on the Properties of Vital Air: and the Curative...Effects, Resulting from the Use of Vital Wine* (London: the proprietor, n.d.).

3 *Malignant Fevers Prevented or Cured* (London: the proprietor, [1806]), History of Medicine Division, National Library of Medicine.

4 J.H. Powell, *Bring Out Your Dead: The Great Plague of Yellow Fever in Philadelphia in 1793* (Philadelphia: University of Pennsylvania Press, 1949): 32-33, 257.

5 Lyman F. Kebler, "United States Patents Granted for Medicines During the Pioneer Years of the Patent Office," *Journal of the American Pharmaceutical Association* 24 (1935): 486-87; James Harvey Young, *The Toadstool Millionaires: A Social History of Patent Medicines in America Before Federal Regulation* (Princeton: Princeton Univ. Press, 1961): 32-33.

6 *Ibid.*, 16-30.

7 Jo Ann Carrigan, "The Saffron Scourge: A History of Yellow Fever in Louisiana, 1795-1905" (Ph.D. dissertation, Louisiana State University, 1961): 438-41.

8 Elizabeth Dwyer Vickers and F. Norman Vickers, "Notations on Pensacola's Medical History, 1873-1923," *Journal of the Florida Medical Association* 61 (1974): 99.

9 Carrigan, "Saffron Scourge," 438-41.

10 Bottle of Tichenor's Antiseptic Refrigerant in author's collection.

11 Charles E. Rosenberg, *The Cholera Years: The United States in 1832, 1849, and 1866* (Chicago: Univ. of Chicago Press, 1962): 23.

12 Young, *Toadstool Millionaires*, 38-79.

13 *New York Tribune*, April 29, 1881.

14 *Harper's Weekly*, January 7, 1882, 14.

15 Young, *Toadstool Millionaires*, 144-62.

16 *Ibid.*; William Radam, *Microbes and the Microbe Killers* (New York: published by the author, 1890).

17 James Harvey Young, *The Medical Messiahs: A Social History of Health Quackery in Twentieth-Century America* (Princeton: Princeton Univ. Press, 1967): 60-62.

18 Carrigan, "Saffron Scourge," 440.

19 Samuel Hopkins Adams, *The Great American Fraud* (Chicago: American Medical Association, 1906): 28.

20 *Ibid.*, 23-31.

21 "Fraudulent Infantile Paralysis 'Cures'," *American Journal of Public Health* 6 (1916): 821.

22 "Exploiters of Fraudulent Cures Prosecuted," *ibid.*, 1247.

23 Scott Ticer, David Hunter, and Reginald Rhein, Jr., "'Fast-Buck' Artists Are Making a Killing on AIDS," *Business Week*, December 2, 1985, 85-86.

24 "AIDS Tests and Cures," *American Family Physician* 28 (December 1983): 250.

25 Advertisement furnished by the Food and Drug Administration (FDA), Rockville, Maryland.

26 "AIDS Tests and Cures."

27 Conceptrol, Rub, and ForPlay Sensual Lubricant advertisements furnished by FDA.

28 Advertisements furnished by FDA.

29 "AIDS: False Hopes?," The MacNeil/Lehrer News Hour, Transcript #2638, November 6, 1985, 12-13.

30 [Miami] *Weekly News*, August 2, 1985, clippings furnished by Douglas Stalker, University of Delaware.

31 "AIDS: False Hopes?," 13-14; Mark L. Fuerst, "AIDS Patients Turn to Unproven Therapies," *Medical World News*, April 28, 1986, 62, 64.

32 Information provided by FDA.

33 Travis Hawk, "Psychic Healer Cures AIDS Victim on TV," unidentified clipping provided by Douglas Stalker.

34 Edward Cody, "AIDS Victims Seek Drugs in Mexico," *Washington Post*, September 10, 1986.

35 Randy Hammer, "The Old Path Leads to Store Closing," *Pensacola News Journal*, March 8, 1986.

36 Fuerst, "AIDS Patients," 62, 64.

37 Robert F. Cathcart, III, "Vitamin C in the Treatment of Acquired Immune Deficiency Syndrome (AIDS)," *Medical Hypotheses* 14 (1984): 423-33; Fuerst, "AIDS Patients," 62.

38 Cathcart, "Vitamin C Treatment Protocol for AIDS," in Michael Weiner, *Maximum Immunity* (Boston: Houghton Mifflin, 1986): 199-201.

39 "AIDS: False Hopes?," 10-12; Patrick McDonnell, "Desperate AIDS Victims Seek a Miracle in Tijuana," *[Los Angeles Times]*, undated clipping furnished by FDA.

40 Cody, "AIDS Victims Seek Drugs in Mexico."

41 McDonnell, "Desperate AIDS Victims Seek a Miracle in Tijuana."

42 Ticer *et al.*, "Fast-Buck Artists," 85-86.

43 "AIDS: False Hopes?," 11.

44 Donna K. H. Walters, "FDA Rejects AIDS Drug, Raps Firm," *Los Angeles Times*, February 22, 1986.

45 A Talk Paper, T86-14, February 20, 1986, and attachments.

46 Michael H. Grieco *et al.*, "In-vivo Immunomodulation by Isoprinosine in Patients with the Acquired Immunodeficiency Syndrome and Related Complexes," *Annals of Internal Medicine* 101 (1984): 206-7; P. Tsang *et al.*, "Immunopotentiation of Impaired Lymphocyte Functions in Vitro by Isoprinosine in Prodromal Subjects and AIDS

Patients," *International Journal of Immunopharmacology* 7 (1985): 511-14; *FDC Reports* 48 (November 3, 1986): In Brief.

47 Walters, "FDA Rejects AIDS Drug."

48 "AIDS Tests and Cures"; Fuerst, "AIDS Patients" 62.

49 Stephen Barrett, "'Strengthening the Immune System' – A Growing Fad," *Nutrition Forum* 3 (1986): 24.

50 Cited *ibid*.

51 Stuart M. Berger, *Dr. Berger's Immune Power Diet* (New York: New American Library, 1985).

52 Barrett, "Strengthening the Immune System."

53 William I. Bennett, "Review," *Harvard Medical School Health Letter* 10 (September 1985): 7.

54 Jean Mayer, "Tough to Swallow," *Wall Street Journal*, October 29, 1985, courtesy of Fredrick J. Stare, Harvard University.

55 James Harvey Young, "The Foolmaster Who Fooled Them," *Yale Journal of Biology and Medicine* 53 (1980): 555-66.

56 Clark Glymour and Douglas Stalker, "Engineers, Cranks, Physicians, Magicians," *New England Journal of Medicine* 308 (1983): 960-64.

57 Douglas Stalker and Clark Glymour, eds., *Examining Holistic Medicine* (Buffalo: Prometheus Books, 1985).

58 William Osler, *Aequanimitas* (Philadelphia: P. Blakiston's Son, 1922), 6.

59 Victor Herbert, "Unproven (Questionable) Dietary and Nutritional Methods in Cancer Prevention and Treatment," *Cancer* 58 (1986): 1934.

339

CHRISTIAN HUMANISM at the END
of the TWENTIETH CENTURY

BY DANIEL TAYLOR, BETHEL COLLEGE (ST. PAUL)

C hristian humanism: to some the term is a paradox, even self-contradictory, almost an embarrassment. Millions are comfort-able with one half of the phrase or the other – Christian or humanist – but precious few would embrace the two together. "What," Tertullian asked 1800 years ago, "has Athens to do with Jerusalem? What concord is there between the Academy and the Church?" "What," we might ask in caricature today, "has Sagan to do with Falwell?"

For most of those 1800 years, reflective Christians in the Church have answered Tertullian's question in a way he would not approve: "Athens has much to do with Jerusalem." We cannot fully know and serve God without participating in the world he created. It is an answer that, in one form or another, we must continue to give. The question today is whether either Athens or Jerusalem cares to listen.

Christian humanism has a long and honored history. It has powerfully shaped Western culture and Western Christendom. The list of people, from Justin Martyr to Augustine to Erasmus to Pascal to Milton to Newton, who could without distortion be called Christian humanists, is, up until the eighteenth century, almost coterminous with those who made the most visible contributions to Western society.

Since that time, Christian humanism has been in retreat, not-withstanding a still distinguished list that includes the likes of Jonathan Edwards, John Henry Newman, T.S. Eliot, Martin Luther King, and Alexander Solzhenitsyn. This retreat has resulted from the ferocious attacks of secularism on the one hand, and, to a lesser degree, funda-mentalist Christianity on the other.

The time is right for Christian humanism to reassert itself. Secular society has exhausted the moral capital it borrowed from Christianity at the same time it was declaring religion irrelevant. The great confidence with which it declared its liberation from traditional notions of transcendence has now almost entirely waned. A few people are still playing with mirrors in an effort to project an optimistic secu-larism, but their credibility is thin.

Before we can decide whether Christian humanism has a con-tribution to make, we must decide what it is. Here, as usual, the person who controls the definitions controls the argument. Tell me what you mean by the terms "Christian" and "humanist" and I will tell you if I am one.

The kind of Christian humanism I am interested in dances no jigs in defining the term "Christian." A Christian is one who believes Christ to be the Son of God, at once fully human and fully divine, and who devotes his or her life to trying to live out the implications of that belief. John Updike speaks for the Christian, I think, in the following passages from his poem "Seven Stanzas at Easter":

> Make no mistake: if He rose at all
> it was as His body;
> if the cells' dissolution did not reverse, the molecules reknit,
> the amino acids rekindle,
> The Church will fall.
> …
> Let us not mock God with metaphor,
> analogy, sidestepping transcendence;
> making of the event a parable, a sign painted in the faded
> credulity of earlier ages:
> let us walk through the door.
> …
>
> Let us not seek to make it less monstrous,
> for our own convenience, our own sense of beauty,
> lest, awakened in one unthinkable hour, we are embarrassed
> by the miracle,
> and crushed by remonstrance.
> …

The definition of "humanism" is more problematic. "Humanism" and "humanist" are terms which appear in all the major European languages in similar forms. Unfortunately, the history of the meaning of the term is different in each language and often varies considerably even within the same language.[1] Being a humanist has meant at one time or another everything from simply being a teacher of Latin and Greek literature to being an atheistic rationalist.

Ironically, both radical secularists and Christian fundamentalists have pushed the latter meaning as the definitive one for our age. At the same time, each is almost entirely ignorant of, or willfully distorts, the more holistic humanism that is the historical legacy of both the Church and the wider culture.

Christian humanists must reject this idiosyncratic equation of humanism with secularism, no matter who propounds it, because it distorts both history and revelation. Going to the radical secularists for a definition of humanism, as Christian fundamentalism does, is like going to the Ku Klux Klan for a definition of Christianity. Each embodies a perversion of what they claim to represent that makes them its opposite.

I offer as a brief definition of humanism the belief in the great value of human beings and of the entire human experience. Such a belief entails an interest in and valuing of the created world, human history and society, human creativity and destiny. It implies getting involved in this world, getting dirt under the fingernails, taking chances.

The Christian humanist differs from all secular humanists in grounding his or her understanding of the human in an understanding of God and of biblical revelation. We cannot answer any of the important questions about humankind without first understanding our position as creatures under God.

On the other hand, the Christian humanist differs from anti-humanistic Christians in being more likely to affirm the value of this world and of human involvement in it. Whereas the anti-humanist believer will focus on the Fall, the Christian humanist will balance that with belief in the original goodness and ultimate redemption of Creation. Whereas the anti-humanist will see the Incarnation as a divine rescue mission to snatch believers from an evil world, the Christian humanist will see God entering time as the clearest symbol of his valuing of the human experience.

Assuming the validity of Christian humanism as a concept, what in the late twentieth century is the state of Western society to which the Christian humanist proposes to make a contribution? Extended diagnoses of modern life abound. No age has more analyzed itself than ours and we are confronted daily with the bleak results of our endless self-appraisal. Recurring themes include the loss of a moral center resulting in a crisis of values, a growing awareness of the darker implications of unqualified pluralism, a waning faith in the ability of science and reason to solve our problems or answer our deepest questions, a feeling of having been cut off from the past yet having no confidence in the future, a growing awareness that education and prosperity do not seem adequate to cure our self-destructiveness. The list goes on and on.

And the Christian church? Rather than playing a leading role in shaping culture as it did for 1500 years, it now reacts to culture. The conservative church has largely withdrawn from a threatening society to cling to an escapist conception of Christ, and the liberal church has essentially abandoned the biblical Christ in a futile attempt to remain palatable to a secular culture.

Christian humanism has contributions to make to these two worlds, just as it has learned much from them. Among these are a sense of transcendence, a realistic understanding of evil, and a commitment to living simultaneously – and graciously – in both the temporal and the eternal.

Christian humanism reminds the secular culture, for example, of the reality and the necessity of transcendence. When we did away with God we were forced inexorably to what Emil Brunner calls "nothing but" definitions of humankind.[2] The human being is nothing but a collection of atoms, nothing but the product of economic and historical forces, nothing but a highly evolved animal, nothing but a genetic code, nothing but the product of unconscious drives, and so on.

Each of these has its logic and evidences, and each has its insights into one part of the complexity of the human condition. But when cut off from an understanding of transcendence, the transcendence of God in which humanity participates, each becomes not only a distortion of truth but potentially an instrument of death. Each contributes to the devaluation of individual human life that characterizes our day. Only if there is something about us which transcends our molecules is there any reason to prefer life to death or a just society to an unjust one.

We have tried living without genuine transcendence for well over a hundred years in our culture. It hasn't worked, and neither has the substitution of false or derivative forms of transcendence (History, Nature, personal self-fulfillment, social and political utopias). T.S. Eliot suggests that modern culture has not only stopped believing in transcendence; it can't even understand the concept any longer. Anyone concerned about our increasingly flattened and mechanistic world – secularist as well as believer – should welcome the efforts of the Christian humanist to keep alive our intuition of and search for something greater than ourselves.

A biblically informed humanism can also help our culture in another crucial task: taking evil seriously. When we no longer understand transcendence, we also no longer understand immanence. As one result we no longer understand evil. Perhaps in no area has orthodox Christianity been more derided in our century than in its conception

343

of evil as expressed in the doctrine of sin.

The very use of the word "sin" in intellectual circles is sufficient to elicit rolled eyes and condescending smiles. We have long
thought ourselves free of such "medieval" conceptions. Evil, if it exists
at all, is simply imbalance – psychological, physiological, or social. It
is to be cured by education, therapy, or laws.

Furthermore, "evil" is only a convenient label for what we individually or collectively do not like. Like "right" and "wrong," it is a
social construct that allows us to declare our preferences but which has
no basis in the ultimate nature of things. "Different strokes for different
folks," and the like.

Alexander Solzhenitsyn, among others, thinks differently. He
speaks as a Christian humanist when trying to answer the question of
what lies at the center of all that he writes:

> I would say that my outlook on life has been formed largely
> in concentration camps.... Those people who have lived in
> the most terrible conditions, on the frontier between life and
> death, be it people from the West or from the East, they all
> understand that between good and evil there is an irreconcil-
> able contradiction, that it is not one and the same thing –
> good or evil – that one cannot build one's life without regard
> to this distinction.[3]

And fundamental to the perception of the Christian humanist
is that evil is ultimately personal, that it lies in the hearts and minds
of each of us – not only in those of our enemies – and that the only
adequate response to this fact lies, again, in the recognition of transcendence and of a right relationship with a transcendent God.

A third contribution the Christian humanist can make at the
end of the twentieth century is to insist on the distinction between the
transient and the eternal. Again, as with notions of transcendence and
evil, modern secular orthodoxy has made quasi-heretical any talk of
eternal verities, absolutes, or unchanging values. This is the age of process, change, flux, and relativism. It is not, of course, a simple question
of either/or. Some things change, some stay the same; some things stay
the same even as they change; and, to be complete, some things change
even as they stay the same.

Christian humanism is in a unique position to affirm both
change and stasis, both time and eternity, both the relative and the
absolute, both the physical and the spiritual, both God and man. It not

344

only can affirm these things; it tries to hold them in tension together, because reality lies not at the extremes or in a lukewarm, mid-way compromise, but in the extremes held simultaneously as one.

In practical terms, the Christian humanist may work to preserve the environment, or for social justice or a strong and fair economy, but will never mistake those things for ultimate ends in themselves. He or she will see these as important symptoms of underlying realities having to do with God's creation and the nature of human beings.

Christian humanism is in a position to recognize, in a way the secularist cannot, what has eternal significance and what has only transient interest, what will make a difference for eternity and what will never make any genuine difference at all. While not foolproof, this perception can help separate the wheat from the chaff as one chooses how to use one's energies in the brief time allotted each individual life.

If Christian humanism has something important to offer Western culture at this point in history, it also has a role to play in the Church. The liberal church must be reminded again that the Gospel was and continues to be "foolishness to the Greeks." If one is afraid to appear a fool to contemporary secularism, there are many safer ways to try to be a good person than claiming to be a Christian.

The conservative church, on the other hand, perhaps needs to be reminded that while one should be willing to seem a fool, it is not an absolute requirement. Foolishness comes easily enough to us all without going out of the way to seek it. The conservative church has been locked into an anti-intellectual, anti-world box for most of this century. At times it has aggressively pursued irrelevance. As it clumsily but legitimately re-enters the public sphere, it needs to moderate its combative defensiveness. It needs to learn again to speak a language the common culture can understand, without diluting the nature of its message.

Christian humanism can help it do so. It can remind the conservative church that the world was created by God and that it is good and right that Christians be at the forefront of exploring and shaping it. It can act as the memory of this church, recounting the long history of Christian risk-takers who in following God found themselves deeply engaged in the life and learning of this world.

Christian humanism can reaffirm and explore the implications of the doctrines of creation and Incarnation. Because all are made in the image of God, all (believers and unbelievers alike) are capable of insight into truth, of the creation of beauty, of the expression of love. Therefore,

DANIEL TAYLOR

we can affirm again with Aquinas that all truth is God's truth and that we will look for it in all the nooks and crannies of the human experience.

And to both the larger culture and to the Church, the Christian humanist can model a keen awareness of the centrality of grace. Life is difficult. Survival, spiritual as well as physical, is not assured. Our failures and failings – our sins – are many. Can we not offer to each other some small part of the grace that God offers us?

Christians, who above all should understand and demonstrate grace, seem to have forgotten how to act graciously toward their supposed enemies. They have adopted and sometimes exceeded the tactics of the battlefield – the arrogant assertion, the sneer of condescension, the vilification of all who disagree. Christian and secularist alike wrap themselves in moral superiority, confident that all truth will die when they do.

The secular version of graciousness is civility, but civility is a lesser virtue and not adequate to the needs of the time. Grace entails a notion of forgiveness, of unmerited favor, that goes beyond the propriety and sophistication of civility. The Christian humanist can look to Augustine with his affirmation of the earthly city even as he showed its limitations, to St. Francis, to Erasmus, to Bonhoeffer, to Martin Luther King, for a tradition of grace under pressure that can bring a healing spirit to our too often internecine struggles.

The task suggested here is not an easy one. The Christian humanist tries to bear witness to what T.S. Eliot calls "the timeless moment," that epiphany in which one experiences the intersection of the eternal and the temporal. Eliot himself testifies to how evanescent and difficult the task of conveying those moments can be.

Will all these potential contributions be welcomed? Most likely not. William Buckley worried aloud, while interviewing Malcolm Muggeridge, that the slightest attempt to introduce specifically Christian perspectives into a conversation at a typical highbrow dinner party risks eliciting knowing looks, and the epithet "Christer." Perhaps the only thing to match the ignorance of most fundamentalist Christians about the "humanism" they deplore is the ignorance of most fundamentalist secularists about the Christianity they reject. If Christian fundamentalists are still fighting nineteenth-century battles over such things as evolution, secularists often deal only in nineteenth-century caricatures of the nature of Christianity.

The truth is that both the Church and secular culture will be much the worse if Christian humanism fades into silence. The Church will lose an essential part of its link to the culture to which it is called to minister. It will lose part of God's intention for His creation and much of its memory of what the Church at its best has been about through the centuries.

The secular culture will lose a sometime ally and needed critic. Though their differences are crucial, there are important values the Christian humanist shares with humanists of any stripe. The world will be a diminished place if one can speak those values only in a secular voice. Similarly, Christian humanism can help the broader culture critique its own orthodoxies and discover unseen implications of its doctrines, just as secularism has forced Christianity to look closely at itself for the last 200 years.

It is not necessary, however, that great numbers embrace the vision of Christian humanism for it to have an important effect. At one time in this century there were fewer than a dozen Russian Marxists. At one time there were only a dozen or so followers of Christ. Western society may never again be Christian in the way it once was, and the Church may be the better for it. But truth has a power beyond numbers. And the truths the Christian humanist has to offer can make a difference even in a society which does not acknowledge their Source.

NOTES

1   Giustinian, Vito R. "Homo, Humanus, and the Meaning of 'Humanism.'" *Journal of the History of Ideas,* 44 (1985), 167-95.

2   Brunner, Emil. *Christianity and Civilization: First Part, Foundations* (London: Nisbet, 1948).

3   Solzhenitsyn, Aleksandr. "The Vision of Solzhenitsyn" (Columbia, S.C.: Southern Educational Communications Assoc., 1976), p. 4. This is a transcript of a *Firing Line* program telecast on March 27, 1976. Produced by Warren Stiebel.

THE COMMUNION of SAINTS:
LEST the JOURNEY BE TOO LONG

BY ROSE HOOVER, THE CENACLE

I believe in the Holy Spirit; the holy Catholic Church; the communion of saints; the forgiveness of sins; the resurrection of the body; and the life everlasting. Amen.

In my Presbyterian youth, when the Apostles' Creed was recited every Sunday morning in church, this last paragraph seemed disconnected, as if left-over bits of doctrine not fitting anywhere else were unceremoniously tacked onto the end. My inclination, however, was to recite it all at once, in a single breath, so that the six articles of faith would have seemed to the uninitiated to be only one. Although there was no theological significance that I was aware of in this rush toward the final 'Amen,' it expressed, perhaps, a truth not yet grasped on a conscious level. For in reality these six are not isolated fragments at all, but are so intimately related that no one of them can stand without the others in the Christian life. What is more, the relatively humble doctrine of the communion of saints seems to me to be a vital expression of our belief in and experience of the other five.

As it was originally used, the term "communion of saints" probably signified a sharing in the "holy things": those mysteries and blessings in which the followers of Jesus participated, including baptism, the breaking of bread, and the hearing of the word of God. It followed that this communion included also the fellowship of God's people.[1] More recently, however, there has been a regrettable tendency to limit the communion of saints to an exchange between individuals here on earth and those who have died. Departing from this narrow notion, I would like to consider the doctrine as embracing the living, the dead in Christ and a very broad expanse of "holy things."

THE COMMUNION of SAINTS, KAIROS and THE HOLY SPIRIT

OCCASIONALLY – very rarely, I imagine, for most of us – we may be given glimpses of beauty, as if a veil were removed or a shade opened to reveal something that has been there all along, but which we do not ordinarily have the eyes to see. These glimpses of beauty, whether of our relationship with creation, with another person or with the dead, witness to what will be in the future which is Christ – and in reality to what already is. It is as if we were being allowed to see with God's eyes. In whatever form they occur, as love, as harmony, as peace, as truth, or simply as beauty itself, these glimpses show us our connectedness in the Spirit with these holy ones and holy things and indicate what our stance toward them is to be.

It is in what we might call "privileged time" that these glimpses of beauty take place. This is time, not in its flow from past through present to future, but time in its fullness. The first sort of time can be expressed by the Greek word *chronos*, chronological time, time which can be measured. For the most part, *chronos* is the way our modern Western culture conceives of time. Privileged time, on the other hand, is more accurately expressed by the word *kairos*, time seen as opportunity. "Behold, now is the acceptable time," says Paul to the church at Corinth; "behold, now is the day of salvation."[2] Although the New Testament uses both words, *kairos* is used almost twice as often as *chronos*, and in both testaments, biblical time tends to be *kairos* time.

It is time experienced as *kairos* which enables our looking back and our looking forward to be more than merely chronological. In the Eucharist we find the primary manifestation both of this privileged looking back (or *anamnesis*) and a privileged looking forward toward the *eschaton*, or last things. Remembering was, for the Hebrew people, much more than the simple exercise of an intellectual faculty. For one thing, it was primarily a communal action, rather than an individual one. And remembering was closely related to the very reality of what was being remembered. For example, past sins remembered were thereby brought into the present to have power over the sinner.[3] Therefore, when Jesus says, "Do this in remembrance [*anamnesin*] of me" (Luke 22:19), he intends more than a mere chronological looking back over time measurable, but lost. On the contrary, this remembrance carries with it into the present the reality of that past event, so that the present moment becomes an "acceptable time," the "day of salvation."

If *anamnesis* is not just the recollection of an event, neither is it the making present of an episode in its barrenness. In the Christian context, it is memory healed and the past redeemed. Thus, in the light of the Resurrection, the horror of the cross is transformed and becomes a revelation of the glory of God. John can show Jesus saying, as Judas goes off to betray him, "Now is the Son of man glorified, and in him God is glorified" (13:31). This past event, transfigured through the Resurrection, is joined to the present moment by means of the communual remembering of the body of believers, so that we also may be one with the paschal mystery in our communion.

It is significant, however, that the "memorial acclamation" or *anamnesis* of the eucharistic celebration looks also towards the future. Past and future both become part of the *now*. Indeed we proclaim the fullness of time:

> Christ has died;
> Christ is risen; [note the present tense: we live in the
> *now* of the post-Resurrection age]
> Christ will come again.

Our communion unites us not only with the past sacrifice of Christ, but also with our future. In his body and blood we have the sign of that consummation of all things, when Christ will come again; and in that sign we may participate even now in the reality to come.

Time as *kairos*, as opportunity, allows us to perceive our own past and future as redeemed in Christ. In ordinary time, our memory, like the Church's collective memory of the Passion, contains fearful and hurtful things, and the future often appears threatening. Memory redeemed and healed, however, transforms the very real pain and evil of the past into liberating signs. In the light of the Resurrection, our own past, like the cross of Jesus, is touched by grace, revealing the beauty and truth that in fact were there, although we did not know it. Our past and those whom we knew and loved are made holy in Christ.

The future, too, is made not only holy, but welcoming. By grace we may experience the validity of Julian of Norwich's declaration that "all will be well, and all will be well, and every kind of thing will be well."[4] That this redeemed future is in some mysterious way a reality even now is beyond our ability to grasp. But in a *kairos* moment, the knowledge that this is so may be glimpsed, and the fear that can overwhelm our human existence is mercifully eased.

When the fullness of the present moment embraces the past and the future, neither of which is seen as menacing, the *other* is no longer viewed as adversary, rather as one participating with us in the love of God. Because of this, communion becomes possible. In his book, *The Go-Between God*, John V. Taylor asks:

> But what is this force which causes me to see in a way in which I have not seen? What makes a landscape or a person

or an idea come to life for me and become a presence towards which I surrender myself? I recognize, I respond, I fall in love, I worship – yet it was not I who took the first step. In every such encounter there has been an anonymous third party who makes the introduction, acts as a go-between, makes two beings aware of each other, sets up a current of communication between them. What is more, this invisible go-between does not simply stand between us but is activating each of us from inside. Moses approaching the burning bush is no scientific observer; the same fiery essence burns in his own heart also. He and the thorn-bush are caught and held, as it were, in the same magnetic field.[5]

This "go-between," Taylor concludes, is the Holy Spirit. It is the Spirit who awakens us to the fullness of the moment, to time as opportunity. It is the Spirit who opens our eyes to mystery and to beauty, who introduces us, so to speak, to each other. It is the Spirit in us and between us who brings about communion and without whom there is no communion. In fact, the early Church seems to find the creation of communication and communion intrinsic to the action of the Spirit. The pouring out of the Holy Spirit at Pentecost was accompanied by an extraordinary gift of communication. And in the trinitarian blessing at the end of the Second Letter to the Corinthians, the Spirit's particular gift is described as communion: "The grace of the Lord Jesus Christ and the love of God and the fellowship of the Holy Spirit be with you all" (13:14). The word *koinonia*, translated here as 'fellowship,' can also be rendered 'communion' or 'participation [in].'

When one participates in the Holy Spirit, there is also a communion with others. Communion with God and fellowship with God's people are inseparable. As we read in the First Letter of John: "That which we have seen and heard we proclaim also to you, so that you may have fellowship with us; and our fellowship is with the Father and with his Son Jesus Christ" (1:3). Because our communion is with God, we may also be in communion with others. What is more, we may even go so far as to say that to refuse communion with others is to refuse it with God.

During the Eucharist, which is the primary sign of our oneness, we glimpse that banquet where our communion will be accomplished and where there will be no division. By praying the "Our Father" ("thy Kingdom come...forgive us our trespasses, as we forgive those who have trespassed against us"), by offering the sign of peace, and by receiving the body and blood of Christ, we express our *desire* to live in that future where all will be one in Christ and our *willingness* to commune with all who are called. Among those invited to the banquet may very well be our worst enemies. A refusal to sit down with them does not exclude them, but on the contrary, represents our own refusal of the banquet.

THE COMMUNION of SAINTS, the HOLY CATHOLIC CHURCH, and the FORGIVENESS of SINS

352　THE SAME SPIRIT who opened the eyes and heart of Moses to perceive the divine through the burning bush works in us to open our eyes and hearts to each other:

> From now on, therefore [says Paul], we regard no one from a human point of view; even though we once regarded Christ from a human point of view we regard him thus no longer. Therefore, if anyone is in Christ, he is a new creation; the old has passed away, behold, the new has come. All this is from God, who through Christ reconciled us to himself and gave us the ministry of reconciliation. [II Cor. 5:16-18]

The Holy Spirit thus brings into being the community of those who have been redeemed. We are not created for isolation. On the contrary, through Christ who became one of us, we are welcomed as part of the family of God. Our relations in this family include Mary the mother of Jesus, the apostles, the martyrs, the saints throughout the ages, known or unrecognized, and a motley assortment of kin. This is the universal communion of all who have lived, however imperfectly, in Christ, and all who have died in him: all who, by the Spirit of Jesus who breaks down barriers and causes strange tongues to be understood, are one in God, whether or not they are conscious of their union.

From time to time a deep sense of our own belonging to this holy assembly may awaken in us. This may happen, for example, when we are made aware of the love of God through another person who accepts us as we are and perhaps calls us beyond where we are. It may happen when we are given the grace to see another or to see ourselves with God's eyes. More often, however, we will have to recall the truth of our unity, letting our *anamnesis* become a means for creating communion in the present moment.

When our eyes are enlightened by the Spirit, so that "we regard no one from a human point of view," when we stand in amazement at the beauty which God sees, then not to forgive is out of the question. Reconciliation is the only alternative for beings who radiate the divine like the burning bush. It is the only option for those who are already fundamentally one. Our ministry of reconciliation is to witness to God's forgiveness with our own and to participate in that reconciliation with God and with God's people which brings everyone into the fullness of communion.

The ministry of forgiveness and reconciliation is basic to the very identity of the Church, herself reconciled by the life, death, and resurrection of Jesus. As God's people we are one even in our sinfulness. Our communion in the holy things necessarily includes communion with each other in mutual repentance and in mutual forgiveness. It is in company with the people of God that we draw near to God and become signs to each other of God's tender mercies.

THE COMMUNION of SAINTS and the RESURRECTION of the BODY

THROUGH THE HOLY SPIRIT who enables us to be reconciled with God and with each other, we experience and begin to make manifest the redemption of the whole world. This redemption is not limited to the spiritual, but embraces as well the bodily aspects of reality. "We know," says Paul, "that the whole creation has been groaning in travail together until now" (Rom 8:22). In ordinary, chronological time – after the Fall, so to speak – we find ourselves alienated from the physical world of which we are a part. Nature, for example, not only provides for us, but destroys us; and we, in turn, pollute the atmosphere and the water, drain the wetlands, replace the forests and jungles with cities. In the cities themselves, there would seem to be an enemy lurking around every corner. Not even in solitude are we safe, for our own bodies betray us.

But if creation groans, it groans "together," and its groans signal a birth. Paul uses two Greek verbs to indicate this: *sustenazo*, to groan together; and *sunodino*, to suffer in pain (as the pain of childbirth) together. There is a sense in which the communion of holy ones and holy things encompasses all of God's creation. All cry out in pain as one, and all benefit from the new life of the children of God. Indeed, according to Isaiah, the messianic age is to be one of harmony among all creatures, when the time of groaning will be past:

The wolf shall dwell with the lamb,
    and the leopard shall lie down with the kid,
and the calf and the lion and the fatling together
    and a little child shall lead them....
The sucking child shall play over the hole of the asp,
    and the weaned child shall put his hand on the adder's den.
They shall not hurt or destroy
    in all my holy mountain;
for the earth shall be full of the knowledge of the Lord
    as the waters cover the sea. [11:6, 8-9]

354   It is through the resurrection of Jesus that we know that the
new age has already been inaugurated. In spite of the very evident remnants of the old, we believe that what was has already been overcome.
While it is true that we must wait for the fulfillment of the Kingdom of
God, Christ's resurrection is the witness to the new life that is ours in
him. It is the gauge that the earth is already full of the knowledge of the
lord. Karl Rahner puts it this way:

> What we call his resurrection – and unthinkingly take to be
> his own private destiny – is only the first surface indication
> that all reality, behind what we usually call experience...has
> already changed in the really decisive depth of things. His
> resurrection is like the first eruption of a volcano which shows
> that God's fire already burns in the innermost depths of the
> earth... The new creation has already started, the new power
> of a transfigured earth is already being formed from the world's
> innermost heart, into which Christ descended by dying. Futili-
> ty, sin and death are already conquered in the innermost realm
> of all reality, and only the 'little while' (which we call history
> 'A.D.') is needed until what has actually already happened ap-
> pears everywhere in glory, and not only in the body of Jesus.[6]

It is more than obvious that our own resurrection has not yet
"appeared everywhere in glory." However, while futility, sin and death
seem to prevail we do, even now, catch glimpses of what is to come,
of what in truth is already ours. There are graced moments when the
harmony of a renewed creation is revealed as already present. It is as
if we beheld the heart of reality. At these times, the mutual trust and
peace of the messianic age can be directly experienced, if only for a
moment.

There are persons whose lives appear to demonstrate in a special way this harmony of what will be. For example, the legends of Francis of Assisi indicate that he was able to enter into the covenant promised in the Book of Hosea "with the beasts of the field, the birds of the air, and the creeping things of the ground" (2:18). Created things which for others would have been threatening, or for which others would have constituted a threat, were for Francis participants in God's love and therefore related to him in a mysterious way: "our brother fire," even "our sister, the death of the body" ("Canticle of the Sun").

Though of a very different style from that of Francis, Ignatius of Loyola was also gifted with a vision into the true nature of created things. For him, this vision was expressed as finding God in all things. In the "Contemplation to attain the love of God," which serves as a transition between the intensity of the Spiritual Exercises and everyday life, Ignatius presents the following point for prayer:

> This is to reflect how God dwells in creatures: in the elements giving them existence, in the plants giving them life, in the animals conferring upon them sensation, in man bestowing understanding. So he dwells in me and gives me being, life, sensation, intelligence; and makes a temple of me, since I am created in the likeness and the image of the Divine Majesty.[7]

When we turn to the Spanish, we see that the one making the Exercises is to do more that just 'reflect' on God's indwelling. Ignatius uses here a word which is one of the favorites in his spiritual vocabulary: *mirar*. The exercitant is, like Ignatius himself, to look, to gaze: "*mirar cómo Dios habita en las criaturas...y así en mí.*"[8] Through the grace of God, one is to contemplate the reality of God's presence in physical creation and in one's own being, the very temple of the divine.

Because of this presence, all creation can reveal God. And the human being, fashioned in the image of the Creator, has a special relationship with the rest of creation. During the First Week of the Spiritual Exercises, when one becomes vividly aware of personal sinfulness, Ignatius makes this relationship clear:

> This is a cry of wonder accompanied by surging emotion as I pass in review all creatures. How is it that they have permitted me to live, and have sustained me in life! Why have the angels, though they are the sword of God's justice, tolerated me, guarded me and prayed for me! Why have the saints interced-

ed for me and asked favors for me! And the heavens, sun, moon, stars and the elements; the fruits, birds, fishes and other animals – why have they all been at my service! [Exx 60]

This is the communion of God's holy ones, a sharing of blessings between creation at all levels and the graced sinner. Creation is in complicity with God to pour out goodness and love on this one who is aware of deserving nothing. Not only the angels and saints, but also physical reality – inanimate objects, plants, animals, themselves held in being by God's indwelling – all work together to support the person whom, like them, God has made and continues to sustain.

356　　　　If nature participates in the brokenness and blessings of creation, so does civilization, or what we might call human creation. In its fallen state, the city always carries with it the risk of misery or menace, both of which are described in Scripture, and both of which are more than evident in modern urban life. Even the biblical Jerusalem becomes the menacing city, "killing the prophets and stoning those who are sent" (Mt. 23:37). The Book of Lamentations, where the poet-author grieves over the desolation of Jerusalem, provides a description of urban misery to rival anything in twentieth-century journalism:

> [Infants and babes] cry to their mothers,
> 　"Where is bread and wine?"
> as they faint like wounded men
> 　in the streets of the city,
> as their life is poured out
> 　on their mothers' bosom. [2:11-12]

It is probably easier to envisage in nature the beauty of what will be than it is to picture it in today's cities. As Hopkins writes, "All is seared with trade; bleared, smeared with toil; / And wears man's smudge and shares man's smell" ("God's Grandeur"). Redeemed, however, the city will become holy, the new Jerusalem, part of the new heaven and the new earth. Here, as in all creation, God will dwell. But God already dwells in the city, as do the saints, God's holy ones. Because of this, we may become aware, even if momentarily, that as the crowds and buildings surround us, so does the love of God. The same Jerusalem where "we must pay for the water we drink" (Lam. 5:4) is also the site of "the river of the water of life" (Apoc. 22:1). She is transformed into the image of eternal life, where "death shall be no more, neither shall there be mourning nor crying nor pain any more, for the former things have passed away" (Apoc. 21:4).

To say that the resurrection of physical creation is already a reality is not to claim that pain and brokenness are unreal. Jesus did not treat them as such in others, nor did he experience his own cross as either unreal or unimportant. Indeed, we are faced with a paradox. On the one hand, all is well, for all is in the hand of God and moves toward the future which is Christ and which is with us even now. On the other hand, our world is not as a good and loving God intended it to be. Curiously enough, the vision of the first half of this paradox does not ordinarily make one content with the second half. Glimpsing the beauty of other creatures and our relationship with them in the Spirit, one can no longer deny that something more is possible: something more than destitution, war, the destruction of the environment; more than sickness, alienation, death. This knowledge can be unsettling. According to Jürgen Moltmann:

> Christianity is completely and entirely and utterly hope... For the Christian faith lives from the raising of the crucified Christ and reaches out towards the promises of Christ's universal future. But that means that the hoping person can never come to terms with the laws and necessities of the world. He can never come to terms with the inescapability of death or with the evil that continually breeds evil. For him the resurrection of Christ is not merely consolation in suffering; it is also the sign of God's protest against suffering. That is why whenever faith develops into hope it does not make people serene and placid; it makes them restless. It does not make them patient; it makes them impatient. Instead of being reconciled to existing reality they begin to suffer from it and to resist it.[9]

In no case, therefore, may we ignore the sufferings of the world in which we live. There are things which can and must be changed in order to make the promised beauty and harmony more visible in everyday life. And because the essential oneness of God's people is actual as well as potential, how can we be other than peacemakers, healers, bearers of mercy and justice? Nevertheless, when all is said and done, there is brokenness which we cannot fix. There is pain beyond our ability to alleviate. Where we have done what can be done, our communion may imply simply gazing in helplessness and in reverence before the mystery of one who suffers.

It is here that we encounter a second paradox, one which originates in the first. Ignatius and Francis both passed by the way of the cross in order to reach that luminous awareness of God in all things and the relatedness of all creatures. But this must be said carefully, as it has in the past been readily translated into a glorification of suffering contrary to scriptural tradition. God's will, after all, is the elimination of death, grief and pain (Apoc. 21:4). It is not by chance, however, that Ignatius' contemplation of God's indwelling in creation comes only after deep prayer on the passion and resurrection of Jesus, or that Francis' love of nature coexists with a profound devotion to, even union with, Christ crucified.

Eloi Leclerc, a twentieth-century descendant of Francis of Assisi, concludes his book-length study of the "Canticle of the Sun" by recounting a personal experience. Near the end of World War II, he and a few of his Franciscan brothers were among thousands being transported by train from Buchenwald to Dachau. It is not necessary to describe the cruel conditions of this voyage, during which hundreds died. It will suffice to quote Leclerc who says, "Everything we can see, every experience we must undergo, tells us we are in the grip of an iron law, handed over to the play of blind forces – and that this, and this alone, is reality." It is, he adds, "reality where the Father has no place!" and, "Black night fills our souls."[10]

On the twenty-first day of a trip which should have taken only a few days, the small group of Franciscans in the packed coal car gathers around one of their brothers who is dying and sings, with Francis, of brother sun, sister moon, brothers wind and air, and "those who grant pardon for love of you." Surprisingly enough, the song is not forced. "It rises spontaneously out of our darkness and nakedness, as though it were the only language fit for such a moment" (p. 234). What has happened? Simple acts of human kindness and ordinary things of nature have taken on a new significance, point to something beyond themselves:

> Where do they come from, this purity and innocence that suddenly lay hold of us through these humble realities? Whence the limpid radiance that bathes the world but is perceptible only amid extreme poverty?... The purity and innocence do not originate in us. They do, however, well up within us, at the deepest level of the soul, and when they do, they restore childhood there. It is not our gaze that brings them into being; on the contrary, it is they that enable us to see things once

again as children do. But this purified vision is attained only through a kind of agony, when we have become poor enough to welcome such purity and innocence. What chaos we must have within us if we are to see the world born once again in the light! It is always in the shadow of the crucified Christ that the Christian, at the end of his journey, recovers the vision of a child. [pp. 235-36]

Leclerc, having been through the horrors of the concentration camps and the hell of a voyage such as this, does not romanticize suffering or seek it out. But his small group had seen a beauty beyond the pain and evil which had threatened to become for them the only reality. When their brother died, he says, "a supernatural peace had filled our hearts" (p. 236).

THE COMMUNION of SAINTS and LIFE EVERLASTING

A CASUAL READING of Scripture, as well as a glance into our own inner being, should be sufficient to convince us of the extent to which fear is prone to take hold of the human heart. Even when our lives are relatively free of difficulty, we tend not to be at ease. God, it seems, must constantly reassure us. Over and over God says, in one way or another, "Do not be afraid" (see Is. 43:1 and Lk. 1:30). Perhaps the deepest fears of the human heart are the fears of rejection and of annihilation. In fact, rejection is a manner of annihilation and annihilation is a radical form of rejection. The communion of saints mitigates both of these fears. It is a way in which God tells us, through his holy ones and holy things, not to be afraid. First, communion is always an experience of acceptance; and acceptance in the Holy Spirit by another being is nothing less than a sign of the unconditional acceptance of God. We are welcome in the world; we are welcome among the company of God's people; and we are welcome in the love of God.

Second, the communion of saints is a witness to that acceptance and love which literally keep us in being. Of course, this continuation of existence is manifested by the continued existence of the saints themselves. But more than that, we are shown that we are loved far too much to be annihilated. The family of God, to which we belong, is not like many families, who for one reason or another stop loving each other. Those who have gone before us persist in caring for us. Their love for us is greater now than when they were in this life. Rahner says that when we pray for the dead, they are also praying their own prayer for us. He imagines them praying like this:

> Lord, grant eternal rest to them whom we love – as never before – in your love...and may your perpetual light shine on them as on us. May it shine upon them now as the light of faith, and then in eternity, as the light of blessed life.[11]

So those who have died remain connected to us. They have entered into the life of God and, as Rahner says, "are silently summoning" us to enter into God's life.[12] They have arrived at home, where we will one day be with them. Our communion with them, the sharing of blessings between living and dead, reveals that, indeed, they have not entirely departed from us. Once again, we may be given glimpses of this truth which our memory may carry with us into ordinary time. More often, we may have to rely on the collective experience of the Church in its *anamnesis* of those who have gone before us.

Of what use, might we ask, are our experiences of communion, our glimpses of what is and what will be? On the one hand, the question itself seems ungrateful, as if one were inquiring about the usefulness of a brilliant sunset. We have already seen that the life and love of those who have died are signs to us that we are loved and held in being by God. Besides this, our union with God's holy ones incites us to forgiveness and love of others. The gifts of God, however, are very purposeful, and the communion of saints has another and very practical function in the divine plan.

When Elijah, discouraged and afraid, fled into the wilderness, an angel brought him food, touched him, and said, "Arise and eat, else the journey will be too great for you." Elijah ate, "and went in the strength of that food forty days and forty nights to Horeb the mount of God" (1 Kg. 19:7, 8). So for us, our moments of communion, our glimpses of beauty, become food for the journey. They are our *viaticum*. Without them, the journey would be too long; but through *anamnesis*, these glimpses can sustain us and carry us forward toward the mountain of the Lord.

Jesus, too, both needed and was given special moments of communion with God and with others. Four obvious times of communion in the life of Jesus were his baptism, his stay in the desert, his transfiguration and his Last Supper. At his baptism, the communion was with God: he heard the accepting and affirming voice of the Father saying, "This is my beloved Son, with whom I am well pleased" (Mt.

360

3:17). Jesus was also given a glimpse into the truth of his own identity before God, as our glimpses suggest to us the graced nature of our being. He went in the strength of this spiritual food for forty days and forty nights, and was sustained through difficult temptations.

At the end of his forty days in the desert, Jesus' communion was with non-human holy ones. We are told that "angels came and ministered to him" (Mt. 4:11). At the transfiguration, Jesus communicated with Moses and Elijah, who had gone before him. What is more, Peter, James, and John were given an extraordinary glimpse of the beauty of Jesus. And at the Last Supper, the communion of Jesus was with his friends. We can imagine that on each occasion he was given the nourishment he needed at the moment.

One of the Church's prayers for the dying person who has just been anointed and has received communion contains the following petition:

> May our brother (sister) N.,
> who has been refreshed with food
> and drink from Heaven,
> safely reach your kingdom of light and life.[13]

Like Elijah, like Jesus, we are given the food we need for our journey. We are fed, and we are drawn toward and into the Kingdom of God – which lies before us, but which, in truth, is already here within us and among us. And like the last paragraph of the Apostles' Creed, nothing is unconnected in the rush to the final "Amen." No, God's creation is not made of isolated fragments, but moves together in the Holy Spirit to that fulfilment when all will be one in God, and God will be all in all.

NOTES

1   In both the Greek and Latin versions the clause is ambiguous. The word *sanctorum*, because it can be construed as either masculine or neuter, may be the genitive plural of *sancti* (Gk. *hagioi* meaning 'holy persons' – 'saints') or the genitive plural of *sancta* (Gk. ta *hagia*, meaning 'holy things'). Jan Milac Lichman, *An Ecumenical Dogmatics: The Faith We Confess*, trans. David Lewis (Philadelphia: Fortress, 1984), 209.

2   II Cor. 2:2. All scripture references are from the Revised Standard Version, *The New Oxford Annotated Bible with the Apocrypha* (New York: Oxford University Press, 1977).

3   See A. G. Herbert, 'Memory' in *A Theological Workbook of the Bible*, ed. Alan Richardson (New York: Macmillan, 1962), 142-43.

4   Julian of Norwich, *Showings*, trans. Edmund Colledge, O.S.A., and James Walsh, S.J. (New York: Paulist, 1978), 225.

5 *The Go-Between God* (London: SCM Press, 1972), 16-17.

6 *The Eternal Year*, trans. John Shea, S.S. (Baltimore: Helicon, 1964), 91-92.

7 *The Spiritual Exercises of St. Ignatius*, trans. Louis J. Puhl, S.J. (Chicago: Loyola, 1951), 235. References are to the marginal numbers.

8 *The Spiritual Exercises of St. Ignatius*, Spanish and English, trans. J. Rickaby (London: Burns & Oates, 1915), 209.

9 *Experiences of God,* trans. Margaret Kohl (Philadelphia: Fortress, 1980), 11-12.

10 *The Canticle of Creatures: Symbols of Union,* trans. Matthew J. O'Connell (Chicago: Franciscan Herald, 1977), 233-34.

11 *The Eternal Year*, 143-44.

12 *Encounters with Silence* (Westminster, Maryland: Newman, 1960), 58.

13 *The Rites of the Catholic Church* (New York: Pueblo, 1976), 642.

362

The editors wish to thank *The Way* for permission to reprint this article, originally published in their July, 1990, issue.

EPILOGUE

PASSION/SUN(SON)

BY PAUL EVANS

W hip + honey, he comes down. Anatomy of ecstasy,
wears us – ourselves, his miracle + threadbare coat.
His white chest: ecology – GARDEN/Gethsemane/
Whitman/Indiana; SKY/eyes/Mind/Plato/Pascal's fire;
ADAMANT/Golgotha/Roccasecca/brick beds in Intensive
Care.

Dry mouth open, mute, to high rain; stutter Word, cry.

Mothering hands, shaking but delivering. From home,
hurled home – traveller (war, far country, north to
south +, ever, fitful, up). All, the long study – revelation,
torn of the book of bones + flesh (night journey, night train).
Fuse, fa(r)thering,
flame.

+ flower. Fair, clear gaze (unmoved mover?) – until, +
yet – descent. Reverie to riven – eyes devouring,
devoured.

To haunt his true + dark illuminating house. Cancer ward,
prison, poverty. Joy! Joy!

Head, sweet spike, driven into God.

A LANGUAGE EXPERIMENT about Christ's passion, since my father's illness is, even more than his scholarship, I think, his gift.

KEY

A= Arthur Evans

Style:
Allusive update of Modernism (Eliot esp. significant for A), crossed w/ Catholic version of César Vallejo's "gnosticism." Tribute, too, to A's patient line-by-line exegesis of poems (ref: Auerbach). Many gerunds, to mimic A's intellectual creativity, swiftness. Gerunds also suggest Christian "becoming," evolutionary theology (de Chardin).

Title:
Christ; also, acknowledgment of A's scholarship, neither dry nor narcissistic, but fruitful, directed (ref: Augustine, more uti than frui). Sun – symbolic centrality in Greek metaphysics (A's apollonian qualities). Son – Christ, all men, A, me.

1st Section.
Anatomy/Incarnation references keyed to my mother's devotion to the symbol of Mystical Body (& Christian corrective to Burton's *Anatomy of Melancholy*). Also, A's athleticism. His white chest, ref: RFK's chest, revealed in assassination. Body-consciousness of the sick, ref: Elaine Scarry, *The Body in Pain* (& Foucault). Ecology, ref: A is nature devotee (Rousseau, Goethe, Jünger). Whitman, ref: A is American/democratic (something Lincolnesque about him, W's hero & hero of A's beloved father-in-law). Indiana, ref: where my brother & I were most obviously A's children. Mind/Plato, ref: Aristotle & a more unrelieved Ideal. Pascal, ref: important to A, vs. Voltaire's mocking. Fire, ref: P's note of his conversion, found in his coat (which echoes "threadbare coat"). Adamant, ref: not only play on Christ as New Adam, but on various twists on "stone" (Parkinson's ability to make the body rocklike; Rilke's "Archaic Torso of Apollo"; that symptom's metaphorical hint of [*memento mori*] toward incipient rigor mortis; Roccasecca [dry rock, Aquinas' birthplace – A's Thomism, Dante]). Brick beds, ref: Parkinson's dystonia (also, reference to St. Lawrence's martyrdom &, hence, pun on T.E. Lawrence, hero of A's).

2nd Section.
Dry mouth, ref. Parkinson' s symptom. Stutter Word, ref: when A was

a child, he had a nervous laugh; also, Parkinson's savages speech. Subliminal inference: Whitman's prophetic "barbaric yawp from the rooftops of the world").

3rd Section.
Mothering, ref: not only is Christ androgynous, but **A** is a maternal man (w/ devotion to his mother). Home, etc., ref: **A** travelled – WWII, Europe, Iceland (Auden), Minnesota to Ga. All, etc. ref: Life itself as his learning (& O' Neill's *Long Day's Journey*). Night journey, ref: Exodus & Koestler (a Parkinson's sufferer). Night train, ref: train trips in Dr. Zhivago & the lamplit "train" of thought of the scholar. Fuse, ref: **A**'s fertility &, obviously, Dylan Thomas (the Evanses are Welsh).

369

4th Section.
Flower, ref: **A** is beautiful. Gaze, ref: at times, A's eyes seemed almost Olympian, detached (& the glance of the real aesthete, e.g. "On First Looking Into Chapman's Homer"). Also, **A** was a scout in WWII. Unmoved, etc. ref: intentionally blasphemous allusion to Aristotle/ Aquinas & their arguably "intellectual" spirituality (curse/blessing of the thinking Christian). Until, etc., ref: all of **A**'s suffering, but esp. Parkinson's (Conversion from Aquinas to Francis). Reverie, etc., ref: orphic passage, from detachment to catharsis, observation to act, sympathy to empathy.

5th Section.
House, ref: the house in which **A** was diagnosed was dark (inferno); his new one, bright (paradiso), plus Teresa's Interior Castle. Also, how **A**'s suffering explodes/expands him toward compassion/union with my mother's cancer (Solzhenitsyn, significant to **A**) & the whole world' s suffering. Prison, ref: Parkinson's paralysis, Pound's madness, Teilhard's notice of how the world' s circumference shrinks for the person in pain. Joy, ref: Pascal's legacy, & Gerard Manley Hopkins' last words.

6th Section.
For operation, staples were driven into **A**'s head (also, wound in **A**'s side, ref: Calvary). Spike, ref: perhaps obviously, horse's mouth in Guernica: intentionally phallic, to emphasize Incarnation.
Finally, I used to wear an ID bracelet, which read "Spike."

NOTE from the DESIGNERS

This book was designed by Robert Evans and Judith Martens, set in Berkeley book and bold typefaces on a Macintosh IIci.

The butterfly and gecko images on the cover were chosen by father to appear on the cover of a lecture on Ernst Jünger. It was his last public lecture to the university. The symbols also were used on his funeral pall.

Our efforts are dedicated to our daughter, Catherine Carson.